Constructive
Knowledge Acquisition

A Computational Model and
Experimental Evaluation

Constructive
Knowledge Acquisition

A Computational Model and
Experimental Evaluation

Franz Schmalhofer

Routledge
Taylor & Francis Group

LONDON AND NEW YORK

First published 1998 by Lawrence Erlbaum Associates, Inc.

Published 2018 by Routledge
2 Park Square, Milton Park, Abingdon, Oxon OX14 4RN
52 Vanderbilt Avenue, New York, NY 10017

First issued in paperback 2018

Routledge is an imprint of the Taylor & Francis Group, an informa business

Library of Congress Cataloging-in-Publication Data

Schmalhofer, F. (Franz), 1952-
Constructive knowledge acquisition: A computational model and experimental evaluation / Franz Schmalhofer.
p.   cm.
Originally presented as the author's thesis (Ph. D.) — Universität Heidelberg.
ISBN 0-8058-2724-2 (cloth : alk. paper)
1. Knowledge acquisition (Expert systems).   2. Computer simulation.   3. Artificial intelligence.   I. Title.
QA76.76.E95S32   1997
006.3'31—dc21   97-5613
                                                                CIP

ISBN 13: 978-1-138-87664-4 (pbk)
ISBN 13: 978-0-8058-2724-8 (hbk)

Contents

Preface

In a way, this book is my resolution of the various disciplinal and cultural differences that I have been exposed to during the last 20 years. I consider myself very fortunate that in the years from 1976 to 1981, I could study at the University of Colorado in Boulder. This was where I first met my wife. There were very nice mountains and many people with whom I could go hiking and skiing. As far as academia was concerned, I learned how to run interesting and well-controlled computer experiments and I acquired practical experience in developing and implementing (symbolic) computer simulation models. In addition to many exiting courses in cognitive psychology, I took classes in computer science and artificial intelligence and completed a PhD thesis under the supervision of Professors Kintsch and Polson.

During my subsequent work as a research associate to Dietrich Albert at the University of Heidelberg, traditional mathematical models played a more essential role than did symbolic computer simulations. In the area of general experimental psychology, computers were mostly used for controlling psychological experiments, performing statistical analyses, and estimating parameters in mathematical models.

Dietrich Albert also provided me with the opportunity to teach a course on computer simulations and artificial intelligence. By teaching this course, I could get students interested in my research. He encouraged me to pursue my own research and gave me the moral support for submitting the sketch of a project proposal to the *DFG-Schwerpunktprogramm Wissenspsychologie*, or the German Wissenspsychologie Project, as it would later be termed in English. This Schwerpunktprogramm was about to be initiated by Professors Mandl and Spada and continued until 1993 when it was completed by an edited volume of

Professors Strube and Wender. The research reported in this book was to a large degree conducted within the academic and financial framework of this *Schwerpunktprogramm.*

At first, the IBM scientific center in Heidelberg provided some financial support to Dr. Thomas Wetter and me to develop computer simulations of cognitive processes. Starting in 1985, the *Deutsche Forschungsgemeinschaft* (DFG) began 7 years of funding for my research. As a result, I could perform my investigations with the assistance of students and researchers. I was lucky enough to continue this research together with Otto Kühn, Stefan Boschert, and Beate Schlenker at different universities. Most of the reported research was conducted at the University of Freiburg, McGill University in Montreal, and at the University of Colorado, where I also visited with Clayton Lewis, and the University of Kaiserslautern. This book thus describes the product of serially distributed research that was performed at five different locations in Germany, Canada and the United States.

In October 1989, I joined the German Research Center for Artificial Intelligence (DFKI) in Kaiserslautern where I led a research group on *knowledge acquisition for expert systems.* I now had the opportunity to more thoroughly study the areas of *knowledge engineering* and *artificial intelligence,* as well as the opportunity to participate in the current research of this engineering discipline. I could now achieve a much more thorough and detailed understanding of the nature and techniques of artificial intelligence than I would ever have acquired had I only conducted psychological experiments and only developed computer models within the area of psychology. At the time, I led two projects, one in the area of psychology (KIWi), and one in the area of artificial intelligence (A-TEC). The researchers of the KIWi-project were psychologists (Otto Kühn, Stefan Boschert, Michael Rohr, and Jörg Thoben) as well as computer scientists (Ralph Bergmann, Bidjan Tschaitschian, and Dr. Stuart Aitken). There was also a computer scientist (Dr. Gabriele Schmidt) and a psychologist (Otto Kühn) in the A-TEC project. With this very balanced set of researchers, I had the chance to obtain some insights into the tensions between the two areas of scientific research. It was quite interesting and challenging.

As the KIWi and A-TEC projects were about to be completed, I began to devote more time to cognitive experimental psychology. Now I could also attempt to relate this research to areas such as intelligent tutoring systems, expert systems, knowledge bases, and more generally epistemology. Again with the academic and moral support of Professor Albert, I began this book project at the University of Heidelberg in December 1992. Dietrich Albert helped me to find the initial organization of my exposition before he left Heidelberg to accept a chair of psychology at the University of Graz.

In order to further pursue my project, I needed a new academic advisor at the University of Heidelberg, and I approached Professsor Weinert who was kind and generous enough to continue with me on this topic. He also invited me to the Max-Planck Institute in Munich and from 1994 to 1996 I had several opportunities to be a guest in his department. During this time. Professor

Weinert was always available for me and I could discuss with him important issues of general concern as well as several quite specific topics. He provided me with invaluable guidance in many different ways. His suggested readings helped me to put pieces together, which in my mind were miles apart from one another. Working at his department in Munich also gave me the much needed psychological research environment. I very much enjoyed the excellent library, various colloquia presentations, and the informal conversations with Professor Elsbeth Stern, Dr. Michael Waldmann, Dr. Ulrich Geppert, Dr. Erik Farin, and several other researchers at the institute. Without Professor Weinert's support I would not have been able to complete this book.

Professor Kintsch provided invaluable advice and a continuous inspiration to me for almost 20 years. His construction-integration theory is the central building block of the research which is reported in this book and without his work this book could not mean much.

As a native English speaker, my wife has proofread every chapter of this book and thereby improved its readability, most often by splitting sentences and deleting commas. When my daughter found out about this, she became very worried and asked: "Is this allowed, mommy?" I must admit I have had much more support for doing my homework than she gets for hers.

Stefan Boschert, Herbert Karlovitz, Isabel Müller, Erich Farin, Anne Schellhorn, Mathias Spinner, Beate Schlenker, Fabian Wilmers, Michael Rohr, Rhona Charron, and Paula Messamer helped in running the experiments and in performing statistical analyses. Otto Kühn, Ralph Bergmann, Bidjan Tschaitschian, Stefan Jäger, and Wolfgang Wilke performed various computer implementations. The experiments of chapter 7 were performed in collaboration with Doris Glavanov. For the past two years, Ludger van Elst has helped me in preparing graphs, editing the manuscript, and discussing various aspects of the reported research.

Within the Wissenspsychologie framework, financial support was provided to me by grants Schm 648/1-1 to Schm 648/1-5 from the DFG. The research on knowledge acquisition for expert systems was funded by grant ITW 8992 #C4 from Bundesministerium für Forschung und Technologie (BMFT) to the DFKI (1989-1993). For conducting this research, the DFG provided the necessary financial support by grants Schm 648/9-1 and Schm 648/9-2. The final touches of this book were done, while I was a visiting professor at the Interdisciplinary Center for Cognitive Studies at the University of Potsdam.

Finally, I want to thank Judith Amsel, Amy Olener and Kathy Scornavacca for their competent help regarding the different aspects in preparing this book for print. I want to acknowledge all of this support and would like to thank everyone who helped me with my work.

Franz Schmalhofer

1

Introduction and Overview

For the last 15 years, I have studied such widely different areas as experimental cognitive psychology and the construction of knowledge-based systems. Although both areas are somehow concerned with human knowledge and human cognition, the research agendas and methodologies of the two areas have been quite different in the past. This is also true for the basic scientific orientations and the underlying philosophical attitudes that are most dominant in the two areas.

Experimental psychology is an empirical science in which human cognition (among other topics) is researched by investigating the information processing that occurs in memorizing, categorizing, problem solving, reading, and other tasks. In order to obtain highly reliable results, psychological experiments are typically performed in laboratory settings where the researchers can systematically manipulate the variables of their interest, such as the number of items on a list that the subjects are asked to memorize. The researcher can then empirically determine how this experimentally manipulated variable influences another variable of interest, for instance the processing time that subjects require to decide whether a newly presented item did or did not occur on the previously presented list. From such data, experimental psychologists may then attempt to infer properties of human information processing (Sternberg, 1969). They may for instance infer that memory search would be serial and self terminating (Theios, Smith, Haviland, Troupman, & May, 1973) or that memory search is indeed a parallel process (cf. Vorberg & Ulrich, 1987). Preference is supposedly given to the process description that can account for the experimental data and that appears to be most parsimonious.

The construction of knowledge-based systems is an engineering effort within the realm of artificial intelligence (AI) and computer science, where methods and techniques are to be developed for solving complex problems in the real world by appropriately designed computer systems. Such complex problems include, for example, production planning in mechanical engineering. These computer systems are also called expert systems. Knowledge-based systems or expert systems may be developed by analyzing the intelligent behavior of human experts (Fischer & Reeves, in press) as well as by applying formal methods (e.g., predicate calculus) without much discussion of the respective human behavior. Although both approaches have been pursued in the past, the behavior of human experts is now often regarded as irrelevant for developing a knowledge-based system. Formal description logics (Brachman, McGuiness, Patel-Schneider, Resnick, & Borgida, 1990) may be employed for developing a knowledge-based system without any reference to human expert behavior. It is therefore often believed that, as a subfield of artificial intelligence, the construction of knowledge-based systems should be performed by analytic and rational methods rather than by investigating human intelligence (Clancey, 1991; p. 359-360).

Given the divergent beliefs, the differences in the agendas of experimental psychology and of expert system research, one could at first think that any attempt of coordination and mutual fertilization between the two areas must necessarily be doomed to failure. Whereas experimental psychology is generally assumed to stand predominantly in the tradition of John Locke's and George Berkeley's empiricism, expert systems research and artificial intelligence are typically viewed as continuing the tradition of Rene Descartes' and Gottfried Wilhelm Leibnitz's rationalism. Descartes' "cogito ergo sum" may thus be contrasted to Berkeley's "to be is to be perceived" as two completely different epistemological foundations. If one wanted to, one easily could argue that any person who is qualified in one of the two areas (experimental psychology or knowledge-based systems) and who values the research agenda of the other area, would automatically disqualify himself because this would imply that the person believes at the same time in empiricism and rationalism, and this would be undoubtedly a contradiction in terms. Such an argument might be quite convincing, had there not been the *cognitive revolution* of the sciences in the middle of this century (cf. Gardner, 1987; Kuhn, 1970), which yielded a research agenda that stresses the coordination of the different methodologies for researching cognition, as well as mutual discussions of different epistemological views. As a consequence of the cognitive revolution there is now an empirically based effort to answer long-standing epistemological questions by applying psychological experiments and computer simulations as research techniques. These questions address the nature of knowledge, its sources, its components, its creation, and its acquisition, development, and utilization (cf. Gardner, 1987).

I should also mention that the relation between contemporary science and the history of philosophy is much more intricate and complicated than what could be expressed by a simple classification or even by a short exposition. For example, Krämer (1988) pointed out that the field of artificial intelligence is a break with the rationalism of Descartes and Leibnitz as well as a continuation of it.

Although Descartes and Leibnitz were very much opposed to a mechanical model of the mind, they viewed their calculi as part of a universal science (*mathesis universalis*) that could be used to generate mechanically all true sentences. Descartes is furthermore also credited as the father of physiological psychology (Sahakian, 1975) and much of physiological psychology is a branch of experimental psychology. The strong separation between empiricist and rationalist traditions in scientific research may therefore not be as unavoidable as it often appears.

1.1 The Cognitive Revolution

There is a general consensus that the most critical event(s) of the cognitive revolution occurred in the year 1956 (cf. Gardner, 1987; Newell & Simon, 1972; Simon, 1991). This year featured two meetings and several influential publications that broke with the ontological and methodological restrictions of behaviorism (Watson, 1913/1994) and created a new orientation in scientific research by introducing the model of symbolic information processing. On September 10-12, there was the Symposium on Information Theory at the Massachusetts Institute of Technology. This meeting was attended by many leading figures in the communication and the human sciences such as Allen Newell, Herbert Simon, Noam Chomsky, and George Miller. In the same year, there was also the so-called Dartmouth Conference, which was organized by John McCarthy and Marvin Minsky. McCarthy had proposed to carry out a study of artificial intelligence at Dartmouth College. This study was to proceed "on the basis of the conjecture that every aspect of learning or any other feature of intelligence can in principle be so precisely described that a machine can be made to simulate it" (Charniak & McDermott, 1985, p. 11). This conjecture of a mechanistic model of the mind stands as the core assumption of the cognitive revolution, and the Dartmouth conference is generally credited as the beginning of artificial intelligence as we know it today.

Newell and Simon's (1956) paper entitled "The Logic Theory Machine", Chomsky's (1956) "Three Models for the Description of Language", Bruner, Goodnow, and Austin's (1956) "Study of Thinking" and Miller's (1956) "The Magical Number Seven " are uniformly credited as the pivotal publications that revealed the *cognitive revolution* to a broader public. As computer scientists, Newell and Simon developed a software computer system that they called the Logic Theory Machine, and reported how they had successfully applied this machine to automatically carry out a complete proof of a theorem. The linguist Chomsky introduced transformational grammars for describing the English language and showed how such a grammar could be used for generating and analyzing natural language expressions. The psychologist Bruner described the subjects of his experiments as active and constructive problem solvers rather than as simple reactors to stimuli, and applied an information-processing analysis to concept formation. The psychologist Miller similarly applied the terminology of information processing to human memory and thereby put forward his claim that the capacity of human short-term memory is limited to approximately seven units.

During this time period, neuroscientists were also achieving seminal progress by beginning to take recordings from single neurons. McCuloch and his associates showed that some neurons of the frog were most responsive to extremely specific forms of information, such as imitations of bug movements across the receptive field of the frog's retina. With the recordings from cells in the visual cortex of a cat, Hubel and Wiesel identified nerve cells that responded to very specific information such as the orientation of lines. In the field of anthropology, the publications of Harold Conklin, Ward Goodenough, and Floyd Lounsburgy started to define the new field of cognitive anthropology, and researchers started to collect data concerning the naming, classifying, and concept formation of people living in remote cultures and then tried to give a formal account for the different linguistic and cognitive practices. Philosophers also applied innovative notions, more specifically the formal notion of a computing machine — generally known as Turing machine — was introduced into philosophy. The Turing machine is the theoretical notion of a quite simple machine (an infinitely long tape, a mechanism for moving right and left on the tape and erasing and printing a slash). Despite its structural simplicity, there is overwhelming evidence that such a machine is most powerful and has indeed the capability of computing any and every conceivable function (Turing, 1936). This relationship is generally known as the Church–Turing thesis. Supposedly such a machine could then be programmed so that its behavior would be indistinguishable from the behavior of a human. If an observer could not distinguish the responses of a computing machine from the responses of a human, the computing machine was said to have passed the Turing test (Turing, 1963). Thereby computers and humans could be compared to one another. Around 1960, the philosopher Hilary Putnam expected that the Turing machine formalism and the use of electronic computers would therefore also help to solve — or dissolve — the classical mind-body problem (see Gardner, 1987).

Looking back at this time period, psychologist George Mandler concluded that "the various tensions and inadequacies of the first half of the 20th–century cooperated to produce a new movement in psychology that first adopted the label of information processing and after became known as modern cognitive psychology: And it all happened in the 5–year period between 1955 and 1960." (Gardner, 1987, p. 29). Basically, what had happened in this critical time period is that researchers from different disciplines had used the concept of a Turing machine and its physical realization in the form of electronic computers as a mediating formalism and a mediating research tool to jointly address quite old epistemological questions. Thereby, (at least partially) new theories of the human mind were developed (cf. Gigerenzer, 1991). The new techniques and tools included the powerful formalisms for expressing logical reasoning that had been developed by Frege, Boole, Hilbrandt, Herbrand, Russel, and Whitehead, and the formal definition of computing machines by Turing and the subsequent development of electronic computers. These methodological innovations started towards the end of the last century. The epistemological questions that were discussed, on the other hand, can be traced much further back in history.

Historical Milestones

The historical roots of the issues that have been at the center of attention since the cognitive revolution have been traced back to the 17th-century philosophy of enlightenment as well as to ancient Greek philosophy. The relationships between the cognitive revolution in the middle of this century and the history of philosophy and science are intricate and complicated, at least as intricate and complicated as the history of philosophy and science itself. For the purpose of this book, it will be sufficient to remind the reader of some of the best known milestones (cf. Gardner, 1987; Sahakian, 1975). Thereby, I show how the research topic of this book relates to more general epistemological questions.

Socrates (470–399 BC) is generally credited with founding the inductive method for acquiring knowledge, a method that has become very important for scientific reasoning. Instead of explicitly answering any of his students' questions, Socrates guided the knowledge-acquisition process of his students by asking additional questions so that his students would themselves generate answers. The Socratic method of responding to questions has become a well-known technique for stimulating creative thought as opposed to teaching by rote. By asking where knowledge came from, what it consisted of, and how it would be represented in the human mind, Plato (427–347 BC) questioned the nature of knowledge. He assumed that the purest knowledge was idealized forms or archetypes and that such genuine knowledge was implanted in the human soul at birth, whereas the mundane reality we perceive with our senses only reflects such genuine knowledge. Aristotle (384–322 BC), on the other hand, asserted that nothing could be in the mind which was not first in the senses and that no one could learn or understand anything in the absence of sense. His syllogisms, furthermore, showed how reasoning can be accomplished by a formal logic, independent of specific information. Aristotle distinguished three types of souls: the vegetative soul of plants, the sensitive soul of animals, and the rational soul of humans. The philosophy of the Middle Ages was more or less an Aristotelian philosophy.

During the Renaissance and Enlightenment periods, epistemological questions were discussed in relation to the findings of the newly flourishing analytic and empirical sciences. Rene Descartes (1596–1650) assumed that the mind is separate from and independent of the human body. He thought of the body as an automaton comparable to artificial machines, and of the mind as unified and not decomposable (i.e., a mechanical body and a rational mind). As a rationalist, Descartes believed the mind to be the arbiter of truth and assumed that ideas were innate rather than coming from experiential sources. These assumptions were soon contradicted by the British empiricist philosophers. John Locke's (1632–1704) epistemology was grounded in the experience of objects in the external world (as opposed to being grounded in a rational mind). George Berkeley (1685–1735) similarly assumed that the experiencing self with a perceiving mind is essential for having sensations and for conceiving ideas. Whereas the rationalists searched for universal principles that were embodied in pure thought, the British empiricists viewed thought only as an instrument to reflect or build on experience. In his *Critique of Pure Reason* (1781), Immanuel Kant (1724–1804) attempted to synthesize the rationalist and empiricist points of view. Kant wrote that knowledge would begin with experience (thus not being purely analytic) and that, nevertheless, it does not directly come from it (thus not being purely a posteriori). "Kant ... saw the mind as an active organ of understanding which molds and coordinates sensations and ideas, transforming the chaotic multiplicity of experience into the ordered unity of thought" (Gardner, 1987, p. 57). Kant also asserted that a science of psychology would not be possible because of the impossibility of experimentation, the absence of a mathematical basis, and because the mind is affected while studying itself. For about a century Kant's epistemology remained without major competition.

Dramatic advances were then achieved in several sciences. In formal logic, the work of George Boole (1815–1864), Gottlob Frege (1848–1925), Bertrand Russell (1872–1970), Alfred North Whitehead (1861–1947), J. Herbrand (1908–1931), and Alfred Tarski (1902–1983) provided the foundations for building powerful computational systems. In mathematics and physics scholars like Niels Bohr (1885–1962), Georg Cantor (1845–1918), Albert Einstein (1879–1955), Max Planck (1858–1947), and Werner Heisenberg (1901–1976) rewrote our understanding of mathematics and the physical universe. In psychology, researchers like Gustav Fechner (1801–1887), Herrmann Helmholtz (1821–1894), Wilhelm Wundt (1832–1920), Hermann Ebbinghaus (1850–1909), and Georg Müller (1850–1934) demonstrated that a science of psychology with mathematical notations and experimental investigations is indeed possible and that general epistemological questions can be investigated within a science of psychology that uses experimentation as well as formal models. The logical-empiricist program (Carnap, 1928) that resulted from these dramatic advances in the different sciences led to much closer ties among the empirical sciences, logic, mathematics, and philosophy (cf. Stegmüller, 1969). It allowed definite answers to certain problems and therefore had the quality of science rather than of philosophy. Instead of inventing at one stroke a complete theory of the whole universe, individual problems could now be tackled one at a time (and in a scientific fashion).

As the writings of John Austin (1911–1960), Gilbert Ryle (1900–1976), and Ludwig Wittgenstein's (1889–1951) *Philosophical Investigations* (1971) showed, epistemology and philosophy can no longer be regarded as meta-disciplines that could legislate topics like knowledge and truth. As Gardner expressed it, philosophy now "participates in the disciplinary matrix by virtue of its dialectical role: a dialectic within the discipline and a dialectic between the analysis put forth by philosophers, on the one hand, and the empirical findings and theories put forth by scientists, on the other" (1987, p. 87). Vera and Simon (1993b) went a step further when they said: "Let's permit the tested science to shape philosophy (as it has done, e.g., in evolutionary theory, cosmology, relativity, quantum theory, and even, in recent years, epistemology) instead of asking the tail of philosophy to wag the dog of cognitive science" (p. 132).

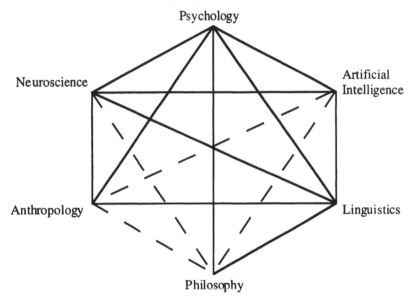

FIG. 1.1. The cognitive hexagon shows the interdisciplinary connections between psychology and other disciplines that perform research on cognition. Unbroken lines indicate strong interdisciplinary ties and broken lines indicate weak interdisciplinary ties (adapted from Gardner, 1987; p. 37).

Human knowledge acquisition can thus be scientifically investigated within the realm of a psychological science without being framed by such restrictive presuppositions as an empiricist or rationalist epistemology. As a science, the field of psychology is defined through the content area that is being researched and by the scientific methods that are thereby applied. The acquisition of knowledge in humans is thus one of the research topics of cognitive psychology (e.g., Anderson, 1989; Chipman & Meyrowitz, 1993). Since the cognitive revolution, computer simulation methods have found increasingly more use in addition to the methods of experimental psychology. The research on the acquisition of knowledge that is presented in this book lies in the areas of cognitive science and cognitive psychology. Computer simulation methods as well as experimental psychology methods are applied. As Simon (1991) described in some detail in his autobiography, the application of computer simulations in cognitive psychology is also a clear consequence of the cognitive revolution (cf. Newell & Simon, 1972).

By virtue of the cognitive revolution of the sciences, there are now closer ties between psychology and other disciplines concerned with cognition. Figure 1.1 shows the relations between psychology and five other disciplines as far as research on cognition is concerned. Unbroken lines represent strong interdisciplinary ties and broken lines represent weak interdisciplinary ties. The so-called cognitive hexagon that is presented in Fig. 1.1 is part of the state-of-the-art report on cognition research that was drafted by a dozen leading scholars under the commission of the Sloan Foundation in 1978. All that time, the goal of research on cognition was defined as discovering "the representational and computational capacities of the mind and their structural and functional representation in the brain" (cf. Gardner, 1987, p.36-37). Whereas the representational and computational capacities of the mind are now investigated in cognitive psychology, research in neuroscience investigates their implementation in the brain (e.g., Kutas & Hillyard, 1980; van Petten & Kutas, 1990).

The Physical Symbol System Hypothesis and Further Developments

For psychological research on cognition, the notion of a *physical symbol system* has become an important concept. The concept of a *physical symbol system* asserts the existence of

> a broad class of systems that is capable of having and manipulating symbols, yet is also realizable within our physical universe... The notion of symbol that it defines is internal to this concept of a system. Thus it is a hypothesis that these symbols are in fact the same symbols that we humans have and use everyday in our lives. Stated another way, the hypothesis is that humans are instances of physical symbol systems, and, by virtue of this, mind enters into the physical universe. (Newell, 1980, p. 136).

Newell's definition postulates that the human mind *is* a physical symbol system and that symbol manipulation and the distal access of complex symbol structures via other symbols is a necessary and sufficient condition for accomplishing intelligent behavior in general (cf. Newell, 1990).

Newell offered his definition of a physical symbol system mostly from the perspective of a computer scientist. Over the years, this concept has been discussed from several other perspectives. Philosophers and psychologists have provided important contributions, which, in my opinion, require certain modifications and extensions of Newell's definition.

As a philosopher, Searle (1983) introduced into the discussion the so-called *Chinese Room,* which is a specific example of a symbol system. The Chinese Room is an isomorph of the Turing machine and thus also of electronic computers in general. The Chinese Room takes Chinese symbols as input; a person without any knowledge of the Chinese language (sitting in the Chinese Room) would then manipulate these symbols according to certain rewrite rules and would thereby generate some other Chinese symbols as output. If the inputs were some questions in Chinese and the output was identical to the correct answers that a Chinese person would give, this symbol system would pass the Turing test. In other words, from the outside, the behavior of the symbol system cannot be distinguished from the respective language behavior of a human. Searle argued that in such a case, one cannot claim that the person in the room or the symbol system as a whole would understand the Chinese language. Searle insists that understanding requires what he called *intrinsic intentionality.* Intrinsic intentionality and intentionality in general is seen as a characteristic of the mental abilities. Because the intrinsic intentionality of humans is tied to properties of the biological substance, and computer systems do not have these properties, computer systems cannot possess intrinsic intentionality. According to Searle, the Turing test is therefore not a sufficient criterion for asserting cognitive states (e.g., intentions and understanding) in a system. Instead of claiming that the human mind *is* (nothing but) a symbol system (i.e., the so-called strong AI position), this claim should be modified. For the psychological research that I report in this book, I only need to assume that the human mind can be *modeled* by a symbol system (i.e., the so-called weak AI position). Just in the same manner as one wants to distinguish between real money and forged money, even when two bills can no longer be distinguished from one another (i.e., the forged money passes the Turing test), we are thus distinguishing between the human mind and the physical symbol system as its model or imitation.

Dennett (1987) proposed the *intentional stance* as a third person perspective that legitimizes the use of mental descriptions when the behavior of humans and computer systems is to be characterized in scientific research. By attributing rationality and purpose to a computer system (or any other machine), the computer system is treated as if it were an intelligent human being. The notion of an *intentional system* is thereby only used to serve as a bridge between the common-sense world of people and the non-intentional domain of physical symbol systems. This notion therefore does not imply that an intentional system (e.g., a computer system) *really* has beliefs and desires, but only that it can be useful to explain and predict the behavior of a machine by *ascribing* beliefs and desires to it. When one adopts such an intentional stance, one is basically allowed to talk about *homunculi*, as long as each homunculus can indeed be replaced by a machine, so that all homunculi are eventually discharged. One may thus say that a chess computer *knows* a certain chess opening. This means nothing more than an abbreviation of the descriptions of the respective symbol-level structures and processes of that chess computer.[1] In addition to a symbol-level description, computer systems can therefore also be described as intentional systems, which has also become known as the *knowledge level description* of a system (see section 2.2; cf. Newell, 1982). Dennett's intentional stance and Newell's knowledge level are thus fundamentally the same.

For a long time, symbol processing was assumed to be a set of purely serial processes (Newell & Simon, 1972). The seminal work of Rumelhart and McClelland (1986) demonstrated that this need not be true for all of cognition. With the same precision as in symbolic models, one may also postulate parallel

---

[1] The intentional stance has sometimes been misunderstood as a mentalistic approach that would be at odds with natural evolutionary mechanisms and as an approach that would have some family resemblance to the argument from design that was used by 19th century theologians. (cf. Blumberg and Wassermann, 1995). However, the design stance of a computer scientist simply says that as the creator of the artifact he or she also knows that the artifact will behave according to the specifications of its design. From an intentional stance, we would thus describe a thermostat in the following way: When it is too hot, the thermostat will shut off the heater. When it is too cold, the thermostat will turn on the heater. The thermostat knows when it is too hot and when it is too cold.

distributed processing (PDP) at a subsymbolic level (Smolensky, 1988). Such connectionist processing components are indeed needed to explain how truly new concepts or conceptual spaces may emerge over time through interactions with an environment that is not described by the same set of symbols (cf. Dorffner & Prem, 1993). With the traditional symbolic models, any newly generated concept is implicitly contained in the conceptual space that is determined by a symbol structure and is therefore not really new. Because every concept must be defined in terms of the specific representational primitives of the conceptual space, symbolic models are basically closed systems, where everything that can be learned from the environment or by deduction was already (knowingly or unknowingly) determined at the time the symbolic system was established. Through the use of a (nonsymbolic) connectionist processing component one may also generate structures that lie outside of a given conceptual space and that are, in addition, grounded in the environment (cf. Brooks, 1991; Wrobel, 1991). Although connectionist models and artificial neural nets were at first seen purely as competitors to symbolic models, over the years it has become obvious that significant progress can be achieved by combining the strengths of the two modeling techniques in hybrid models (e.g., Holyoak & Thargard, 1989; Schneider & Oliver, 1991).

One important question concerning the symbol-level hypothesis that was originally ignored is how symbols come into existence. A symbol system is basically a sort of calculus. At the time the calculus is designed, everything that can be processed and derived is already fixed. Such a system cannot generate anything truly new, in the sense that a new symbol would not again be defined in terms of the old symbols. A symbol system that contains the concept of a *mother-child relation*, may thus learn the concepts of *grandmother*, *great-grandmother*, *great-great-grandmother*, and *female ancestor*, as the *transitive closure* of the *mother-child relation* (cf. Bürckert, Hollunder, & Laux, 1993) but it could not invent any novel conceptions like the height of mothers if such a concept were not at least implicitly contained in its conceptology (e.g., by having some sensor or measuring procedure that yields heights of people from some system input and an induction procedure that yields generalizations).

The generation of new representations that are grounded in the environment is currently being investigated in the field of situated cognition, situated action, and situativity theory (Clancey, 1993; Greeno, 1995; Suchman, 1987).[2] In order to

---

[2] Although some proponents of situated action are very explicit about their view that all cognition is situated and that assumptions about mental symbol processing are generally flawed (Clancey, 1993), we have, nevertheless, chosen to view situated cognition as a means for curing some insufficiencies of the symbolic approach rather than replacing it by some methodology that is not yet as mature. Despite the existing controversy between the proponents of situated action and the proponents of symbolic cognition, it can be said that "these two traditions do not seem to be contradictory: They emphasize different behaviors and different methods of study. They do not conflict." (Norman, 1993; p. 3). I agree with Greeno and Moore (1993; p. 57) when they stated that "breaking completely" from symbolic cognitive theories would be the wrong thing to do, but that something like "departing fundamentally" could be required. They stated correctly that a symbol or symbolic expression can be a physical as well as a mental structure, that is interpreted as a representation of something. Obviously, there are systematic relations (cf. Kintsch, 1974; Perfetti and Britt, 1995) between physical symbol structures (e.g., a text written by a specific author) and

describe how new representations emerge, one needs to step outside the notion of symbol processing. It requires an interactionist view (Gibson, 1954; Greeno, 1994) where the external physical and the internal mental processes are part and parcel rather than being factored apart. In such situations where a new symbol structure is being generated, knowledge acquisition cannot simply be viewed as the process of transferring information from the environment or another person into the system. The symbol grounding problem (Harnad, 1990) indicates that one cannot simply copy the concepts (and usages) of one cognitive system into a second system and expect that the second system thereby acquire the functionality of the first system. Instead, a person's newly generated knowledge should be viewed as the result of a longer dialectic process in the real world where cycles of perception and action are simultaneously coordinated and some specific symbol structure emerges from this coordination (see Maturana & Varela, 1990). This symbol structure can then be understood as an abstraction of the behavior patterns that resulted from the dialectic process. The generation of new symbol structures may thereby be described as attunements to the constraints of the already existing symbol structures and the affordances of the specific situations (cf. Greeno, 1995).

This process can be termed *knowledge creation* or *knowledge acquisition*. The term *knowledge acquisition* has sometimes been misunderstood to imply that some commodity (i.e., knowledge) that is outside in the world would simply be transported into the system (i.e., acquired) and then stored in memory. I do not, however, imply this *commodity view* of knowledge when I use the term *knowledge acquisition*. To avoid this misunderstanding, the reader should remember that I use the terms *knowledge creation* and *knowledge acquisition* more or less synonymously.

In summary, the physical symbol level hypothesis of the strong AI position has matured over the years into a set of modeling techniques for describing human cognition, which in addition to symbol-level processing includes the parallel processing of subsymbolic entities in connectionist nets, as well as situativity theory, which can describe how completely new symbol structures that lie outside any prestored ontology may emerge during knowledge acquisition. With this set of modeling techniques, one can now indeed investigate knowledge acquisition as an act of creativity rather than by assuming that all knowledge acquisition must consist of searching and chunking in predetermined representation spaces (Laird, Newell, & Rosenbloom, 1987). A general framework for discussing such creative knowledge acquisition in terms of computational concepts was recently proposed by Boden (1991).

1.2 Computational Description of Creative Processes

Boden (1991) distinguished two broad types of creativity, which she called *improbabilist* and *impossiblilist* creativity. Improbabilist creativity occurs when

---

some mental symbol structures (e.g., the symbol structure that a psychologist may ascribe to the subject who has just read this text).

familiar ideas are combined in a surprising way and this combination is positively valued. The surprise is thereby due to the apriori improbability of combining these ideas. Impossibilist creativity is a deeper type of creativity. Impossibilist creativity is defined with respect to a conceptual space. With impossibilist creativity, one can generate novel ideas that could not have been generated before because these ideas lie outside the conceptual space that was originally available. Such novel ideas can be made possible by creating a new conceptual space. A new conceptual space (or representation space) may be obtained by mapping and transforming some already available representation space to representational units that emerge from a collection of subsymbolic units (McMillan & Smolensky, 1988) or that immerse into a different representation space (cf. Schmalhofer, Bergmann, Boschert, & Thoben, 1993; Schmalhofer & Tschaitschian, 1993). Thereby a representational redescription of some given problem may be obtained, thus enabling novel ideas. Boden's thesis that creativity can be described in computational terms has recently been supported by Ram (1993) and his associates who developed the SINS and the ISAAC systems (Moorman & Ram, 1994). These systems, which are instantiations of computational theories about creative conceptual changes, describe two kinds of creative processes: the construction of new concepts from input information, and the extrapolation of existing concepts in novel and unfamiliar situations. Discrete symbolic representations are thereby used in combination with continuous metric information.

A historical example of *impossibilist* creativity is Kekule's discovery of the benzene ring (cf. Boden, 1991; chapter 3). For a long time, Kekule had assumed that all organic molecules were based on strings of carbon atoms. His representation space for finding the structural equation of the benzene molecule was thus restricted to linear sequences, and, for benzene, the valences of the constituents were such that no solution could be found in this representation space. A change in the representation space was brought about by imagining these linear sequences as snakes that would perform twining and twisting motions until they seized hold of their own tails. There was thus an immersion from another conceptual space that was mapped onto his representation space for organic molecules, followed by a creative representational redescription. In terms of Greeno's (1995) situativity theoretical framework, this representational redescription may be understood as an attunement among the constraints of the initial conceptual space and the affordances of snakes. Greeno defines an *affordance* — a concept taken from Gibson's (1954) ecological psychology — as a resource in the environment that supports an interactive activity by a person. In order to describe such creative thought in terms of a strictly symbolic processing model, the description of such attunements would require cheating, because some of the constraints represented in the model must be broken. This fact has already been pointed out by Boden. Because we do not want to cheat in our modeling, we have to extend our description techniques. Relative to the style of thinking in a particular conceptual space, what immerses into this space appears to be quite random.

Kekule's discovery is an example of what Boden called a *historical creative act*, which means that no one else in all human history had ever had this creative thought and knowledge before. A *psychological creative act*, on the other hand, is only creative with respect to an individual. Boden pointed out that as far as psychological processes are concerned there is no difference between historical and psychological creative acts. Creative knowledge acquisition may therefore also be investigated in a quite mundane subject area, such as for example acquiring new knowledge about a specific computer system. As long as the learners have the opportunity to step outside of their current representational spaces, knowledge acquisition processes may involve a creative act for the particular individual.

There are general frameworks for the study of creativity (Feldman, Csiksentmihalyi, & Gardner, 1994) as well as a large variety of cognitive studies on this topic (cf. chapter 11 of Sternberg, 1996). For example, Weisberg (1995) held the view that there is nothing special about creativity. What distinguishes creative individuals from less remarkable people is their expertise and commitment to a creative endeavor. Finke (1995), on the other hand, argued that it is insight that distinguishes the magical from the mediocre. He distinguished between two types of creative thinking. In *convergent insight,* a person converges on a unifying structure from a scattered assortment of data. In *divergent insight,* on the other hand, a person diverges from a particular form or structure to explore what kind of uses can be found. Langley, Simon, Bradshaw, and Zytkow (1987) researched creativity as it can be found in scientific discoveries. Weinert (1993) undertook a comprehensive and general review of the psychological literature on creativity. He included several different research areas in his analysis: personality traits and individual differences, aging, diagnostic tests of creativity, the social structures and the working environment of an individual, as well as training programs for creativity. Weinert found that the processes that generate creative products are in no way special. There is no specific psychological force, ability, or mechanism that could be trained and then would guarantee the generation of creative products. Creativity, therefore, can be researched only by describing, in combination, the qualities of the products, processes, and persons that are commonly described as creative. His review shows that for generating creative solutions in realistic subject domains (as opposed to the toy problems that are used in psychological tests), intelligently usable domain knowledge is required in combination with skills for divergent thinking. The use of solid domain knowledge and divergent thinking are therefore not so much exclusive alternatives as component processes that are used jointly when substantive creative products are obtained.

1.3 Knowledge Acquisition and Experimental Psychology

The previous sections of this chapter have shown that knowledge acquisition was first researched as an issue of philosophical epistemology and that a scientific methodology can now be applied to investigate knowledge acquisition in the area of cognitive psychology. In the research reported in this book, psychological experiments and computer simulations were conducted in order to investigate how humans construct new knowledge from different materials and how the creation of new knowledge depends on knowledge that already exists. Thus, the topic of this book lies mostly in the area of general experimental psychology. Computer simulations are employed as analytical tools that allow us to compensate for some of the weaknesses that might arise from purely empirical investigations.

The field of cognitive psychology has dealt with the issue of knowledge acquisition mostly in terms of memory and concept formation processes but left relatively untouched the topic of knowledge acquisition as a creative process. Also, experimental psychology has investigated various components of human knowledge acquisition, such as memory and concept formation processes rather isolated from one another. From the perspective of knowledge acquisition research these isolated results would need to be integrated into a unified model, and computer simulations provide the methodology for doing so (Newell, 1990). Despite the many publications in which computer models were tested with psychological data (Anderson, 1993; Mannes & Kintsch, 1991; Newell & Simon, 1972), the issue of how the methods from experimental psychology and computer simulations are best used in combination with one another is still not resolved (cf. Greeno & Moore, 1993).

We propose the *levels approach to cognitive modeling* (see chapter 3). With this approach, psychological experiments and computer simulations can be integrated in a quite balanced manner. At the highest level of consideration (i.e., the *knowledge level*) it is assumed that through evolution the human cognitive system is well adapted to its environment (see Anderson, 1990a). In other words, the human mind acquired its functional organization through an evolutionary process (Cosmides & Tooby, 1994) by which the cognitive system and its environment evolved together and are therefore well adapted to one another. To a large degree, the cognitive system and its environment therefore mutually define one another, and a *rational analysis* (Anderson, 1990a) can be performed to determine the *knowledge level characteristics* of a cognitive system and its environment. At the *symbol level*, the cognitive system is then further specified by processing mechanisms. By executing these mechanisms at the implementation level, experimental predictions are obtained and compared to specifically designed psychological experiments.

1.4 Previous Research

New knowledge about a domain can be acquired by learning from an expository or technical text (Dee-Lucas & Larkin, 1988; Kieras & Bovair, 1984; Kintsch, 1986; Reder, Charney, & Morgan, 1986), as well as by studying specific examples or cases of a subject domain (Chi, Bassok, Lewis, Reiman, & Glaser, 1989; Gentner, 1983; Kolodner, 1993; Ross & Kennedy, 1990). For instance, a programming language like LISP is often learned by studying a text, such as an introductory chapter of a LISP book. Similar or identical domain knowledge may also be acquired from examples by induction and case-based inferences. From several specifically selected interactions with a LISP interpreter, the rules of the programming language LISP may thus be inferred. Whereas in learning from text, the relevant facts and general rules of the domain are described in natural language, in case-based learning (Weber, 1994) learners are directly confronted with specific situations of the domain. While expository texts usually consist of a sequence of true sentences about the domain, success cases (positive examples) as well as failure cases (negative examples) may be important in case-based learning.

In the area of general experimental psychology, learning from texts and learning from cases have typically been investigated in isolation. Research with texts was mostly concerned with the cognitive representations of texts in memory (Kintsch, 1974) and how encoding processes (e.g., Cirilo & Foss, 1980) and text memory (Ratcliff & McKoon, 1978) are influenced by such variables as text structure, prior domain knowledge (Bower, Black, & Turner, 1979), and pragmatic relevance (McKoon, Ward, Ratcliff, & Sproat, 1993). Text comprehension was thus investigated within a memory paradigm for language materials, with recall, recognition, and summarization being the most dominant criterion tasks to measure comprehension.

Research on learning from examples (or cases), on the other hand, was mostly concerned with hypothesis-formation processes and how the identification of a concept depends on the saliency of the various cues of the examples (Bower & Trabasso, 1964). This research was concerned primarily with inductive thought processes (Bourne & Restle, 1959). The form of the memory representation and the use of natural language was only of secondary interest (Bourne, Ekstrand, & Dominowski, 1971). Learning from examples was thus typically researched with simple geometric figures within the well-known concept-identification paradigm (Levine, 1975). To determine the success of learning, verification tasks, such as whether some example would or would not belong to a concept, were predominantly used as criterion tasks.

In experimental and cognitive psychology, text comprehension and learning from examples (or cases) thus were investigated only under artificially constrained conditions, separate from one another and with different emphases — memory and language in one paradigm and hypothesis sampling and concept formation in another paradigm. However, in non-laboratory environments, texts are not read primarily to be recalled at some later point. Similarly, situational cases or examples are studied not only to determine category memberships of an arbitrary case.

Texts and examples therefore should be seen more realistically as informational sources for acquiring knowledge about a domain. Learning from text and learning from examples may have more in common than the language/memory and concept formation paradigms indicate. Despite the obvious differences between the two types of instructional materials that can be characterized in terms of affordances, learners very well may have the same global processing goal when they study a text as when they study examples. Because in both instances learners seek to acquire the relevant knowledge about the domain, learning from texts and learning from examples should be investigated in a general framework so that a *unified theory* (Newell, 1990) may be derived of the acquisition of knowledge from different types of learning materials. Also, there may be several interdependencies between learning from text and learning from examples, which can hardly be investigated without such a framework.

There is a third type of learning that should also be included in such a unified theory, namely learning by exploration (e.g., Carroll, Mack, Lewis, Grischkowsky, & Robertson, 1985). Learning by exploration is rather similar to learning from examples. The main difference is that in learning by exploration, the learners themselves must instigate an interaction with their environments. The learners' actions, together with the reactions from the environment, constitute a case or an example from which the learner may acquire knowledge in a manner similar to learning from examples.

When a text and/or examples are intentionally studied in order to acquire the relevant domain knowledge for some future tasks, learners often do not know with which tasks they will be confronted or exactly what knowledge they will need for these tasks. Thus, under normal circumstances the goal of knowledge acquisition is only ill-specified and depends on the learners' vague expectations about the criterion tasks. Learning materials, such as a text or examples, and the learner's prior knowledge are the givens in knowledge acquisition from which the desired new knowledge is to be formed. In order to construct the desired knowledge in their minds, learners apply encoding and inference operations to the learning material. Knowledge acquisition can thus be understood as a goal-driven process in which the knowledge structures that are appropriate for the anticipated test tasks are formed from the available learning material and the learner's prior knowledge. Often, the ill-defined class of anticipated tasks may be quite large and heterogeneous.

1.5 The LISP System as a Learning Domain

The theory of knowledge acquisition that we propose is quite general and is not restricted to any specific domain. One could therefore test this theory in a variety of different domains, such as biology (cf. Mannes & Kintsch, 1987), medicine (cf. Patel & Groen, 1986; Schlenker, Schmalhofer, Kühn, & Rohr, 1989), or computer programming. The application of the model requires, however, that the learners' prior domain knowledge is coded, so that it can be used as an externally provided (symbolic) parameter in the application of the computer simulation. Unlike in the more traditional types of mathematical models, in which such external parameters are usually specified by numerical values (e.g., Albert, Aschenbrenner, & Schmalhofer, 1989), here the learners' prior domain knowledge is represented by symbols and symbol structures.

Nevertheless, these external parameters of the model must somehow be elicited (cf. Mannes & Kintsch, 1991) or estimated before model predictions can be derived. If each experiment employed a different application domain for testing the model, we would also have to estimate the learner's prior knowledge for each of the different domains anew. On the other hand, if the same application domain is used across the several different experiments, we will obtain a stronger test of the model. Because of the specific consistency requirements that arise with respect to the specification of the learners' prior knowledge and the different learning materials, there are fewer degrees of freedom when only one subject domain is used.

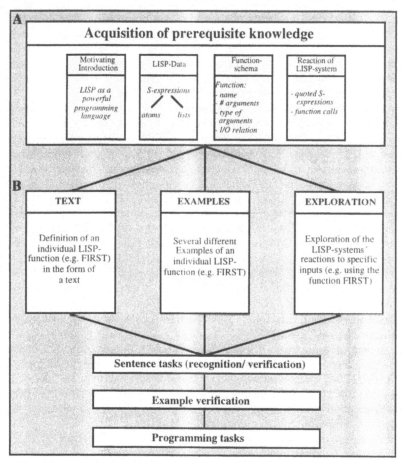

FIG. 1.2. Overview of the experimental study and test materials. Depending on the specific experimental question, various sections of these materials were employed. See text for more details.

Such an application domain should be selected so that a learner's prior knowledge can be relatively easily estimated. By picking a programming language that was not known to any of the learners, the relevant domain knowledge could be systematically induced in these subjects in the first phase of each experiment. Elementary constructs of the programming language LISP were therefore selected as the main subject domain for testing the model. To show that the model can also be applied to different subject areas, results from additional experiments are reported in chapter 12 as part of the general discussion.

The fundamental concepts of the programming language LISP can be learned in a modular way, with each module being relatively small and relatively independent of previous modules. LISP is therefore a very good subject domain for achieving good experimental control in the various studies (cf. Anderson, Farrell, & Sauers, 1984). Because a small number of such LISP modules suffices for writing realistic and useful LISP programs, knowledge acquisition can be investigated in an ecologically valid setting while exerting a large degree of experimental control on the learner's prior knowledge and the specific learning materials. The acquisition of knowledge of elementary LISP functions is therefore well suited for the purpose of the present research.

Figure 1.2 gives an overview of the learning materials and the test tasks that were used in the various experiments. The learning materials were obtained by editing a published programmer's manual on LISP (see McCarthy, Abrahams, Edwards, Hart, & Lewin, 1976), so that it would suit the experimental purposes. The learning material can be subdivided into a part A, namely the section used for acquiring some prerequisite LISP knowledge, and a part B, the section in which different LISP functions (FIRST, REST, EQUAL, LIST, SET) were to be acquired, in general from different types of materials (text, examples, exploration). Depending on the specific experiment, different sets of test tasks were employed. Figure 1.2 shows some typical test tasks in a typical order (cf. experiments 4, 8, and 9).

Part A of the material was used for the acquisition of the prerequisite LISP knowledge. It consisted of the following instructional modules:

1. A paragraph with a motivating introduction. This paragraph basically said that it is important to learn LISP.
2. The general definition of LISP data. It was said that atoms and lists are the two sub-classes of S-expressions. Basically, atoms are symbols like words (e.g., *FRIENDS, JOHN,* or *FRED*). By following some syntactic rules, lists like *(FRIENDS (JOHN FRED))* can be formed from these atomic symbols. This paragraph presented the detailed rules for building atoms and lists. Specific examples were also presented.
3. A third paragraph explained the mathematical notion of a function. An analogy to a simple mathematical function was used to explain the concept of a function. From this paragraph a subject was supposed to acquire a function schema, which states that a specific function is defined by value assignments to the following four attributes: (a) the function name, (b) the type of argument, (c) the number of arguments, and d) the input/output mapping between the argument(s) and the result of the respective function call.
4. The behavior of the LISP system was explained. More specifically, the syntax specifications for two types of acceptable inputs to the LISP interpreter, namely, *quoted S-expressions* and *function calls* were described: A quoted S-expression consists of a single quote followed by an atom or list, like *'JOHN* or *'(FRIENDS (JOHN FRED))*. In response to such an input, the LISP system returns the respective S-expression without the quote. A *function call* consists of "(" and a *function name* followed by one or several *argument*

specifications and ")". The argument specification must be an acceptable input to the LISP system and must satisfy the requirements of the specific function.

In part B of the learning materials, the specific definition of the LISP functions under consideration (LIST, FIRST, REST, and EQUAL) were presented by text. Examples of these functions could be explored by the learners. The definitions given in the text described the respective values of the four attributes of the function schema. For instance, the sentence, *First has one argument*, would describe the value of the attribute, *number of arguments* of the *function schema*. In the example condition, on the other hand, a collection of examples (typically about 12 examples) such as *(FIRST'(A B))* → *A* would be presented. From such examples, the *values* of the *attributes* of the *function* (e.g., the number of arguments) may be *induced* or *abducted* when sufficient prior knowledge is available.

With appropriate prior knowledge (for details see chapter 8), each of the four LISP functions can thus be defined by a few sentences that express the specifications for the attributes of the function schema. For instance, the following four sentences may be used:

1. The function LIST is used to construct lists from simpler S-expressions.
2. The function LIST can have any number of arguments.
3. Both atoms and lists can be used as arguments.
4. The value of the LIST function call consists of "(", the arguments of the function call, and ")".

Alternatively, a function definition may be inferred from a number of positive (and/or negative) examples of interactions with the LISP interpreter, which may include the following:

1. (LIST 'A 'B)   →   (A B)
2. (LIST 'C 'D 'E)   →   (C D E)

Although the surface form of the sentences are very different from the surface form of the examples, our theory suggests that the two types of learning materials may be constructed to be *informationally equivalent* (Larkin & Simon, 1987). From either material, a learner may therefore acquire the relevant *situation knowledge* about a function. Situation knowledge is the knowledge about the state of affairs that is described by the text. This situation knowledge is also exemplified by the sequence of examples, which is said to be informationally equivalent to the text.

In the various experiments, one or several of the following test tasks were employed: Sentence recognition and verification tasks, example verification tasks, and programming tasks. In a *sentence recognition task*, a subject is asked whether a given sentence appeared verbatim in a text. In a *sentence verification task*, on the other hand, a subject is asked whether a presented sentence is true or false with respect to the situation that was described by the learning material (see Fig. 1.2).

According to the specific experimental question under investigation, a somewhat different selection of paragraphs from the text and test tasks was used in the various experiments: The influence of a learner's processing goals was investigated by using section A of the materials followed by *sentence recognition tasks* (see chapter 7). To compare learning from text with learning from examples, parts A and B of the materials were employed. Because a sentence recognition test is not a sensible task when knowledge has been acquired from examples, *sentence verification* and *example verification* tasks were administered to investigate knowledge acquisition from different learning materials (see chapter 8). The transformation from text to examples and vice versa was investigated by selecting all those sentences and examples that, according to our model, were required to perform this task (see chapter 9). In order to investigate the influence of prior domain knowledge, expert subjects who were knowledgeable about the general concept of a function were compared to novice subjects who supposedly did not posses such knowledge. In these experiments, instruction module 3 (function schema) was therefore not included in the learning materials (see chapter 10). In order to compare the predictions of the *integrated knowledge acquisition hypothesis* with the *example dominance hypothesis*, certain sentences that could supposedly be inferred from the examples were similarly deleted from the instruction materials. Whether these statements would indeed be inferred from the examples and whether information from the text would be integrated with the examples was tested (chapter 11).

1.6 Cognitive Modeling of Human Learning Processes

In our research, we developed a *unified theory of knowledge acquisition*, which describes the purposeful acquisition of new knowledge in the different kinds of learning situations. The need for developing unified theories of cognition was emphasized by Newell (1990). Newell proposed striving for unified theories, because it is more useful to provide the total picture than to study related phenomena in isolation. Much of experimental psychology yields more and more differentiated results whose scope of reference becomes increasingly smaller. By providing a means for integrating the research results from different experimental paradigms, unified theories can help to counterbalance the trend toward differentiation in experimental psychology. Unified theories can also help to design new experiments, which allow us to jointly investigate different experimental phenomena that had previously only been researched in isolation.

In this book, we report research on learning from text, learning from situation-examples (cases), and learning by exploration. Figure 1.3 shows the general framework that was used for theorizing and empirically investigating knowledge acquisition. This framework determines the sets of observations and theoretical constructs that are regarded as interesting and important. It portrays the worldview that during knowledge acquisition a learner's prior knowledge is used in combination with the learning materials for developing and/or updating cognitive representations. In knowledge utilization, these cognitive representations are then employed to yield a person's performance for specific tasks in some given environment. Within traditional cognitive psychology, this worldview is quite uncontroversial (but see Clancey, 1993; Greeno, 1995; Suchman, 1987; and section 1.1 of this chapter). Some of Greeno's suggestions were incorporated into this framework. In particular, the newly generated cognitive representations are understood as the products of goal-driven attunements of the specific learning situation and the learner's prior knowledge.

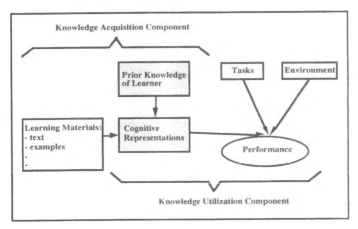

FIG. 1.3. A general framework for theorizing about the acquisition and utilization of knowledge. Cognitive representations are understood as the products of goal-driven attunements of the specific learning situation (text, examples, etc.) and the learner's prior knowledge.

We now give an overview of the contents of the different chapters of this book. The first part of this book, which consists of chapters 2 through 6, continues the discussion of cognitive modeling of human learning processes. The second part of this book is concerned with the experimental evaluation of the model that was proposed in the first part. The book concludes with a discussion of prospects and applications of the conducted research.

Chapter 2: As Newell pointed out, a uniform set of principles is required for developing a general theory. In particular, a unified theory must be precisely stated, and a corresponding computational model must be developed. In chapter 2, we therefore first review some selected computational models of learning that have been developed within the machine learning community (Shavlik & Dietterich, 1990). On the basis of this review, we then decide which type of computational model should be employed as a seed for developing the desired unified theory of knowledge acquisition.

The algorithmic descriptions of the computational models are often quite complex. A knowledge-level perspective (Newell, 1982) and the *Knowledge Acquisition and Design Structuring* (KADS) description formalism (Wielinga, Schreiber, & Breuker, 1992) abstract away many algorithmic details and are therefore better suited for characterizing the previously developed models of learning. From a knowledge-level perspective, models of learning can be roughly classified into three different groups. Namely, *case-based* (e.g., Riesbeck & Schank, 1989), *search-based* (e.g., Laird, Newell, & Rosenbloom, 1987), and *comprehension-based* (e.g., Kintsch, 1988) theories of learning can be distinguished.

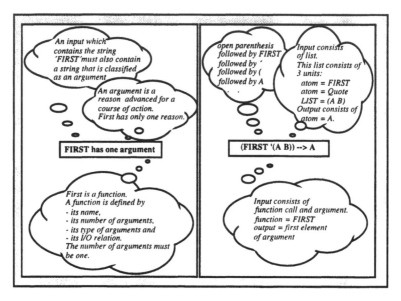

FIG. 1.4. Hypothetical mental constructions (shown as clouds) that may arise when studying the sentence about the LISP function FIRST or the specific LISP example. For instance the thought that "an argument is a reason advanced for a course of action" would be an immersion from a different conceptual space, namely from common sense knowledge. The statement that *FIRST has only one reason* can be seen as the product of an attunement. In this case the attunement is quite inappropriate.

In our research, the comprehension-based theory (Kintsch, 1988, 1992; Mannes & Kintsch, 1991) that underlies the processing assumptions of the *construction–integration (C–I)* simulation model (Mross & Roberts, 1992) is used as the seed for developing the unified theory for the acquisition of knowledge from text, cases, and by exploration. An important assumption of this comprehension-based theory is that learning is a *constructive process* in which different and possibly contradictory and redundant knowledge units are first creatively constructed. Figure 1.4 gives an example of such partially redundant and contradictory knowledge constructions, which may occur to various degrees, when a learner studies the sentence, *FIRST has one argument*, or the LISP-example, *(FIRST '(A B))* → *A*. After such knowledge *construction processes*, a context-sensitive *integration process* attunes these knowledge units so that, according to very global considerations, a coherent whole is obtained. All the knowledge units that do not fit into the "gobal picture" that emerged from the relatively arbitrary collection of knowledge units are thereby eliminated. In other words, global coherence and consistency determine the representation that will be maintained after the integration processes. In the terminology of Gestalt psychology, one could also say that those knowledge units that together yield a good Gestalt are maintained in memory, whereas the other knowledge units vanish.

A computational model of comprehension-based learning will consequently describe the creative processes by which new representations are formed. *Comprehension-based theories* thus differ from *case-based reasoning*, which emphasizes the importance of veridical storage of concrete real-life episodes and their later reuse for solving new problems as well as from *search-based theories*, which stress the importance of searching problem or representation spaces for specific solutions and subsequently compiling the search result into a more efficient representation.

Chapter 3: Unfortunately, computational models have sometimes been viewed as a way of theorizing that does not harmonize with the methods of experimental psychology (e.g., Dörner, 1989). We believe, however, quite to the contrary, that computational models and psychological experiments fit together very well and do indeed mutually compensate for their respective weaknesses. They should therefore be understood as two sides of the same coin. This view has, for example, been taken for the definition of cognitive modeling (cf. Schmalhofer & Wetter, 1988). In chapter 3, we first evaluate the criticisms against computational models in the area of experimental psychology. On the basis of the research of Gregg and Simon (1967), we show that computational models are in principle no different from (other) mathematical models and that in many cases they can be more appropriate and more specific than a more traditional mathematical model. In particular, computational models can be empirically evaluated by psychological experiments and experimental psychology may greatly benefit by employing such modeling techniques. Computational models can be systematically developed and experimentally evaluated according to the levels approach to cognitive modeling (cf. Anderson, 1990a). Thereby, descriptions at the (a) *knowledge level*, (b) *symbol (or algorithm) level*, and (c) *implementation level* are distinguished.

Computational models basically consist of the algorithms and data structures that are implemented by a computer program that predicts or models certain aspects of human cognition. Computer models further require implementation in some specific computer language, such as C, PROLOG, or PASCAL and execution on some computer such as a personal computer, a workstation, or a mainframe. Although such an *implementation* in a specific programming language that runs on a particular computer is a prerequisite for obtaining a (testable) computational model, it is not really the essential part of the computational model. It does not matter whether the computer model is implemented in PROLOG or PASCAL. Essential for the computer models are the algorithms and the data structures. Computer models are therefore specified at the *symbol level* (Newell, 1980) or at the *algorithm level* (Anderson, 1990a).

A *computational theory*, on the other hand, is specified at the *knowledge-level* and has a somewhat different cut (system and environment are jointly described). A *knowledge level* description of a computer model can be best understood as an abstract description of a computer program together with its environment, where *goals, knowledge, skills, and performance* are attributed to the computer program (Schmalhofer, Aitken, & Bourne, 1994). We thus clearly distinguish between *computational models* and their respective *computational theories*. The relation between a computational model and a computational theory is similar to the relation between a computer program and its well-written (and possibly formally specified) documentation. The distinction between these levels is also of particular importance for the empirical evaluation of a cognitive model (see Fig. 3.2), which is also discussed in chapter 3. Finally, a *rational analysis* (Anderson, 1990a) of knowledge acquisition is performed. This analysis yields an initial knowledge level description for the unified theory. Because empirical results from experimental psychology are mostly ignored by a rational analysis, it is a top–down approach for deriving a knowledge-level description.

Chapter 4: In this chapter we pursue a more bottom-up approach for obtaining a knowledge-level description. We first review the research literature on verbal learning and text comprehension. The results show that over the years experimental research has progressed from investigating memory for relatively simple and isolated verbal materials, such as words, to the acquisition of knowledge from texts. Important progress was achieved by Kintsch's (1988) C–I model. However, because the distinction between *knowledge* and *symbol level descriptions* is relatively new in cognitive research, the C–I model has not yet been described according to the *levels approach to cognitive modeling*. After the C–I model has been described in its conventional way, we characterize this model in the abstract terms of the knowledge-level. A knowledge-level description of comprehension-based learning is thereby obtained. This description is presented in the form of a KADS inference structure (cf. Fig. 4.2) that is termed the C–I theory. Fortunately, the C–I theory turns out to be completely consistent with the initial knowledge-level description that was obtained by the rational analysis of knowledge acquisition.

A knowledge-level description also identifies the major experimental manipulations, which can (and should) be performed for validating the theory as well as the corresponding models. In particular, (a) the manipulation of the learner's processing goal, (b) the variation of the learning materials and (c) the manipulation of the learner's prior knowledge (i.e., the knowledge net) are determined as the three sets of variables that need to be experimentally investigated. By following the assumptions of the C–I theory, we then develop the KIWi model for the acquisition of LISP knowledge from texts. The acronym KIWi stands for "Konstruktion und Integration von Wissen" which translates to *construction and integration of knowledge*. The KIWi model is presented by its symbol-level description. For learning from text, the KIWi model is quite similar to the C–I model, but it has been implemented in such a manner that it can be easily extended to learning from other materials. The presentation of implementational details, however, is postponed until after the presentation of the extended KIWi model.

In **chapter 5**, the extended KIWi model for learning from cases, learning by exploration, and the subsequent utilization of knowledge in verification, evaluation, programming, and problem-solving tasks is presented. This chapter has a structure similar to its predecessor: After a review of the previous research on learning from examples, a description of the extended KIWi model is presented (at the symbol level). Again, the model description is applied to the learning of LISP. Learning from examples is described, as well as learning by exploration. Learning by exploration is thereby viewed as consisting of two components. At first, the learner instigates some interaction with his or her environment and the environment reacts to it. The learner's action, together with the reaction of the environment, constitutes a case (or an example). The second component of learning by exploration is therefore assumed to be identical to learning from examples. It should be noted that with the KIWi model, the various learning methods can be arbitrarily interspersed. The KIWi model thus allows the derivation of predictions of the cognitive products of learning from any sequence of text, examples, and exploration. Toward the end of the chapter a description of how these cognitive products are utilized in the different test tasks is given.

Chapter 6 is dedicated to presenting the KIWi model as a unified cognitive model of the acquisition of knowledge, from which very definite experimental predictions can be derived. After a concise model description, the various implementation modules are described. Furthermore, we show how the knowledge-level description of the model can be used to design experiments that test the core assumptions of the theory and the model. For these experiments, model predictions are derived and the results of individual simulation runs are presented. The predictions of the model address the effect of a person's learning goal, the effects of different learning materials as well as their combination, and the effect of a learner's prior domain knowledge. These predictions are later tested by the experiments presented in the second part of the book (on experimental evaluation): Chapter 7 addresses the predictions about a learner's goals; chapter 8 and 9 are concerned about the different types of study materials; chapter 10 investigates the various interrelationships between a learner's prior knowledge and the different types of learning situations (learning from text, examples, and by exploration); and in chapter 11, the predictions of the KIWi model are compared to the example–dominance hypothesis that has been derived from the assumptions of case-based learning (cf. LeFevre & Dixon, 1986).

1.7 Experimental Evaluation

Chapter 7: The experiments presented in this chapter examine the specific prediction of how the knowledge acquisition process, as indicated by sentence-reading times, depends on the learner's processing goal (experiment 1) and how the memory strengths at the various representation levels are thereby affected (experiment 2). In particular, the verbatim representation of a text is distinguished from the representation of its propositional meaning (i.e., the textbase) and the representation of the situations described by the text (i.e., the situation model). Experiment 3 tested, in addition, the time course of the information retrieval from the three representation levels. The results showed that the processing goal of writing a text summary yielded a relatively strong textbase and the processing goal of having to apply the knowledge for writing a computer program produced a relatively strong situation model. The analysis of the sentence reading times supported this conclusion.

Chapter 8 addresses the question of the acquisition of equivalent situation knowledge from different types of study materials. Thereby, the KIWi model is tested in the following way. A text and a set of examples were developed so that the KIWi model would construct the same situation representations from either one of the two sets of materials. In learning from text, this knowledge is basically constructed by elaborative processes. In learning from examples, this knowledge is basically constructed by inductive and abductive processes. From the simulation runs of the KIWi model, it could thus be predicted that the same situation knowledge would be obtained in both conditions (learning from text versus learning from examples), but that there should be clear differences with respect to the more material-related knowledge representations (textbase and template base; cf. Fig. 6.1). Predictions were also derived with respect to the different types of cognitive processes that would be executed during learning in the two conditions.

Experiment 4 clearly confirmed these hypotheses. The situation knowledge was indeed found to be identical when the different types of materials were studied. In order to further examine the cognitive processes that operate on the different learning materials, experiment 5 employed a think-aloud method (Ericsson & Simon, 1984) for the same experimental design that was used in experiment 4. For the analysis of the verbal protocols, a model-based category system was developed. The verbalizations of each category could thus be associated with a specific component process of the KIWi model. Additional categories were subsequently developed so that all verbalization episodes of the protocol could be uniquely classified. The verbal protocols provided clear indications for the psychological reality of the component processes that are postulated by the KIWi model. Furthermore, indications of additional processes were found that are not described by the KIWi model.

Chapter 9 addresses the question of informationally equivalent learning materials even more directly. Larkin and Simon (1987) pointed out that different types of materials can be viewed as informationally equivalent when they contain the same information even though they differ with respect to which information is explicitly stated and which information can only be derived from the learning material. When they are appropriately designed, text and examples can be regarded as such informationally equivalent materials. It was therefore investigated how well subjects can transform a text into examples and vice versa. Thereby, many component processes should occur which are also used in learning from these materials. Experiment 6 investigated these predictions by collecting think-aloud protocols. In experiment 7, the individual differences that occur in performing these transformational processes were assessed. In this experiment, the KIWi model was not only applied to develop the experimental materials (so that they would indeed be informationally equivalent on the basis of the model), but was also used as an analysis tool for assessing the knowledge that was acquired by the individual subjects. This experiment thus also shows how the KIWi model can be applied as a tool for knowledge diagnosis to assess individual knowledge differences. Thereby, it was determined which component processes are very error prone in human subjects and which processes are more reliable.

Chapter 10 investigates the effect of prior knowledge on learning from text, from examples, and by exploration. The C–I theory and the KIWi model assume that learning is a constructive process. Prior domain knowledge as well as general processing heuristics are thereby responsible for constructing knowledge from the learning materials, which is then further processed by the integration processes. If the constructed situational knowledge coheres and is consistent, the integration processes will yield an appropriate situation model in addition to the more material-related representation. This prediction of the KIWi model was tested in experiment 8. In four different experimental conditions, computer users who were assumed to have a function schema, as well as novices who did not have such prior domain knowledge, studied either a text or a set of examples. (Starting with this experiment, module 3 of part A of the learning materials, which described the concept of a function, was removed from the learning materials; see Fig. 1.2.) The experiment confirmed the predictions of the KIWi model: Although the formation of a situation model depended quite strongly on the prior domain knowledge, the more material-related representations, such as textbase and template base, were even formed when the most significant prior domain knowledge was lacking (i.e., by the novices). Experiment 9 showed that when text and examples are studied together, the expertise differences were much less pronounced. According to the KIWi model, the heuristic processes will construct more and also more coordinated knowledge when two different materials, rather than only one learning material are studied. With two different learning materials (text and examples) it is therefore more likely to form an adequate situation model, even when significant prior domain knowledge is lacking. In other words, when two study materials are presented and more time and effort is exerted, even novices may succeed in forming an appropriate situation model in a bottom-up fashion. In experiment 10, learning from examples and learning by exploration were compared in programmers and novices. The results showed that different skills are required in the two learning situations. Whereas programmers are more successful in learning by exploration, novices perform better when they learned from examples.

Chapter 11: Several researchers have emphasized the importance of examples for acquiring new knowledge (Anderson, Farrell, & Sauers, 1984; Chi et al., 1989; LeFevre & Dixon, 1986). The KIWi model acknowledges the importance of examples but, at the same time stresses that texts may be equally important in knowledge acquisition. In this chapter, predictions derived from case-based reasoning assumptions are compared to the predictions derived from a comprehension-based theory and the KIWi model. More specifically, the example–dominance hypothesis of case-based reasoning was compared to the integrated knowledge-acquisition hypothesis of the KIWi model. In experiment 11, more or less complete texts were presented in combination with examples. Rather than being informationally equivalent, text and examples were constructed to supplement each other. The integrated knowledge-acquisition hypothesis was thus tested against the assumption that learners would prefer to study examples and only process the text in a shallow fashion. The experimental results supported the integrated knowledge-acquisition hypothesis. In addition, it was shown under which conditions the KIWi model would predict that subjects ignore or only shallowly process a text while focusing on the examples.

Chapter 12: In this chapter, we investigate whether the results that were achieved by our research in experimental cognitive psychology could possibly have valuable implications on the development of instructional materials for teaching purposes as well as for the development of tutoring and expert systems. We thereby distinguish between tutoring systems that were developed from a point of view of symbolic cognition and tutoring systems that can be motivated by the worldview of situated cognition. We then report the results from a quite large research project on the development of expert systems that has been conducted from 1989 to 1993 by the knowledge acquisition group at the German Research Center for Artificial Intelligence (DFKI) in Kaiserslautern. Because this expert system research was motivated by the reported results from cognitive experimental psychology, it is well suited to demonstrate how such research can be applied to expert systems.

Chapter 13: In this final chapter, we summarize and discuss the proposed solution to the methodological problem of integrating the results from increasingly more detailed psychological experiments. In addition, the proposed model of constructive knowledge acquisition that we have developed according to the proposed methodology is compared to alternative models as well as to alternative theories and frameworks. This discussion includes the various experimental results. We conclude with the assertion that an evolutionary perspective may very well serve as the seed for a synthesis of the rationalist and empiricist research traditions that have fragmented research on cognition for such a long time (cf. Cosmides & Tooby, 1994; Fischer, McCall, Ostwald, Reeves, & Shipman, 1994; Lesgold, 1993).

1.8 Summary

In this introductory chapter, we have presented an overview of *what* research we have performed, *why* it was done, and *how* it was conducted. Creative knowledge acquisition was researched in the area of cognitive experimental psychology. Due to the dramatic scientific advances at the turn of this century and the cognitive revolution of the sciences at the middle of this century, the question of knowledge acquisition is no longer only an issue of a philosophical epistemology but can indeed be researched by scientific methods. Techniques from experimental psychology and computer simulation methods were therefore used to investigate this topic.

The research: The research topic was characterized as the development of a cognitive model about creative knowledge acquisition in the form of a computer simulation and its empirical evaluation by psychological experiments. The resulting model was called the KIWi model.

Why it was performed: In the area of general experimental psychology, different ways of acquiring knowledge, such as text comprehension and concept formation from examples and cases, have typically been investigated in isolation. In order to integrate the experimental research findings of the different areas, a unified model is required. A unified model is furthermore needed to utilize previous and future research results in practical applications that are more complex than the controlled laboratory situations that are so well suited for performing systematic research. Therefore, the cognitive model was developed in a manner that would integrate learning from text, learning from examples, and learning by exploration into a unified theory. In other words, a unified model was obtained that bridges the gap between the systematic but isolated observations from the psychological laboratory and the more complex real-world situations.

How it was conducted: In reporting this research, we must first deal with the methodological issue of using computer simulations together with psychological experiments and the assumptions from situativity theory that are essential for creative knowledge acquisition. In chapter 2, we therefore review results from computational technology. In particular, computational models of knowledge acquisition are presented together with knowledge-level descriptions of computer systems. In chapter 3, the levels approach towards cognitive modeling is presented. This approach combines computer simulation techniques, methods from experimental psychology and constructionist assumptions from situated cognition in a balanced way. It can be applied in a more top–down or a more bottom-up fashion. A so-called rational analysis is the first step in a top–down application, and the acquisition and utilization of knowledge was analyzed in this manner. Chapters 4 and 5 address learning from text and learning from cases. These chapters use the levels approach towards cognitive modeling in a bottom-up fashion: From the results of psychological experiments our discussion progresses toward psychological processing models, and a knowledge-level description (that we also refer to as the C–I theory) is abstracted out of these models. This C–I theory is then used to develop the KIWi model (once again in a top–down manner). In chapter 6, we evaluate whether the results of the rational analysis are consistent with the assumptions of the C–I theory. The KIWi model is then presented as a model that unifies the different kinds of knowledge acquisition. In this chapter, the model is also presented at the implementation level. Its knowledge-level description is then employed for obtaining experimental designs that provide representative empirical tests of the model. The second part of the book, which consists of chapters 7 to 11, reports the experiments that have been performed for testing the model in the subject domain of learning a new programming language. In chapter 12, we assess how the results of this research can be applied. Chapter 13 concludes the book with a general discussion and a perspective for future work.

Part I

Cognitive Modeling of Learning

Something old,
something new,
something borrowed,
something blue.

2

Computational Models of Knowledge Acquisition

In the area of machine learning, which is a very prominent research topic in the field of artificial intelligence, numerous computer programs have been developed that are capable of learning. Especially within the last 15 years, much progress has been made and powerful computational models of learning have been developed (cf. Carbonell, 1989; Morik, 1993; Schmalhofer, 1996). Whereas early systems were pretty much restricted in their applications to toy problems (e.g., Samuel, 1959), more recent machine learning systems perform learning processes in quite complex domains. These complex application domains include criminal justice (Bain, 1986; Riesbeck & Schank, 1989) as well as the acquisition of new knowledge from texts (e.g., Mooney & DeJong, 1985). Shavlik and Dietterich (1990) collected the descriptions of the most important learning systems that have been developed over the years. Each of these learning systems may be considered as a possible starting point for developing a computational model of human knowledge acquisition.

In this chapter, we attempt to give some insights and an overview of machine learning systems. Due to the limitations in space, we certainly cannot describe all the systems and not even all of the most important systems. We therefore proceed in the following way. In order to provide some insights on how machine learning systems operate, we first present three particular learning systems in some detail. Then, a more comprehensive overview of the available systems is given by analyzing the general characteristics of a larger number of different learning systems.

Newell (1982) suggested that artificial intelligence systems should be described at a more abstract level, which he termed the knowledge level. One of his motivations was to provide a description level independent of implementation and symbol-processing details. Knowledge-level descriptions are therefore well suited for characterizing machine learning systems. First, we present Newell´s knowledge level and the KADS notational system, which has been proposed by Breuker, Wielinga, and their research group (Breuker & Wielinga, 1989; Wielinga, Schreiber, & Breuker, 1992) for specifying such knowledge-level descriptions, together with some extensions that were suggested by Schmalhofer, Aitken, and Bourne (1994). For a relatively representative sample of learning systems, which we select from the collection of Shavlik and Dietterich (1990), we thus establish knowledge-level descriptions by determining goals (purpose), knowledge, skills, and performance as the four abstract parameters of such knowledge-level system descriptions. By using these paramenter descriptions, are able to distinguish roughly three classes of learning systems, in which each class has its own characteristic parameter values. As seen at the end of the chapter, this classification allows us to deliberately select the fundamental learning assumptions, on which we base the development of our unified theory of knowledge acquisition.

2.1 Some Typical Examples of Machine Learning Systems

In this section, we describe three systems, which learn in quite different ways. The descripitons of the three systems are intended to provide some insights into how machine learning systems operate, without requiring the reader to have any technical knowledge about computer programming. The JUDGE system is a typical case-based reasoning system. The INDUCE system uses inductive reasoning. GENESIS (Mooney & DeJong, 1985), finally, applies deductive reasoning for learning. All of these systems are in different ways relevant for psychological research on learning: The JUDGE system was developed on the basis of interviews with human judges (cf. Riesbeck & Schank, 1989) and results from psychological research (e.g., Pennington & Hastie, 1981). The INDUCE system, on the other hand, has been evaluated regarding how well it can describe human inductive learning, and GENESIS describes processes that may occur in learning from text.

JUDGE

The JUDGE system, which was developed by Bain (1986), determines the criminal sentences for adverserial interactions in which a crime has (supposedly) been committed. JUDGE is a typical case-based reasoning system. In case-based reasoning, learning occurs by storing cases. Cases are basically episodes of problems and their respective solutions. These cases are stored in combination with appropriate indices, so that they can be retrieved easily when a similar problem arises. The old problem solution (e.g., the specific criminal sentence) is then modified, so that it becomes a solution for the new problem (e.g., the verdict or criminal sentence for the new case). A case-based reasoner thus learns to solve new problems by adapting the solutions that were used to solve problems previously. The new problem and its solution are then again stored as a case in the knowledge base.

This is basically the method by which JUDGE operates. JUDGE stores the descriptions of crimes together with the verdict of the sentence and its legal justification. The following description is a typical case of an adverserial interaction that can be processed by the JUDGE system. We refer to this description as case x.

> First, Randy struck Chuck with his fists several times. Chuck was only slightly hurt. Next, Chuck struck Randy with his fists several times. Randy was only slightly hurt. Then, Randy slashed at Chuck with a knife one time. Chuck's skin was cut. Next. Chuck slashed at Randy with a knife one time. Randy's skin was cut. Finally, Randy stabbed Chuck with a knife several times. Chuck died.

In order to use this case for solving future problems, a specific criminal sentence needs to be attached to it. Five processing stages are distinguished in the JUDGE system: (a) the *interpretation phase*, (b) the *retrieval* of previous cases from memory, (c) the *comparison* and differentiation of the retrieved cases, (d) the *modification* phase, and (e) a *generalization* phase.

During the *interpretation phase* the motivations of the different persons who are involved in the description are analyzed. For example, the reason the person started a fight is explained. Subsequent actions are then interpreted according to whether the outcome of an action was as intended, not as severe as intended, or accidental (i.e., more severe than intended). For example, in case x an episode is found in memory that closely corresponds to the descriptions given by the first two sentences in the case. On the basis of this memory retrieval, Randy's action is interpreted as an unprovoked assault.

In the subsequent *retrieval phase*, the memory is searched for a case that is similar to the current case with respect to the interpretations that were established in the interpretation phase. Only cases that satisfy some minimal similarity criterion are retrieved from memory.

During the *comparison phase*, the differences between the current case and the cases retrieved from memory are evaluated. If no differences exist at all, the same verdict would be suggested as in the case retrieved from memory. More generally, the result of this comparison determines which modifications of the proposed verdict are proposed in the next phase.

In the *modification phase*, the verdict of the old case is adjusted according to the differences determined in the comparison phase. For cases that are not completely identical but rather similar, an extrapolation procedure is used that takes into account the minimum and the maximum sentences that are allowed by law. More generally, when the JUDGE system transfers a sentencing strategy from one case to another, it modifies the sentence to accomodate the feature differences between the two cases. In the *generalization phase*, several similar cases are analyzed to obtain more general rules by inductive processes. Thus, inductive processes also occur in case-based reasoning. Inductive processes are the central component of the INDUCE system, that is described in the next section.

INDUCE

An important learning procedure consists of inducing general rules from a limited number of specific examples (cf. chapter 5). It is well known from the literature on the philosphy of science (cf. Westermann & Gerjets, 1994) that there is no unique solution to solving such induction problems. In other words, there is a large number of quite different rules that may be induced from a given set of examples, and on purely logical grounds, there are no good reasons why one rule should be preferred over another. For instance, if we had to induce a general rule for the number sequence which starts by "1, 2, 4," we may induce the general rule "increasing sequence of integers which are not divisible by 3" and hypothesize that 5 would be the next element of the sequence. Alternatively, we could induce the general rule "$a_{n+1} = 2*a_n$; $a_1 = 1$" and predict that the next element would be 8, or the general rule "$a_{n+1} = a_n^2 - a_n + 2$, $a_1 = 1$" and predict that the next element would be 14. When we learn by induction, we can form rules that have only the status of a hypothesis. Further evidence may show that a given hypothesis was incorrect.

Computer programs that learn by induction also have this limitation (see: Medin, Wattenmaker & Michalski, 1987). Inductive learning programs are generally characterized by their inductive bias. The inductive bias determines which of the many possible generalizations formed are from a given set of examples. In describing the learning bias of an induction procedure, one can distinguish between the *representation bias* and the *search bias* (Rendell, 1986). In other words, the learning bias of a machine learning program is determined by the specific knowledge representation used in the system and by the manner in which the space of possible hypotheses is searched. INDUCE is a specific learning system developed by Michalski (1983).

INDUCE takes positive and negative examples as input (i.e., classified examples) and produces a general description of the target concept that is delineated by the class of positive examples. INDUCE may for instance be presented with two groups of trains, which are supposed to define the concept of east trains and west trains (see Fig. 2.1). Thereby, each example (i.e., each train) is described by several attributes. For instance, the cars of a train may be described as short or long, by their shape, and by the number of wheels. INDUCE can process several types of attributes: Nominal attributes (e.g., left, right), ordinal attributes (e.g., short, medium, long), and metric attributes (e.g., the length in cm) can be used, as well as hierarchically structured attributes (e.g., "a train consists of a locomotive with several cars; each car consists of wheels, the body and the roof; the roofs come in various shapes" would be an instance for a *part-of* hierarchy; *is-a* hierarchies may be used as well).

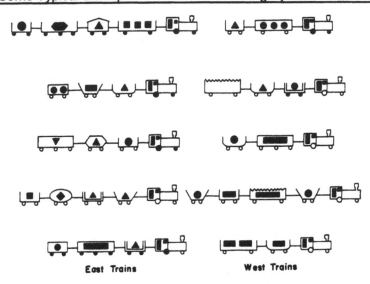

FIG. 2.1. East trains and west trains as two sets, which are preclasssified as positive and negative examples of the concept that is to be identified by the INDUCE learning system (reprinted from Medin, Wattenmaker, and Michalski, 1987; Figure 1).

To obtain a general description of the target concept, INDUCE applies several generalization processes:

1. A specific value of an attribute may be replaced by a variable (e.g., the color red is replaced by any color).
2. A given attribute is deleted from the description of the target concept (i.e., it is assumed that this attribute is irrelevant with respect to the definition of the target concept).
3. For metric attributes, two specific values can be replaced by the interval defined by these values (the description that a west train has 2 or 4 cars is thus generalized to the description that a west train has between 2 and 4 cars).
4. For hierarchically structured attributes, generalizations are obtained by climbing one level up in the hierarchy (from the description "VW or OPEL or BMW," one may thus obtain the description "German car").
5. Under specific circumstances, INDUCE can also apply negation. If there is an example of the target concept (e.g., east train) together with a counterexample (e.g., west train), INDUCE can generate the negation of all those attribute descriptions that are satisfied by the counter examples, which at the same time do not occur in the description of the example. Thereby, the most general description of the target concept is obtained that excludes all the instances of the counter examples.
6. Finally, there is a procedure called *constructive generalization*. With this procedure, explicit descriptions can be transferred into descriptions with numbers. Instead of the description of a trains as *car and car and car and car*, one thus obtains the description *four cars*. These generalization rules are

applied according to the following induction algorithm, which is called the *star algorithm.*

Star algorithm: At first, a positive example is selected (e.g., the first east train of Fig. 2.1). This example is termed the *seed.* The different generalization processes are then applied to the seed, so that a description is obtained, which is not satisified by the negative examples (i.e., the west trains). For instance, the description *long train with hectagon as load* may be obtained. The set of the produced descriptions are termed *the star.* In the next step, the descriptions that are contained in the star are evaluated with respect to different representation criteria (e.g., one may prefer conjunctions over disjunctions) and the description with the best evaluation is maintained. If the obtained description applies to all positive examples, the induction procedure is finished. Otherwise, a second positive example is included as a *second seed*, the induction procedure is repeated with this seed, and a disjunction of the two obtained concept descriptions is formed. INDUCE may thus produce a concept description that consists of the disjunction of terms, which themselves consists of conjunctions. The description of this algorithm clearly shows that the learning result depends on how the examples were described (representational bias) as well as on the order in which the different examples were processed (search bias).

GENESIS

GENESIS is an abbreviation of *Gen*eralizing *E*xplanations of *S*tories *into Schemata* (Mooney & DeJong, 1985). The GENESIS system takes stories written in English as input and produces an action schema, which represents the interactions of the various agents in the story. The following story is an example of an input that can be processed by GENESIS.

> Fred is the father of Mary and is a millionaire. John approached Mary. She was wearing blue jeans. John pointed a gun at her and told her he wanted her to get into his car. He drove her to his hotel and locked her in his room. John called Fred and told him John was holding Mary captive. John told Fred if Fred gave him $250,000 at Trenos then John would release Mary. Fred gave him the money and John released Mary.

This text is first processed by a parser (Dyer, 1983), which generates a conceptual represenation in terms of semantic primitives (Schank, 1982; Schank & Abelson, 1977; chapter 1, this volume). The major task of the understanding component is to generate a complete representation of all causal connections that exist within the given story. Several inferences may be required to recover the complete causal structure. To accomplish this task, a collection of schemata is used as background knowledge. Learning occurs by generating a new schema that is then stored in the schema collection. Finally, a simple question-answering component has been implemented, so that different questions can be answered.

For generating a schema, an explanation-based learning procedure is applied (see DeJong & Mooney, 1986). Explanation-based learning (EBL) is a method in which generalizations are formed from a single case by employing a body of background knowledge and a desired description level, which is defined by a so-called operationality criterion. In explanation-based generalization, which is a special form of EBL, a target concept is also explicitly given. In the more general EBL method, the target concept is formed during learning. EBL explains or proves that the case (*training example*) satisfies the requirements of a target concept (*goal concept*) using the background knowledge as the *domain theory*. In other words it is deduced from the domain theory that the training example is an instance of a goal concept. The deduced proof is generalized to a more usable concept definition in terms of the desired description level (*operationality criterion*). This generalization is guided by the background knowledge rather than by some unknown inductive bias, and brings the relevant features of the case in focus whereas irrelevant features are ignored.

For the GENESIS system, the story serves as the training example. The background knowledge is stored as part of the collection of schemata. It describes objects and their properties, which occur in the story, as well as general inference rules for deriving other properties and relations. In order to process the specific story, the backgound knowledge must describe actions like TO_DRIVE, TO_CAPTURE, TO-TELEPHONE. In addition, inference rules like FATHER(X,Y) --> PARENT(X,Y) are required. The target concept consists of a sequence of actions that accomplish the final result of the story. The current story thus yields an action schema for getting money by kidnapping a person. Figure 2.2 shows the complete explanation structure (all nodes and edges are included) as well as the generalized explanation structure (only the nodes and edges which are bold and solid are included). The generalized explanation structure constitutes the schema that is learned from the story. The acquired schema can subsequently be used to understand similar stories or stories in which kidnapping is only part of a larger plot.

Each of the three described learning systems is a complex computer program that has been designed according to some general idea concerning how learning may be accomplished. Each of the systems uses a certain algorithm for achieving a particular learning result, and finally, each system has been implemented in some some specific programming language. Because these processing models are quite complex systems, their functioning is often quite difficult to understand if one has not implemented or at least worked with such a system.

For the development and the documentation of such knowledge-based systems, Newell (1980) proposed so-called *knowledge-level descriptions* that abstract away from the specific processing and implementation detail and simply ascribe knowledge and goals to a system. Skills and performance may also be included in such a description (Schmalhofer et al., 1994). In the following section, we describe Newell's proposal as well as the pragmatically oriented notations for the knowledge-level descriptions proposed by Breuker, Wielinga, and their collegues.

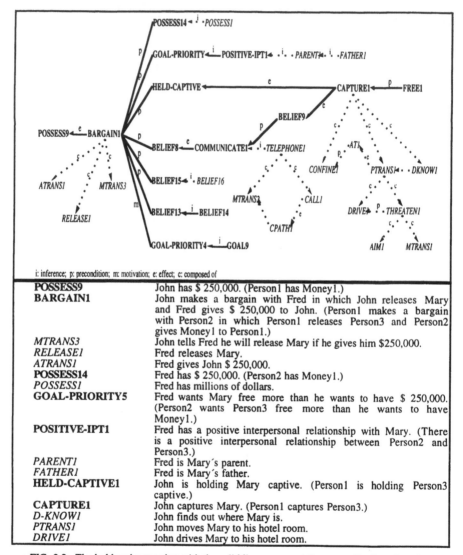

POSSESS9	John has $ 250,000. (Person1 has Money1.)
BARGAIN1	John makes a bargain with Fred in which John releases Mary and Fred gives $ 250,000 to John. (Person1 makes a bargain with Person2 in which Person1 releases Person3 and Person2 gives Money1 to Person1.)
MTRANS3	John tells Fred he will release Mary if he gives him $250,000.
RELEASE1	Fred releases Mary.
ATRANS1	Fred gives John $ 250,000.
POSSESS14	Fred has $ 250,000. (Person2 has Money1.)
POSSESS1	Fred has millions of dollars.
GOAL-PRIORITY5	Fred wants Mary free more than he wants to have $ 250,000. (Person2 wants Person3 free more than he wants to have Money1.)
POSITIVE-IPT1	Fred has a positive interpersonal relationship with Mary. (There is a positive interpersonal relationship between Person2 and Person3.)
PARENT1	Fred is Mary's parent.
FATHER1	Fred is Mary's father.
HELD-CAPTIVE1	John is holding Mary captive. (Person1 is holding Person3 captive.)
CAPTURE1	John captures Mary. (Person1 captures Person3.)
D-KNOW1	John finds out where Mary is.
PTRANS1	John moves Mary to his hotel room.
DRIVE1	John drives Mary to his hotel room.

FIG. 2.2. The bold nodes together with the solid lines represent the generalized explanation structure. GENESIS produces this structure from the complete explanation structure that consists of all the nodes and links (including dotted lines) that are shown in the upper panel. The lower panel presents a description of selected nodes from the complete explanation structures as well as the nodes from the generalized explanation structure. They are shown in parentheses (adapted from DeJong and Mooney, 1986; Figure 8).

2.2 Knowledge Level Descriptions

Newell's Knowledge-Level

In his influential paper, Newell (1982) introduced a level of computer system description called the *knowledge level*. Since this time, describing artificial and human systems as a knowledge system has become an important goal in expert system research (Clancey, 1985; Breuker & Wielinga, 1989) as well as in cognitive psychology (Anderson, 1990a). When establishing a knowledge-level description, a natural or artificial system "is viewed as having a body of knowledge and a set of goals, so that it takes actions in the environment that its knowledge indicates will attain its goals" (Newell, 1992, p. 426). Knowledge systems are one level in the hierarchy of systems that make up an intelligent agent. Lower level descriptions such as the symbol level specify how a knowledge level system is realized in mechanisms (i.e., information processing and representation). The symbol level is described by memory, symbols, operations, interpretation processes, and perceptual and motor interfaces (Newell, 1980). Through knowledge-level descriptions, Newell provided us with a possibility for uniformly characterizing natural and artificial systems.

The key assumption underlying the knowledge level is the notion of an idealized rational agent. A rational agent is assumed to have the following attributes: (a) The agent has the ability to perform a set of actions in some environment; (b) The agent has goals about how its environment should be; (c) The agent has a body of knowledge about the evironment, its goals, its actions, and the relations between them, and knows all those facts that are a deductive consequence of its body of knowledge; and (d) The principle of rationality is its single law of behavior. It describes which actions the agent will perform: "If an agent has knowledge that one of its actions will lead to one of its goals, then the agent will select that action" (Newell, 1982, p. 102). The behavior of an agent is a sequence of actions taken in the environment over time. By applying the principle of rationality, one can presumeably predict the future behavior of an agent from its knowledge and its goals.

According to Newell (1980, 1992), the *symbol level* is described with the following attributes: (a) a memory, containing independently modifiable structures that contain symbols; (b) symbols (patterns in the structures) providing the distal access to other structures; (c) operations, taking symbol structures as input and producing symbol structures as output; and (d) interpretation processes, taking symbol structures as input and executing operations (the structures thereby representing these operations); and (e) perceptual and motor interface to interact with an external environment.

Although there are some open questions as to whether Newell's conception of the knowledge level may possibly be too idealistic (cf. Schmalhofer et al., 1994; Sticklen, 1989), there is no doubt that in general, such knowledge-level descriptions are very useful for cognitive psychology (Anderson, 1990a) as well as for the purpose of developing knowledge-based systems. Within the last decade, Breuker, Wielinga, and their collegues have developed the KADS notational system for documenting and designing computer systems at the knowledge level. KADS and similar notational systems are also very useful for documenting machine learning systems at the knowledge level without having to consider all the symbol processing details of these systems.

The KADS Methodology

KADS is a methodology for developing knowledge-based systems. The KADS methodology has matured during more than ten years of research that included several ESPRIT projects (e.g., COMMON-KADS and ESPRIT P5248). ESPRIT is a *European Specific Programme for Research in Information Technology*. In Europe, KADS has indeed become the de facto standard for developing knowledge-based systems. In KADS, the development of a knowledge-based system is viewed as a modeling activity. For our current purpose, it is not necessary to describe this methodology in detail. Here, we are only interested in some of the knowledge-level descriptions that have been proposed in KADS and, in particular, the distinction between *domain knowledge* and *inference knowledge*. According to KADS, knowledge-based systems should be described so that the domain knowledge can be considered to be relatively task neutral. In other words, the domain knowledge is represented in a form so that it is independent of its use by particular problem solving actions. Domain knowlege can thus be used in a variety of different ways, such as for problem solving, for explanation, for teaching, and so on. In addition to the domain knowledge, one also specifies the inference knowledge. The inference layer describes the control knowledge that is abstracted from the specific domain knowledge. "An inference specified at the inference level is assumed to be primitive in the sense that it is fully defined through its name, an input/output specification and a reference to the domain knowledge that it uses." (Wielinga et al., 1992, p. 18). Because the inferences are specified at the knowledge level, the actual way in which the inference is carried out is irrelevant. An inference structure is a combination of several inferences which achieve a certain goal. Inference structures are expressed in terms of *basic inference actions* (often also referred to as *knowledge sources*) and *metaclasses*. A basic inference action is the entity that carries out an action in a primitive inference step. In graphical representations (see Fig. 2.3) inference actions are usually indicated by ellipses. The data elements, which are operated on by the knowledge sources, are called metaclasses.

> A knowledge source performs an action that operates on some input data and has the capability of producing a new piece of information ("knowledge") as its output. During this process it uses domain knowledge. The name of the knowledge source is supposed to be indicative of the type of action that is carried out. . . .
> A metaclass description serves a dual purpose: (i) it acts as a placeholder for domain objects, describing the role that these objects play in the problem solving process, and (ii) it points to the type(s) of domain objects that can play this role. (Wielinga et al., 1992, p. 18ff)

Figure 2.3 shows a simple inference structure in which a specific hypothesis about which component of the system is faulty is obtained by decomposing a system description. The inference structure does not specify which actual system is being diagnosed. This is only represented at the domain layer.

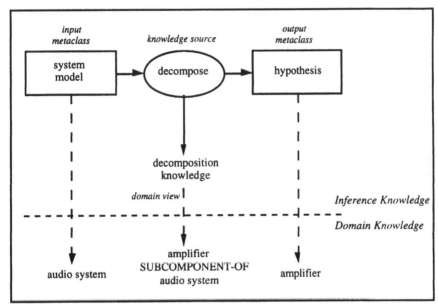

FIG. 2.3. A simple KADS inference structure: In KADS the generic inference knowledge is separated from the domain-specific knowledge (here an audio system, which has, among other components, an amplifier). The inference knowledge is represented by "system model" and "hypothesis" as metaclasses, and "decompose" as a basic inference action. In the complete system description, the relation between the domain knowledge and the inference structure is defined by a respective mapping (reprinted from Wielinga, Schreiber and Breuker, 1992; Figure 5).

KADS inference structures thus provide us with a means of describing learning systems independent of the specific application domain. The KADS notational system has also been formalized (Angele, Fensel, Landes, & Studer, 1991; Wetter, 1990). When we review some of the psychological learning models in chapters 4 and 5, we also develop KADS inference structures to characterize these models at the knowledge level.

So far we have presented an overview of knowledge level descriptions of computational systems as well as the KADS inference structures, which can be used to describe the processing of learning systems at the knowledge level. A more representative overview of the computational models of knowledge acquisition follows.

2.3 Knowledge Level Characterization of Learning Systems

To obtain a more comprehensive overview of the available learning systems, a respresentative sample of systems was selected from a reader on machine learning and these systems were then analyzed at the knowledge level. Because knowledge-level descriptions do not depend on the specific type of information processing (e.g., connectionist or symbolic), symbolic learning as well as connectionist learning systems were included in this analysis. More specifically, from the *Readings in Machine Learning*, edited by Shavlik and Dietterich (1990) the following systems were selected for this knowledge level analysis: As systems that are representative of *inductive learning*, Quinlan´s ID3, and Mitchell´s versionsspace procedure (VS) and Rumelhart, Hinton, and Williams' backpropagation (BP) were included. Fisher's COBWEB, Rumelhart and Zipser's competitive learning (CL) and Langley, Simon, and Bradshaw's BACON were included as examples for *unsupervised concept learning and discovery systems*. Mitchell, Keller, and Kedar-Cabelli's EBG and Laird, Rosenbloom, and Newell's SOAR were included as *systems that improve the efficiency of a problem solver*. Gentner's structure mapping engine (SME), Carbonell's derivational analogy in the PRODOGY system (DA-PRODIGY), Anderson's (1990b) analogical reasoning in PUPS, and Hammond's CHEF were included as *systems that use preexisiting domain knowledge inductively*. In addition, the previously described systems — JUDGE, INDUCE, and GENESIS — as well as Anderson's (1993) knowledge compilation procedure in ACT (ACT-R/KnCo), the theory revision (TR) system of Richards and Mooney (1991) and van Lehn and Jones' (1993) CASCADE system were included. This collection of learning systems is a small but quite representative sample of the various types of learning systems that are actively being discussed in the current research literature.

It has recently been suggested that knowledge-level descriptions should also include the actually observed performance of a (natural or artificial) system and that *knowledge, goal, skills,* and *performance* should be viewed as parameters of such descriptions (Schmalhofer, Aitken, & Bourne, 1994). Because such parameter descriptions are particularly suited for obtaining a coarse-grained characterization of a system, we have analyzed the selected systems in this manner. More specifically, the selected systems were described in terms of (a) the *knowledge* that is used during learning, (b) the learning *goal* in terms of the required input and the desired output, (c) the learning *skills*, and (d) the *result* that is achieved through learning. For each system, it was thus asked which value is best suited for documenting the respective parameter in a system description. A more detailed account about how these parameter values have been determined, was presented in Schmalhofer (1996). An overview of the obtained results is presented by Fig. 2.4.

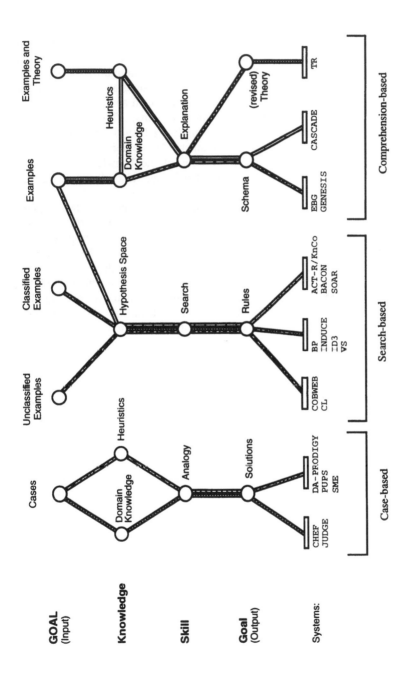

FIG. 2.4. Knowledge-level descriptions of a representative sample of machine learning systems. The systems are characterized by the parameters goal (i.e., input/output), knowledge, and learning skill. The connecting lines indicate relations among the parameters of a system description.

The bottom of Fig. 2.4 shows the names of the different systems that were analyzed. For each system one can follow a line upward and thereby read which learning result (*output*) is achieved by the system, what kind of *skill* is applied for achieving this learning result, which *knowledge* the system utilizes, and what kind of *input* is required for learning. Figure 2.4 thus presents an overview of the different learning systems, that is quite easy to understand and does not require any special knowledge about machine learning systems. This overview was achieved in a systematic manner, namely by applying Newell's concept of the knowledge level (in a somewhat extended manner). This extension was required because previous descriptions of learning systems at the knowledge level have revealed certain insufficiencies (Dietterich, 1986; see also Schmalhofer & Auerswald, 1994).

Because it was derived according to some general method, the present characterization of machine learning systems is more objective than the previous distinctions of different machine learning paradigms which was largely based upon the distinction of various research communitities. Systems had thus been classified according to the research community within which they had been developed. For example, Carbonell (1989) distinguished the inductive, analytic, genetic, and connectionist paradigms. Because implementational and symbol processing details are, however, not important from a knowledge-level perspective, symbolic induction and connectionist learning may not be all that different.

Our knowledge-level analyis showed for example, that connectionist learning by back propagation (BP) is basically identical to symbolic induction as it is performed by INDUCE. In Fig. 2.4, both learning systems are described in the same way. Both learning procedures require classified examples as input. Both procedures use a hypothesis space. In symbolic learning, the hypothesis space is represented by the set of all rules that can possibly be expressed by the symbolic representation language. In connectionist learning, the hypothesis space is given by the network architecture and the various values that can be assumed by the different nodes and links. In both systems, learning occurs by searching the hypothesis space. Back propagation is basically a hill-climbing procedure (cf. Minsky & Papert, 1988). The learning result is finally a collection of rules that differentiate between different sets of examples (McMillan & Smolensky, 1988).

From Fig. 2.4, we can also see that the different learning systems can be basically grouped into three classes, namely *case-based*, *search-based*, and *comprehension-based* systems. Case-based systems typically apply some sort of analogical reasoning procedure to obtain solutions for a new problem. Thereby domain-specific knowledge or general heurisitics may be applied. Search-based learning systems, on the other hand, typically search a space of hypotheses for a general rule that is consistent with the one or several examples that are available as learning materials. Comprehension-based learning systems generate new structures and new representations in the form of schemata or theories. The learning result is thus all encompassing and not just an individual rule or a specific solution. Forming new structures and establishing an explanatory coherence is therefore the important skill in comprehension-based learning.

Domain-specific knowledge as well as heuristic knowledge can be applied in executing this learning skill.

Some authors have recently developed integrated learning architectures. For instance, Anderson's (1990b) integrated learning system (ACT and PUPS) can learn by knowledge compilation as well as by analogy. ACT and PUPS are acronyms which stand for *adaptive character of thought* and *pen-ultimate production system*. So far, integrated learning architectures have been mostly developed for case-based systems (Veloso & Carbonell, 1993) and for search-based systems (Anderson, 1993; Newell, 1990). On the basis of comprehension-based learning, no unified model of learning has yet been developed.

2.4 Summary

We have presented an overview of recent developments in *machine learning* and *knowledge-level modeling*. At first, three selected systems, namely the JUDGE, INDUCE, and GENESIS systems, were presented in some detail, showing how such systems operate in specific application domains. To obtain a more comprehensive description of such learning systems, we then introduced the notion of *knowledge-level* descriptions, as it has been proposed by Newell (1982). Furthermore, the notation of an *inference structure* as it has been developed in the KADS project (Wielinga et al., 1992), was introduced for representing machine learning systems at the knowledge level. For several representatively selected machine learning systems, such knowledge-level descriptions were then established, by describing (a) *the purpose (or goals)* of these systems in terms of their input–output behavior, (b) *the knowledge*, and (c) *the skills* that are applied during learning. The descriptions of the various systems revealed that roughly three classes of learning systems can be distinguished on the basis of such knowledge-level characterizations: Case-based learning systems, search-based learning systems, and comprehenstion-based learning systems. In previous research, unified theories were developed on the basis of case-based and search-based reasoning. For comprehension-based learning, no such unified theories have yet been developed. A unified theory for the acquisition of knowledge could thus be developed on the basis of the knowledge-level assumptions of comprehesion-based learning. However, it still remains an open question as to how such models can be employed as psychological theories. This is the topic discussed in the next chapter.

3

The Levels Approach
Toward Cognitive Modeling

For developing and empirically evaluating models of human cognition, a levels approach towards cognitive modeling is proposed in this chapter. This approach combines methods from three different research areas in a balanced way. More specifically, we will use methods from *experimental psychology, computer simulation* techniques, and constructionist assumptions from *situated cognition* as the building blocks of this approach.

The three methodologies have often been seen as being in competition with one another. We must therefore review and reconcile the controversial views about experimental psychology, computer models, and situated cognition before we present our synthesis. Basically, our synthesis consists of viewing the human mind as a biologically evolved architecture (Cosmides & Tooby, 1994) that is well adapted to its environment. Based on this view, we then derive certain high-level properties of a cognitive system in its natural environment by a so-called rational analysis (Anderson, 1990a). This high-level description is usually called knowledge-level description. However, in order to take the recent criticism from the field of situated cognition into account (e.g., Clancey, 1989), the concept of knowledge-level descriptions must be revised. Instead of a knowledge level that lies directly above the symbol level (Newell, 1982), a revised knowledge-level description is employed. This knowledge-level description can be understood as a (third-person) description of a cognitive system in a given environment (Clancey, 1993). At a lower level (i.e., the symbol level), knowledge-level descriptions are split and refined into a description of the cognitive system and a description of a specific experimental environment. These descriptions must remain consistent

with the knowledge-level description. Computer simulation techniques can then
be employed to obtain more precise symbol-level descriptions of the cognitive
system. Experimental psychology techniques are used to test the predictions that
are derived from the computational model. The symbol-level description of the
cognitive model will contain symbolic as well as subsymbolic components.
According to a constructionist view of cognition (Greeno, 1995; Kintsch, 1988),
(creative) knowledge acquisition and comprehension are viewed as the attunement
or integration of the learner's prior knowledge (represented as symbolic
constraints) and the affordances of the particular learning materials. Such
attunements can be modelled by sub-symbolic (Rumelhart & McClelland, 1986)
and symbolic (Freuder, 1978; Lassez, 1987; Mackworth, 1977) constraint
satisfaction processes.

The levels approach toward cognitive modeling thus presents a systematic
way of integrating an evolution-based theory of development with the advantages
of experimental psychology research and computer simulation techniques. The
levels approach is presented by discussing the empirical evaluation of computer
simulations and by describing the distinction between *implementation-, symbol-,
and knowledge-level* descriptions of a *cognitive model*. Finally, we describe how
Anderson's *rational analysis* can be applied to obtain an initial knowledge-level
description of a cognitive model for the acquisition and utilization of knowledge.

3.1 Symbolic and Situated Cognition

Several prominent researchers have recently asserted that the human cognitive
system cannot be appropriately described as a physical symbol system and have
thereby challenged one of the most fundamental assumptions of traditional
cognitive psychology. In traditional cognitive psychology, human cognition is
thought of as a physical symbol system that

> interacts with its external environment in two ways: (1) It receives sensory stimuli from the
> environment that it converts into symbol structures in memory; and (2) it acts upon the
> environment in ways determined by symbol structures (motor symbols) that it produces. Its
> behavior can be influenced both by its current environment through its sensory inputs, and
> by previous environments through the information it has stored in memory from its
> experiences. (Vera & Simon, 1993a, p. 9)

Criticisms have been voiced on several different accounts. Cosmides and
Tooby (1994) pointed out that the human mind obtained its functional
organization through the process of biological evolution. The human mind would
consequently not be a general purpose formalism that is completely detached
from its environment and its evolutionary history. We should therefore focus on
the adaptive function of the mind and perform detailed analyses of those tasks for
which the various cognitive mechanisms have been developed during their
evolution. Cosmides and Tooby suggested developing rigorous evolutionary
theories of the adaptive function of the mind, rather than arbitrarily proposing
general purpose mechanisms that are content-independent.

Suchman is an anthropologist who used ethnomethodological considerations
for analyzing plans and situated actions (Suchman, 1987). Whereas in artificial

intelligence it is typically assumed that (mental) plans would determine actions, Suchman found that actions are indeed structured in relation to the specific environmental circumstances. She therefore asserted that plans should be predominantly understood in terms of the specific environmental circumstances. Suchman proposed that the purpose of a plan is only to get an initial orientation toward a specific situation so that certain embodied skills can be executed in this situation. Instead of the assumptions of traditional cognitive psychology, namely that plans would determine actions, Suchman assigned the primacy not to plans but to situated actions and, among other things, proposed that situated actions would produce plans. According to Suchman, plans are generated by continuously ongoing processes of prospective and retrospective sense-making. Such sense-making is required to obtain an observable–reportable accountability of reasoning and practical action.

From his experience in developing expert systems, Clancey concluded that knowledge acquisition is not a matter of storing symbol structures in memory. Supposedly, the description of a human reader who comprehends a text cannot be reduced to a storing and matching process. He postulated quite to the contrary, that knowledge acquisition should be viewed as a constructive and creative process, and that this constructive process is a physical process of activation, selection, and subsumption, which is not ontologically grounded in some set of primitive symbols, properties, or relations. The grounding would be the other way around. Regularities are developed through interactions in the environment where the actions of individuals are not governed by rules. The psychologists Greeno and Moore (1993) similarly pointed out that, according to situativity theory, cognitive activities such as understanding a text or solving a specific task, should be viewed primarily as interactions between agents and physical systems and with other people. The research on situativity theory thus addresses the question of how symbols are constructed and used in activities rather than assuming that there would exist a fixed (symbolic) ontology, which is the underlying assumption of the symbolic approach to cognition (cf. Gruber, 1994).

Although symbolic and situated cognition are currently seen as two competing worldviews (Agre, 1993) with a state of tension between the two camps, this does not necessarily mean that one of the camps is right and the other camp wrong. The assumptions of symbolic cognition are not completely outdated and Vera and Simon (1993a) may also not get their wish of completely subsuming situated cognition by the symbolic approach. As Greeno and Moore (1993) correctly stated, breaking completely from symbolic cognitive theories would be the wrong thing, but some fundamental modifications may be required. In particular, computer models should be seen as *descriptive simulations* rather than as *demonstrative simulations*. By demonstrative simulations it is claimed that the target system (i.e., the human cognitive system) does indeed have the same properties as the symbolic system. In descriptive simulations, on the other hand, it is only claimed that the target system would have those properties that are described by the symbolic system.

In summary, computer simulation techniques can be very useful for describing human cognition, but human cognition does not necessarily have the properties of a computer system. The symbols of a computer system are not identical to the symbols in our heads. The crucial operations that are performed "on symbols in our heads have to do with analogy, association, and reference," rather than with the "marks on a Turing machine's tape, where the basic operations are copying and composition" (Touretzky, 1993, p. 167). In other words, humans use symbols that are grounded in their environment rather than symbols that are grounded in some fixed ontology. The classical cognitive theory must therefore be extended by describing how new symbols and new representation spaces emerge through a person's interactions in some environment. In chapters 4, 5, and 6 we develop such a constructionist theory of human knowledge acquisition on the basis of previous research results from experimental psychology.

3.2 Experimental Psychology and Computer Simulations

Although computer simulations of human cognition have a 30-year tradition in experimental psychology, these modeling techniques are still not equally appreciated by every experimental psychologist. The criticisms that have been brought forward by experimental psychologists, however, do not reveal any (major) weaknesses of this method. The criticisms seem to be mostly based on certain views that stem from an empiricist and associationist philosophy that constitutes an important part of the heritage of experimental psychology.

It has been argued that the methods of experimental psychology and computer simulation techniques would not be compatible. On the one hand, experimental psychologists have criticized computer simulations for their lack of simplicity. Because computer programming languages provide very powerful representational constructs and simulation programs are (supposedly) very complex, it has been argued that any given empirical phenomenon could be quite easily modelled by a (relatively arbitrary) computer program and that computer models could hardly be falsified by empirical data. Dörner (1989), on the other hand, argued against using the methods of experimental psychology when the behavior of time-dependent systems (i.e., typical information processing systems) is to be empirically investigated.

We herefore evaluate these criticisms of using computer simulation techniques in combination with the factorial designs of experimental psychology. This evaluation shows that the criticism of the computer simulation techniques as well as the criticisms of experimental psychology are not free of misunderstandings, and that computer simulation techniques and experimental psychology do indeed supplement each other quite well as the theoretical and the empirical sides of one and the same research agenda, which has been called cognitive modeling (cf. Anderson, Boyle, Corbett, & Lewis, 1990; Schmalhofer & Wetter, 1988). Rather than being two exclusive alternatives, computer simulations and psychological experiments should therefore be viewed as the two sides of a coin. By using computer simulations, more theoretically relevant psychological experiments can be designed and more precise predictions can be derived from a psychological theory. By testing computer simulation models against the well-known effects from experimental psychology research, the empirical validity of computer simulations can be assessed by data that have been collected according to strict methodological standards. Furthermore, the results from rather isolated experiments can thereby be integrated into a unified theory. After almost 30 years, the most convincing evaluation of the suitability of computer simulation models as psychological theories in experimental psychology is still the analysis that was performed by Gregg and Simon (1967).

A Typical Psychological Experiment

Gregg and Simon considered a very well-known set of experiments on concept attainment, that had been conducted by Bower and Trabasso (1964). A brief description of these experiments will therefore suffice: In a total of six experiments, subjects were presented with N-dimensional stimuli. There were two possible values for each dimension and only one of the dimensions was relevant for determining whether the stimulus did or did not belong to the concept. On each trial, an instance of a stimulus (positive or negative) was shown to the subject. The subject then had to respond by saying "Positive" or "Negative," depending on whether he or she believed that the stimulus belonged to the concept. The experimenter then replied "Right" or "Wrong," as appropriate.

In their research, Bower and Trabasso (1964) presented a verbal description of what they assumed about the behavior of a subject in these experiments:

> The subject in a concept-identification experiment is viewed as testing out various hypotheses (strategies) about the solution of the problem. Each problem defines for the subject a population of hypotheses. The subject samples one of these hypotheses at random and makes the response dictated by the hypothesis. If his response is correct, he continues to use that hypothesis for the next trial; if his response is incorrect, then he resamples (with replacement) from the pool of hypotheses. (Bower & Trabasso, p. 39)

Mathematical Model

Bower and Trabasso (1964) had furthermore formalized these processing assumptions by developing a mathematical model. This mathematical model can basically be described by two assertions — a performance assumption and a learning assumption (cf. Atkinson, Bower & Crothers, 1965, pp. 33-34):

1. On each trial the subject is in one of two states, K or $\overline{K}$. If the subject is in state K (i.e., knows the correct concept), he will always make the correct response. Otherwise he does not have the correct concept. An incorrect response will then be made with probability p (performance assumption).

2. After each correct response, the subject remains in his previous state. After an error, with probability π, a shift from state $\overline{K}$ to state K is made (learning assumption).

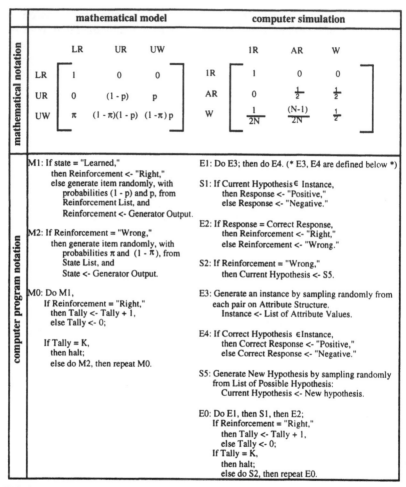

FIG. 3.1. A comparison between two different formalizations (conventional mathematical model and computer simulation) of one and the same informal processing assumptions about concept attainment. The upper left panel shows the mathematical model. The lower right panel shows the computer simulation. The remaining two panels present the translations of these two models into the other notional system (i.e., transition matrix or production rules; adapted from Gregg & Simon, 1967, p. 253–257).

This model can be mathematically stated by a transition matrix. After the subject has made a response, he or she is in one of three different states: LR is the state in which the subject has learned the concept and has given the right answer; UR is the state in which the subject has not yet learned the concept (unlearned) and has (incidentally) given the right answer; UW is the state in which the subject has not yet learned the concept and has given a wrong answer. The transition matrix of this mathematical model is shown in the upper left section of Fig. 3.1. There are two free parameters in the model, namely p and π, that must be estimated from the experimental data.

Computer Simulation Model

Instead of developing a traditional mathematical model, Gregg and Simon (1967) formalized the verbal process descriptions into computer simulation models (written in the information processing language IPL-V). At first, the following variables and constants were defined:

Variables

Instance: Its value is a *list* containing a value (e.g., "large," "square") for each of N attributes.

Attribute Structure: Its value is a *list* of pairs of values (e.g., "red–blue") for each of N attributes.

Correct Response: Its value is one of the two *constants*: "Positive," "Negative".

Correct Hypothesis: Its value is one of the $2N$ attribute values.

Current Hypothesis: Its value is one of the $2N$ attribute values.

Response: Its value is one of the two *constants*: "Positive," "Negative".

Reinforcement: Its value is one of the two *constants*: "Right," "Wrong".

New Hypothesis: Its value is one of the $2N$ attribute values.

List of Possible Hypothesis: Its value is the *list* of $2N$ attribute values.

Tally: Its value is a positive *integer.*

Constants

"Positive," "Negative," "Right," "Wrong"; the integers; K, the criterion of solution; and the symbols for the $2N$ attribute values.

Although production systems and production rules are terms that had not been used at that time (cf. Newell, 1973), Gregg and Simon's simulation program, which is shown in the lower right section of Fig. 3.1, is best characterized in these terms. Their model basically consists of eight production rules, where each production rule describes a possible behavior of the subject (rules S1, S2, and S5) or the experimenter (rules E1, E2, E3, and E4). An additional rule (E0) determines the order in which these rules are to be executed (executive process).

By comparing the transition matrix of the mathematical model (upper left section of Fig. 3.1) to the production rules of the computer simulation model (lower right section of Fig. 3.1, in combination with the presented definitions of variables and constants), it does indeed look like the computer model would be more complex than the mathematical model. However, this is not a fair comparison, because the production rules must make every detail explicit so that they can be executed on a computer and the transition matrix leaves many aspects implicit. It certainly cannot be executed on a computer in the form that has been presented and a human must also have some basic knowledge of Markovian processes to understand this process description.

Comparison of Mathematical Model and Computer Simulation

In order to perform a fair comparison between the two types of models, Gregg and Simon (1967) translated each of the two models into the other notional system (production rules and transition matrix, respectively). Because each production rule basically describes a transition between states, the construction of a state space and a respective transition matrix is straightforward. Thereby, a state space with many different states was obtained. With respect to the possible transitions, many of the constructed states were equivalent. Many states could therefore be collapsed into a few different states, which were termed 1R, AR, 2W and AW. Finally, the states 2W and AW could be aggregated into the state W, so that the transition matrix, which is shown in the upper right section of Fig. 3.1, was obtained. The comparison of the two models in terms of a transition matrix yields the following result:

> Comparing this matrix with the one for the Bower-Trabasso theory, we see two differences, one large and one small. The big difference is that the Bower-Trabasso matrix has two free parameters, the new aggregate matrix has none - it predicts exact numerical values for π and p. The small difference is that the Bower-Trabasso matrix predicts no difference, prior to learning, between the probability of a right guess following a right guess and a right guess following a wrong guess, respectively. The matrix derived from P_0 [i.e. the computer simulation model] predicts that the former probability will equal 1/2, the latter $(N-1)(2N-1)$. ... This difference, of course, could be detected only in very large samples. (Gregg & Simon, p. 257)

The comparison thus showed that for the parameters $\pi = 1/2N$ and $p = 1/2$ the computer simulation and the mathematical model are virtually identical. It is furthermore seen, that for a given set of experimental data, the computer simulation will make more detailed predictions than the mathematical model, because the mathematical model allows the parameters to be separately estimated for each of the various experiments.

Conversely, Gregg and Simon (1967), also stated the Bower and Trabasso model in terms of a computer simulation. This resulted in three rules, which are shown in the lower left section of Fig. 3.1. One rule represents the executive process (M0). Each of the other two rules combines descriptions of the behaviors of the experimenter and the subject.

> Hence there is no clear separation between those processes that define the experimental design, on the one hand, and those that define the subject's behavior on the other. If the experiment is altered in any respect, there is no direct way, in this representation, of deriving the corresponding changes in the process description or in the transition matrix. Matters are quite different with the detailed model [i.e. the computer simulation model]. For any change in the design of the experiment *which does not cause the subject to change his response strategy*, the process model [i.e. the computer simulation model] can be used to predict outcomes simply by modifying the input constants and the experimenter processes to fit the new description of the experiment. This procedure does not introduce any new degrees of freedom into the assumptions about the subject's behavior, since the modifications are strictly determined by the conditions of the experiment. (Gregg & Simon, p. 257)

For a typical set of experiments from the area of general psychology, Gregg and Simon showed:

1. Verbally described processing assumptions can be formalized by computer simulations as fully as one pleases.
2. Computer simulation models are empirically distinguishable. Gregg and Simon also developed and empirically evaluated three different computer simulation models, which they called P_0, P_1, and P_2. These models differed with respect to the rule S5.
3. Computer simulation models make stronger predictions about behavior than the previously developed Markovian models, which contaminated important distinctions.
4. Markovian models can be derived from computer simulations as formally as one pleases (p. 254).

Since Gregg and Simon's publication, it has therefore become generally recognized, that computer simulations are an important means for developing formal models in psychology. Today, computer simulation methods play a very important role in the area of general experimental psychology. The following quote from Gregg and Simon (1867) nicely explains, why simulation models had originally been misunderstood as being less formal than conventional mathematical models.

It is often objected to (...) computer simulation models (...), that they are too 'flexible,' hence weak and not falsifiable. They have, it is argued, too many degrees of freedom so that, by simple adjustment of parameters, they can be made to fit the data no matter how the data come out.
This impression seems to arise from the fact that simplicity is sometimes equated with parsimony, and that process models [e.g. computer simulations], when compared to mathematical theories, have the appearance of being decidedly garrulous and not parsimonious at all. For example, Bower and Trabasso's stochastic theory appears to be based on only two equations containing two parameters; while a computer program that is a literal translation of [this model] contains about 200 instructions in IPL-V, a list processing programming language, in addition to a substantial amount of input data to specify the stimulus structure.
Appearances in this case are decidedly deceptive. A large part of the program and the data in the process model are required to make explicit things that are only implicit - but of necessity assumed - in the stochastic theory. Our earlier comparison of the formalized descriptions of the models with the program implementing the theory shows that the differences in parsimony are more apparent than real as soon as both formulations are held to the same standard of explicitness. . . .
We add one comment of a more pragmatic kind. Persons who claim that it is "easy" to modify a process model, because of its garrulousness, to fit experimental data simply have never tried. The usual result of modifying a computer program, for any reason, is that the program behaves nonsensically. A program that is put together at random will give every evidence of being a random device - until it stops entirely or loops. Hence, modifying a program to fit particular discrepant observations without destroying the fit elsewhere is a good deal harder than estimating parameters, and probably at least as hard as modifying a mathematical theory by introducing new degrees of freedom via new parameters. Even if we give the theorist wide privileges of "fitting" them, process models in the form of computer programs are highly falsifiable. (p. 272–274)

In a tutorial, Kieras (1985) once more highlighted the two major reasons for performing computer simulations.

> The first is the traditional one, that constructing a rigorously specified computer program is an excellent way to convert a set of vague ideas into a more specific and precise theory. It is important to keep in mind, however, that the simulation program is *not* the theory, but only a specific realization of the theory. That is, we normally have a set of theoretical ideas that we are *really* interested in, but which are usually stated in a very general and imprecise way. In constructing a simulation model (and also, a traditional mathematical model), we are specifying a precise system that is based on these ideas. Attempting to specify the system in a way that runs on the computer reveals the consistency, completeness, or clarity of our theoretical ideas. . . . I believe that cognitive theory would advance much faster if, for this reason alone, more researchers constructed simulation models.
> The second reason for constructing a simulation model is to account for empirical data. Clearly, this is the standard goal for the traditional mathematical modeling approach; but simulation models have traditionally been excused from this standard, or questions have been raised about whether they could ever be held to it. However, recently efforts have been made to use simulation models in a serious and thorough way to account for data. These efforts are especially interesting because both the model and the cognitive processes are quite complex, and the accounting is done at a very fine level of detail in the data. (p. 279–280)

The Use of Experimental Designs for Evaluating Computer Models

Dörner (1989) presented a hypothetical research situation, where the factorial designs, which are so frequently used in general experimental psychology, would supposedly not be adequate. He applied a so called Monte Carlo method (cf. Coombs, Dawes, & Tversky, 1970, p. 270). Dörner ran several (basically identical) computer programs (which he called "little green turtles") as virtual subjects in experiments with a factorial design. The collected "experimental data" did not yield any significant effects and it was concluded that case studies would be better suited for researching such systems than a well controlled experimental design.

There is a very good reason why Dörner's experiments did not yield systematic results. His experiments were not guided by any theoretical assumptions about the "little green turtles." More specifically, there was no deliberation at all about which independent variables should be included in the experiment. Instead, the independent variables were arbitrarily selected and did not include one of the most central factors that determined the turtles' behavior. The turtles' behavior was influenced by a mediating internal variable (i.e., whether or not the turtles had been charged with sufficient energy and whether they were currently being charged). Because of the contamination of this determining factor with the experimental variables, the turtles' experimentally investigated behavior appeared to be quite erratic. Dörner thus demonstrated that psychological experimentation can be quite ineffective, when the design of the experiment is not guided by an (appropriate) theory.

From Dörner's demonstration one can, however, not conclude that computer simulations and the factorial designs of experimental psychology should not be applied together. There are several research examples, where the two methods have been applied together very successfully. For instance, Fletcher (1981) employed a computer simulation whose system characteristic was actually quite similar to the type of system assumed by Dörner. However, Fletcher did not design his experiments completely independent from the theoretical assumptions about the system. Instead, he ran computer simulations and thereby determined the different levels of the independent variable in his experiments. In the experiments, he could then determine whether the different levels of the independent variable indeed influenced the dependent variable, in the way it was predicted by the computer simulation. Fletcher thus designed an experiment that hardly could have been conducted without a simulation model. More specifically, Fletcher has employed the Miller and Kintsch (1980) simulation to determine the level of activation of a proposition, according to the previous processing history of this proposition. In the experiment, cued recall, recognition, and response times were then collected as dependent measures.

Dörner could have similarly used a simulation of a turtle's behavior history for assessing the specific state of a turtle and thereby determine the different levels of a respective independent variable in his experiment. He would then have also obtained very systematic experimental results. Dörner's demonstration can, therefore, not be taken as an argument against experimental methods, but rather highlights the importance of precise processing theories for experimental psychology research. This discussion, nevertheless, shows that the relation between computer simulation techniques and experimental psychology research can be easily misunderstood (see Herrmann, 1990, for additional justifications of applying experimental methods). In the following section, we therefore describe how computer simulations are empirically evaluated according to the levels approach to cognitive modeling.

3.3 The Empirical Evaluation of Computer Simulations

There is another similarity between computer simulations and mathematical models. Similar to the so-called identifiability problem, which arises with mathematical models (Greeno & Steiner, 1964), there is an identifiability problem with computer simulations. Anderson (1990a) pointed out that such identifiability problems arise when the computer implementations themselves are regarded as psychological theories. For example, it has been shown that it is not possible to decide between different claims of competing implementations, such as whether the information processing is performed sequentially or in parallel (Townsend, 1974), or claims about which kind of representation language ought to be used in the simulation (Anderson, 1978).

In other words, given some empirical data, we can produce a computer simulation with parallel or serial execution, or with propositional or analogue representations, so that each of the simulation programs will reproduce the data equally well. Because writing computer simulation programs is a very time consuming activity, this may take a long time, but it can be done. The deeper reason behind this identifiability problem lies in the fact that the relationship between a computer implementation and behavioral data is too indirect. The large degree of indirectness prohibits identifiability (Anderson, 1990a). Given this arbitrariness about the various features of an implemented program, not every property of a computer implementation can be considered as psychologically meaningful. Some properties of a computer simulation must thus be viewed as necessary (or at least convenient) technical details, which do not carry psychological meaning.

A related problem is known from using Markov models as models for human memory (Greeno & Steiner, 1964). With somewhat different terminology, the identifiability issue was also addressed in mathematical measurement theory. When an attribute (e.g., temperature) of a set of items is scaled, the numerical values that are assigned to the different items are also not unique (cf. Baird & Noma, 1978; Suppes & Zinnes, 1963). A simple example may clarify this similarity between cognitive modeling and mathematical measurement theory. Let us assume, that we determined the temperature on two consecutive days as being 10 and 20 degrees. This result would probably allow us to claim that it was clearly warmer on the second day than on the first day. As is well known from measurement theory, the claim that it was twice as warm on the second day is, however, not justified, because this relation between the two numbers is not substantive or meaningful but only a superficial aspect that is due to relatively arbitrary details of the specific implementation of the scaling procedure. For example, it might have been relatively arbitrarily decided, that zero degrees is set as the temperature where water freezes and 100 degrees is set as the temperature where water boils (for a more formal treatment of this example, see Narens & Mausfeld, 1992).

In measurement theory we consider only those relational structures that can be identified from the empirical data to be meaningful. Thereby some technical assumptions are often presupposed. As described in the next section, the same rationale is followed in the levels approach towards cognitive modeling. All the relational and temporal structures that are assumed to be psychologically meaningful are used to define or determine the symbol or algorithm level of a cognitive model, whereas the other properties of the simulation program are viewed as the implementation level, which mostly describes the technical details, needed for "running" the computer model. Our review of the research by Gregg and Simon has already shown, that it is the implementation level, that makes computer models more complex than other models. The implementation level thus corresponds to the technical assumptions, which are necessary in any mathematical model (cf. Krantz, Luce, Suppes, & Tversky, 1971), without carrying any psychological significance. There is a third level of description, the knowledge level, which is said to lie above the symbol level (Newell, 1982).

3.4 Symbol- and Knowledge-Level Descriptions

In the levels approach towards cognitive modeling, a computational model is described at different levels (see Fig. 3.2). Such descriptions encompass knowledge, symbol (or algorithm), and implementation levels. A computational model, which is described in this way, is also called a cognitive model. The distinction between the symbol and the implementation level allows for a more systematic way of describing and empirically testing a model. The knowledge level is of particular importance for developing a unified theory that integrates results from several different types of experiments.

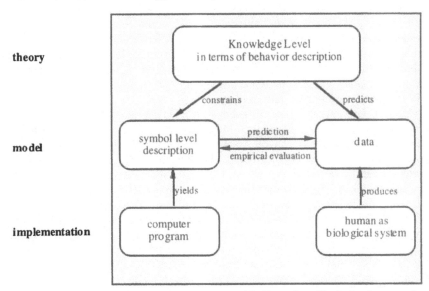

FIG. 3.2. How computer simulation models are empirically evaluated in the levels approach to cognitive modeling.

In its objective, a levels approach is thus rather similar to a measurement theory approach, where theoretical structures, such as various numbers that are assigned to different items, are analyzed with respect to which relations among theses numbers would be empirically meaningful, and which relations are only superficial and do not carry any meaning. With the levels approach to cognitive modeling, we want to differentiate between the (relatively arbitrary) implementational details of a process model and the relations among the various symbol structures that can be related to the results of psychological experiments in a meaningful way. We thus distinguish between the implementation level and the symbol level of a cognitive model. For the same reason that it is not admissible to claim that 20°C would be twice as warm as 10°C, it is also not meaningful to claim that "funcall(Input,first, ArgSpecs):-Input=[first | ArgSpecs]" would be more difficult to remember than "lisp_function(first)." Similar to the ratio of two temperatures in centigrade, the implementational detail of one string being longer than the other does not carry any meaning for making predictions about human memory.

In addition to the implementation of the computer simulation, we also describe the cognitive model at the symbol level. The symbol-level description of the cognitive model specifies which aspects of the computer simulation are assumed to be psychologically meaningful. A symbol-level description of a cognitive model should therefore provide the same type of results that are obtained from the discussion of the meaningfulness in measurement theory.

In the levels approach to cognitive modeling, symbol-level descriptions thus characterize the symbols, symbol structures, and cognitive processes of human learners in specific situations. Propositions (Kintsch, 1974) are good examples of such symbols. The textbase and situation model would be examples of symbol structures, and the formation of a textbase (e.g., Miller & Kintsch, 1980) can be taken as an example for a cognitive process in a symbol-level description. The symbol level thus "refers to a description of cognition in terms of the general steps of cognition" (Anderson, 1993, p. 11).

In addition to the symbol and implementation levels of a cognitive model, we also describe a cognitive model at a more abstract level, which Newell has termed the *knowledge level*. At this level, information processing systems (humans as well as artificial systems) can be described as rational agents. The knowledge level sits directly above the symbol level (Newell, 1982). A knowledge-level description can be obtained as the result of a so-called *rational analysis*. At the knowledge level, a cognitive model is described in terms of goals, knowledge, skills (the fundamental computational limitations of the system), and the predicted behavior. Knowledge-level descriptions thus abstract away many details of symbol-level descriptions and are well suited as a starting point for developing a unified theory for learning from different instructional materials.

It should be noted that we deviate from Anderson with respect to what we call the implementation level. Anderson (1993) stated: "The implementation level refers to a lower level description of cognition in terms of the factors that determine whether a specific production rule will fire and the speed with which it fires" (p.12). When Anderson talked about the implementation level, he meant the implementation level of the human mind. "Because cognition must be implemented in the human brain, it seems transparent that the implementation of ACT-R should be in terms of neural-like computations. Thus, the constraint used to choose among behaviorally equivalent proposals is that the mechanisms proposed correspond to what is known about neural processing" (Anderson, 1993, p. 12–13). The present research is, however, not concerned with such questions. By implementation level, we simply mean the implementation of the symbol-processing model (i.e., the symbol-level description) in some specific programming language. Unlike Anderson, we do not require that the computer implementation should be in terms of neural-like computations. Our implementations are only a technical convenience for implementing the information processing that is described at the symbol-level in the form of a running computer program.

3.5 Anderson's Rational Analysis

In the previous sections of this chapter, we have shown how a computer simulation can be evaluated with respect to whether or not its predictions are consistent with some given set of data. In this respect, there is basically no difference between the empirical evaluation of a computer simulation and any other kind of formal model. Before we can empirically evaluate a computer simulation, we must, however, develop it. Because developing a computer simulation is very time consuming and requires a lot of resources, we are not particularly interested in developing a simulation model that would be quickly falsified by the first experiment that is conducted for its empirical evaluation. A review of previous experimental findings can certainly help in developing the model, so that it would at least be consistent with several of the already known empirical effects. Accomplishing such a computer simulation may be quite difficult or even appear to be impossible. As Anderson (1993, p. 12) put it: "There is a huge space of possible implementation proposals and little guidance for finding the correct one. It sometimes seems impossible to discover one that is consistent with the data. It is like trying to find a needle in a haystack."

By reviewing the literature, "one can try to find a theory consistent with the data, but what reason is there to believe it will be consistent with the next empirical phenomenon?" (Anderson, 1993, p. 13). Especially when trying to develop a unified theory that cuts across different experimental paradigms (such as learning from text and learning from examples), it is desirable to have at least some plausible argument that the core assumptions of the model may also hold up in new experiments. As Anderson (1993) pointed out correctly: "Any infinite number of theories that are consistent with any finite body of data will make different predictions about data yet to be collected. We need some reason to believe that when we commit to one of these theories it will hold up when the new data come in" (p.13). In our particular research, we would like to have some reason to believe that the knowledge acquisition model that we develop for learning from text may also be confirmed by experiments that investigate learning from cases.

Anderson proposed to provide guidance for developing a cognitive model by performing a so-called *rational analysis*. A rational analysis provides relatively global constraints for developing a cognitive model by introducing the thesis that cognition is adapted to the structure of the environment. We can thus begin with the description of the environment in which the human cognitive system operates. By assuming that the human cognitive system is goal-driven and well adapted to this environment, we can infer certain global properties of the cognitive system. These properties may be used as knowledge-level descriptions of the cognitive model. This knowledge-level description can then provide guidance in specifying the symbol-level and implementation-level descriptions of the cognitive model. More specifically, the symbol level and implementation level will be developed so that they are consistent with the knowledge-level description. The rational analysis and the resulting knowledge-level description thus provide guidance for specifying the algorithm and the implementation levels of the cognitive model.

Because the knowledge-level description is derived from the general postulate that human cognition is adapted to its natural environment, it is at least plausible to assume that restrictions that are derived from this postulate would hold true across different experimental settings. It is then furthermore plausible to assume that a cognitive model that is developed on such restrictions may also hold up its predictions in newly conducted experiments. Therefore a rational analysis will be performed for guiding the development of the mechanistic theory (i.e., the symbolic and the implementation level). In conducting the rational analysis, Anderson's proposal is largely followed. Therefore, the following six steps are used to develop a theory:

1. Specify the goals of the cognitive system.
2. Describe the environment to which the system is adapted. The environment description is presented in much less detail than the description of an experimental situation.
3. Make the minimal assumptions about computational limitations that supposedly result from the constraints of its evolutionary history. For instance, the properties of a working long-term memory, which have been described by Ericsson and Kintsch (1995), may be employed as such computational limitations.
4. Derive some abstract behavior description from the specifications that were made by items 1 through 3.
5. Examine the empirical literature to see if the predictions of the behavior descriptions are confirmed.
6. If the predictions are not confirmed, iterate.

There are only three differences between these six steps and the six steps presented by Anderson (1990a, p. 29). Unlike Anderson, we do not require and do not even recommend that formal descriptions of the environment be established. Because formal representations contain hidden biases (Rendell, 1986), verbal descriptions are better suited for expressing the essential characteristics without committing to some technical details that may later become a hindrance. As has been pointed out elsewhere, preference is given to early verification rather than to early formalization (Schmalhofer, Kühn, & Schmidt, 1991). In philosophy, the argument has also been made that precision can be achieved in ordinary language and that precision does not necessarily require a formal language (e.g., von Savigny, 1969).

Second, Anderson viewed his rational analysis as "a new methodology for doing research in cognitive psychology" (1990a, p. 1). We would like to emphasize that rational analyses are quite similar to the more traditional task analysis. The difference between a rational analysis and a task analysis is that the scope of reference in a rational analysis is not a specific task, but rather the natural environment to which the cognitive system is adapted. We thus believe that rational analysis can be viewed as having emerged quite naturally from the more traditional task analyses.

Third, we do not see that the rational analysis and the cognitive architecture approaches must challenge each other (Anderson, 1990a, p. xi). Instead, we propose a coordinated approach: The rational analysis is only used to obtain an initial knowledge-level description. The algorithm and implementation levels are (pretty much) developed in the way in which cognitive architectures have traditionally been developed and tested by experiments. Special considerations are, however, taken so that the cognitive architecture that is developed is consistent with the knowledge-level description obtained from the rational analysis.

3.6 Rational Analysis of the Acquisition and Utilization of Knowledge

The current research issue concerns the question of how humans with different amounts of prior knowledge acquire additional knowledge from different learning materials and how these persons perform subsequent criterion tasks. In Fig. 1.1, we showed a quite uncontroversial framework for conceptualizing this research issue. On the basis of this framework, we now perform a rational analysis. Thereby, a general characterization of the goals of the cognitive system, the environment, the computational limitations of the cognitive system and even some behavioral predictions are obtained.

Goals of the Cognitive System

The goal of learning is defined in relation to future yet unknown problem-solving situations. In particular, a cognitive system engages in learning in order to acquire knowledge that will assist in solving future problems. Because the problems that may arise in the future cannot be precisely predicted but only approximately anticipated, the cognitive system needs to prepare itself for a relatively large class of only vaguely specified problems. If additional information were available about which tasks will have to be solved, the cognitive system should acquire that knowledge that is most pertinent to the expected tasks. Learning thus serves the purpose of preparing oneself for future situations.

Abstract Description of the Environment

The environment provides different clues that may be exploited by the learning system in order to prepare itself for the future tasks. Humans are situated in rich environments in which experiences accumulated by other individuals are available in the form of texts or examples selected by an instructor. Furthermore, they may learn by exploration from interactions with the environment. Typically, a combination of the different learning materials is available.

Basically, there are three types of learning materials that would yield different ways of learning. The learning material may consist of general statements, usually presented in the form of a text (learning from text), from which the solutions to all the relevant tasks can supposedly be inferentially derived by the learner. Alternatively, the learning material may consist of a sequence of examples (learning from situation examples) from which the learner can induce the general principles that can also be used to solve new problems. In a third type of learning (learning by exploration) no learning material is presented, instead the learner must engage in an interaction that may provide some answer to his questions.

Another important characteristic of the environment is the fact that the information presented in the learning situation may be useful for solving a large variety of tasks, some of which may be quite different from the situation in which the knowledge was acquired. Also, the time interval between the learning situation and the knowledge utilization may vary in length. In addition, there are different time constraints for the two situations. Whereas the learner typically is allotted sufficient time when acquiring knowledge, a new problem that arises in the environment must often be solved under severe time constraints.

Assumptions About Computational Limitations and Computational Facilities

It is well known that the human cognitive system has a rather limited ability to memorize isolated facts. Several studies have shown that human memory is not particularly capable of remembering isolated pieces of information (e.g., Bower, 1970). In fact, a new piece of information can be remembered better when more links to existing knowledge structures can be established. When the cognitive system operates in an environment and with learning materials to which it is well adapted (e.g., written texts are studied rather than a list of nonsense syllables), the information that is stored in long term memory can be relatively easily accessed with the assistance of so-called retrieval structures (Ericsson & Kintsch, 1995).

General Behavioral Predictions

Because only a limited amount of novel information can be stored in human memory at any given time, the presented learning materials should be appropriately prepared during the knowledge acquisition phase. Through such a preparation, exactly that information can be stored that will supposedly be most useful for solving future, yet unknown tasks. A well-adapted learning system must integrate the information of the different learning materials into its prior knowledge in such a way that it is readily available when a new task must be solved. This is implied by the characteristics of the described environment, the goals of the learner, and the processing limitations of the system. The knowledge that is acquired from the various sources (text, examples, by exploration) should therefore become closely related to the anticipated tasks, as well as being closely related to the learner's prior knowledge.

When learning from examples, the specific information presented in the examples must be generalized so that it can be applied to a wider range of tasks. This generalization should be performed on the basis of relevant prior knowledge, because generalizations that are not guided by knowledge would be relatively arbitrary and therefore not very useful.

When learning by exploration, a learner should fill the gaps in the knowledge that is relevant for the future tasks. In particular, in learning by exploration, rational learners can use the opportunity to improve the correctness and the generality of their knowledge.

More or less the same knowledge could thus be acquired from quite different learning materials. When learning from a text, more specific knowledge that can more easily be applied in different kinds of test situations must be derived. Furthermore, the individual statements should be linked with each other and with the related prior knowledge so that they are likely to be remembered in the relevant context.

The results of this (relatively crude) rational analysis can be seen as part of a knowledge-level description, or as a relatively general theory for which specific models can then be developed and tested by psychological experiments.

3.7 Summary

When computational models are applied to the area of experimental psychology they should be viewed as *descriptive* rather than as *demonstrative simulations*. Whereas by demonstrative simulations it is postulated that the human mind would have the same properties as a respective computational model, in descriptive simulations it is claimed only that human cognition has those properties that are described by (the symbol level of) the computational model. The levels approach toward cognitive modeling was then introduced and the knowledge, symbol and implementation levels of a cognitive model were thereby explicitly distinguished. Whereas the symbol level describes those properties that are regarded as psychologically meaningful, the implementation level contains additional technical details that are required for running the model on a computer. At the knowledge level, on the other hand, the environment is viewed as being part and parcel of the cognitive system. A rational analysis, which assumes that a cognitive system is well adapted to its environment, can therefore be applied to obtain a knowledge level description for specific tasks. In the following, knowledge-level descriptions are also referred to as *theory*. The symbol processing specifications for specific situations are called *models*. And a running computer program is then called the implementation level or simply the *implementation*. With this levels approach, cognitive models can be empirically evaluated by comparing predictions at the symbol level to respective experimental data. Some more general experimental predictions can already be derived from the knowledge level.

For the purpose of cognitive modeling, computer simulations and psychological experiments should be viewed as two sides of a coin: Through the use of computer models, psychological experiments can be designed that are theoretically more relevant. In addition, more precise predictions can be derived from a psychological theory. By testing computational models with psychological experiments, empirical validity can be assessed by data that have been collected according to strict methodological standards.

By performing a rational analysis of the acquisition and utilization of knowledge, we have furthermore derived an initial knowledge-level description for the desired cognitive model. Such a rational analysis, which is motivated by concerns from situated cognition, can be understood as the first step in a top–down application of the levels approach. In the two following chapters, we follow the concerns of experimental psychology. We thus take a fresh start toward developing the cognitive model that is supposed to unify learning from text and learning from cases as two different classes of knoweldge acquisition. In a more bottom-up fashion, our discussion of psychological experiments on text comprehension (chapter 4) and learning from cases (chapter 5) progresses toward psychological processing models. A knowledge-level description that will be termed the C–I theory is then abstracted out of these models. This C–I theory is subsequently used to develop the KIWi model (once again in a top-down manner). As a knowledge-level description, the C–I theory can then be compared to the results of the rational analysis that were obtained in the current chapter. Based on this comparison, chapter 6 subsequently presents the KIWi model as a model that unifies the different kinds of knowledge acquisition.

4

Learning From Text

In the previous chapter, we introduced the levels approach to cognitive modeling. This methodology is now applied to develop a cognitive model of knowledge acquisition. In the current chapter, we first summarize the research in experimental psychology that is most relevant for the purpose of building a cognitive model. Thereby, the results of research on learning from text originating from investigations of human memory for verbal materials (such as word lists) and the update of an early information processing model of human memory explaining memory for texts are seen. Currently, the most influential model of text comprehension is Kintsch's (1988, 1992) construction integration (C–I) model. It was applied successfully to a large variety of data sets (Britton & Eisenhart, 1993; Doane, McNamara, Kintsch, Polson, & Clawson, 1992; Kintsch, Welsch, Schmalhofer, & Zimny, 1990; Mannes & Kintsch, 1991; Singer & Halldorson, 1996; Weaver, Mannes, & Fletcher, 1995). We therefore perform a knowledge-level analysis (cf. Newell, 1982) of this model. The resulting knowledge-level description is termed the C–I theory and is described by a KADS inference structure. By applying a top–down development, the KIWi model of learning from text is then described as a symbol-processing model that is a specific realization of this C–I theory. Most importantly, the knowledge construction processes that may occur in learning the programming language LISP is thereby modeled at the symbol level. At the end of the chapter, we discuss the specific advantages of expressing psychological theories in terms of knowledge-level descriptions. Thereby, we also discuss previously developed C–I models.

4.1 Memory for Verbal Materials

In experimental psychology, research on learning from text originated from investigations of human memory with lists of unrelated items. At the beginning of this research, the nonsense syllable was much appreciated, because it allowed memory to be investigated in a very controlled way. Memory could be investigated by controlling for prior exposure, familiarity, and meaningfulness of the material (cf. Ebbinghaus, 1885/1971, p. 20 ff.). Because nonsense syllables do not occur in real life, the learning materials presented to the subjects were completely new, and therefore not contaminated by a learner's prior experiences. After the fundamental characteristics of human learning, such as primacy, recency, proactive, and retroactive inhibition were discovered in such tightly controlled situations (cf. Murdock, 1974), memory for more realistic verbal materials could be investigated.

By building meaningful associations, subjects could form richer relations between words than between nonsense syllables, and more items could thereby be remembered. At the same time, researchers developed information-processing models that could account for the various experimental effects. One of the best known models is the buffer model of Atkinson and Shiffrin (1968). Through the assumption that short-term memory consists of a buffer of limited size, in which the to-be-learned material had to be held in a number of processing cycles, the memory for the individual items could be predicted: The more rehearsal cycles an item would participate in, the more likely it was to be stored in long term memory. The primacy effect was thus predicted by the fact that at the beginning of learning a list, the buffer was empty and therefore, the first items would remain longer in the buffer than the items that replaced them (i.e., the items in the middle of the list). The items at the beginning of the list were therefore better remembered, because they had a better chance of being stored in long-term memory. The items at the end of the list, on the other hand, were better remembered because they remained in short-term memory after the whole list had been presented. In retrospect, the buffer model has some features of a unifying model in that it binds together a number of different experimental phenomena and explains them by a single data structure (i.e., the buffer) and a respective process (i.e., rehearsal). Of course the scope of unification is in no way comparable to the scope of the unified theories that were proposed by Newell (1990).

After much successful research with lists of verbal materials, the field of experimental psychology had prepared the ground to study the memory for more complex materials, such as sentences and complete texts (Kintsch, 1974). With simple lists, the possible kinds of relations among the various items was quite limited (e.g., the predecessor and successor relation between two items or the position of an item in the list). With materials like texts, there are many more possible relations. In addition, memory tests for text are more difficult to score. Whereas a syllable or word was scored as correctly reproduced when it matched letter for letter with the presented item, this letter-for-letter match criterion tends to be too strict when the reproduction of a text is concerned. With such a strict scoring rule, the sentence "The car was speeding" would be simply scored as incorrectly reproduced if the sentence "The automobile was driving too fast" were presented in the study phase. However, the more appropriate conclusion is that the sentence was actually remembered quite well with respect to its meaning, although it may not have been recalled verbatim. Such modifications in the reproductions of a text may indicate which representational units are used when a meaningful sentence or a complete text is stored in memory.

One important issue in investigating memory for text was to determine the nature of the *cognitive units* that humans use for storing and remembering a text. This question has been carefully researched, and numerous experiments have been conducted (for a review, see van Dijk & Kintsch, 1983, chapter 2). Fortunately, these experiments provided us with a clear answer. To a large degree, texts are stored at the meaning level. The basic units for representing a text by its meaning are *propositions*. Propositions are cognitive units in human memory that basically represent elementary sentences (or clauses). The proposition (speeding, car) would thus represent the sentence "the car was speeding" as well as the sentence "the automobile was driving too fast." Because propositions represent the meaning of sentences, different paraphrases of a sentence are mapped on to the same proposition. There also exist definite guidelines of how propositions are constructed from a text (Bovair & Kieras, 1983; Turner, 1987). Now that the units for representing the meaning of a text are known to be propositions, a learner's recall protocols could be scored in a more informative way than requiring the verbatim reproduction of a text, which had been the criterion that Ebbinghaus (1875/1971; p. 43) used for scoring his memory for text segments of Byron's Don Juan.

How closely research on list learning and memory for text is related is also indicated by the fact that the processing assumptions of the Atkinson and Shiffrin model were also used as a foundation for models of text processing. In the Kintsch and van Dijk (1978) model, memory for the various propositions of a text is again predicted by the number of processing cycles. According to this model, the items held in short term memory are propositions. However, because a text is more structured than a list of unrelated items, and because this structure is important, a learner must also recover the relations among the different propositions. Therefore, the items in short-term memory cannot be randomly replaced when a new item is entered, as had been the case in the Atkinson and Shiffrin model. The Kintsch and van Dijk model employs a strategy for determining which propositions are held over in short-term memory for the next processing cycle. The so-called leading edge strategy holds those propositions in short-term memory that, at the time, appear to be most likely to relate to propositions that will appear in the subsequent sentences of the text. In addition, memory reinstantiations are performed on those occasions where the leading-edge strategy did not select the relevant propositions. The likelihood that a given proposition is remembered is thus again a function of the number of processing cycles. However, the number of processing cycles of a proposition is now not simply determined by its sequential position, but more strongly by the meaning relations among the propositions according to the text structure. The task demands of recovering the meaning structure of a text thus interact with the specific limitations of human memory. The Kintsch and van Dijk model has been empirically supported by a variety of different experiments. We mention only two of these studies. Fletcher (1981) demonstrated that the propositions that the model predicts to be in short-term memory in a given processing cycle are indeed more readily available, independent of how far back in the text the proposition had occurred. Britton and Gülgöz (1991) showed that when texts are rewritten so that they become more coherent according to the processing assumptions of the model, subjects are better able to recall these texts than the original texts, where the model had diagnosed several coherence breaks.

Texts can also be summarized. In addition to the already described construction of a propositional textbase, which represents the meaning of the text, a reader also forms a representation of the gist of the text, which is called the macrostructure. The formation of the macrostructure of a text is basically done in the same fashion as the microstructure except that only selected propositions (some of which may have been constructed as abstractions of some other propositions) participate when the macrostructure is formed. Although the psychological reality of these processes became well established by several psychological experiments (e.g., Guindon & Kintsch, 1984), additional experiments showed that in the way it had been stated in 1978, the Kintsch and van Dijk model is by no means complete. In other words, there are systematic experimental data that cannot be accounted for by the model, because they reflect some other cognitive processes, which had not been integrated in the processing model.

4.2 Knowledge Acquisition From Texts

Texts are usually not read for the purpose of reproducing or summarizing them at some later time. Because texts are most often studied to acquire new knowledge about a situation or a domain, the formation of this new knowledge also needs to be modelled. This is especially true when we concern ourselves with learning from text. But this fact has also been demonstrated by well-controlled experiments with quite simple materials. Bransford, Franks and their colleagues provided such an experimental demonstration (Bransford, Barclay, & Franks, 1972). When subjects studied the sentence *Three turtles rested on a floating log, and a fish swam beneath them*, the subjects knew that the fish swam under the log because they had built a referential mental model of the text. Such referential mental models of a text have been termed *situation models*. In addition to a textbase, consisting of a micro- and a macrostructure that represent the meaning of a text and its gist, it was therefore postulated that learners would also form situation models, which are mental representations of that section of reality which is described by the text (van Dijk & Kintsch, 1983). A situation model is thus a cognitive structure which represents the knowledge about a domain, whereas a textbase represents the (intensional) meaning of a text.

Knowledge Construction Processes

To a certain degree, a text may be remembered word by word (verbatim representation) and by its meaning (propositional representation). Furthermore, learners will utilize their prior knowledge in combination with the new information provided by the text and construct a knowledge representation of the situations described by the text. Constructive processes, like various types of inferences, thereby play an important role. A typology of such constructive processes was presented by Graesser, Singer, and Trabasso (1994). These constructive processes are strategies rather than algorithms. Whereas an algorithm can be assumed to calculate a certain type of result from some given input, strategies operate according to a rule of thumb and use only local information to produce quite varied results. The cognitive results produced by such strategies may therefore be contradictory and inconsistent. As van Dijk and Kintsch (1983) and Kintsch (1988) argued, such knowledge construction strategies should be modelled by *weak* production rules. Production rules are said to be *weak*, when they function independent of context, (i.e., their firing is only determined by local information). In support of this assumption, Till, Mross, and Kintsch (1988) found that when reading short texts, sense activation functions independently of context.

When reading a text, some strategies will construct a linguistic representation of the text: The so-called propositional strategies will construct the various propositions, and the so-called macrostrategies will construct the macropropositions. Schematic and other strategies will build the *situational units*, from which a situation model will be formed on the basis of one or several selected schemata. The construction and or activation of situational units may increase reading time. Rinck and Bower (1995) have shown that a situational unit that is not as directly available yields a longer reading time. The activation of situation knowledge during reading has also been shown in several other experiments (e.g., Morrow, Bower, & Greenspan, 1989). In addition to these strategies or production rules that generate knowledge units in memory, there are strategies that generate connections among the various knowledge units. Argument overlap is one such strategy, which would connect various propositions to one another. Another strategy may connect situational units to propositions, whenever a situational unit can be viewed as the referent or extension of the intensional meaning that is encoded by the respective proposition.

From a given text segment like a phrase, many more units are thus constructed than just the propositions, which were processed by the Kintsch and van Dijk (1978) model. With all these different knowledge construction processes, a simple buffer model is no longer viable. Ericsson and Kintsch (1995) showed that for performing complex tasks, people must indeed maintain access to large amounts of information. After reviewing research of skilled memory, they concluded that a general account of working memory has to include a mechanism for the skilled use of storage in long-term memory, that they referred to as *long-term working memory*. Because text comprehension is such a skilled activity, models of text comprehension should also include a long-term working memory.

Knowledge Integration Processes

In his C–I model, Kintsch (1988) assumed that the knowledge that was formed by the *construction processes*, is subsequently processed by a *context-oriented integration process*. This process determines which units fit together well and can thus be combined to one whole and which units are at odds with that structure and are therefore dropped out. In the C–I model, the integration process is modelled by a spreading activation or connectionist constraint-satisfaction process (Rumelhart & McClelland, 1986) that interactively activates and sometimes also inhibits the various representational units before the network settles. The long-term memory links are then determined on the basis of the results where the network settled its activation in combination with the original link strengths in short-term memory. In particular, the long-term memory link strengths are obtained by multiplying the final activation values of the nodes, which are connected by the link with the original link strength (Kintsch & Welsch, 1991).

The C–I model thus assumes a distributed memory. The contents of working memory are modelled by a network of interconnected nodes. The integration process is described as a spreading activation process and the node strengths of the settled network determine the strengths of the links in the long-term memory representation. With a somewhat modified strategy, it may again be determined which nodes will be carried over to the next processing cycle. The processing of the next cycles can then proceed in the same fashion and additional processing cycles are performed until the whole text has been processed.

In the older Kintsch and van Dijk (1978) model (cf. Schmid, 1994), memory for text was simply predicted by the propositional representation in combination with the buffer model: The more processing cycles a proposition had participated in, the more likely it was to be remembered. With the newer distributed memory model, the memory for some probe (e.g., a proposition or a sentence) is determined by a comparison of the probe to the whole memory pattern. The comparison between a test probe and memory is determined by the amount of activation that flows from the memory representation into the representation of the test probe. Thereby it is assumed that the processing of the test probe is similar to the processing during the comprehension phase: The same type of constructive processes are performed and the constructed units are then connected to the network in the same manner that was used for modeling the comprehension processes. Thereafter the spreading activation process is performed. The amount of activation that flows back into the nodes that represent the test probe determine the memory score for that test probe. Because the test probe is compared to the whole memory representation rather than to a single memory unit, the C–I model is also in agreement with the current models of recognition memory (Gillund & Shiffrin, 1984; Hintzman, 1988) that share the same property.

TABLE 4.1

The Sentences That Were Processed by the C–I Model

Nick	decided	to go to	the movies.
V1	V2	V3	V4
(NICK)	(DECIDE, P1, P3)	(GO, P1, P4)	(MOVIES)
P1	P2	P3	P4
S1	S2	S3	S4

He	looked at	the newspaper		to see	what	was playing.
V10	V5	V6		V8	V11	V9
	(LOOK, P1, P6)	(NEWSPAPER)	(CAUSE, P5, P8)	(SEE, P1, P9)		(PLAY, IN MOVIES)
	P5	P6	P7	P8		P9
	S5	S6	S7	S8		S9

Note. It is shown which verbatim, propositional, and situational nodes correspond to the various units of the sentences (adapted from Kintsch, Welsch, Schmalhofer and Zimny, 1990; Figure 3).

Kintsch applied the C–I model to explain text memory (Kintsch et al., 1990). When subjects study the two sentences shown in Table 4.1, they are assumed to construct units that represent the text at the verbatim level (i.e., nodes V1 to V11). These units become connected according to simple phrase structure rules, which yield the additional linguistic nodes L1 to L8 (see Fig. 4.1). Propositional strategies generate the propositions P1 to P9. Schematic strategies generate the situational units S1 to S10, which are connected according to a well-known schematic structure (Galambos, 1983). Further knowledge-construction processes connect corresponding nodes of the verbatim and propositional representation as well as between the propositional and the situational representation by referential links (see Table 4.1). The resulting network is shown in Fig. 4.1. Activation is now spread through this network until a stable activation value is reached for each node. In Fig. 4.1, the relative strengths of the final activations are shown for each node. Higher activation levels are indicated by darker nodes. It can be seen that S5 is a node with a very high activation, actually the highest activation. Node V10 is a node with a very low activation. Nodes in the center of the network (such as node S5) thus collect more activation and are therefore predicted to be better remembered than peripheral nodes (such as node V10). With this application of the C–I model, sentence recognition data that had been collected by Zimny (1987) could be modelled quite well. It thus appears that constructive processes that form a situation representation even play a role for sentence memory.

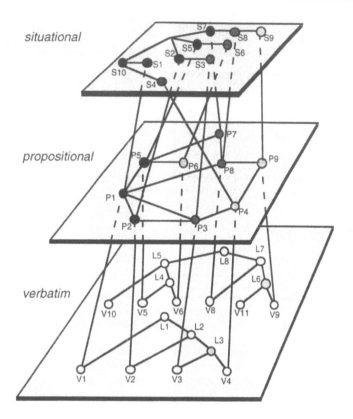

FIG. 4.1. According to Kintsch's C–I model, texts are encoded at different representation levels. It can be seen how the knowledge about a domain (i.e., the extensional meaning of the text at the situation level) is distinguished from the representation of the (intensional) text meaning (propositional level) and the wording of the text (verbatim representation); adapted from Kintsch, Welsch, Schmalhofer and Zimny, 1990; Figures 3, 4, and 5.

Inference Processes

A particular interest in text research concerns the cognitive processes that occur when two consecutive sentences are not related according to the information that is directly presented by the sentences themselves. The following two sentences are an example of such a sequence: *The spy threw the report in the fire. The ashes floated up the chimney.* These two sentences would be completely disjoint, if the reader did not make a causal inference, such as *The report burned to ashes* (Singer & Ferreira, 1983; Singer & Halldorson, 1996). In order to generate a coherent representation, readers must therefore apply their prior domain knowledge. As mentioned earlier research has shown that texts are more easily read and better remembered when they are (causally) coherent according to the assumptions of the Kintsch and van Dijk model (Britton & Gülgöz, 1991; Miller & Kintsch, 1980) and no such knowledge intensive (and possibly unreliable) inference processes have to be performed. It has also been shown that the inferences that are drawn during the reading of a text depend on the purpose of reading (Noordman, Vonk, & Kempff, 1992).

From the postulates of the C–I model, in particular the assumption that subjects also construct a situation model, additional predictions can be derived. Coherence breaks in the surface of a text should stimulate the use of prior domain knowledge. For readers with appropriate prior domain knowledge, texts that do not cohere at the surface level should therefore be better at provoking the formation of a situation model and consequently improve the acquisition of knowledge from text. For readers with little or no prior domain knowledge on the other hand, superficially coherent texts are more useful because they yield a better text memory. Because of the lack of domain knowledge, these subjects are not capable of forming an adequate situation model (Kintsch, 1994). These predictions were confirmed with both 8th-grade students and adult readers as subjects (McNamara, Kintsch, Songer, & Kintsch, in press; McNamara, 1995). The C–I model has thus been able to account for a variety of different experimental findings.

In all important aspects, the theory that underlies the KIWi model is identical to the basic assumptions of Kintsch's C–I model. There is, however, a difference that concerns the manner in which we describe the model. Whereas in the description of the C–I model, general theoretical assumptions have not been clearly separated from the more specific processing assumptions and the implementational details by which the various cognitive processes have been described in the computer simulation, the KIWi model will be presented according to the levels approach of cognitive modeling. Because the C–I model has not yet been described in this way, it is sometimes difficult to assess whether the successful model predictions are due to the general theory, to the symbol processing assumptions, to a specific computer implementation, or to some specific combination of the three levels. In the next section, we provide a knowledge-level description of the C–I model in terms of a KADS inference structure, which we will also refer to as the C–I theory. This C–I theory will then be used as the framework within which the KIWi model (i.e., symbol-processing descriptions) and the KIWi implementations are described.

4.3 The C–I Theory in Terms of the Knowledge-Level

To obtain a knowledge-level description of the C–I model, skills, goals, and knowledge are attributed to the information-processing model, so that this attribution provides an appropriate description or documentation of the performance of the model (see chapter 2, section 2.2). Such a knowledge-level analysis was performed by taking some related models into account, namely the NETWORK model by Mannes and Kintsch (1991), the UNICOM system by Doane et al. (1989) and Kitajima and Polson's (1995) comprehension-based model of human-computer interaction. The NETWORK model describes how subjects solve routine computing tasks such as sending e-mail. The UNICOM system describes how subjects combine various commands in UNIX, a well known computer operating system. Kitajima and Polson's model describes the errors that experienced computer users make while performing some task with a graphical user interface. All of these models could be appropriately described by the KADS inference structure shown in Fig. 4.2.

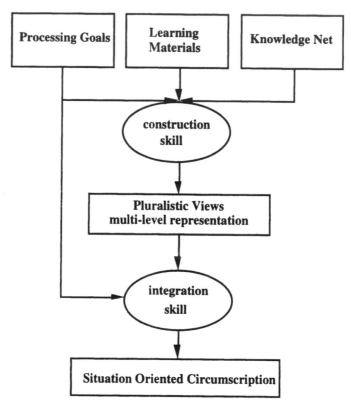

FIG. 4.2. The C–I theory in terms of a knowledge-level description.

As can be seen from Fig. 4.2, two different skills are assumed in these models, a *knowledge construction skill* and *knowledge integration skill*. Both of these skills are shown as basic inference steps. For the construction skill, three input metaclasses are assumed. A learner's prior knowledge is organized in the form of a knowledge net (cf. Mannes & Kintsch, 1991). The learning materials are another input metaclass. In addition, the processing goal influences how the construction skill utilizes the information from the knowledge net and the learning materials.

The construction skill forms a multilevel representation with pluralistic views of the learning materials. One piece of text information may thus be represented from different perspectives and in different ways. A specific person that was mentioned in the text may be represented as the argument of a text proposition as well as a situational unit representing the person as being part of some section of reality. These pluralistic views may furthermore contain opposite and contradictory information. Knowledge construction in the C–I theory is thus a very creative process and not so much a fixed algorithm that is applied to some predetermined sets of inputs.

The integration skill then evaluates how the pluralistic views can be best fit together in a multilevel description, so that a coherent and consistent abstract structure is obtained. Thereby, the abnormalities (i.e., inconsistencies) that existed in the pluralistic views are eliminated or at least substantially reduced. The product of the integration skill is termed a *situation oriented circumscription* and presents the (relatively abstract) knowledge that is acquired from the learning materials in combination with the learners' prior knowledge. The network that was shown in Fig. 4.1 is an example of a specific symbol-level instantiation of such a situation-oriented circumscription.

It should be noted that the presented knowledge-level description is quite generic, and no specific symbols or symbol structures are identified. In particular, this description is neutral with respect to whether the integration skill is modelled in terms of a connectionist or a symbolic constraint satisfaction process. Also, no temporal sequence of the application of the different skills is identified in the inference structure. The connecting lines and arrows only denote the general dependencies among the metaclasses and the basic inference actions.

We have now described the C–I theory in terms of a KADS inference structure. We have shown that the C–I theory can be understood as a knowledge-level description for possible symbol processing models, which is completely independent of any specific learning domain. As is shown in chapter 6, important empirical predictions can already be derived from this knowledge-level description. In order to obtain additional testable predictions, we have to specify the symbol-level processing for a specific application, such as the learning of the programming language LISP. The following symbol-level description that was developed under the guidance of the C–I theory is called the KIWi model.

4.4 The KIWi Model as a Symbol-Level Description

The KIWi model is an information-processing model that is described at the symbol level. It specifies the various symbols and symbol structures that are being processed. We must therefore become more specific about the particular learning materials as well as about the learner's prior domain knowledge that is organized in the knowledge net. The KIWi model is presented for the learning of elementary LISP functions from text descriptions. We thus describe the specific symbols and symbol structures that are postulated by the KIWi model as well as the information processes that are assumed to operate on them. Thereby, a sample of the learning materials, the knowledge net that contains a learner's prior knowledge, and the construction and integration processes are discussed.

Learning Materials

A set of possible learning materials may, for instance, consist of the following sentences:

FIRST is a LISP function.
It requires exactly one argument.
The argument must be a list.
The function FIRST returns the first element of the argument.

Prior Knowledge (Knowledge Net)

In applying such an information-processing model, it is important that a learner's prior knowledge can be estimated. One possibility to obtain such an estimate was demonstrated by Mannes and Kintsch (1991). They used a representative sample of subjects and had these subjects freely associate to the key notions that occurred in the learning materials. From the information units that were produced by their subjects, Mannes and Kintsch then constructed the knowledge net that the learners would supposedly use. With these estimates for the knowledge net, the performance could be predicted for a new set of subjects, who were assumed to have the same knowledge net as the subjects from which the parameters of the information-processing model were derived. For a quite different model and a quite different area of research, the same rationale and a similar method for independently estimating the parameters of a processing model was used by Albert, Aschenbrenner, and Schmalhofer (1989).

For the current research, we selected a learning domain (namely LISP) that would allow us to determine the learners' prior knowledge by theoretical considerations rather than by an additional empirical investigation. Subjects were selected who did not have any prior knowledge about this particular language. The prior knowledge that was important for learning the LISP functions such as FIRST, REST, LIST, or EQUAL could thus be experimentally induced in a preceding learning phase, and the KIWi model could be used to predict the knowledge net that would be available when the criterion materials (i.e., the LISP functions) were subsequently learned.

Three types of knowledge are distinguished: (a) known rules and facts, (b) hypotheses, and (c) heuristics that can generate hypotheses. Each knowledge unit incorporates two numerical scores. One score represents the confidence in the correctness of the knowledge unit and the other score represents the usefulness of the knowledge unit. The three different types of knowledge can thus be denoted in the following manner:

(1) known(Domain, FactOrRule, Confidence, Usefulness)
(2) hyp(Domain, FactOrRule, Confidence, Usefulness)
(3) heur(Domain, FactOrRule, Confidence, Usefulness)

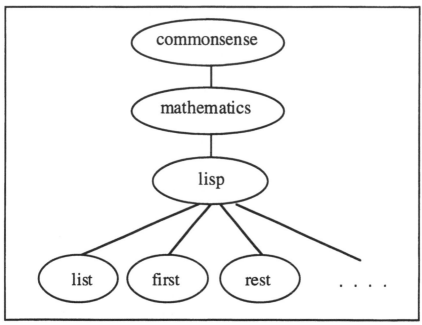

FIG. 4.3. Hierarchical organization of the knowledge that is relevant for learning elementary LISP (knowledge net).

For the subject domain of LISP functions, the relevant prior knowledge is assumed to consist of commonsense, general programming knowledge, and the LISP knowledge that was acquired by the preceding learning materials. To facilitate access to this knowledge, each knowledge unit is assigned to a domain that may be selectively accessed. Domains are furthermore hierarchically organized. For the area of elementary LISP, the relevant knowledge is structured according to the hierarchy shown in Fig. 4.3.

Commonsense knowledge includes the transitivity of subclass relations, counting, and general heuristics. An example of such a heuristic would be the wishful-thinking heuristic: It says that if something is not known in general, then just assume that whatever is given in the specific case would be true in general. The wishful-thinking heuristic is particularly important in learning from examples. The argument overlap strategy (Kintsch & van Dijk, 1978) is a heuristic that plays an important role in the construction of the propositional textbase. It compares the various propositions in working memory and connects those propositions by a link (i.e., which share an argument or where one proposition is embedded in the other; cf. Schmid, 1994).

For the particular programming language under consideration, the function schema is most important for the learning of new LISP functions. The function schema says:

IF (the actual number of arguments corresponds to the number of
arguments required by the specific function) and
(the type of argument corresponds to the type of argument
required by the specific function) and
(the given input–output relation corresponds to the
input–output relation prescribed by the specific function)
THEN (the current function-call is correct)

Schemata have also been assumed in previous research (e.g., Bower, Black, &
Turner, 1979). For instance, Galambos (1983) collected script norms, which are
schemata for action sequences of routine activities like going to a restaurant,
going to a doctor, or going to the movies. These schemata encode the default
assumptions that people have about these routine activities. The function schema
that we postulate for the learning of LISP functions also has this property.
However, the function schema is, in addition, represented in such a way that it
can model generative processes. In previous work, the statements that a learner
would supposedly infer were explicitly coded into the schema. For instance, a
restaurant script has explicitly coded that the customer will usually pay the
waiter, unless some abnormal conditions occur (such as the customer being
extremely annoyed by the service). With this coded default inference it is thus
predicted that a reader assumes that the customer paid, even when this was not
explicitly stated in the text.

Our proposed function schema works in a somewhat different fashion. It does
not have any presupposed inferences that are explicitly coded into the schema.
Instead, the function schema is used in combination with other knowledge, and
the inferences are actually generated on line by the construction processes.

Construction Processes

The construction processes operate at the surface, the propositional, and the
situational levels. The construction of the linguistic structures is assumed to
operate as was described by Kintsch (1988) and Kintsch et al. (1990). The focus
of the present work is, however, more on the propositional and especially the
situational levels. The propositional strategies generate the respective
propositions from the text. Because no text parsers are yet available that would
automatically generate such propositions, the propositions are manually
constructed according to the specifically developed guidelines (Bovair & Kieras,
1983; Turner, 1987). The various problems that arise in such
propositionalizations have been discussed by Perfetti and Britt (1995). For the
specific text on the function FIRST, the following list of propositions was
obtained. The argument overlap strategy can furthermore link the various
propositions so that a propositional net is obtained.

P0: function(first).
P1: argument(P0)
P2: exactly(one)
P3: number_of(P1,P2)
P4: require(P0,P3).

P5:   is_list(P1)
P6:   must(P5)
P7:   element(P1)
P8:   first(P7)
P9:   returns(P0,P8).

Situational units are similarly constructed. These situational units are expressed in a logical form, so that inference processes can operate on them. Again, there is no parser that would directly build the situational units from the text. But the transcription of the presented sentences into situational units is straightforward. The situational units are:

FIRST is a LISP function.
The required number of arguments of the function FIRSTis one.
The required type of argument of the function FIRSTis a list.
The required input–output relation of the function FIRST is that the
    output is the first element of the argument.

Basically, the situational units consist of some recoding of the text sentences, so that inference processes can operate on them. In particular, the KIWi model focuses on such situational inference processes. These inferences are elaborative inferences (cf. Reder et al., 1986) in which the situational knowledge units that are currently in working memory and knowledge from the most closely related subject domains are used to form new elaborations. When such inferences are generated, the knowledge net of prior knowledge is searched from the specific to the more general domains. Within a domain, the most recently acquired knowledge is given preference over the older knowledge. For any set of knowledge units, only a limited number of inferences are constructed. The constructed inferences can then be used to construct further inferences. Whenever an inferred rule is used during further inference processing, its usefulness counter is incremented by 1.

From the situational unit *FIRST is a LISP function*, and other knowledge about LISP, the following inference was thus obtained by the KIWi simulation:

IF (the Input to the LISP system is of the form
    (first Argumentspecification)) and
    (an evaluation of the *Argumentspecification* yields the *Arguments*) and
    (the function *first* with the *Arguments* yields some *Result*)
THEN (the specific *Input* will indeed yield the specific *Result*.).

This elaborative inference can already be called a partial template, because it is knowledge that is operational. The original statement was so general that it is quite difficult to see how one should operate on it, for instance, to generate an input to the LISP system. The inferred knowledge on the other hand says that one can produce an input to the LISP system by typing *first* . Furthermore,

Arguments and a corresponding *Argumentspecification* must be found, so that the application of the function *first* will yield the desired *Result*. With further reasoning it may be concluded that by using '(A B) as the *Argumentspecification*, the result *A* can be obtained. The situational elaboration processes thus construct a large number of inferences, some of which are quite useful, like the one which we have just described. Others are irrelevant or have a high degree of redundancy with other knowledge units.

An additional construction process concerns the generation of links among the situational units. Each newly constructed situational unit is linked to those units that were employed for its construction. The usefulness parameters are employed to determine the strengths of the links. Thus in addition to the propositional level, the situational level contains interconnections as well. Finally, the propositional units are connected to corresponding situational units. As a result of the various construction processes, one thus obtains pluralistic views with a three-level representation on the learning materials. In the manner in which the KIWi simulation is currently executed, no contradictory knowledge is formed, but the constructed knowledge varies in its degree of redundancy and usefulness.

Integration Processes

At the symbol level, the integration skill is described as a constraint-satisfaction process. Between all the knowledge units that are connected, certain compatability or incompatability relations exist. The constraint satisfaction process then determines which knowledge units fit together well and which knowledge units are at odds with the structure that emerges from propagating the constraints among the various knowledge units. At the symbol-processing level, the specific implementation of constraint satisfaction is thus not determined. The constraint satisfaction process can indeed be implemented in two different ways: It can be implemented by a connectionist spreading activation process (cf. Rumelhart & McClelland, 1986; Strube, 1990) or by a symbolic constraint satisfaction procedure (Freuder, 1978; Lassez, 1987; Mackworth, 1977).

In the C–I model, the integration process is simulated by a connectionist constraint satisfaction or spreading activation process. Some nodes of the network are activated and this activation then spreads along the links of the network until the activation in the individual nodes has stabilized. An example for the application of a connectionist constraint satisfaction process is shown in Fig. 4.1. Such a spreading activation process is easily implemented by representing the nodes of the network by a vector. Each element of the vector thus represents an individual node and the numerical value represents its activation. The links and their strengths can then be represented by a corresponding matrix. A zero in column i and row j of the matrix would thus mean that node i and j are not connected. A specific number like the number 3 would mean that the nodes are connected with strength 3. Typically (e.g., Kintsch et al., 1990), it is assumed that each linguistic and propositional node is connected to itself by strength 5. The situational nodes are connected to themselves by strength 4. Four is also the strength of the connections between the different levels (i.e., from the linguistic to the propositional level and from the propositional to the situational level). Different nodes within one level are connected by strength 3. Furthermore, at the situational level, the units of a schema are assumed to be tied together more strongly. Therefore, nodes that are two links apart are additionally connected directly with a link of strength 2, and nodes that are three links apart are directly connected with strength 1. The construction of the nodes and the links are both part of the construction processes of the C–I model.

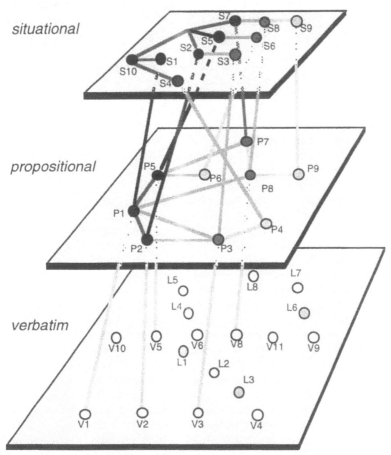

FIG. 4.4. Long-term memory storage of the multi-level representation that was shown in Fig. 4.1. It is seen that propositional and situational links have a better chance of being stored than the links at the verbatim level. At the verbatim level, only 5 of 17 nodes are part of the long-term representation.

On the basis of these node strengths, the strengths of the nodes of the network that are moved to long term memory is then determined. Kintsch and Welsch (1991) suggested that the long-term connections should be calculated by multiplying the original connection strength by the activation strengths of the nodes that it connects. A node that was relatively inactive when the network settled will thus tend to be disconnected from the network in the long-term memory representation. Figure 4.4 shows the long-term memory representation that is obtained from the network is shown in Fig. 4.1. In Fig. 4.4, dark connections indicate strong links and light connections indicate weaker links. Links below a certain value were cut and several nodes were thereby disconnected. Figure 4.4 shows that the nodes of the verbatim level were more likely to be disconnected or only weakly associated than the nodes at the propositional or situational level. This observation may be understood as an indicator for the representational strengths of the three different levels (see chapter 7, experiments 1, 2, and 3).

For some of the simulation runs of the integration process of the KIWi model, we used the spreading activation process of the C–I model (Mross & Roberts, 1992; Rodenhausen, 1992). For these simulation runs we combined the knowledge construction processes of the KIWi model with a re-implementation of the spreading activation process of the C–I model. Each node in the network thus contained one or several PROLOG expressions, which could be operated on by the different production rules (Jäger, 1992). The construction and integration processes were therby dynamically interconnected.

Modeling the knowledge integration processes by a connectionist constraint satisfaction procedure is quite appropriate and sufficient for most purposes. However, when structurally complex knowledge is to be acquired and utilized at some later point in time, the typical topologies of connectionist networks do not provide a rich enough structure and are therefore not sufficient for producing the critical task performance. For instance, Schmalhofer and Tschaitschian (1993) modelled the knowledge acquisiton processes that occur when subjects solve different problems. The experimental research of this study showed that subjects acquired an abstract procedure schema, which allowed learners to solve tasks that are quite different at the surface level. In order to provide a sufficient processing model for the subjects' performance according to the assumptions of the C–I theory, Schmalhofer and Tschaitschian employed a symbolic rather than a connectionist constraint satisfaction process that yielded a richer structure.

However, this symbolic constraint satisfaction process had the same general properties as the connectionist process. By propagating local information to achieve global consistency, it constructed a coherent and consistent structure and it eliminated those knowledge units that were not consistent or did not cohere with this structure. It is thus seen that, depending on the particular requirements, knowledge integration can be modelled by connectionist or by symbolic constraint propagation.

4.5 Discussion

Kintsch's (1988) proposal of modeling comprehension by construction and integration processes stimulated the development of several different processing models. Mannes and Kintsch (1991) implemented the NETWORK model and were also successful in modeling how subjects solve routine computing tasks. Doane, Kintsch and Polson (1989) developed the UNICOM model. Goldman and Varma (1995) proposed the 3CI model for explaining how macrostructures are generated. Kintsch et al. (1990) applied the C–I model for modeling sentence memory. Singer and Halldorson (1996) have recently proposed a model of generating inferences during text comprehension, which they called the validation model. Their model states that readers would first generate inferences on the basis of coherence breaks in the text (similar to the Kintsch and van Dijk model) and that these inferences are then validated by the reader's world knowledge. Singer and Halldorson then employed Mross and Robert's C–I program to obtain empirical predictions from their model.

An obvious question that arises when one studies all this modeling work concerns the similarities and the differences among the models. These models differ with respect to the experimental data to which they have been applied. They also differ concerning which particular simulation program was used to generate the experimental predictions. For instance, the NETWORK implementation differs in many respects from the C–I implementation.

By using the levels approach to cognitive modeling, the similarities and differences among such models can be determined in a systematic way. In particular it can be shown that NETWORK, UNICOM, C–I, the 3C–I model, and the KIWi model are all consistent with the C–I theory, where the C–I theory has been specified as a knowledge-level description in terms of a KADS inference structure (see Fig. 4.2). All of these models can thus be understood as different instantiations of Kintsch's C–I theory. The models differ in that they have been applied to various domains, and the specific symbols and symbol structures that are processed in these models must consequently also differ. The symbol structures in learning UNIX are necessarily different from the symbol structures in learning the programming language LISP.

In Singer and Halldorson's validation model, the inference generation process is a typical construction process in the sense of the C–I theory. The inference validation, on the other hand, is simply a match of the generated inference against the subject's background knowledge. It is therefore not generated by an integration skill or a constraint satisfaction process that would produce a situation-oriented circumscription from the pluralistic views generated in the construction process. Singer and Halldorson basically used the C–I model as a special purpose programming language for simulating their validation model. It is thus seen that the levels approach toward cognitive modeling is very useful for analyzing the relations among various simulation models.

The C–I theory, in terms of a knowledge-level description, may also be quite useful for evaluating alternative views about online inferences during reading. Both the minimalist (McKoon & Ratcliff, 1992) and the constructionist positions (Graesser, Singer, & Trabasso, 1994) are in general agreement with the assumptions of the C–I theory. They only differ with respect to their assumptions about the construction processes. Whereas the minimalists assume that the construction of a situation model is not a regular component of text comprehension, the constructionists postulate such inference processing to be an essential part of understanding a text. By discussing the differences between the two positions within the framework of the C–I theory, much more progress can be made than by discussions that do not assume such a common ground.

4.6 Summary

In this chapter, we have indicated how the C–I theory can be understood as an abstraction of representative results from experimental psychology in the areas of memory and text comprehension. We have shown how experimental psychology research on texts has emerged from research with simpler verbal materials such as lists of unrelated words or syllables. One of the central issues in this research concerns how texts are represented in memory. The early research of the 1970s focused on the representation of the meaning of the text by its propositions. More contemporary formulations of text-processing theories, like Kintsch's C–I theory, assume that knowledge acquisition is a constructive process in which a multiple level representation is formed: (a) a representation of the surface structure of the text, (b) the propositional representation of the meaning of the text ,and (c) the situation model is thereby distinguished.

The levels approach toward cognitive modeling that was introduced in the previous chapter was applied for analyzing various simulation models of text comprehension. The knowledge-level description, or C–I theory, could thus be distinguished from the specific symbol-level processing. At the symbol level, the construction skill is modelled by production rules and the integration skill is modelled by a constraint satisfaction process (which may be implemented in a symbolic or connectionist fashion). The KIWi model was introduced as an instantiation of the C–I theory for the application domain of learning a programming language like LISP. The KIWi model differs from other implementations of the C–I theory in that it automatically generates elaborative inferences. In other implementations such inferences have to be handcoded and are not generated by the program itself. Like previous implementations, the KIWi model uses a connectionist integration process. When a structurally more complex learning product must be achieved, a symbolic constraint satisfaction process is also postulated.

In the next chapter, we similarly review experimental and theoretical research in the areas of concept formation and learning from cases. More specifically we then attempt to extend the C–I theory and the KIWi model so that learning from text and learning from cases can be unified.

5

Integration With the Acquisition
of Knowledge From Cases

In the previous chapter, we showed that historically the research on learning from
text can be traced back to investigations of memory for verbal materials, such as
nonsense syllables, word lists, and sentences. Within the area of experimental
psychology, the investigations of learning from complex cases can similarly be
traced back to research that employed quite simple materials. In the research on
concept identification, simple-structured examples were employed for
investigating how subjects would identify the relevant attributes and respective
rules that represent the underlying concept. In the absence of a sophisticated
theoretical foundation, simple materials were essential for conducting well-
controlled experiments that would lay a solid foundation for future work. Whereas
the early experimental research with text materials had focused on memory and
memory representations, the research on concept identification investigated the
processing strategies that subjects would employ when learning new concepts
from positive and negative examples.

In this chapter, we first summarize some of the classical work on concept
identification and show how this work relates to the more recent research on
learning from cases and learning by exploration. Thereafter the most important
computational models are reviewed. We then show how learning from cases and
learning by exploration can be integrated into the C–I theory and how the KIWi
model is thereby extended to also describe learning from cases, learning by
exploration, and how the acquired knowledge is subsequently utilized in various
test tasks (sentence verification, example verification, program evaluation, and
program development tasks).

5.1 The Identification of Concepts From Examples

In the research on concept identification, subjects were typically put into well-specified closed-world situations. Because the experimenters had completely defined these closed-world situations, they also had complete knowledge about all aspects of these artificial situations. The well-known investigations by Bruner, Goodnow, and Austin (1956), and the subsequent research with mathematical learning theories (e.g., Bourne & Restle, 1959; Bower & Trabasso, 1964) are good examples of this type of work. In a typical experiment, subjects were presented with a sequence of simple examples, such as different geometric shapes (i.e., triangles, squares, circles, etc.) that may appear in one of several different colors (i.e., red, blue, green, etc.). A green square, a red triangle, and a red circle may thus be presented simultaneously or sequentially, and for each example the learner was informed whether or not the example was an instance of the concept to be learned. On various test trials, subjects were then shown selected examples and they had to decide whether an example was or was not an instance of the concept to be learned. Thereby, the various component processes that subjects would use to identify a concept such as *a red object* or *a square* were investigated (cf. Levine, 1975).

In Bruner et al.'s (1956) study of thinking, the experimenter could present examples (i.e., a stimulus card) one at a time, and the subject had to say whether the example would or would not belong to the concept. Subsequently, the experimenter would provide feedback about the correctness of the subject's response. Bruner et al. called this presentation, where the subjects would learn from a prearranged sequence of examples, the *reception method.* In another procedure, which was called the *selection method*, subjects themselves could select one of several stimulus cards. Rather than studying a sequence of predetermined examples, the subjects could thus select those examples that appeared particularly suited for exploring some specific hypothesis.

Several strategies were identified by Bruner et al. With the reception method of presentation, two strategies were identified. Subjects could apply a *wholist strategy* and remember all the attributes that were common to the positive examples while ignoring all other attributes. With the *partist strategy*, subjects focused on one hypothesis and would maintain this hypothesis until a contradicting example was encountered. At that time a new hypothesis was selected on the basis of their memory of past experiences.

With the selection method of presentation, four strategies were identified. With the *simultaneous scanning* strategy, the subject would begin by assuming the correctness of all possible hypotheses. After selecting a new example, all those hypotheses that were inconsistent with this example would be eliminated. The simultaneous scanning strategy has several similarities to Mitchell's *version-space* algorithm (see chapter 2). With the *successive scanning strategy* on the other hand, a subject would begin with a specific hypothesis and maintain this hypothesis until it was contradicted by some example. At that time, a new hypothesis that would consistently account for all previously studied examples is selected. This procedure is more similar to Michalski's INDUCE algorithm, which was described in chapter 2. With the *conservative focusing strategy*, a learner would start with a single positive example and would subsequently select examples that differ by one attribute at a time. Finally, with the *focus gambling strategy*, a learner would again start with only one positive example, but then select examples with several different attributes at a time.

The described strategies thus differ in whether they use the whole space of possible hypotheses, a single hypothesis, or a particular instance as a starting point. They also differ in how additional information is selected and how the hypothesis updating is performed on the basis of the presented feedback. When subjects are allowed to generate their own examples, they often form concepts that are unnecessarily specific, because they tend to generate examples that are expected to confirm rather than refute their current hypothesis. In learning by exploration, this is generally known as the confirmation bias (Klayman & Ha, 1987; Wason, 1960).

The research on concept identification with mathematical learning theories showed that discovering the relevant attributes (called attribute learning) and discovering the logical rules by which the attributes are connected to define the target concept (called rule learning) are two component processes for a successful concept identification. Although the saliency of an attribute is an important factor for attribute learning, the rule-learning experiments in which the subjects were a priori informed about the relevant attributes showed that conjunctive rules are generally easier to identify than disjunctive, conditional (i.e., logical implications), and bi-directional rules (i.e., the logical equivalence).

During the 1970s, the view of concept identification as a hypothesis-testing and rule-learning process was criticisized on several grounds (cf. Eckes, 1996). This view assumes that concepts could be defined in a very simple manner. Namely, it is assumed that all the examples of a category would share some common properties and that these properties are the necessary and the sufficient conditions that an example must satisfy in order to belong to the concept. According to Smith and Medin (1981), this has become known as the *Classical View* of a conceptual structure. The *Probabilistic View*, on the other hand, assumes that concepts are organized by characteristic properties, which are neither necessary nor sufficient conditions. Whether an example belongs to a concept is thus a matter of degree rather than being all or none. The shift from the *Classical* to the *Probabilistic View* was very much motivated by the research of Rosch and her colleagues on natural categories (Rosch & Mervis, 1975). A third view of conceptual structure is the *Exemplar View*, which assumes that categories are represented by their individual exemplars. A new example is thereby classified by determining whether it is sufficiently similar to one of the category's known exemplars (e.g., Heit, 1992; Nosofsky, 1988).

In a recent review, Medin and Heit (in press) pointed out that the different views of conceptual structure invite different processing assumptions. Whereas hypothesis testing or rule-based models are more compatible with the Classical View, a learning procedure that forms the central tendency of category examples is more compatible with the Probabilistic View. As Medin and Heit remarked, the Probabilistic View can also be referred to as the *Prototype View*. According to the Exemplar View, the similarity measure is the determining factor for deciding about class memberships. The Exemplar View is thus quite similar to case-based reasoning.

Common to all three views of conceptual structure is the assumption that all the information that is needed for classifying the examples is directly observable from the examples. In particular, it is assumed that all the features that are relevant for classifying the examples would be directly observable to the learners. Because the similarities among the surface features thus determines the classification, the three views can be jointly described as similarity-based learning (cf. Medin & Heit, in press). Explanation-based learning (see chapter 2), on the other hand, assumes that the learners use their prior domain knowledge to determine the relevant features of the examples. Concept learning may thus consist of highly interactive processes that involve mutual influences of prior knowledge and experience from the examples (Wisniewski & Medin, 1994).

Although we have presented only a very selective summary of the extensive research on concept learning, this is quite sufficient to show how the results from laboratory studies on the learning of artificial categories can be integrated with learning from text, and how a more unified theory of a much broader range of human thought can thus be obtained. In the following section, we are concerned with knowledge acquisition in more real-life-like situations. In this setting, the learning materials have usually been denoted as cases rather than as stimuli. We therefore refer to these real-life stimuli as cases.

5.2 Knowledge Acquisition From Cases

A *case* is a specific situation, which is described in terms of a problem and its solution. It represents knowledge that is at an operational level and that is tied to a context. We can thus define a *case description* as a contextualized piece of knowledge that represents some important experience (cf. Kolodner, 1993). Therefore, cases also can be used to teach lessons. When a problem and a solution are produced or selected by a teacher in order to be demonstrated to a student, they are also referred to as (situation) examples (cf. VanLehn & Jones, 1993). Although cases and examples are not exactly the same, for most purposes, we can and will regard cases and examples as synonyms.

Empirical Results

The cases and concepts that occur in real life can be quite complex. The research by Rosch on natural concepts has shown that although objects could be classified into one of several hierarchically structured categories (e.g., a given object may be classified as a stool, as a chair, or as furniture), humans tend to use the basic level categories (e.g., chair). The basic level is that level in a class hierarchy in which the objects of a class share a maximum number of attributes with one another that distinguishes them from the objects of the other classes at this level. In other words, basic level categories are those categories in which the attributes of an object have the maximum predictiveness for the class membership of the object.

Chi, Feltovich and Glaser (1981) furthermore demonstrated that the classification of problem cases in physics depends on a person's prior domain knowledge. Whereas novices classified the problems by their literal features (e.g., whether springs or vertical motion were involved in the problem), expert subjects classified the problems on the basis of more abstract physics knowledge that was relevant for solving the problems (e.g., conservation of energy consideration and work-energy theorem). As it turns out, such differences also play an important role when we investigate the influence of prior knowledge on the acquisition of knowledge from different learning materials (see chapter 10).

Wertheimer's (1945) research on productive thinking had similarly shown that quite different knowledge can be acquired from problems and their solutions (i.e., from cases) by different learners. When a student achieves an in-depth understanding of a problem and grasps the inner structural relationships of the problem, the student can then solve a variety of superficially quite different problems. Students who do not achieve such an understanding, on the other hand, are only able to solve a relatively narrow class of (superficially similar) problems. Students who solved the problem of calculating the area of a parallelogram in an insightful way could also reason out and calculate the areas of trapezoids and other less regular figures. On the other hand, students who had only memorized a formula for calculating the area failed to solve these transfer problems altogether. The scope of transferring a problem solution that was acquired from a specific case thus depends on the kind and depth of comprehension that is achieved when a case is studied.

The self-explanation effect that was reported by Chi, Bassok, Lewis, Reimann and Glaser (1989) furthermore confirms this conclusion. Chi et al. observed that those students who were able to solve more problems after having studied some worked-out examples happened to be the students who had generated self-explanations when they studied the worked-out examples. The other students were mostly paraphrasing the statements of the example and were not as capable in solving new problems. It may thus be concluded that the self-explainers had achieved a deeper level of understanding (cf. Chi, de Leeuw, Chiu, & LaVancher, 1994) by grasping the inner structural relationships of the problems through so-called self-explanations. Pirolli and Recker (1994) achieved the same results in the area of computer programming (LISP), and Pirolli (1991) reported that elaborations of the underlying program structure would produce more efficient learning than elaborations on how the code worked (cf. Bergmann, Boschert, & Schmalhofer, 1992).

In a investigation on learning to program a computer-controlled robot, Klahr and Dunbar (1988) used a think-aloud method. Their subjects had to formulate hypotheses based on their prior knowledge, conduct experiments with the robot (i.e., program the robot), and evaluate the results of their experiments. The results showed that the learners used one of two main strategies. One strategy was to search memory. This strategy yielded a search in the space of the concepts (also referred to as hypothesis space). The other strategy was to generalize from the results of previous experiments. This strategy yielded a search in the space of the specific cases (also referred to as experiment space).

Computational Models

Various computational models have been developed to describe the cognitive processes that occur in learning from cases. Lewis (1988) developed the EXPL system, which models how subjects form explanation-based generalizations from various interactions of humans with a computer. EXPL does not assume any prior domain knowledge. Instead, general heuristics are applied. These heuristics generate causal attributions for the various events. A causal attribution can be made on the basis of the so-called *identity heuristic*. For instance, after a human user has typed the name of an object and this object disappears from the computer screen, it is attributed that the user's action was the cause for the object to disappear from the screen. Other heuristics that are implemented in the EXPL system are: The *obligatory previous action heuristic*, the *loose-ends heuristic* and the *previous action heuristic*. We do not describe here what each of these heuristics does, but simply point out that these heuristics are quite general and do not have any domain-specific knowledge encoded into them. Nevertheless, Lewis could demonstrate that these general heuristics are sufficient for explaining a number of different human–computer interactions. The causal attributions that are generated by EXPL coincide to some degree with the causal attributions from human subjects. However, human subjects also used domain-specific knowledge, which was not represented in EXPL. On the basis of his results, Lewis speculated that people may shift between different styles of domain theory in an explanation-based framework (cf. Ellman, 1989; also chapter 2), or between two different generalization methods. One generalization method may rely more on general heuristics and the other one more on domain-specific knowledge.

VanLehn and Jones (1993) developed the CASCADE system. This system also uses an explanation-based learning paradigm and models the self-explanation effect. Rather than using general heuristics, VanLehn and Jones encoded the information from the prose parts of the textbook, which subjects had read "in a predigested form" (p. 26), and used this information as a domain theory. Thus they did not model the text comprehension processes. Instead they simply assumed that their learners would have acquired certain knowledge from the text. They then asked an independent set of subjects whether it would be reasonable to assume that this knowledge can indeed be acquired from the specific text. As it turned out, their subjects confirmed this question. Furthermore, VanLehn and Jones assumed that their learners had indeed used this knowledge to self-explain the physics examples.

Basically, CASCADE models only two different tasks, namely explaining examples by applying previously acquired domain knowledge and solving new problems. In both tasks new knowledge is acquired. Both tasks are implemented by a rule-based, backward-chaining theorem prover (like in PROLOG). The self-explanation of physics examples is modelled by proving a given line of the worked-out example (like "The magnitude of the tension force on Block-ix due to

String-ix is ...") with the already available domain knowledge. The absence of a self-explanation is modelled by ignoring the specific line of the proof. In problem solving, which occurs after the studying of the examples, analogical search control (also known as *derivational analogy*; Carbonell, 1986) and *transformational analogy* are employed. At impasses, explanation-based learning of correctness (EBLC) and analogy abduction can be applied. In EBLC an overly general rule is applied, and whenever such an application is successful, its context-specific specialization is saved as new domain knowledge. For instance, domain-specific knowledge could be derived from the overly general rule "If an object is composed of parts, the *property values of the parts* and the *property values of the whole* must be identical." When this rule was applied for reasoning about pressures in containers, the following more specific rule was obtained: "If the container has a part, then the pressure in the part is equal to the pressure in the whole container." Finally, in analogy abduction, a transformational analogy is performed and the results are stored for future use in the form of a rule. For modeling the self-explanation effect, a fixed ordering of the various learning processes was applied: If regular problem solving (i.e., the search processes) failed due to missing domain knowledge, EBLC was applied. Transformational analogy was only used as a last resort.

Although there are many more models that describe the storage and indexing of cases and other case-oriented learning processes (Kolodner, 1993), we do not need to concern ourselves with these models in any detail, because they are not particularly suited as processing components for an integrated model within the framework of the construction-integration theory. The learning processes, which were proposed by Lewis (1988) and VanLehn and Jones (1993), on the other hand, were developed for modeling understanding processes. As long as we have one model for understanding text and another model for understanding cases, it will, however, not be possible to predict how learning from text and learning from cases interact with one another. It is therefore a promising endeavour to integrate the various learning processes into a unified model of learning within the framework of the knowledge-level description of the C–I theory.

5.3 Knowledge-Level Descriptions of Learning From Cases

The C–I theory, as it was described in Fig. 4.2, is a very appropriate framework for modeling learning from cases. The postulate of *construction* and *integration phases* can be applied very well to the described computer models. The self-explanations that are modelled by the CASCADE simulations describe knowledge-construction processes in which some segment of a worked-out example is used in combination with some domain knowledge that was acquired from previously studied materials. In terms of the C–I theory, this means that the learner's knowledge net is activated and together with the new information from the example, numerous inferences are constructed. EBLC and analogy abduction, which occur at impasses in problem solving, are also knowledge-construction processes. The formation of an analogical search control schema can be seen as the result of a comprehension process, in which the different knowledge constructions have become integrated into a well-formed procedure schema (Schmalhofer & Tschaitschian, 1993). All the major processes that were proposed in the CASCADE model can thus be understood as processing components in a unified comprehension model.

There is only one essential difference to the assumptions of the CASCADE model. CASCADE assumes that each of the component learning processes occurs at the "right" time so that a smart solution is obtained. Self-explanations thus occur when examples are studied, and EBLC occurs when an impasse is encountered during problem solving. EBLC then yields exactly that knowledge that is needed to overcome the impasse. According to the assumptions of the C–I theory, the different knowledge construction processes would occur on various or almost all occasions. As a consequence, not only the knowledge that is needed under the particular circumstances is constructed, but instead pluralistic views are obtained that may be redundant and even contradictory. It is then up to the integration process to select and rework the constructed knowledge so that a consistent and coherent whole is obtained. Unlike in the CASCADE model, where transformational analogies are only applied after everything else has failed, according to the C–I theory, we would assume that both transformational and derivational analogies would be constructed. Thereafter, the integration processes would yield the target structure, which may consist of one of the two structures or some coherent combination of the two structures.

In addition to the domain-specific explanation processes from the CASCADE model, we also postulate that learners would apply such general, domain-independent heuristics as were described by Lewis (1988) for knowledge construction. But again, the integration processes would then decide which combination of the constructed knowledge would form the situation-oriented circumscription.

We are thus proposing a unified theory for the acquisition of knowledge from different learning materials. A common set of processes is assumed to operate in the different learning situations. Learning from demonstrations, learning by exploration, and even the utilization of knowledge in such tasks as the verification of statements or problem solving are not viewed in isolation. With the knowledge-level view, we can now identify how the different components are related in the different tasks.

Learning From Examples

In a demonstration, a sequence of examples is presented, in many respects similar to the sequence of examples (stimulus cards) that is presented in a classical concept identification experiment. However, there is now a large body of background knowledge that can be utilized in processing these examples. Learning from examples in interaction with background knowledge is therefore a much more creative process than the identification of concepts according to the *Classical View* of conceptual structure. In knowledge-intensive learning, construction processes may occur at the level of the domain-specific knowledge, at the level of related domain knowledge, and at the level of general heuristics. After the various constructions have been performed, the context-sensitive integration process forms a coherent whole with the presented example and the various knowledge elaborations.

Learning by Exploration

The identical component processes that occur in learning from demonstrations are also assumed to operate in learning by exploration. However, rather than studying examples that have been presented by an instructor, the learner must first instigate some action in his or her environment (e.g., pushing a disk on a pool table for learning about the underlying physical laws; Spada, Stumpf, & Opwis, 1989; or producing some input to a computer system in order to learn about a specific programming system). The instigated action together with the reaction from the environment (e.g., the trajectory of the disk on the pool table or the output of the computer system) constitutes an example. Such examples are assumed to be processed in the same way as an example that was presented by an instructor during a demonstration. With this unified approach, we thus only need to add the processes of example generation (i.e., the instigation of an interaction with the environment) or experimentation (Klahr & Dunbar, 1988) to the already outlined processes of learning from examples.

In example generation, the construction and integration processes yield externally visible results. The construction processes are used to elaborate the hypothesis. After knowledge integration, an action that is appropriate for testing the hypothesis in the specific environment (e.g., a syntactically correct input to a computer system) may be obtained. The construction and integration processes are thereby driven by the goal to obtain new information from the environment. This goal may be guided by a confirmation or disconfirmation strategy. The processes of knowledge utilization, as they may occur in verification, evaluation, or problem-solving tasks are similarly viewed as being composed of the component processes that are used for the acquisition of knowledge.

Verification Tasks

Verification tasks are basically performed by the same construction and integration processes that occur during learning. The verification of sentences is thus very similar to the comprehension of a sentence. The only difference really is that in the verification task, an explicit judgement about the sentence (e.g., its correctness) must be given. This judgement is based on how well the sentence is integrated with all of the relevant knowledge. A sentence that is coherent and consistent with all of the activated knowledge would thus be judged as true. A sentence that is inconsistent to a large body of activated knowledge, on the other hand, would be judged as incorrect. The verification of examples would proceed in exactly the same manner.

Programming as Problem Solving Tasks

The process of generating a computer program that would realize some specific input–output relation is quite similar to the process of learning by exploration. The major difference lies in the specific processing goals. Whereas in learning by exploration the generation of an example (or computer program) is driven by the goal of acquiring new knowledge (e.g., testing a specific hypothesis), programming is driven by the goal of solving a specific task. Therefore, it is important that the program that is assembled by the construction and integration processes will satisfy the specific task goal rather than the goal of testing a particular hypothesis. (cf. Mannes & Kintsch, 1991). Learning may also occur during the solution of programming tasks.

5.4 The Extended KIWi Model as a Symbol-Level Description

We now describe the extended KIWi model. Thereby, we present the symbol-level processes that supposedly occur in the learning of the programming language LISP from cases, as well as the various symbol structures that are involved. We describe how particular learning materials are processed during knowledge acquisition and how the acquired knowledge is utilized in verification and problem-solving tasks.

Learning From Examples

Assume that a learner has studied the prerequisite LISP knowledge (cf. Fig. 1.3; learning materials of block A) and is now presented with a LISP example such as *(first '(A B)) ->A.* How would knowledge acquisition occur from this example?

The learner obviously has the goal of acquiring knowledge from this example. This goal would drive the construction as well as the integration processes. The knowledge net contains specific LISP knowledge, more general programming knowledge, and common-sense knowledge. Some of the production rules respond to the surface features of the examples, others may respond to conceptual entities that are defined by the slots of a schema that may be considered to be relevant. All of this knowledge is used by the construction processes. Production rules would thus combine the information from the example and the knowledge net to elaborate and obtain new knowledge units. By the application of one of these production rules, the knowledge *(A B) is a list* is obtained. Other production rules generate *(A B) is the argument of the function.*

Figure 5.1 shows how this particular LISP example is processed by a learner with low domain knowledge and a learner with high domain knowledge. With low domain knowledge, the knowledge construction processes operate on the surface features of the LISP example. Thereby, a knowledge unit is constructed that states that *'(A B) is a quoted S-expression.* With high domain knowledge, on the other hand, a learner can construct a knowledge unit that affords a deeper level of understanding of the example, such as: *'(A B) is the argument specification.* This knowledge unit expresses the role of *'(A B)* with respect to its role for the function call, rather than simply saying that it is a quoted S-expression. The features that are used to describe an example are thus highly dependent on the mutual influences between the learner's prior knowledge and the specific example (cf. Wisniewski & Medin, 1994). The features of an example are therefore not simply a property of the example but they emerge from the interaction between a learner's prior knowledge and the example.

As can also be seen from Fig. 5.1, several redundant and even contradictory knowledge units may be obtained by the knowledge-construction processes. For instance, *(A B) is the argument* is contradictory to *quote (A B) is the argument*. The collection of these knowledge units thus constitute the pluralistic views on the particular learning material on the basis of the knowledge in the knowledge net.

The integration process subsequently analyzes the collection of constraints that exist among the various knowledge units. A globally coherent and consistent structure is thus obtained. This structure is called the situation-oriented circumscription. In the situation-oriented circumscription, the abnormalities (inconsistencies, redundancies) that existed in the pluralistic views are largely reduced. As can also be seen from Fig. 5.1, with low domain knowledge, the more surface-oriented template *(first '(?X ?Y)) -> ?X* was obtained from our particular example. With high domain knowledge, a template is obtained that portrays a deeper level of understanding. This template states that a *function call* with the *function first* consists of the *function name* and the *argument specifications*, that it yields a *result* so that *certain restrictions* hold between the *argument specification* and the *result*.

In addition to the integration process, which analyzes the constraints among the constructed knowledge units, we postulate an additional integration process, which supposedly occurs mostly in high-knowledge subjects. This integration process analyzes the sequence of knowledge constructions that were successful in the sense that they contributed to some section of the resulting situation-oriented circumscription. This integration process may yield a procedure schema (cf. Schmalhofer & Tschaitschian, 1993). Procedure schemata are sometimes represented as derivation trees and are used to perform derivational analogies (Carbonell, 1986; VanLehn & Jones, 1993). The situation-oriented circumscriptions may thus consist of knowledge that is stored in the situation model (see Fig. 5.1; high domain knowledge), a specific template that is stored in the template base (see Fig. 5.1; low domain knowledge), or even a procedure schema that can be used for forming derivational analogies. All of these situation-oriented circumscriptions are entered into long-term memory and can then be used for solving future tasks.

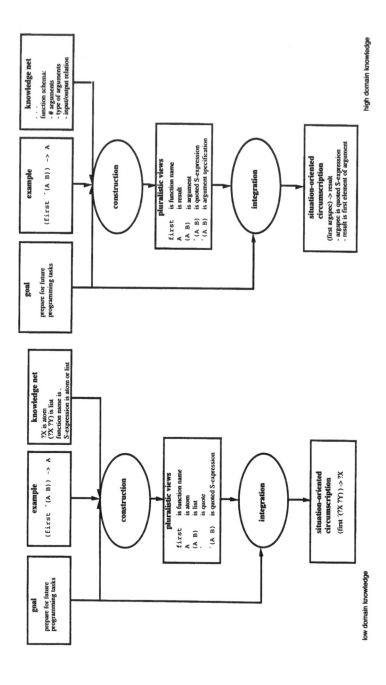

FIG. 5.1. Description of learning from examples according to the extended KIWi model. It is shown how low and high domain knowledge may influence the pluralistic views that are constructed as well as the situation-oriented circumscription that is obtained by the integration process.

Learning by Exploration

In learning by exploration, the learners themselves have to instigate an interaction with the LISP system. Again, these learners have previously acquired the prerequisite LISP knowledge.

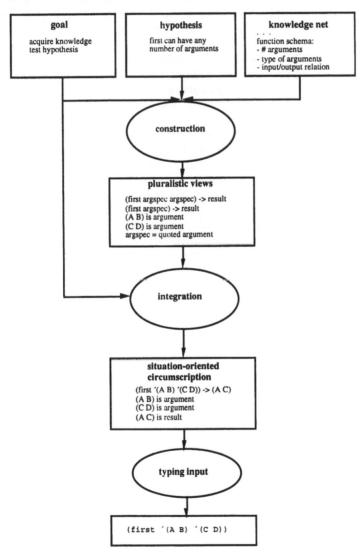

FIG. 5.2. The symbol processing of generating an input to an environment (i.e., the LISP system) in learning by exploration.

The generation of an input to the LISP system is driven by the goal to acquire knowledge that is most useful for solving future programming tasks. From the knowledge net, the possibly relevant knowledge units are selected. These knowledge units may be taken from the conceptual description space as well as from the description space of surface structures. From the conceptual description space, abstract statements or hypotheses such as *the function first has one argument* may be retrieved. With such a statement, concrete specializations such as *(first '(A B))*, and *'(A B) is an argument specification* may be derived with the use of additional background knowledge. From the surface-oriented knowledge (i.e., the template base), relevant information can be retrieved more directly. Complete templates such as *(first '(?X, ?Y)) --> ?X* may be retrieved from this knowledge. All of these knowledge constructions become part of the pluralistic views. Fig. 5.2 shows some of the knowledge units that may thus be constructed.

From the quite diverse knowledge units, a consistent and coherent structure must again be formed by the integration processes, so that it can be entered into the LISP system. This integration process is centered on certain knowledge units that are of particular importance. For instance, if the hypothesis that *the function first has one argument* is to be tested, this hypothesis will be included in the situation-oriented circumscription. As can be seen from Fig. 5.2, the possible input to the LISP system of *(first '(A B))* may then be obtained. In the case of generating an input to a system, the integration processes are similar to editing processes, where the global aspects of syntactic and semantic constraints are to be coordinated.

Learning is also assumed to occur when an example input to the LISP system is constructed. Again, the knowledge construction processes that contributed to generating an input to the LISP system may also yield a procedure schema, which is then used to generate additional examples (i.e., by applying derivational analogy). This process is assumed to occur mostly in high-knowledge subjects. As has already been pointed out, the generated input together with the response from the LISP system build an example that can be acted on by the processes that have already been described in the section on learning from examples.

The Verification of Sentences and Examples

It is a characteristic property of a unified model that there is a large degree of overlap among the sets of component processes that are used for performing different tasks. Most of the component processes that were used to describe learning are also postulated to occur in knowledge utilization. For instance, the component processes that were used to describe the comprehension of a sentence are also used for sentence verification tasks. There are basically only three differences between sentence (or text) comprehension and sentence verification tasks.

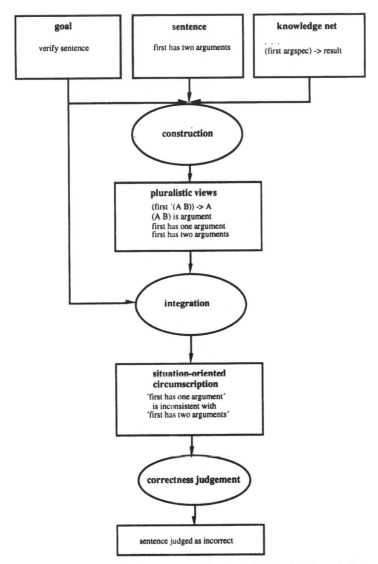

FIG. 5.3. The symbol processing in sentence verification tasks (i.e., deciding whether or not a sentence is true with respect to some state of affairs). The processing in sentence recognition tasks (i.e., deciding whether or not a sentence was presented in a text) is assumed to follow the same structure. The verbatim and propositional processing components carry more weight in recognition than in verification tasks. The situational component carries more weight in verification than in recognition tasks.

Whereas in text comprehension, the statements of a sentence are presupposed to be true (cf. Grice, 1967), a sentence verification task requires that the truth of the sentence be assessed on the basis of the previously acquired knowledge. Therefore, the following three differences must necessarily exist between the two tasks: (a) In sentence verification, there is an additional decision component, which judges the correctness of the test sentence on the basis of the achieved comprehension result; (b) whereas in text comprehension, the knowledge that is acquired from the sentence is stored in long term-memory, we do not assume such a storage process in sentence verification tasks; (c) the different processing goal of comprehension versus verification influences the construction as well as the integration processes.

Figure 5.3 shows how the particular sentence *The function first has two arguments* is processed in a sentence verification task. The construction processes activate all the relevant knowledge that was acquired during the study phase. These knowledge units are then related to one another by elaborative inferences. The various knowledge units such as, (a) *(first '(A B))--> A*, (b) *(A B) is the argument*, (c) *first has one argument*, and (d) *first has two arguments* thus form part of the (partially incorrect) pluralistic views in relation to the test sentence.

The integration processes then attempt to form a coherent and consistent structure between the knowledge units from the test sentence and the knowledge units that were activated from the knowledge net. If the test sentence is a central and integral part of the situation-oriented circumscription that was obtained by the integration processes, it will be judged as a correct sentence. If the situation-oriented circumscription contains major global inconsistencies between the constraints resulting from the test sentence and the constraints provided by the activated knowledge, it will be judged as incorrect. The correctness judgement component utilizes the harmony or the lack of harmony (cf. Britton & Eisenhart, 1993) that exists in the situation-oriented circumscription to decide whether a test sentence is correct or false. For the present test sentence, the knowledge unit of *first has one argument* would obtain much support from the other units of the knowledge net. At the same time, this unit is in clear conflict with the knowledge units constructed from the test sentence, namely *first has two arguments*, which itself obtains less support from the knowledge net. A connectionist as well as the symbolic constraint satisfaction processes would thus similarly yield the judgement that the test sentence is incorrect.

The verification of examples proceeds in the same way as the verification of a test sentence. The only difference is that different production rules (knowledge construction processes) would fire when an example is to be tested as opposed to a sentence. With respect to the knowledge construction processes, example verification is therefore more similar to learning from examples, which has already been presented in Fig. 5.1.

Programming as a Problem-Solving Task

Writing or developing a computer program that performs some task is best understood as a problem-solving task (Soloway, 1985). The givens of this problem-solving task consists of the description of the possible inputs of the program and a description of the outputs that the computer program should calculate. In other words, the input–output specifications are given. The goal is to write a computer program in a language that would produce the respective output for each possible input. In the current research, we only consider relatively simple programs, such as an input to the LISP system that would extract the second element from a list (i.e., the function SECOND; cf. Anderson et al., 1984).

Here again, we can see the advantages of a unified model. In particular, the cognitive processes of generating a simple input to the LISP system, which would produce a certain output, is viewed to be quite similar to learning by exploration. The major difference lies in the goal. Whereas in learning by exploration, a specific hypothesis may have to be generated and/or tested, computer programming requires that a specific task be solved. The learning goal that drives the construction and integration processes in learning by exploration is thus replaced by the performance goal of the programming task, namely the goal of producing a certain program. In all other respects, the cognitive processes proceed in the same way as has been shown in Fig. 5.1. The learning that occurs during such computer programming or problem-solving episodes is usually called discovery learning (cf. McDaniel & Schlager, 1990). Kitajima and Polson (in press) have recently developed a model where instruction taking and action planning or problem-solving have been linked in a unifying manner. Their Linked model of Comprehension-based Action planning and Instruction taking (LICAI model), simulates the comprehension of instructions and then generates the goals for performing actions.

5.5 Summary

We have shown how the KIWi model can be extended so that learning from text and learning from cases can both be viewed as knowledge acquisition processes. We have described the similarities and differences between the traditional experimental psychology research on concept identification, in which subjects are required to identify artificial concepts in toy domains and the acquisition of knowledge from real-life cases. It was thereby found that the Classical View, the Probabilistic View, and the Exemplar View of conceptual structure usually assume that all the relevant features of an example are more or less directly presented by the example itself and that learning is therefore assumed to be similarity-based rather than explanation-based (cf. Medin & Heit, in press). Many psychological models have thus ignored the role of prior knowledge in learning from examples. VanLehn and Jones' CASCADE system and Lewis' EXPL system were then described as two systems in which domain-specific and heuristic prior knowledge are applied for building more realistic conceptual structures.

Inspired by these models, we then developed knowledge construction and knowledge integration processes for learning from cases as well as for knowledge utilization. Thereby, the KIWi model that was presented in the previous chapter was extended to learning from examples, learning by exploration, and to example and sentence verification tasks as well as programming tasks. All of these tasks could be modelled according to the knowledge-level assumptions of the C–I theory. The construction and integration processes in the different tasks were exemplified for the domain of acquiring elementary LISP knowledge. The extended KIWi model was thus presented from a knowledge-level as well as a symbol-level perspective. From the description of the model, it could be seen that several component processes were used for different types of tasks, indicating that the KIWi model does indeed satisfy the requirements of a unified model.

6

Unified Model of Knowledge Acquisition and Experimental Predictions

So far, we have proposed a computational model that specifies the various cognitive processes of acquiring new knowledge. This model was derived from the general assumptions of comprehension-based learning (see section 2.3 and Fig. 2.4) together with the more specific assumptions of Kintsch's (1988) construction–integration theory. The model was first described for the acquisition of knowledge from text (chapter 4) and then extended to include learning from cases, learning by exploration, and the utilization of knowledge in different verification and problem-solving tasks (chapter 5). In describing the model, we have applied the levels approach to cognitive modeling (see chapter 3). The knowledge level, the symbol level and the implementation (see section 3.3 and Fig. 3.2) were clearly distinguished in the description of the cognitive model. Whereas the presentation of the implementation had been postponed for the current chapter, symbol and knowledge-level descriptions have already been presented.

A rational analysis (see section 3.6) showed that knowledge acquisition would be driven by the supposed demands of future, yet-unknown tasks. Knowledge acquisition would therefore be a constructionist process in which a learner's prior knowledge, the specific learning material, and the anticipated tasks become related to one another. When a definite learning goal is present, the acquired knowledge may consequently be quite independent of the specific learning material. A similar and consistent knowledge-level description was also obtained by reviewing and abstracting research results fom experimental psychology in the areas of text comprehension and concept formation, giving further support for the levels approach.

A major reason for developing this model is the fact that the field of experimental cognitive psychology has yielded many detailed results that have not yet been integrated into a single formal model. Research topics that are obviously closely related have therefore often been treated in isolation, resulting in criticism of some of the experimental psychology research in this respect. As Newell (1973) said, one cannot play 20 separate questions with nature and win. In order to integrate the various results, a unified model is needed in which the scope of reference extends over several different experimental paradigms.

The development of the current model can thus be understood as a reaction to Newell's (1973) criticisms and his constructive suggestions (Newell, 1990). By extending an appropriately developed computational model to different experimental paradigms, we hope to integrate the inherently related experimental findings into a uniform formal description. The consistency of different experimental findings can thus be more precisely tested and additional progress can be achieved. The memory research with texts (cf. chapter 4) and the concept formation research with cases (cf. chapter 5) are examples of such inherently related research. By applying the proposed model, we show that memory for texts and the formation of concepts from cases can indeed be uniformly characterized as the acquisition of knowledge from two different types of materials (texts or cases). The same general theory (i.e., a knowledge-level description) can thus be applied to learning from text and learning from cases (cf. Fig. 4.2). Various component processes that occur in learning from text also occur in learning from cases. Of course, there are also some other component processes that must be unique to a specific type of learning material. For example, because of the different structures of the input materials, the parsing of a sentence must necessarily be different from the processes that parse a case.

In the present chapter, we first show that the proposed unified model (that we continue to call the KIWi model) does indeed provide a unified cognitive model in the sense of Newell (1973, 1990). For this purpose, the representational and symbol processing assumptions of the KIWi model are first summarized, and its implementation is described in some detail. We then address the question of how the proposed model can best be evaluated by psychological experiments. At first, we discuss which of the many possible experiments one should conduct so as to test the most central assumptions of the model and not merely peripheral details. As it turns out, knowledge-level descriptions in terms of KADS inference structures (see section 2.2) can be used as guidelines for designing such experiments. By employing the knowledge-level description of the KIWi model (see Fig. 4.2) general experimental designs are thus obtained. These designs also show that the KIWi model does indeed unify different experimental investigations. Finally, predictions for the outcomes of these experiments are derived from the KIWi model. Respective experiments are reported in the second part of the book.

6.1 The KIWi Model

Figure 6.1 presents an overview of the representation and processing assumptions of the KIWi model. It shows the particular information processes and the resulting symbol structures that are formed and utilized in different tasks. In learning from text, a textbase is formed en route to the construction of a situation model. For the construction of a situation model, related domain knowledge as well as commonsense knowledge are utilized. In learning from cases, on the other hand, a template base is formed en route to the construction of a situation model, while related domain knowledge and common sense knowledge are similarly employed.

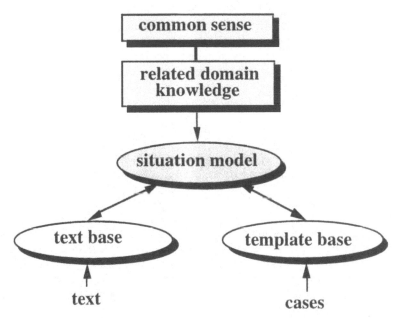

FIG. 6.1. Overview of the representational assumptions of the KIWi model: Textbase and template base are formed when the respective learning material is presented. A situation model may be built from either one or a combination of learning materials. Its formation depends more strongly on the prior domain knowledge. Textbase, template base, and situation model are formed by satisfying the various constraints (*integration process*) that were generated from the given learning material and the prior knowledge (domain knowledge and common sense) by the *construction processes*.

In learning from text, the following information processes may thus be distinguished: (a) the parsing of a text and the textbase formation, (b) the selection of prior knowledge (domain or common sense knowledge), (c) the situation-oriented instantiation of prior knowledge, and (d) the operationalization of abstract situation knowledge for some specific purpose. Thereby a more specific template may be formed, which can then be stored in the template base.

In learning from cases, we distinguish the following processes (a) the generalization of cases and the formation of templates, (b) the selection of prior knowledge (domain or common sense knowledge), and (c) the formation of abstractions which are then stored as part of the situation model.

The KIWi model postulates that a situation model can be formed in learning from text, in learning from cases, and from the combination of the two materials. In both instances, common sense and more domain-specific knowledge are involved. Whereas in learning from text a textbase is formed as an intermediate representation, in learning from cases a template base is formed as the intermediate representation. Each of the postulated processes consists of construction and integration phases.

The knowledge utilization processes that occur in the verification tasks and the programming tasks are very similar to the respective knowledge acquisition processes. The major difference concerns the last processing component. Whereas in knowledge acquisition a memory storage is performed as the last processing component, a decision or performance component is executed in the knowledge utilization tasks. In the description of the implementation, these differences are described in more detail.

6.2 Description of the Implementation

The KIWi model has been implemented in LPA-PROLOG and runs on Macintosh computers. It has furthermore been adapted for SEPIA-PROLOG and was then interfaced with C and now also runs on SPARC workstations under UNIX. Figure 6.2 shows a typical screen image as it arises when the KIWi model is executed in the Macintosh environment. As can be seen from this figure, there are several pull-down menus that are used for entering the learning materials, running the simulation, and inspecting the resulting knowledge representations. In the present simulation run, the learning by exploration component is being executed after the simulation has already acquired some knowledge from a text and some examples. The exploration component has just completed several steps of the exploration episode. The program now requires a decision as to whether the exploration episode should be continued. Instead of continuing the exploration episode, one may now execute a different component of the KIWi model, such as learning from examples, learning from text, or performing a sentence verification or programming task. The results of the processing are always shown in the output window.

As can be seen from the output window, the results of learning by exploration currently consist of a number of hypotheses and respective confidence values (see *Output Window*). The other five windows on the screen show the domain-specific knowledge (see window *Knowledge*) that has already been acquired, the general heuristics (i.e., commonsense knowledge) that are available for deriving new knowledge (see window *General Heuristics*), and three different learning procedures (the windows *Learn from Text, Learn from Examples,* and *Explore*). The pull-down menu *Knowledge* shows which additional windows (e.g., different learning materials) can be inspected. With the *Simulation* pull-down menu, one can select which simulation component should be performed next.

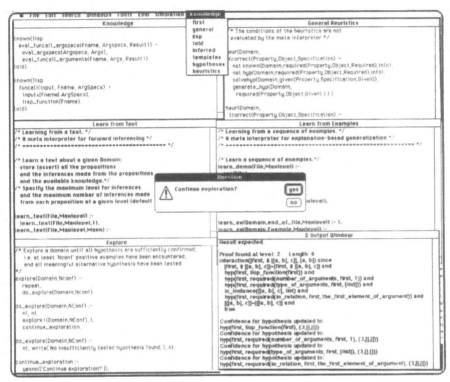

FIG. 6.2. A typical screen image as it arises during the execution of the KIWi simulation program. See text for further explanation.

In order to automatically perform the different knowledge construction processes, the situational units that are supposedly contained in a text or the learner's prior knowledge must be entered in a PROLOG notation. The propositions that are used to construct a textbase must similarly be entered. The KIWi model thus does not accept any input in natural language. The examples or cases, on the other hand, do not require such preprocessing and can be directly entered into the simulation program according to their surface structure. Of course, this surface structure is again encoded according to the syntax requirements of PROLOG.

The different simulation components can be performed at any time and in any order. One can thus simulate any arbitrary sequence of *learning from text*, *learning from examples*, or *learning by exploration*. Also, each learning component can be applied to learning materials of any length. The component *learning from text* can therefore be applied to the propositions and situational units of a single sentence, of a paragraph, or of a complete text. The simulation program thus provides a high degree of flexibility for modeling human learning.

The order in which one should execute the different components for a specific learning situation are, however, clearly restricted by the specifications of the KIWi model.

knowledge acquisition tasks

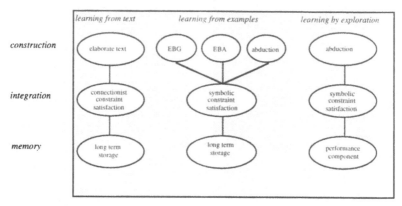

knowledge utilization tasks

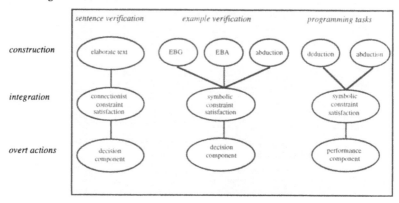

FIG. 6.3. Combination of components for simulating different knowledge acquisition and knowledge utilization tasks. The re-use of the various components (e.g., elaborate text, EBG, EBA) for different tasks (e.g., learning and verification tasks) is a consequence of the unified modeling approach. Any other learning situation (i.e., combination of text, examples, and exploration episodes of any arbitrary length) can be similarly modelled by combining and executing the respective model components.

Figure 6.3 shows in which order the different components should be executed for simulating the cognitive processes in the different knowledge acquisition and knowledge utilization tasks. For each task, there are between one and three construction components that are followed by an integration process. In the knowledge acquisition tasks, the last processing component concerns the storage of knowledge in long term memory. In the knowledge utilization tasks, the last processing components concern the generation of some overt response, such as generating a binary decision (in sentence and example verification tasks) or typing the generated solution (in the programming tasks). Although an additional long term storage may be performed in the knowledge utilization tasks, this storage of knowledge is not relevant here.

Components for Knowledge Integration, Long-Term Storage, and Output Generation

Several processing components that are used in the KIWi model have previously been implemented by other researchers. The *connectionist constraint satisfaction process*, which is used for simulating *knowledge integration*, has already been programmed by Mross and Roberts (1992). Therefore, we only needed to re-implement this process so that it could be integrated with the different knowledge construction processes. This re-implementation was conducted by Jäger (1992). The most important aspect of this re-implementation is that each node of the connectionist network (implemented in C) also addresses one or several PROLOG clauses that can be used by the *knowledge construction* process. This implementation thus required the design of an appropriate interface between C and PROLOG.

In addition to the *connectionist* constraint satisfaction process, we also implemented a *symbolic* constraint satisfaction process in which symbolic information is passed among nodes and a consistent network is established that satisfies the symbolic constraints that are obtained from the learning material and the learner's prior knowledge. Different applications of this *symbolic constraint satisfaction* process were reported by Schmalhofer and Tschaitschian (1993) and Tschaitschian (1993). This symbolic constraint satisfaction process has become necessary because several tasks required that the types (cf. Norvig, 1989) rather than only the strengths of the relations (i.e., the links in the network) would determine which units are maintained as a result of the integration process. The symbolic constraint satisfaction process thus allows that the consistency among various logical relations determines which knowledge units are maintained by the integration process (cf. Meyer, 1994).

The long term storage component was also obtained by re-implementing the respective parts of the program by Mross and Roberts. Only one change was made. In the program by Mross and Roberts, the link strengths between nodes that have participated in more than one processing cycle are simply added up in the long-term memory representation. If for example, the nodes P1 and P2 had participated in the first and the second processing cycles, the long-term connection between these nodes will be on average (approximately) twice as strong as the long-term connection that would result when the nodes P1 and P2 had participated in only one processing cycle. This is psychologically unrealistic because the long-term representation is too dominated by the pairs of nodes that participated in several processing cycles. In the current implementation, we have therefore restricted the maximum increase of a link strength in long-term memory that occurs when a node pair participates in more than one processing cycle. The components for generating the overt responses are relatively straightforward so that they do not need to be described here.

Components for Knowledge Construction

The more novel implementations of the KIWi model are the ones that simulate the knowledge construction processes (see Fig. 6.3). The knowledge construction processes in *learning from text* and in *sentence verification tasks* are simulated by elaborating a sentence at the level of the situation model. This component is therefore called *elaborate text* (cf. Kühn, 1991; Schmalhofer & Kühn, 1991).

For *learning from examples* and for the *example verification tasks,* three components are available for knowledge construction: (a) An explanation-based generalization component *(EBG),* which adheres to the *Classical* and *Probabilistic Views* of concept formation and is therefore quite similar to similarity-based learning (cf. section 5.1). This component can be executed without requiring that much domain-specific knowledge has been stored in the knowledge base that represents the learner's prior knowledge (cf. Kühn, 1991; Schmalhofer & Kühn, 1991). (b) An explanation-based learning component that adheres to the view that learners use their prior domain knowledge to determine the relevant features of the example. Thereby, they also determine an explanation of the example in terms of the more abstract description language that is used for denoting the situation model. This component has been called *EBA,* for *explanation-based abstraction,* and PABS, which stands for program abstraction (cf. Bergmann, 1990; Bergmann & Wilke, 1995; Schmalhofer, Bergmann, Boschert & Thoben, 1993; Schmalhofer, Reinartz & Tschaitschian, 1995). (c) A component that performs knowledge abductions *(abduce).* Abduction is an inference process that generates hypotheses so that a given example can be derived from the newly created hypothesis and the already existing prior knowledge. This component thus generates hypotheses that fill the gaps in the learner's prior knowledge. It generates hypotheses that are needed to explain (i.e., prove) the correctness of a given example by an (otherwise) incomplete knowledge base (i.e., an incomplete domain theory). The component *abduce* is used in combination with the EBG as well as in combination with the EBA component.

Whereas EBG performs generalizations of examples (e.g., replacing constants by variables) that are then stored as part of the template base, EBA constructs true abstractions (i.e., descriptions in a more abstract representation language) that are then stored as part of the situation model. We thus follow the distinction that was pointed out by Michalski and Kodratoff (1990). Whereas generalizations transform a description along a set–superset dimension, abstractions change the level of detail of a description (see also Tenenberg, 1987). Abstraction usually involves a change from a detailed representation space (e.g., the example and template representation space) to a more coarse-grained representation space (e.g., the representation of situation models). Because the application of EBA requires prior domain knowledge, it is predicted that novices would not be able to perform such knowledge construction processes.

The abduction component is also used in *learning by exploration* and when a specific *programming task* is to be solved. In both of these tasks, specific instantiations must be derived from more general or more abstract domain knowledge, so that they satisfy the requirements for a solution of the particular task. These processes are simulated by the component *deduce*. Whenever there is a gap in the prior knowledge, the abduction component is employed to fill this gap by an appropriately generated hypothesis. We now describe the application of several knowledge construction components to specific learning materials. Thereby, one can trace the execution of the specific program component in more detail.

Individual Simulation Runs

In order to understand the presented individual simulation runs in some detail, the reader should be knowledgable of PROLOG. A good introduction to PROLOG is given by Sterling and Shapiro (1986). For the specific needs of developing knowledge-based systems, Puppe (1991) presented a very readable and concise summary of PROLOG. If one is not familiar with PROLOG one may still obtain a valuable impression of the flavor of the implementation and how the experimental predictions were derived. These readers should note in particular that in PROLOG, variables start with a capital letter, and constants start with a lower-case letter. PROLOG rules are denoted by stating the conclusion (or action) of the rule, followed by ":-" and the condition part. The condition part consists of a conjunction of conditions separated by comas. Simulation runs are now described for the following components: *elaborate text*, *EBG*, *EBA*, *Abduction*, and for the deductive processes of solving a programming task.

Elaborate Text. Consider as learning material the following sentences that define the LISP function FIRST: The function FIRST is used to select an s-expression from a list. It requires exactly one argument. The argument of FIRST must be a list. FIRST returns the first s-expression of the given argument. At the situational level, this text is initially represented by four situational units that are encoded in PROLOG as is shown at the upper left side of Table 6.1. As part of the learner's prior domain knowledge there is also a clause that states that a function consists of a function name and argument specifications. In PROLOG, this prior knowledge is represented as is shown at the upper right side of Table 6.1. From this prior knowledge and the first clause of the learning material (i.e., lisp_function(first).), the elaborate text component infers for instance the clause that is shown at the lower left section of Table 6.1. In a subsequent inference step that employs the newly constructed inference together with additional prior domain knowledge (not shown), the inference that is shown at the lower right section of Table 6.1 is obtained. This inference can be understood as a production rule (cf. Richter, 1989) that specifies the constraints that must be satisfied for the function FIRST. This knowledge is much more operational than the clause from which it was derived.

TABLE 6.1

Segments of the PROLOG Implementation

Situational Encoding of Text	Prior Knowledge
lisp_function(first).	funcall(Input) :-
required(number_of_arguments,first,1).	Input = [Fname I ArgSpecs],
required(type_of_arguments,first,list).	lisp_function(Fname).
required(io_relation,first, the_first_element_of_argument).	

Acquired Knowledge	
Inference	Subsequent Inference
funcall(Input) :-	eval(Input,Result) :-
Input = [first I ArgSpecs].	Input = [first I Argspecs],
	eval_argspecs(Argspecs, Arguments),
	correct_function(first,Arguments, Result).

Note: Shown are the Situational Encoding of a Text, the Learner's Prior Domain Knowledge, and Some Situational Inferences That Are Constructed by the Elaborate Text Component

The *elaborate text* component generates several more inferences in this manner. Many of them are quite redundant and not very useful. But this is exactly a requirement of the knowledge construction processes in the C–I theory and the KIWi model. The *elaborate text* component thus generates inferences promiscuously and it is left up to the *integration process* to separate the useful inferences from the others. The simulation run also shows that the generation of situational inferences requires prior domain knowledge. We may therefore expect that the subjects who do not possess this domain knowledge will not be able to construct an appropriate situational representation.

EBG — Explanation-Based Generalization. Consider now as learning materials the following examples, which may be used for learning about the LISP function LIST:

(LIST 'A 'B) --> (A B)
(LIST '(A B) 'C '(D E)) -->((A B) C (D E))
(LIST A B) --> ERROR

In the simulation program the three examples are represented as shown in Table 6.2. From these examples, the EBG component produced the generalization that is shown in Table 6.2. Basically, this generalization describes a typical pattern for a *function call* with the function LIST (cf. prototype view of concept formation). According to the KIWi model, such generalizations are referred to as *templates* and are stored in the *template base*. In such *templates*, the specific atoms (e.g., A, B) or lists (e.g., (D E)) that occurred in the examples have been replaced by their common generalization (i.e., by the class of *s-expression*). For generating the generalization, the EBG component used commonsense knowledge and only very little domain-specific knowledge, namely that A and B are instances of S-expressions. We may therefore expect that even subjects without prior domain knowledge may perform generalizations and then store respective templates in the template base.

TABLE 6.2

Segments of the PROLOG Implementation For the Example Materials

Learning Material	*Templates as Generalizations*
interaction([list, $ a, $ b], [a,b]).	interaction([list, $ X, $ Y], [X,Y]) :-
interaction([list, $ [a,b], $ c, $ [d,e]],	is_instance(X, s_expr),
[[a,b],c,[d,e]]).	is_instance(Y, s_expr).
interaction([list, a, b], error).	

EBA — Explanation-Based Abstraction. In order to process the same examples by the EBA component, additional situation knowledge must already be available in the knowledge base. One of the most important parts thereof is knowledge about functions in general (i.e., a function schema with the slots: number of arguments, type of arguments, and input–output relation). Table 6.3 (left-hand side) shows the function schema in PROLOG notation. This function schema is employed to express and thereby *redescribe* a given example in terms of the more abstract description language. The example *interaction([list, $ a, $ b], [a,b])* is thus characterized in terms of *number of arguments, type of arguments*, and *input–output relation of the function.* The given example is then explained in terms of this abstract description language. Technically speaking, it is proven that the example is a correct function call in LISP. The result of the first proof step is shown on the right side of Table 6.3.

When there are only small gaps in the learner's prior knowledge, *abduction* is used as a process for filling these knowledge gaps by generating appropriate hypotheses so that it can be proven that the given example is a correct function call. After several of these deductive steps have been performed, a complete proof tree is obtained. This proof tree presents a justification for the fact that the given example is a valid function call in terms of the abstract language of the situation model. This proof tree thus connects knowledge units of the situation knowledge to knowledge units of the template base and is accordingly stored in long term memory. A complete description of this explanation-based abstraction procedure has been presented by Schmalhofer, Bergmann, Boschert and Thoben (1993) and Schmalhofer, Reinartz and Tschaitschian (1995). Bergmann and Wilke (1995) showed that the abstraction procedure is correct and complete and that it yields better learning results than explanation-based generalization. Because the application of this component requires prior domain knowledge (e.g., the function schema), it is expected that novice subjects would not be able to perform such processing.

TABLE 6.3

Segments of the PROLOG Implementation

Function schema	Abstraction of example
incorrect_function(Fname,Arguments, Result) :- correct(number_of_arguments, Fname,Arguments), correct(type_of_arguments, Fname,Arguments), correct(io_relation,Fname, (Arguments,Result)).	interaction([list, $ a, $ b], [a,b]) since funcall([list, $ a, $ b], list, [$ a, $ b]) and eval_argspecs([$ a, $ b], [a,b]) and correct_function(list, [a,b], [a,b]).

Note: Shown are the the Learner's Prior Domain Knowledge (Function Schema) and the Knowledge That Is Newly Constructed by the *EBA* Component (Abstraction of Example).

Abduction. Assume that the example *(LIST 'A 'B) --> (A B)* is studied and there is a gap in the knowledge about the number, the type of required arguments, and the input–output relations. Together with the EBA component, heuristics that are part of the commonsense knowledge will then generate the following three hypotheses:

1) hyp(list,required(number_of_arguments, list,2),(1,[],[])).
2) hyp(list,required(type_of_arguments,list,[atom,atom]),(1,[],[])).
3) hyp(list,required(io_relation,list, list_of_arguments),(1,[],[])).

By these hypotheses it is expressed that the required number of arguments would be two, that the required type of arguments would be atoms, and that the output of the function call would be a list that contains as elements the arguments of the function call. The first hypothesis is obviously incorrect. The abduction component thus generates incorrect as well as correct assertions and thus satisfies the postulates of the construction processes in the C–I theory.

When additional examples of the function LIST are processed by the simulation program, the generated hypotheses are modified so that they are also consistent with the newly processed examples. This resulted in the following modified hypotheses:

1) hyp(list,required(number_of_arguments, list,at_least(2)), (2,[1],[])).
2) hyp(list,required(type_of_arguments, list,s_expr),(1,[atom],[])).

These modified hypotheses express that the function LIST would have *at least two arguments* and that *lists* and *any s-expression* can be used as the arguments in the function call. The modified hypotheses are thus more adequate and closer to the truth. The generated hypotheses are stored as part of the situation model. Because the generated hypotheses are in the terms of the abstract description language of situational representations, they become stored as part of the situation model. It should be noted that the generated hypotheses contain the same type of information that was contained in the text learning material. With an appropriate sequence of examples, therefore, we obtained hypotheses that expressed the same information as the sentences from the text. It may thus be seen how a learner may acquire an identical (or equivalent) situation model either from a text or from a sequence of examples.

Programming Task. As a last example of a simulation run of the KIWi implementation, we now show how simple programming tasks are solved. Consider the following task:

Generate an input to the LISP system that deletes the atoms A and B from the list (A B C) which is bound to l; i.e., the function call should return the list (C).

This task requires that a specific interaction be performed with the LISP system. More specifically, an Input to the LISP system is to be found so that the list (C) is obtained as an output while two constraints are observed. As part of the Input, the argument specification is given by l and l is bound to the list (a b c). This is represented in PROLOG by the expression that is shown on the left-hand side of Table 6.4.

For this expression, the KIWi simulation now infers a solution from the available knowledge. Deductive as well as inductive processes can be used. Thereby a specific substitution for the variable Input is obtained. More specifically, the variable Input is replaced by the expression (rest (rest l)) and this is indeed the correct solution of the programming task (see right-hand side of Table 6.4).

For determining this solution, the inference tree shown on the right-hand side of Table 6.4 is obtained. This inference tree describes how and why (Rest (Rest l)) is the solution of the programming task. Such inference trees are then abstracted into a procedure schema, which is stored in long-term memory as part of the situation knowledge. When a related programming task is to be performed at some later point in time, this procedure schema can be employed for performing derivational analogies (cf. Carbonell, 1986). Again, prior domain knowledge was required in the knowledge base for obtaining a solution of the programming task and the inference tree. Novices who lack such prior domain knowledge must rely on commonsense heuristics. Because of several random type search processes, one does not obtain a nice, clean inference tree when novice subjects are simulated. It is therefore expected that novices do not form a procedure schema. Instead, they will only store a generalization of the task solution (i.e., a template) in the template base. When solving related tasks, novices will therefore rely on transformational (i.e., more surface-related) rather than derivational analogies.

TABLE 6.4

Representation of a Programming Task (Left Side) and Its Solution Together With the Inference Tree (Right Side)

Programming Task	Solution of Programming Task

solve_task((is_result([c]), is_argspec(l), bound_to(l,[a,b,c])), interaction(Input,Result)).	interaction([rest, [rest,l]],[c]).
	
	interaction([rest, [rest,l]],[c]) since
	  funcall([rest, [rest,l]], rest, [[rest,l]]),
	  eval_argspecs([[rest,l]],[[b,c]]),
	  correct_function(rest,[[b,c]],[c]).
	  eval_argspecs([[rest,l]],[[b,c]]) since
	    eval([rest,l],[b,c]).
	    eval([rest,l],[b,c]) since
	      funcall([rest,l], rest, [l]),
	      eval_argspecs([l],[[a,b,c]]),
	      correct_function(rest,[[a,b,c]],[b,c]).
	      eval_argspecs([l],[[a,b,c]]) since
	      eval(l,[a,b,c]).
	      eval(l,[a,b,c]) since
	        bound_to(l,[a,b,c]).

Note: These representations were generated when simulating subjects with prior programming knowledge. The inference tree can be abstracted into a procedure schema which then become part of the situation knowledge. Such procedure schemata can be used for solving related tasks, even when they look quite different on the surface.

The simulation runs show that the execution of the components that construct situation knowledge (elaborate text, EBA, deduce, and abduction in programming tasks) depend quite strongly on the availability of prior domain knowledge (e.g., a function schema). The execution of the components that contribute knowledge to the material-related knowledge representation (e.g., the construction of a template by EBG), on the other hand, do not require such prior domain knowledge.

In learning from text, learners with prior domain knowledge (whom we also call *advanced learners* or *expert subjects*) are therefore predicted to construct situation knowledge by elaborative inferences, whereas this is not possible for novices who lack such knowledge by definition.

In learning from examples, a template base may even be constructed by novices. Advanced learners, who by definition possess a function schema, may, in addition, acquire situation knowledge by performing explanation-based abstractions (EBA) in combination with abductive processes.

In programming tasks as well as in learning by exploration, procedure schemata that become part of the situation knowledge may be constructed by advanced learners whose prior knowledge includes a function schema. Novices, on the other hand, will only form a template from the specific solution that is then stored in the template base.

From the computer simulations, it may also be seen that the application of the EBA and the abduce components may construct the same situation knowledge (in the form of hypotheses), which can also be stated in a respective text. The KIWi simulation thus provides the possibility of writing a text that is informationally equivalent (cf. Larkin & Simon, 1987) to a given sequence of examples.

6.3 Experimental Predictions

In order to derive more precise predictions from the proposed model, we must first decide which measures should be recorded as dependent variables, and which independent variables should be manipulated in the various experiments that are employed for testing the model. In general terms, we must decide which of the many possible experimental designs one should employ to test the model. This is the question of finding an experimental design that is representative for testing the model. Thereafter it can be decided how the experimental variables are connected with the theoretical constructs of the model. The model can then be applied for predicting the outcomes of the specified experimental situations.

For making such decisions we should take into consideration the specific purpose of the proposed model. Namely, the KIWi model was developed for integrating empirical results from different experimental paradigms so that a unified account can be presented for a larger scope of empirical findings. Previous models usually addressed the results from various studies within a single experimental paradigm (e.g., *either* text memory *or* concept formation). The proposed unified model, on the other hand, concerns the consistency of experimental findings across different experimental paradigms. It thus addresses the question of how one can give a consistent account of the results from studies on text memory *and* studies on concept formation.

Dependent Measures

In cognitive psychology, a variety of different variables have already been employed for assessing the cognitive processes of human subjects. Thereby, online measures, which directly tap cognitive processes during their execution or determine their relative duration, can be distinguished from variables that measure the product of some cognitive process. Because the purpose of a *unified model* is to integrate several different measures through a coordinated and common set of theoretical assumptions, we also need to use several different measures for testing such a model, so that the integrative aspect of the unified model can indeed be demonstrated.

In particular, the following dependent measures are considered. A comparison of reading times between different experimental conditions or between different materials will be employed to determine the relative duration of some selected encoding processes (cf. Cirilo & Foss, 1980). The relative number of regressive eye movements (cf. Kliegl & Olson, 1981) can be used as an indicator of the degree of bottom-up versus top-down processing. Alternatively, subjects can be asked to think-out loud, while they are performing some task, because the subjects' verbalizations may indicate which information was indeed being processed in the specific task at the various points in time (cf. Ericsson & Simon, 1984).

In addition to the described online measures, various test tasks can be employed to determine the acquired knowledge. In sentence recognition tasks, subjects may be asked whether a given sentence occurred in a text. Such recognition tasks test a subject's memory. Recognition tasks need to be distinguished from verification tasks. In a sentence verification task, a subject has to assess whether or not the sentence is true with respect to a subject domain. Verification tasks therefore examine subjects' knowledge of a domain rather than their memory for the specific learning materials (cf. Shoben, Wescourt, & Smith, 1978). Unlike recognition tasks, which are more closely connected to the particular study material, verification tasks can be used to compare the knowledge that was acquired from different materials such as from a text or from examples. Similarly, one can ask subjects to determine the correctness of examples (i.e., a verification task) independent of whether any examples have or have not been presented in the learning materials. The learners' acquired knowledge can furthermore be evaluated by having them solve problems (i.e., programming tasks) that require the application of the knowledge that was presented by the learning materials.

Recently, time-course characteristics have become an important means for testing the processing assumptions of memory models. For instance, Ratcliff and McKoon (1989) recently showed that the time course of retrieval in sentence recognition can provide critical tests for such models. Time-course characteristics are most economically collected by a tapping speed–accuracy trade-off procedure that was developed by Wickelgren, Corbett, and Dosher (1980). This procedure was adapted for sentence tasks by Schmalhofer (1982). In this procedure, a subject must first guess the correct answer for the next test stimulus. These guesses can be used as a baseline control measure. Thereafter, a rapid sequence of probe signals is presented (e.g., a tone is presented every 1500 msec) and the subject is required to answer each probe signal with an appropriate binary decision and a judgement of how confident the subject is in his decision. From the collected data, time-course characteristics can be calculated (cf. Schmalhofer, 1986a; also see Kliegl, Mayr, & Krampe, 1994). Such time-course characteristics appear to be particularly suited for testing the time-course predictions of the connectionist constraint satisfaction process (cf. Kintsch et al. 1990, experiment 2). The procedure for collecting time-course characteristics is described in more detail in the second part of the book (i.e., experimental procedures described in sections 7.2 and 8.1).

We have thus identified a number of quite different dependent variables, which can be compared to specific predictions from the model. In order to obtain useful measurements with these variables, we furthermore need to specify relevant experimental manipulations. In order to obtain a sensitive empirical evaluation of the model, the experimental manipulations should be closely related to the most fundamental theoretical constructs of the model.

Experimental Manipulations

The knowledge-level description of the KIWi model in terms of a KADS inference structure (see Fig. 4.2) characterizes, at a global level, which variables and theoretical constructs are of central importance in the model. This knowledge-level description can therefore also be employed to decide which general types of experimental manipulations should be conducted to test the fundamental model assumptions. In general, all the metaclasses, which are the input for the application of a *knowledge source* (i.e., *an inference action;* cf. sections 2.3 and 4.3, in particular Fig. 4.2) should be taken as a source for defining a respective experimental manipulation. As can be seen from Fig. 4.2, one should thus induce *different learning goals* in subjects and then determine whether the knowledge acquisition processes and the resulting knowledge structures change according to the predictions of the cognitive model. Similarly, one should employ *different types of learning materials* and *learners with clearly specified knowledge differences* and again compare model predictions with the respective empirical measures. The knowledge-level description thus also prescribes which kinds of experiments are best suited for designing strict tests of the model.

For each of the suggested manipulations, we designed several experiments and derived respective experimental predictions. In general, the experimental manipulations concern: *The effect of different learning goals* (see chapter 7), *the equivalence between different learning materials* (chapters 8 and 9), and *the effect of prior knowledge in relation to different learning materials* (chapter 10). Thereby, learning from text, examples, exploration, and the different combinations of these learning materials will be investigated. In addition, we designed two experiments for performing a competitive test (cf. VanLehn, Brown & Greeno, 1984) between a central assumption of the KIWi model (i.e., the integrated knowledge acquisition assumption) and the assumptions of case-based reasoning (or exemplar) models (i.e., the case or example dominance hypothesis). These experiments are reported in chapter 11.

The Relation Between Empirical Variables and Theoretical Constructs

There are different ways in which a cognitive model can be evaluated by experiments. If one no longer wants to keep the three levels of the model (knowledge level, symbol level, and implementation level) separate, one can simply run the simulation program and thereby obtain very detailed predictions of the subjects' behavior. A comparison with the experimental data will then show whether or not the model is successful in describing the data. This approach has been used for a long time (cf. chapter 3; Gregg & Simon, 1967), for instance by Schmalhofer and Polson (1986) in comparing the frequencies of the various problem states that subjects visited in a problem-solving task (i.e., river-crossing problems) to the frequencies of the state visits that were obtained by running their production system model. Instead of simulating subjects' behaviors in very specific situations in all their gory details, Ohlsson and Jewett (1995) suggested testing computer models at a more abstract level and applying sensitivity analyses on what they called abstract computer models. The quantitative simulations that do not attempt a complete identification of the parameters of the C–I implementation (cf. Kintsch et al., 1990; Singer & Halldorson, 1996) are clearly in agreement with the suggestions put forward by Ohlsson and Jewett.

The levels approach toward cognitive modeling provides a more systematic way of examining the abstract assumptions, the symbol processing postulates, and the concrete model implementation. Deviations between model predictions and observed data may thus be used constructively for determining which level and/or component of the model is to be blamed for the incorrect predictions. We therefore conduct experiments that are more focussed on knowledge-level assumptions, as well as experiments where the symbol-level processing model is employed for constructing the experimental materials and for obtaining predictions from the model.

When comparing the empirical variables with theoretical constructs we sometimes transform the variables so that the transformed variable corresponds more closely to a theoretical construct. For instance, the performance of different foils in a sentence recognition task can be used to identify the representational strength of verbatim, propositional, and situational representations. On other occasions, we combine the various simulation components so that they predict a specific empirical variable.

Model Predictions

We now describe the general experimental designs of the different experiments together with the predictions that were derived from the KIWi model.

The Effect of Different Learning Goals. The first three experiments address the role of learning goals in acquiring new knowledge. It is well known that sentences from a higher level in the text hierarchy yield longer reading times than sentences from a lower level in the text hierarchy. This so-called levels effect (cf. Cirilo & Foss, 1980) has been explained by the processing mechanisms that construct a textbase. Because the KIWi model assumes that knowledge acquisition is driven by the goal of preparing oneself for future tasks, the levels effect should be clearly observed when a textbase plays an important role for the anticipated test task. When on the other hand, the situation model is more important for the anticipated test task, the levels effect should not be observed even when exactly the same text is being studied. By telling one group of subjects that they would have to summarize the text and another group of subjects that they would have to write computer programs, different learning goals were induced for studying an identical text and reading times were recorded as dependent measures.

The same manipulation of learning goals was also applied in the second and the third experiments and the learners' memory was assessed by a sentence recognition task with different sentence foils. The sentence foils were constructed so that the strengths of the verbatim and propositional text memory and the representation of situation knowledge could be determined. In addition, a tapping speed–accuracy trade-off method was applied and time-course characteristics were calculated for the activation of verbatim and propositional text information as well as for the situational knowledge. The following predictions were derived from the KIWi model:

> *Whereas an expected summarization task enhances the formation of a text representation, an expected problem-solving task enhances the formation of a situation model. Respective processing differences should be indicated by reading time measures as well as by measures of the strength of the different knowledge representations.*

Equivalence of Learning Materials. In experiments four and five (reported in chapter 8), an *identical learning goal* was induced in all learners but *different learning materials* were applied in different subject groups. In particular, all subjects were told that they should study as if they were preparing for a mid-term examination. Text and examples were used as two different types of instruction materials. The KIWi model was applied in the development of these study materials. More specifically, the initially designed text and examples were iteratively modified, until the construction processes of the KIWi model yielded the same situation knowledge from either one of the two learning materials. An application of the integration processes to the two different learning conditions would produce different strength values for the nodes of the situation knowledge in the two conditions. In the experiment, it was therefore attempted to minimize the influence of the integration processes by having all subjects repeatedly study the learning materials, so that each subject would spend about an equal amount of time with the respective learning material.

According to the KIWi model, verbatim and propositional text representations should only be constructed from the text. On the other hand, a template base should only be constructed from the examples. These model predictions were then assessed by having all learners perform the same sentence verification tasks and a programming task. It was thus predicted that neither with respect to the situation representation nor with respect to the programming task, should there be significant differences between the two subject groups. Differences were, however, expected with respect to the text representation and the template representations. In a third condition of this experiment, which lies in between learning from text and learning from examples, subjects were given both materials but with the same total amount of study time available as the subjects in the other conditions. These predictions were tested in experiment 4.

In experiment 5, subjects similarly studied either the text or the examples while they were asked to think out loud. For the different verbalization episodes, it was then determined whether they could be described by one of the different processing categories derived from the KIWi model (cf. Fig. 6.1). Thereby, we could determine the percentage of verbalizations, that are described by the KIWi model, and which other processes exist that are not covered by the model. The experiments of chapter 8 (i.e., experiments 4 and 5) employed the symbol-level processing model for deriving predictions about the effect of different learning materials.

The experiments of chapter 9 (i.e., experiments 6 and 7) are similarly concerned with the two types of learning materials. Rather than having subjects only acquire knowledge from these materials, these experiments required that the subjects transform one material into the other. A (general) text had to be transformed into (specific) examples and a set of examples had to be transformed into (more abstract) sentences. Again, the KIWi model was applied to construct the text and the set of examples, so that the KIWi model would indeed be able to construct selected sentences from the given examples and that it would similarly be able to construct selected examples from the given text.

In experiment 6, thinking aloud was employed to determine which information subjects would process when they do these transformation tasks. It was predicted that, by and large, the verbalizations should be relatively similar to the verbalizations that are observed in the learning tasks of experiment 5. The verbalizations were therefore classified according to the classification scheme that was already used in experiment 5.

Experiment 7 employed exactly the same materials as experiment 6. However, in experiment 7 subjects were not instructed to think out loud and a larger number of subjects was employed. The sentences and examples that were constructed by the subjects were then analyzed with respect to the different errors subjects would make and concerning the individual variations that may exist between different subjects. Here, the KIWi model was, in addition, applied as a diagnostic tool for assessing the cognitive representations that were supposedly indicated by the constructed examples. The four experiments of chapters 8 and 9 were thus conducted to test the following model prediction:

> *Text and examples can be equated on the basis of the situation knowledge that is constructed by the KIWi model with some given prior knowledge. Such materials are then called informationally equivalent with respect to this prior knowledge. The KIWi model predicts that subjects with the respective prior knowledge should acquire essentially the same situation knowledge from either one of the two materials. This situation knowledge is, however, acquired along different processing routes. Therefore, there should be clear differences in the textbase and the template base. The different processing routes should thus be reflected by the measures which indicate the strength of the different knowledge representations as well as by the think-aloud protocols.*

Effect of Prior Knowledge in Combination With Different Learning Materials. The learning materials from the experiments of chapter 8 were shown to be informationally equivalent (according to the KIWi model) when the (simulated) learners possessed some prior knowledge that also included knowledge about functions (i.e., the function schema). To induce this prerequisite knowledge, the subjects of those experiments were required to first study respective paragraphs about functions in general.

In order to investigate the differential effect of prior domain knowledge, these paragraphs were now deleted from the instructional materials. Computer programmers and novices were then identified as two subject populations that would supposedly differ in their knowledge about functions. Whereas the prior knowledge of novices would supposedly not contain a function schema, a function schema was assumed to be part of the prior knowledge of the computer programmers. For this experimental situation (experiment 8), predictions from the KIWi model can thus be obtained by running the simulation program, once with a function schema and once without a function schema. In a 2 * 2 design (prior knowledge * instruction materials), computer programmers and novices studied a text or a set of examples. It was predicted that only the programmers would succeed in building an appropriate situation model, whereas the novices would be equally successful in forming the material-related knowledge representations (a textbase or a template base).

In experiment 9, all subjects studied text *and* examples, but the order of presentation was manipulated. In one condition, the text was presented before the examples and in the other condition the examples were presented before the text. Again, two subject groups, advanced learners and novices, participated in the experiment. Predictions can again be derived from the KIWi model. For the novices, the presentation of a second learning material yields additional *knowledge construction* processes that are based on the knowledge that was acquired from the first learning material. These additional knowledge construction processes provide further constraints on the *knowledge integration* so that some relatively appropriate situation model may even be obtained by the novices. For the computer programmers this was already achieved by their prior domain knowledge. The computer programmers will therefore not benefit as much from the second material. The performance differences between advanced learners and novices will therefore be diminished by the presentation of a second type of learning material. In experiments 8 and 9, time course characteristics were again collected with sentence and example verification tasks. Again, a componential analysis was applied to the responses from the different foils, so that the different representational strengths could be assessed. Experiments 8 and 9 are used to test the following predictions:

> *According to the KIWi model, the material-related knowledge representations are constructed by general heuristic processes. The formation of these knowledge structures should therefore be relatively independent of learners' prior domain knowledge. The formation of a situation model, on the other hand, is more strongly dependent on prior domain knowledge. Expert–novice differences should, therefore, arise in the situational rather than in the material-related knowledge representations. When the knowledge construction processes are, in addition, stimulated by presenting a second type of learning material (examples in addition to text, or text in addition to examples), the knowledge integration processes may be further constrained towards forming a more appropriate situation model. The KIWi model, therefore, predicts that expert–novice differences can be reduced when a second type of learning material is supplied. A second type of learning material can therefore (partially) compensate for insufficient domain knowledge.*

In experiment 10, computer programmers and novices acquired new knowledge either from examples or by exploration. In learning by exploration, a learner's prior knowledge has a twofold effect. First, the prior domain knowledge assists in performing an action in the environment (i.e., generating an input to the LISP system). It is therefore predicted that the advanced learners would generate qualitatively better inputs (examples). From the generation processes, the programmers will secondly form a procedure schema that facilitates the solution of programming tasks. Because of the lack of prior domain knowledge, this is not possible for novices. The advanced learners should therefore be particularly successful in solving the programming tasks.

In learning from examples, even the novices will be able to form appropriate templates. These templates will be sufficient for solving program evaluation tasks. In a program evaluation task, a subject is presented with an input to the system and is asked to determine the output that is produced as a response by the system. This task can be solved by matching the input to a respective template and reading out the respective output. In program evaluation tasks, novices should therefore perform relatively well. The advanced learners should be particularly successful in solving the programming tasks. Experiment 10 is used to test the following model predictions about learning from examples and learning by exploration.

> *The KIWi model specifies that advanced learners with sufficient prior domain knowledge can create a possible interaction with their environment from their situational knowledge. Novices, on the other hand, must rely on templates that were acquired from previous examples. In learning by exploration, prior domain knowledge is therefore a prerequisite for the formation of a procedure schema. The KIWi model thus predicts that advanced learners will acquire more knowledge in learning by exploration and novice learners are better off learning from examples that are supplied by an instructor and that are therefore qualitatively better.*

Integrated Knowledge Acquisition Versus Example Dominance. Whereas the KIWi model emphasizes how the information from text and the information from examples becomes integrated during the course of learning, other research has often stressed the importance of cases and examples (e.g., Chi et al., 1989; Riesbeck & Schank, 1989), while playing down the cognitive impact of a text (e.g., LeFevre & Dixon, 1986). We have therefore designed two experiments in which a central prediction of the KIWi model was competitively tested against a central assumption of case-based reasoning. For these experiments, the following competitive predictions were made.

> *The KIWi model can be empirically supported by confirming the integrated knowledge acquisition hypothesis, which states that the information from the text and the information from the examples become mentally integrated during learning.*
>
> *Models of case-based reasoning, on the other hand, are empirically supported by confirming the example dominance hypothesis, which states that readers would often focus on the examples (cases) and ignore the information from the text (or only process it in a shallow manner).*

The design of the experiments of chapters 7 through 10 were thus guided by the input knowledge sources of the knowledge-level descriptions of the KIWi model (see again Fig. 3.2), namely processing goals (chapter 7), learning materials (chapters 8 and 9), and the interaction of knowledge net and learning materials (chapter 10). The experiments of chapter 11 were designed to perform a competitive evaluation between comprehension-based and case-based theories of learning.

6.4 Summary

It was found that the predictions that were obtained by rational analysis (of chapter 3) were indeed consistent with the general assumptions of the KIWi model as it was developed in chapters 4 and 5. The KIWi model could thus be presented as a unified model for the acquisition of knowledge from different learning materials. It was shown how a number of implemented simulation modules are available for obtaining empirical predictions from the model. Experimental variables and paradigms were then delineated that would be suited for testing the predictions of the model in a representative fashion. A total of 12 specific experiments were conceptualized. These experiments address the three central concerns of the KIWi model: Processing goals (chapter 7), learning materials (chapters 8 and 9), and prior knowledge in combination with different learning materials (chapter 10). In addition, some experiments were designed to perform a competitive evaluation between comprehension-based and case-based theories of learning (chapter 11). The respective experimental studies are reported in the following part of this book.

In the investigation of the processing goals, predictions were made from the knowledge-level perspective. In the investigation of the influence of the learning materials, the learning materials were constructed on the basis of runs of the KIWi model and predictions about the knowledge acquired by the subjects were obtained. For one of the experiments in chapter 9, the KIWi model was, in addition, applied to perform a cognitive diagnosis of the subjects' knowledge. In chapter 10, predictions were again obtained from the symbol-level descriptions of the model. In addition to these direct empirical tests of the model, in chapter 11, we perform a competitive comparison of the predictions of the KIWi model to the predictions that are derived from more case-based reasoning assumptions.

We have thus demonstrated how computational models can be applied to experimental psychology. More specifically, it was shown how the levels approach toward cognitive modeling combines methods from experimental psychology, computational modeling, and concerns from situativity theory in a balanced way. It was furthermore exemplified how this approach is applied to a specific research topic, and the KIWi model together with experimental predictions were thus obtained.

Part II

Experimental Evaluation

Denn, wenn du sie anschaust, wirst du zwar nicht etwas
sehen, was *allen* gemeinsam wäre, aber du wirst Ähnlichkeiten,
Verwandschaften, sehen, und zwar eine ganze Reihe.
Wie gesagt: denk nicht, sondern schau!

Ludwig Wittgenstein

7

The Influence of Different
Learning Goals

It is a central postulate of the KIWi model that knowledge acquisition is driven by the goal of preparing oneself for solving future tasks. The knowledge construction processes are consequently driven by the expected task demands (see sections 3.6; 4.3, and 6.3). If a learner is a priori informed that he or she will have to solve a particular type of task, it is thus predicted that the learner will more strongly engage in constructing the knowledge representation that is most useful for solving the particular type of task. In learning from text, the task of summarizing the text *(text summarization* or *TS readers)* and the task of applying knowledge in concrete problem situations *(knowledge application* or *KA readers)* may be seen as two such different types of tasks. Because a textbase is more useful for generating the summary of a text, and a situation model is more useful for applying the acquired knowledge to specific problems in the domain (cf. Mannes & Kintsch, 1987), we predict that *TS readers* would develop a comparably stronger *textbase* and *KA readers* would develop a comparably stronger *situation model.*

The C–I theory and the KIWi model furthermore assume that knowledge representations are the products of cognitive processes that perform an attunement of the specific learning material (e.g., a text) and the learner's prior knowledge. This attunement yields a composite memory trace of *verbatim* and *propositional text representations* together with a *situation representation* (or situation model). Whereas early memory models had assumed that separate memory stores would be relevant for different types of tasks (e.g., episodic memory for recognition tasks, and semantic memory for verification tasks), it has now been clearly demonstrated that *semantic information* intrudes into *episodic judgments* and that *episodic associations* intrude into *judgments of semantic relatedness* (Dosher & Rosedale, 1991). A rememberer can therefore not directly segregate episodic memories from semantic memories (for a review see Hintzman, 1990). Similarly, learners do not directly segregate judgments about a text from judgments about a situation. Text information has been shown to intrude into judgments about a situation and situational information has been shown to intrude into the judgments about a text (Reder, 1987; Schmalhofer, 1986a). In the C–I theory and the KIWi model it is therefore assumed that a test probe (e.g., a sentence of a recognition or verification task) is indeed compared to all memory traces (possibly with different weights). As theoretician observers we may, however, apply a process dissociation procedure (cf. Jacoby, 1991) and partition such a composite knowledge representation into its verbatim, propositional, and situational components. Such decomposition procedures have been successfully applied by Schmalhofer (1986a), Schiefele (1991), and Zwaan (1994).

Because the textbase and the situation model are constructed by presumably interacting, but nevertheless separate, mental processes, it is expected that subjects who study a text in order to write a summary thereafter (TS subjects) would emphasize propositional text encoding by enhancing the macro- as well as the microprocessing of a text. These subjects should therefore show different reading time patterns than subjects who study the same text in order to apply the knowledge in the respective subject domain (KA subjects). Whereas the reading times of subjects who read a text for text memory have been shown to be longer for text segments that are located high in the text hierarchy (Cirilo & Foss, 1980), subjects who study a text for knowledge application are expected to spend relatively more time processing those subordinate paragraphs that present crucial information about the subject domain itself.

As a consequence of these differential encoding processes, TS subjects are predicted to show better propositional text memory, even for micropropositions, than KA subjects. On the other hand, KA subjects should develop a more accurate situational representation than TS subjects. Because the formation of a situation model is an integral part of the text comprehension processes (Garnham & Oakhill, 1992; Graesser, Singer, & Trabasso, 1994), even TS subjects may develop stronger situational than propositional representations.

The information retrieval from the two cognitive structures may also show differences in the time characteristics of knowledge utilization. For example, Reder (1987) postulated that a textbase may be searched until some propositions match the propositions of the test sentence. Subjects would therefore more efficiently judge a test sentence by its plausibility, which is supposedly based on situational information, than searching memory for an exact propositional match (but see Singer, 1991 for a different point of view). If, however, TS and KA subjects did not differ by their development of a situation model, no structural differences in the encoding processes, cognitive structures, and retrieval processes would be expected between the two subject groups.

In order to examine whether or not the construction of verbatim and propositional text representations on the one hand, and representations of the situations referred to by a text on the other, depend on the specific learning goal, Schmalhofer and Glavanov (1986) performed three experiments, which we report in this chapter. Rather than investigating some fully developed knowledge structure for expert programming, this study investigated how verbatim, propositional, and situational representations are formed when people without prior domain knowledge study a programmer's manual for the first time. By instructing subjects to either study the manual for text summarization or for knowledge application, the first experiment investigated differences in the encoding processes of text and situational information, whereas the second experiment examined differences in the resulting cognitive structures. In order to test the different information retrieval speeds from verbatim, propositional, and situational representations, a speed–accuracy trade-off analysis was performed in a third experiment. The three experiments thus investigate the encoding processes, the resulting cognitive structures, and the retrieval processes of three components of text understanding.

7.1 Experiment 1

In order to investigate the construction of propositional and situational representations in a realistic but controlled setting, subjects who did not know anything about LISP were given part of a LISP programmer's manual to study. This text was well suited for investigating the initial construction of situational representations during text comprehension. The experimental text had a clearly identifiable hierarchical structure which is shown in Fig. 7.1. Whereas the paragraphs at the highest level (level 1) in the text hierarchy expressed the text's macrostructure, substantive LISP information, which is needed for the construction of a situational representation, was presented at the lower levels of the text hierarchy. Because the most important information for constructing a textbase and a situation model were contained in different paragraphs, differences in the cognitive processing of TS and KA readers can be assessed by comparing the reading times of different text segments. TS readers supposedly emphasize macroprocessing in their construction of a textbase, and should therefore spend more time reading the sentences of the level 1 paragraphs than the other paragraphs (Cirilo & Foss, 1980). KA readers, on the other hand, are assumed to emphasize the construction of a situation model and therefore should spend relatively more time on the lower level paragraphs than on the level 1 paragraphs. Consequently, a hierarchical text level by subject group interaction is expected. No prediction, however, can be made, as to which group will show longer overall reading times: If the construction of a macrostructure is relatively more time consuming than the development of a situation model, the overall reading times of KA readers would be faster and vice-versa.

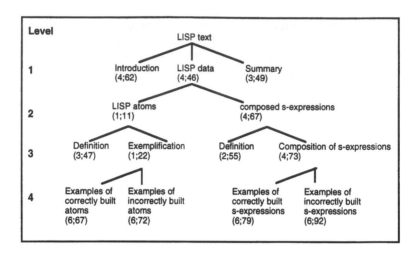

FIG. 7.1. The hierarchical structure of the paragraphs of the LISP programmer's manual. (The two numbers under the paragraph headlines refer to the number of sentences and the number of words contained in the paragraph, respectively).

Method

Subjects. Sixty-four University of Colorado undergraduates, who did not have any knowledge about LISP, participated in the experiment in order to fulfill an introductory psychology course requirement.

Material. A short programmer's manual (742 words) that introduced LISP data representations (atoms and S-expressions) was constructed based on the first couple of pages of McCarthy, Abrahams, Edwards, Hart, and Levin's (1976) LISP 1.5 Programmer's Manual. The hierarchical structure of the text thus obtained is shown in Fig. 7.1. In this figure, each paragraph of the text is represented by a node at one of the four different levels in the text hierarchy. The three paragraphs at the highest level (level 1) consisted of an introduction that motivated the reader to study the text, an outline of the material to be presented, and a summary of the presented material. These three paragraphs, which presented the text's macroinformation, occurred as the first, second, and last paragraphs of the text, respectively. The subordinate paragraphs at levels 2 and 3 introduced and elaborately refined more substantive information about the programming language LISP that should be most useful for the construction of a situation model. The lowest level (level 4) in the text hierarchy presented specific examples of correctly and incorrectly formed LISP data together with brief explanations.

Procedure. The experiment, which was conducted on Visual 200 terminals controlled by the VAX 11/780 computer of the Computer Laboratory for

Instruction in Psychological Research at the University of Colorado, was subject paced.

The subjects first read the instructions for the experiment on the terminal screen in order to familiarize themselves with the mode of presentation of the experimental materials. All subjects were told to study the LISP text in a way that would enable them to do very well on the test that would follow. The only difference in the instructions to the two subject groups concerned the study goal. Half of the subjects were told that the test would involve writing a brief summary of the LISP text (text summarization or TS readers) and the other half were told that the test would involve a programming task that would consist of writing and verifying LISP expressions (knowledge application or KA readers).

The LISP text was presented one sentence at a time. In order to indicate the start of a new paragraph, a heading that introduced the topic of the next paragraph was presented before each new paragraph. The headings were presented in all capital letters so as to distinguish them from the text sentences. When subjects had finished studying a sentence, they pressed a button to request the next sentence. They had been informed that they could not return to previously presented sentences and that they should not take any breaks while studying the sentences. Sentence reading times were collected by the computer.

Results and Discussion

A sentence by reading instruction analysis of variance (ANOVA) revealed that the sentences were read significantly faster by KA subjects (325.8 sec) than by TS subjects (406.8 sec), $F(1,62) = 11.1$, $MS_e = 191.1$, $p <. 005$, and, as would be expected, that the 50 sentences yielded different reading times, $F(49,3038) = 64.3$, $MS_e = 16.3$, $p <. 0001$. Because a significant sentence-by-reading instruction interaction, $F(49,3038) = 1.96$, $MS_e = 16.3$, $p <. 0001$, was found, KA readers (who read 136.6 words per minute) could not have simply applied the same comprehension processes as TS readers (who read 109.4 words per minute) at a higher speed. Because the TS readers were slower, these results suggest that TS readers were more thoroughly engaged in some relatively time consuming processing component that affected the processing of the 50 sentences differently. KA readers, on the other hand, could have emphasized a different processing component, yielding a sentence-by-subject group interaction and overall reading time differences between TS subjects and KA subjects.

In order to determine which processing components were emphasized by each of the two subject groups, average word reading times were calculated for each level of the text hierarchy. Thus, how the average reading times of the two subject groups depended on the hierarchical level of the segments in the text could be analyzed. Because the sentences at the lowest text level (level 4) contained long formulas, level 4 was excluded from the analysis. In addition to significant group differences, $F(1,62) = 9.39$, $MS_e = 0.073$, $p < .005$, and differences between the text levels, $F(2,124) = 11.32$, $MS_e = 0.010$, $p < .0001$, a significant interaction was again found, $F(2,124) = 3.67$, $MS_e = 0.010$, $p < .05$, indicating structural processing differences between the two subject groups.

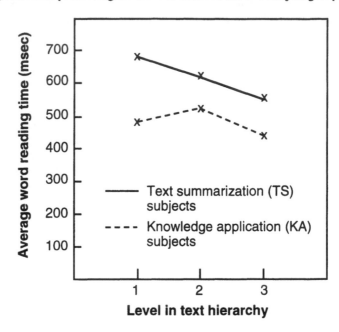

FIG. 7.2. Average reading times per word (ms) as a function of the level in the text hierarchy for each of the two study instructions (studying in order to write a text summary, or studying in order to acquire knowledge about a subject domain).

The average word reading times for each of the two subject groups and the different text levels are shown in Fig. 7.2. TS readers showed a clear levels effect with the longest word reading times for the highest level in the text hierarchy. Newman-Keuls tests showed that the TS readers' word reading times for the three text levels differed significantly from one another ($p < .05$). KA subjects, on the other hand, showed the longest word reading times for the second text level, which presented substantial information about the programming language LISP. The Newman-Keuls test yielded a significant difference ($p < .05$) only between level 2 and level 3. Thus, unlike TS readers, KA readers did not show a clear levels effect in their reading times. Although it was expected that KA readers would study the level 2 and level 3 paragraphs approximately equally intensively, a significant difference was observed between the two levels. Because the level 2 paragraphs introduced some basic LISP concepts for the first time, this result could possibly indicate that the generation of new knowledge elements in a situation model requires more time than further elaborating or updating already existing knowledge elements. A similar result was obtained by the experiments that investigated expert–novice differences (see chapter 10).

These results suggest that, by emphasizing macroprocessing, TS readers were more thoroughly engaged in constructing a textbase, whereas KA readers focused on developing a situation model by processing the more substantive information about LISP. It is thus seen that the different learning goals influenced the encoding processes that are indicated by the reading times in the predicted manner. Because the textbase and the situation model are the cognitive products of these encoding processes, the information-processing differences demonstrated in this experiment should also be reflected in the respective cognitive products. In order to test the prediction that KA readers emphasize the development of a situation model whereas TS readers stress the construction of a textbase, these cognitive products were examined in a second experiment.

7.2 Experiment 2

If the verbatim memory, the textbase, and the situation model are indeed the cognitive products of verbatim, propositional, and situational processing components, subjects can also utilize the information of these three cognitive products in a sentence recognition task. Although a recognition task asks the subjects to examine whether a sentence occurred in a text literally, in addition to verbatim memory, propositional and situational information may be utilized for answering this question (Reder, 1987; Singer, 1991). The relative strength of verbatim, propositional, and situational representations can be determined by applying the retrieval model that was introduced in the previous section of this book. It is therefore assumed that during the recognition processing of a sentence, the retrieval results of the three structures are repeatedly constructed and integrated (see Fig. 5.3) to yield the currently accumulated recognition strength at any point in time. In addition, it is assumed that the accumulated recognition strength determines a subject's recognition decision (cf. Kintsch et al., 1990). By presenting subjects with test sentences that differ only by the contribution of one of the three cognitive structures, the strength of the respective structure may be examined. Four different types of test sentences can be constructed: A sentence may be presented in the form it occurred in the text (O-sentences); it may be paraphrased (P-sentences); its meaning may be changed while preserving its situational correctness (M-sentences); and its situational correctness could be changed in addition (C-sentences). As shown in Table 7.1, the O–P, P–M, and M–C sentence pairs differ only by the contribution of the verbatim, the propositional, and the situational representations, respectively.

Under the assumption that the accumulated recognition strengths are normally distributed with equal variances, the strength of verbatim, propositional, and situational representations may be assessed in a signal detection analysis by d' (Egan, 1975). The strength of the verbatim representation may be measured as the difference between the response distributions of original and paraphrased sentences. A d' value for the verbatim component will be calculated by using the hit rate to O-sentences and the false-alarm rate to P-sentences. Similarly, a d' value for propositional information may be calculated from the percentage of "yes" responses to P-sentences and the false-alarm rate to M-sentences. Finally, a d' value for situational information may be derived from the percentage of "yes" responses to M- and C-sentences.

TABLE 7.1

Contribution of Verbatim, Propositional, and Situational Representations
to Each of the Four Sentence Forms

| | Test sentence | | | |
	Correctness changed	Meaning changed	Paraphrased	Original
Verbatim	-	-	-	+
Propositional	-	-	+	+
Situational	-	+	+	+

Note. This table defines a specific process dissociation procedure within the framework proposed by Jacoby (1991).

The strengths of the three cognitive structures were examined for text summarization (TS) and knowledge application (KA) readers. Possible trade-off effects of response-time and response accuracy were eliminated by determining the asymptote of recognition performance for TS and KA readers with the use of a tapping speed–accuracy trade-off paradigm (Dosher & Rosedale, 1991; Ratcliff & McKoon, 1989; Schmalhofer, 1982; Wickelgren, Corbett & Dosher, 1980).

Method

Subjects. Sixty-four subjects were recruited from the subject pool used in experiment 1.

Material. The programmer's manual prepared for experiment 1 was also used as the text in this experiment.

The ten affirmative and ten negative sentences on examples of LISP data, that occurred in the level 4 paragraphs of the text, were used to construct the recognition test. Affirmative sentences consisted of two clauses which stated that a given LISP data example is a correctly built type of LISP data (clause 1), with a specific element (clause 2). Negative sentences stated that a given LISP data example is incorrectly formed (clause 1), because of a specific element (clause 2). For each of these original (O-) sentences, three distracters were constructed: Paraphrased (P-), meaning-changed (M-), and correctness-changed (C-) sentences (see Table 7.2).

Distracter sentences were created by exchanging words or clauses among the 20 original sentences, so that the distracter sentences consisted only of words and phrases that had occurred in the text. P-sentences were constructed by replacing words of the second clause with synonyms. M-sentences were obtained by exchanging the second clauses of O-sentences in such a way that the constructed sentences were still correct with respect to the rules of LISP. For C-sentences, changes of the LISP example that are difficult to recognize, such as deleting or inserting a dot (Schmalhofer, 1982), were applied in addition to exchanging the second clauses; thus the resulting sentences were incorrect with respect to the rules of LISP. In addition, this construction ensured that the LISP data example was consistent with the information presented by the second clause.

The 80 sentences thus obtained were divided into four different versions of the test, with every set containing exactly five sentences of each form so that each of the 20 original sentences was represented in each version by one of the four different forms (O-, P-, M-, and C-sentences).

TABLE 7.2

An Example of an Original Affirmative and an Original Negative Sentence and Their Respective Distracters

Test sentence	Affirmative	Negative
Original	PSY100 is a legal atom, that concludes with a number.	BIO.-200 is not a legal atom, because it contains a dot.
Paraphrased	PSY100 is a legal atom, which ends with a numeral.	BIO.-200 is not a legal atom because it has a period.
Meaning-changed	PSY100 is a legal atom, which begins with a letter.	BIO.-200 is not a legal atom because it has a dash.
Correctness-changed	PSY.100 is a legal atom that contains a dot. a number.	BIO200 is not a legal atom, because it concludes with

Procedure. The entire experiment was run under the control of a computer. Subjects were told that the experimental session consisted of two independent experiments: A general knowledge test and an experiment on text comprehension. In reality, the general knowledge test served as a practice of the speed–accuracy trade-off procedure that would later be used in the recognition test.

Both subject groups, TS and KA readers, then read the instructions and studied the LISP text exactly as in experiment 1. Then they reviewed the text, paragraph by paragraph, until they had studied the text for a total of 9 minutes. Thus, differences in overall study times between TS and KA readers were eliminated as a confounding factor in the recognition test. Although the overall study time was held constant at 9 minutes, the individual paragraph reading times, which were controlled by the subjects themselves, could vary.

Recognition test instructions and the recognition test directly followed. In the recognition test, subjects were asked to determine whether a test sentence had occurred verbatim in the text. In order to provide a warm-up and to increase the proportion of old sentences, the test began with four filler sentences. The actual test consisted of one of the four test versions. Each test version was presented to eight TS and eight KA readers. The order of presentation of the sentences in a test version was newly randomized for each subject.

The procedure for the recognition test was modeled after Wickelgren et al.'s (1980) tapping speed–accuracy trade-off method. With this method, seven old–new responses were collected for each sentence. The subjects' responses were probed by response signals (tones) that occurred two seconds apart from each other. With each response signal, a subject had to press either the yes or the no button. Unlike Wickelgren et al.'s method, no confidence ratings were collected, that is, for every response signal a subject had to press only one button (Such confidence ratings were, however, collected in the experiments that are reported in chapters 8,10, and 11). Because the subjects gave their first response in the form of a guess, which caused a test sentence to appear on the screen one second later, subjects' recognition responses were collected 1, 3, 5, 7, 9, and 11 seconds after the presentation of the test sentence.

Results

Because a performance asymptote was reached approximately 5 seconds after the presentation of a test sentence, relative frequencies of "yes" responses were calculated by pooling the responses that had occurred at least 5 seconds after the sentence presentation. For TS readers, the relative frequencies of "yes" responses were 0.726 for O-sentences, 0.732 for P-sentences, 0.489 for M-sentences, and 0.165 for C-sentences. For KA readers, the respective frequencies were 0.760 for O-sentences, 0.636 for P-sentences, 0.564 for M-sentences, and 0.161 for C-sentences.

TABLE 7.3

The d' Accuracy Scores of Each Processing Goal for the Three Different Representations

	Representation		
Processing goal	*Verbatim*	*Propositional*	*Situational*
Text summarization	-0.10	0.84	1.15
Knowledge application	0.38	0.25	1.42

For every subject, d' scores for the three cognitive representations were calculated. The mean d' scores of verbatim, propositional, and situational representations thus obtained for TS and KA readers are shown in Table 7.3. A 2×3 reading goal by cognitive representation ANOVA revealed differences in the strength of the three cognitive representations, $F(2,124) = 13.64$, $MS_e = 1.58$, p $< .0001$, as well as a significant interaction between reading goal and cognitive representation, $F(2,124) = 3.23$, $MS_e = 1.58$, p $< .05$. The two reading goals did not produce overall performance differences, however, $F < 1$. Newman–Keuls tests showed that the interaction effect was due to the two reading goals producing significant effects in different directions for the three memory representations. Newman–Keuls tests furthermore revealed that, for TS readers, the strength of the verbatim representation differed significantly from the propositional and the situational representation, which were not significantly different. For KA readers, only the situational representation was significantly different from the verbatim and propositional representations, which were about equal.

Discussion

The significant interaction between learning goal and cognitive representation shows that TS and KA readers emphasized different components of text processing. Whereas TS readers developed a better propositional text representation, KA readers emphasized the construction of a situation model. By demonstrating how the development of cognitive structures depends on a reader's processing goals, it was shown that learning from text is a goal-driven process.

Contrary to the experimental predictions, however, KA readers showed better verbatim memory than TS readers. Although this result is surprising, it could possibly be explained by KA readers having studied the example sentences more extensively. Because the sentences employed in the recognition task provided examples of LISP data, they were more relevant for the construction of a situation model than for the formation of the text's macrostructure. By the end of the study phase, TS and KA readers may therefore have differed with respect to the verbatim information held in working memory that was relevant for the recognition test. The fact that the test phase immediately followed the study phase in this experiment may thus have caused KA readers to correctly reject about 10% more paraphrased sentences than TS readers.

7.3 Experiment 3

In order to eliminate the influence of short-term memory and to further examine the speed with which information is retrieved from the three cognitive structures, an experiment with an interfering task between the study and the test phase was performed. Because in a recognition task a textbase must be searched for a propositional match between the test sentence and textbase, the information retrieval from a textbase has been predicted to be relatively time consuming (Reder, 1982). In comparison, situational information, which may be used to judge a sentence by its plausibility, may be accessed more directly without elaborate searching. For example, in a recognition task the information of a situation model may be utilized by translating the test sentence into its situational representation and comparing it with the situation model. With a consistency check (Johnson-Laird, 1980, 1983) a person may thus judge whether the test sentence occurred or could have occurred in the text. Because of these possible differences in the cognitive representations of the textbase and the situation model, it is predicted that the information of a situation model is retrieved faster and more accurately. This prediction will be tested by examining the speed–accuracy trade-off relation of verbatim, propositional, and situational retrieval components in the recognition of sentences.

Method

Sixty-four subjects from the same subject pool, the same materials, and the same procedure were used as in experiment 2. The only difference was that in the present experiment subjects were given an interpolated task between the study and test phase of the text. The interpolated task, which took about 15 minutes, consisted of a study and test phase with an unrelated text.

Results and Discussion

Table 7.4 shows the percentage of "yes" responses for the two subject groups and the four sentence types. The average d' retrieval scores of verbatim, propositional, and situational information that were obtained for the different processing times are shown in Fig. 7.3.

TABLE 7.4

The Relative Frequencies of "YES" Responses at Different Processing Times for the Four Types of Test Sentences Under the Two Learning Goals

Pr(yes)	TS Readers				KA Readers			
	O	P	M	C	O	P	M	C
After 1 s	0.711	0.637	0.644	0.589	0.781	0.744	0.713	0.658
After 3 s	0.722	0.706	0.638	0.333	0.805	0.745	0.681	0.419
After 5 s	0.738	0.675	0.550	0.181	0.794	0.709	0.603	0.219
After 7 s	0.776	0.695	0.484	0.164	0.802	0.723	0.586	0.138
After 9 s	0.800	0.665	0.467	0.146	0.813	0.716	0.558	0.125
After 11 s	0.800	0.651	0.430	0.150	0.813	0.730	0.552	0.106

Note: O, P, M, and *C* refer to original, paraphrased, meaning-changed, and correctness-changed sentences, respectively.

For each of the three information retrieval components, separate subject group by processing time (2 × 7) ANOVAs were performed upon the respective d' values. In these analyses, the first level of processing time, which consisted of the subjects' guesses before they even saw the specific test sentence, may be used as a baseline for evaluating the retrieval strengths at 1, 3, 5, 7, 9, and 11 seconds after the presentation of the test sentence.

Comparison of Subject Groups. For verbatim memory, neither reliable main effects nor a significant interaction effect were obtained, demonstrating that, after the interfering task, verbatim memory was very weak or had vanished. Subjects, however, showed reliable memory for propositional information, $F(6,372) = 8.59$, $MS_e = 0.67$, p < .0001. Because neither subject group nor interaction effects were significant, TS and KA readers showed about the same retrieval performance of propositional information. Situational information was also reliably remembered, $F(6,372) = 29.3$, $MS_e = 0.86$, $p < .0001$. Although no significant group differences were found, a significant interaction, $F(6,372) =$

2.36, $MS_e = 0.86$, $p < .05$, demonstrated differences in the retrieval of situational information between TS and KA readers. As seen in Fig. 7.3, these differences are mostly due to KA readers showing a higher final level of accuracy than TS readers. In summary, the three analyses demonstrated that instead of verbatim information, subjects based their recognition decisions mostly on propositional and situational information, and that KA readers retrieved more situational information than TS readers.

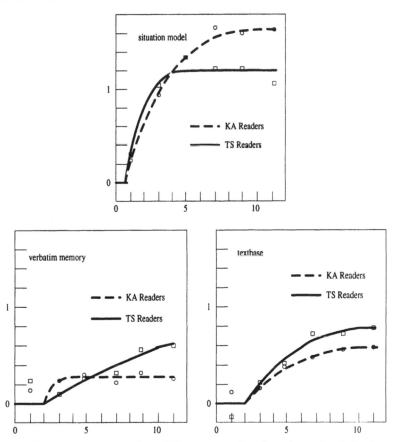

FIG. 7.3. The accuracy scores (d') at different processing times for each of the three retrieval components (verbatim memory, textbase, and situation model) and the two study instructions (studying in order to write a text summary (TS) or studying in order to acquire knowledge (KA)). The smooth curves represent best-fitting speed–accuracy trade-off functions.

Comparison of the Propositional and the Situational Retrieval Components. In order to compare the relative strengths and the time characteristics of propositional and situational information retrieval, d' difference scores between propositional and situational d' values were calculated for the retrieval results at 1, 3, 5, 7, 9, and 11 seconds after the presentation of the test sentence. Whereas KA readers retrieved more situational information, $F(5,155) = 2.51, MS_e = 2.01$, $p < .05$, a one-way ANOVA did not show a significant processing time effect for TS readers. However, for both subject groups, the relation between the accuracy and the retrieval speed was different for propositional and situational information. KA readers had retrieved significantly more situational than propositional information after 5 ($t = 2.18$, $p < .05$), 7 ($t = 2.81$, $p < .01$), 9 ($t = 2.59$, $p < .05$) and 11 ($t = 2.65$, $p < .05$) seconds. Even TS readers had retrieved significantly more situational than propositional information at five seconds ($t = 2.31$, $p < .05$). Since for TS and KA readers, the maximum difference score occurred at five and at seven seconds, respectively, rather than at 11 seconds, it may be concluded that both subject groups retrieved situational information faster than propositional information. As Fig. 7.3 shows, the retrieved propositional information increased rather slowly but constantly with processing time. Situational information, on the other hand, was accessed much faster, and soon reached a performance asymptote.

In order to reveal the differences in the speed and accuracy of propositional and situational information retrieval, the d' scores observed at different processing times t were approximated by a function with speed and accuracy parameters (λ ,β ,δ):

$$d(t) = \begin{cases} \lambda\left(1 - \exp\{-\beta[t - \delta]\}\right) & for \quad t > \delta \\ 0 & for \quad t \leq \delta \end{cases} \qquad (1)$$

In this function, $d(t)$ represents the d' accuracy at processing time t and δ specifies the minimum processing time required for achieving a d' accuracy different from zero. λ specifies the performance asymptote and β is the exponential rate parameter, determining the speed with which this asymptote will be approached. This exponential approach to a limit, λ, has successfully been used for describing memory retrieval processes (Dosher, 1982; Wickelgren et al., 1980).

The parameters of the verbatim, the propositional, and the situational retrieval components were estimated by the STEPIT minimization program (Chandler, 1965). A least-square criterion was applied to determine the retrieval functions that best described the observed d' values. The number of free parameters was reduced by assuming that the δ parameter for each of the three retrieval components was the same for both subject groups. Figure 7.3 shows the retrieval functions thus obtained for verbatim, propositional, and situational information. For the propositional and situational retrieval components, the parameters of these functions are presented in Table 7.5.

TABLE 7.5

The Values of the Speed and Accuracy Parameters of the Different Functions

Retrieval component	Subject group	Intercept (ms)	Retrieval rate (d'/ms)	Performance asymptote (d')
Propositional	TS	1847	0.00027	0.81
	KA		0.00029	0.63
Situational	TS	684	0.00095	1.20
	KA		0.00034	1.74

Although the interpretation of the λ-, β-, and δ-parameters of the present model is often problematic because the parameter estimates may show artifactual interactions (Wickelgren et al., 1980), the parameter estimates shown in Table 7.5 are consistent with the statistical results reported previously: A comparison of the δ-parameters indicates that situational information is more readily accessible than propositional information. Also, the β-parameters are consistent with the hypothesis that situational information is retrieved at a faster rate than propositional information. For reasons of completeness, the parameters obtained for verbatim memory that may be artifactual are also reported. For example, the performance asymptote of verbatim memory of TS readers, $\lambda=0.94$, may be inflated by a low retrieval rate, $\beta=0.0001$, and a large δ-parameter, $\delta=2136$ msec. For KA readers, the respective values were: $\beta=0.0018$, $\lambda=0.28$. Because for verbatim memory, no significant effect of processing time was obtained by the ANOVA, these parameters should not be interpreted.

In order to evaluate the goodness of fit of the six curves to the 36 data points, the percentage of variance accounted for was determined by a measure that adjusts for the number of parameters estimated from the data (Reed, 1973). This measure is described by:

$$r^2 = 1 - \frac{\sum_{i=1}^{N}(x_i-\hat{x_i})^2/(N-K)}{\sum_{i=1}^{N}(x_i-\overline{X})^2/(N-1)},$$

where N is the number of data points x_i, $\hat{x_i}$ are the respective predicted values, $\overline{X}$ is the grand mean of x_i, and K is the number of parameters estimated from the data. With an $r^2 = .94$, the fit between the model and the data can be considered quite good.

When the results of experiments 2 and 3 are jointly analyzed by a $2 \times 2 \times 3 \times 7$ ANOVA with the factors delay between study and test phase, reading goal, memory representation, and processing time significant differences were found among the three memory representations, $F(2,248) = 20.39$, $MS_e = 6.96$, $p < .0001$, the different processing times, $F(6,744) = 173.75$, $MS_e = 0.22$, $p < .0001$, the interaction between processing time and memory representation,

$F(12,1488) = 9.20$, $MS_e = 0.98$, $p < .0001$, as well as a marginally significant memory representation by reading goal interaction, $F(2,248) = 2.53$, $MS_e = 6.96$, $p < .1$. With the exception that the representation by reading goal interaction was only marginally significant, this analysis replicated the results of the individual analyses of experiments 2 and 3.

It appears that the interpolated task succeeded in clearing short-term memory: Although the second experiment only confirmed the predictions about propositional and situational representations, the predicted pattern of results was fully obtained in experiment 3. Thus, the verbatim memory scores of experiment 2 may indeed have been influenced by different information being held in working memory at the end of the study phase.

7.4 General Discussion of Experiments

When readers study a text such as a programmer's manual, three processing components can be distinguished. A reader may process the wording and the meaning of a text as well as the situations addressed by it. For each of the three components, the influence of a reader's processing goal on the encoding processes, the cognitive products, and the retrieval processes were examined.

Experiment 1 showed that the goal of text summarization (TS) resulted in subjects spending most time processing the text's macroinformation. Under knowledge application (KA) instructions, however, subjects most intensively processed substantive situational information. The present results clearly indicate that the intensity of macroprocessing depended on the two processing goals, which were induced by different reading instructions. Unlike TS readers, KA readers did not show the longest word reading times for the paragraphs at the highest text level ("levels effect"; Cirilo & Foss, 1980). The levels effect of reading times could thus be a result of the construction of a text's meaning representation and its macrostructure. Whereas TS readers may have constructed the text's macrostructure by applying heuristic comprehension strategies such as micro- and macroprocesses, KA readers, besides constructing the text's microstructure, emphasized the processing of situational information. Because TS readers studied the text much longer than KA readers, heuristic comprehension processes appear to be more time consuming than the processing of the situations addressed by the text. The encoding time differences between propositional and situational information could be explained by differences in the mode of processing: Whereas the heuristic comprehension processes that construct a propositional textbase (Kintsch & van Dijk, 1978) are more likely to proceed mostly bottom-up, knowledge application more directly depends on a reader's prior domain knowledge (Schmalhofer, 1982), and may thus be faster because of the reader's expectations about the situations to be introduced next in the text.

Experiments 2 and 3 showed that TS and KA subjects also differed by the cognitive products constructed during reading. Whereas TS subjects better remembered propositional information than did KA subjects, KA subjects retrieved more situational information. In the third experiment it was found that accessing text information. Even for recognition decisions, situational information is more important than verbatim or propositional text information. In addition to verbatim and propositional text representations, the cognitive representation of situational information is thus an important component of acquiring domain knowledge from studying a text. Although text summarization and knowledge application goals influenced the three processing components in the predicted fashion, the differences among verbatim, propositional, and situational representations were relatively stable for TS and KA goals. For a technical text such as a programmer's manual, the present study thus provides an intriguing pattern of experimental results for the encoding, memory storage and retrieval of text and situation information that need to be explained by current theories of knowledge acquisition and discourse comprehension.

7.5 Theoretical Analysis and Simulation Results

We attempted to replicate the present experimental results by applying the computer simulation to the learning materials, the manipulation of learning goals, and the four sentence foils of the recognition task in a uniform manner. More specifically, we wanted to account for the systematic differences in the strengths of the (verbatim and propositional) text representation and the situation representation as they were determined by the asymptotic values of the respective memory retrieval functions in experiment 3 (see Fig. 7.3).

At first, we simulated the reading process for the TS and the KA readers. There was only one difference in the simulation of the two conditions. It occurred in the construction phase of the reading process. Of course, this difference will also propagate its effects to subsequent phases. TS readers were assumed to construct stronger intralevel links at the verbatim and propositional levels than KA readers. On the other hand, KA readers were assumed to construct stronger intralevel links at the situational level than TS readers. In both conditions, an identical integration process then generated the situation-specific circumscription of the learning material that was processed in a given processing cycle. The propositional and situational nodes which were associated to the learning material of a subsequent processing cycle (e.g., by an argument that occurred in two propositions), also participated in the subsequent processing cycle. When a pair of nodes participated in more than one processing cycle, their connecting link became subsequently strengthened in long-term memory (see section 6.2).

The processing of a test sentence in the recognition task proceeded in the same manner as a processing cycle during the reading of the text. At first, the verbatim nodes and their connections were constructed. The corresponding propositional and situational nodes were then identified in the long-term memory net of the learning material. If corresponding nodes were not available, new nodes were constructed. The (identified and newly constructed) nodes were then connected according to the same rules that applied for the processing cycles of the learning phase. As a consequence of the specific characteristics of the different learning phase. As a consequence of the specific characteristics of the different sentence foils, original (or O-) sentences, paraphrased (or P-) sentences, meaning-changed (or M-) sentences, and correctness-changed (or C-) sentences thus became connected to the long-term memory net in different ways: All the propositional and situational nodes of the O-sentence already existed in the long-term memory net. In addition, the verbatim nodes of the O-sentences were connected to the identical verbatim nodes of the long-term memory net. P-sentences were like O-sentences, except that there were no verbatim nodes in the long-term memory net that could have been connected to the verbatim nodes of the P-sentence. For M-sentences, only one half of the situational nodes existed already in the long-term memory net. All other nodes had to be newly constructed. For C-sentences, all nodes had to be newly constructed and only the situational nodes were connected to (the situational nodes of) the long-term memory net. Because the situational contents of the C-sentences contradicted the situational contents of the net, these links had negative values.

Just like in a processing cycle during knowledge acquisition, an integration process was then performed with the newly constructed nodes and the nodes that were identified in the net (i.e., carried over from the net). Thereby the strengths among the various links between the test sentence and the long-term memory net were determined (cf. Kintsch & Welsch, 1991). The collection of these links is essential for comparing the test sentence to the long-term memory net. This collection of links corresponds to what is typically called a *retrieval structure* in other memory models (e.g., Ericsson & Kintsch, 1995; Gillund & Shiffrin, 1984). The comparison between the test sentence and the long-term memory net is taccomplished by running a joint integration process on the test sentence and the complete long-term memory net. The sum of the resulting activation values in the verbatim, propositional, and situational nodes of the test sentence (all traces combined) is then used as the familiarity value of the specific test sentence.

The simulated familiarity values of the four sentence foils can thus be compared to the percentages of the subjects' yes responses for the respective sentences. Alternatively, we may also compare the difference of familiarity scores of the O- and M-sentences to the empirically determined strengths of verbatim and propositional traces (as determined by the d' values), and the difference of the familiarity scores of the M- and C-sentences to the empirically determined strength of the situational trace (see Table 7.1). Before we report the simulation results, we present the implementational details about how the simulation was executed.

Reading Processes of TS and KA Readers

Rather than engineering all the details of the cognitive representations for the specific experimental materials (text and test sentences), we followed Ohlsson and Jewett's (1995) suggestion of capturing only the essential structural features in the simulation. Consequently, we did not represent each and every verbatim, propositional, and situational node together with all the relevant connecting links, but instead we identified the general qualitative structure of the patterns of nodes and links that typically exist in the cognitive representations of texts (see for instance, Fig. 4.1 for the fully engineered connectivity pattern of the Zimny materials). Instead of modelling the complete experimental text by some 3,000 nodes that would be processed in approximately 150 input cycles, we could thus characterize the structure among verbatim, propositional, and situational nodes with only 45 nodes. A typical connectivity pattern was then constructed among the various types of nodes, and three input cycles were sufficient for processing these nodes.

The connectivity pattern that was used in performing the simulations can be seen in Fig. 7.4. The verbatim representation basically consists of trees as they are obtained when parsing (the syntactic structure of) sentences. Many of the terminal nodes of these parse trees represent content words and are therefore connected to the respective conceptual entities at the propositional level. The links at the propositional level were determined according to more or less typical coherence relations among the propositions of a text (as determined by argument overlap). The links among the situational nodes represent the temporal, spacial, and causal continuities that exist in the referential situation that is addressed by the text (cf. Zwaan, Magliano, & Graesser, 1995). They constitute a partially directed graph. About every second propositional node is connected to the situational level.

In chapter 3, we showed that computer simulations do indeed provide quite determinate predictions, and the claim that by adjusting parameters, computer simulations could easily be fitted to data was shown to be a myth. But unfortunately, in experimental psychology, this myth has persisted for more than three decades and we have no guarantee that we have really convinced every experimental psychologist of its falsehood. Therefore, we decided to abstain from any parameter estimation at all. Instead we simply used as external parameters the particular parameter values that were determined by Kintsch for an experiment by Zimny. The values of Kintsch were used for simulating the TS subjects (cf. Kintsch et al., 1990). All nodes were linked to themselves with a strength of $c_{ii}=5$. At the verbatim and propositional levels, nodes that were one step apart had a value of $c_{ij}=3$. At the situation level, strength values of 3 and 2 were used for the links between nodes that were one or two steps apart, respectively. Finally, a value of 4 was used to tie together the related nodes from adjacent levels of representations (e.g., V8 to P8 and P8 to S8). For simulating the data of the KA subjects, only one change was made. Connecting links at the situational level were increased by one at the expense of the verbatim and propositional link strengths, which were reduced by one. For simulating the KA subjects, nodes that were one step apart were thus assigned strength 2 at the verbatim and propositional levels and strength 4 at the situational level. Situational links between the nodes that were two steps apart were assigned the value 3.

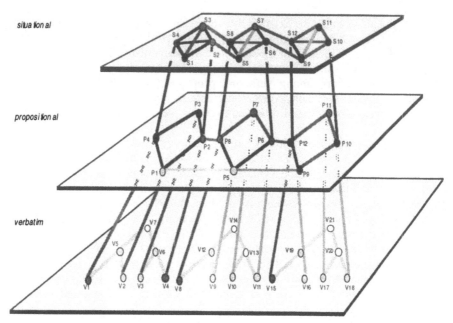

FIG. 7.4. Connectivity patterns among the various nodes and composite long-term net of the text summarization (TS) condition, as it was derived by the computer simulation. The darkness of the nodes indicates the activation level at which a node settled when it was (last) processed in short-term memory. The different shades represent values of 0.0–0.2 (white); 0.2–0.4; 0.4–0.6; 0.6–0.8; and 0.8–1.0 (black). The degree of darkness of the links indicates their long-term memory strengths. The different shades represent strengths of 0.0–0.5 (light); 0.5–1.0; 1.0–2.0; 2.0–3.5; and 3.5–5.1 (black).

Three input cycles were assumed for processing the text. Nodes V1–V7, P1–P4, and S1–S4 were processed in the first cycle. After performing the spreading activation process, the long-term representation was calculated and stored. A long-term memory link strength m_{ij} between a node i and a node j was obtained by multiplying the original link strength c_{ij} of the short-term representation by the final activation values a_i and a_j that were obtained by the spreading activation process for the connected nodes i and j. In sum: $m_{ij} = c_{ij}*a_i*a_j$. Let us consider a specific example: For the TS as well as for the KA conditions, the short-term link between node P4 and S4 was assumed to have strength 4 (see previous description). In the TS condition, node P4 settled with a value of 0.99 and node S4 with a value of 1.00. The long-term memory connection between nodes P4 and S4 was consequently 3.96. In the KA condition, node P4 settled with a value of 0.45 and node S4 with a value of 1.00. The long-term memory connection between nodes P4 and S4 was consequently 1.80. The nodes P2, S2, and S3 were carried over to the next cycle. In addition to the nodes that were carried over, the nodes V8–V14, P5–P8, and S5–S8 were processed in the second cycle and a long-term representation was calculated accordingly. The nodes P6, S6, and S7 were then carried over to the third cycle, the remaining nodes were processed, and the long-term representation was calculated and stored.

Recognition Processes for Different Sentence Foils

The simulation of the recognition tasks were completely identical in both conditions except that the representations of the test sentences were connected either to the TS or the KA long-term net. The various recognition tasks were simulated independently of each other. For the link strengths of the construction phase of the test sentences, the same parameter values were used as in the TS learning condition. All test sentences were represented by 7 new verbatim nodes, 4 propositional nodes and 4 situational nodes. The representation of the O-sentence consisted of the nodes P5, P6, P7, P8, S5, S6, S7, and S8, and the 7 new verbatim nodes, each of which was connected to one of the nodes V8–V14. The representation of the P-sentence also consisted of the nodes P5, P6, P7, P8, S5, S6, S7, and S8, but the 7 new verbatim nodes were not connected to any verbatim nodes of the long-term net. The representation of the M-sentence consisted of the 7 new verbatim nodes, 4 new propositional nodes, two new situational nodes, and the nodes S5 and S8. The representation of the F-sentence consisted of the 7 new verbatim nodes, 4 new propositional nodes, and 4 new situational nodes. Each of these situational nodes was connected to one of the nodes S5, S6, S7, or S8 by a link strength of -3, representing a situational inconsistency between the long-term net and the test sentence.

For each sentence, a retrieval structure was then determined by performing an integration process with all the nodes that represented that particular sentence. The link strengths m_{ij} of the retrieval structure were then calculated according to the formula: $m_{ij} = c_{ij}*a_i*a_j$. These links were then added to the long-term net in the same manner as links are added during learning. In the case of a test sentence, these links only persist for the duration of the specific recognition trial. Depending on the specific type of test sentence, the multilevel representation of the test sentence is now more or less tightly connected to the composite long-term memory representation. Through an integration process in working long-term memory (cf. Ericsson & Kintsch, 1995), it is then determined how much activation flows into the verbatim, propositional, and situational nodes of the test sentence. For each sentence type, we then calculated the sum of the activation values of the verbatim, propositional, and situational nodes.

Simulation Results

Figure 7.4 shows the long-term memory representation in the TS condition and Fig. 7.5 shows the long-term memory representation in the KA condition. From these graphs it can be easily seen that there is a tighter interconnectivity (i.e., stronger links) at the situational level in the KA condition than in the TS condition. At the verbatim and propositional levels, on the other hand, there is a stronger interconnectivity in the TS than in the KA condition. Also, the connections between levels are stronger in the TS condition than in the KA condition. These simulation results elucidate how different processing goals, such as reading for text summarization or knowledge application, can affect the cognitive representations that are formed during reading. In particular it is seen that the TS goal yields relatively strong verbatim and propositional representations and the KA goal yields a relatively strong situation representation.

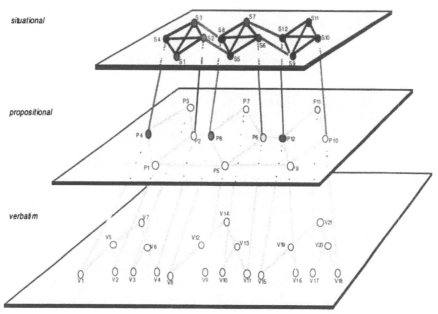

FIG. 7.5. Composite long-term net of the knowledge application (KA) condition, as it was derived by the computer simulation. For a more detailed explanation of the various node and link strengths see Fig. 7.4.

Table 7.6 shows the simulation results for the four different types of test sentences and the two reading goals. Again, there was no parameter fitting involved in this simulation. With the exception of the P-sentence in the TS condition, the accumulated activation values (all traces combined) account for the experimental data very well. With this exception, the familiarity values decreases monotonically from the O- to the M- and C-sentences. In addition, the TS group obtained higher values for the verbatim and propositional representations and the KA group obtained higher values for the situational representation. The simulation results furthermore indicate that verbatim, propositional, and situational levels are not completely separable (which obviously contradicts the conceptualization that was given in Table 7.1) so that the connectivity of the nodes yields intrusions from one level to the other (cf. Dosher & Rosedale, 1991). When we look at the sums of the activation values of all three levels of representations, we can, however, recognize that the simulation results follow very closely the theoretical decomposition that was given in Table 7.1, as well as the pattern of the experimental results in Table 7.4.

TABLE 7.6

**Computer Simulation Results of the Recognition Performance
of Four Different Types of Sentences**

	TS learning goal				*KA learning goal*			
Type of node	*O*	*P*	*M*	*C*	*O*	*P*	*M*	*C*
verbatim	0.33	0.15	0.07	0.003	0.01	0.00	0.40	0.003
propositional	2.87	2.08	0.48	0.011	0.35	0.28	0.40	0.021
situational	1.50	2.89	1.47	0.000	3.60	3.60	2.66	0.026
familiarity value	4.70	5.12	2.02	0.014	3.96	3.88	3.46	0.050
(all traces combined)								

Note: Shown are the sums of activation in the different types of nodes of the test sentences that determine the recognition response after a text had been studied with a text summarization (TS) or knowledge application (KA) learning goal. The higher the overall familiarity value the more likely a sentence is judged as an old sentence. O, P, M, and C refer to original, paraphrased, meaning-changed, and correctness-changed sentences, respectively. According to the mathematical model defined by equation 1 and Table 7.1, the right upper triangle of the matrix would be equal to zero and the rows of the left lower triangle would be equal to the asymptotic value λ of the verbatim, propositional, and situational traces.

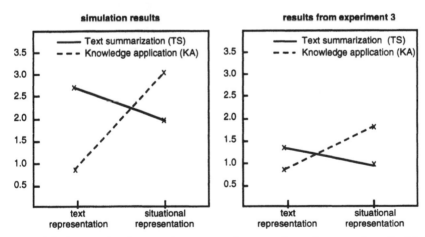

FIG. 7.6. A comparison between the representation strengths as they were determined by the computer simulation and the representation strengths as they were determined by the results of experiment 3. See text for further explanation.

The close correspondence between the simulation results and the experimental data can be seen in Fig. 7.6. The left side of the figure shows the simulation results. For each of the two learning conditions, the value for the text representation was obtained by subtracting the familiarity value of the M-sentence from the familiarity value of the O-sentence (see Table 7.6). Correspondingly, the value for the situational representation was obtained by subtracting the familiarity value of the C-sentence from the familiarity value of the M-sentence. The experimental results show the respective differences in terms of d' values (calculate d' values from Table 7.4 or compare to Fig. 7.3). Thus, there is a clear correspondence between the predicted and observed text and situation representations in the TS and KA conditions. When a text summarization task is expected, a relatively strong text representation is formed, and when a knowledge application task is expected, a relatively strong situation representation is formed. This is true for the simulation results as well as for the experimental data.

7.6 General Discussion

The prediction of the KIWi model that knowledge acquisition is driven by the goal of solving future tasks was tested in three experiments. This prediction was obtained by a postulate of the knowledge-level description of the model. By using straightforward experimental designs and various operational measures, this central model prediction could thus already be tested without having to run any computer simulations. A simple mathematical model (see equation 1) and a process dissociation procedure (see Table 7.1) were applied to the experimental data, and the representational strengths of verbatim, propositional, and situational representations were thus empirically determined as a function of two different learning goals (text summarization or knowledge application). The predictions of the model were thereby confirmed by reading time measures, the strength values for the various representations, and the time course of memory retrieval.

Secondly, we applied the symbol-level processing specification of the model (i.e., the computer simulation) to the specific learning and test materials that were used in the three experiments. This resulted in a much more detailed and differentiated account of the experimental data. In particular, it turned out that differentiations that were lumped together in the mathematical model and that must be of necessity assumed were now made explicit by the model. In the mathematical model, which has also been successfully applied by other researchers (e.g., Dosher & Rosedale, 1991), the processes that occur in the study phase were not distinguished from the processes that occur in the test phase. Instead, the whole complex of study and test phase was characterized by strength values for verbatim, propositional, and situational representations.

The KIWi model, on the other hand, described very clearly the cognitive representations that would exist after the learning phase (see Figs. 7.4 and 7.5), how retrieval structures are dynamically generated for the various sentence foils, and how the performance in the sentence recognition tasks is determined by a matching process between the representation of the test sentence and the cognitive representation of the learning material (see Table 7.6). Although the KIWi model gives a more differentiated account of the relevant psychological processes, no additional degrees of freedom were introduced. All the implementational details were fixed by using external parameters, which had previously been published. No degrees of freedom were thus lost by estimating parameters from the data.

The application of the simulation model to the experimental learning and test materials also demonstrated that the ontological primitives of the KIWi model are more appropriate than the theoretical constructs that were used in the mathematical model. Because the mathematical model lumped the processing of the study phase and the test phase into one parameter, the mathematical model can hardly be used to derive a definite prediction when a verification task had been applied instead of a recognition task. The mathematical model is therefore hardly suited to unify experimental findings across different experimental paradigms.

On the other hand, we developed the KIWi model as a unified model and the ontological primitives of the model were chosen so that they can be canonically composed to yield predictions for a large set of experiments on knowledge acquisition. From the KIWi model we can therefore easily predict the performance in the sentence tasks when verification instead of recognition instructions are given. Obviously, the simulation of the study phase is completely identical, because no change occurred in this phase (because the verification instructions were presented to the subject only after the study phase). And there is only one difference in the simulation of the verification task. Changing the task instructions from recognition to verification changes the emphasis from processing the text representation to processing the situation representation. This change is therefore analogous to changing the learning goal from text summarization to knowledge acquisition. We must consequently only change the short-term link strengths that are assigned for nodes of the test sentence when the retrieval structure is calculated. Instead of using the values of the TS condition that were used for the recognition task, for the verification tasks we now use the values of the KA condition. Again no parameters are estimated from the data.

In order to demonstrate this essential property of a unified model, we performed these simulations. The respective results of the verification task are shown in the left panel of Fig. 7.7. The predictions for the recognition tasks were of course identical to the predictions of the text summarization condition in Fig. 7.6. The experimental data for the verification task is taken from a respective experiment by Schmalhofer (1986a) and the data for the recognition task is identical to the text summarization condition shown in Fig. 7.6. It is thus seen how a unified model can describe the data from different experimental paradigms by using a uniform set of modeling primitives. How these primitives are combined for the different experiments is quite strictly determined by the properties of the experimental design.

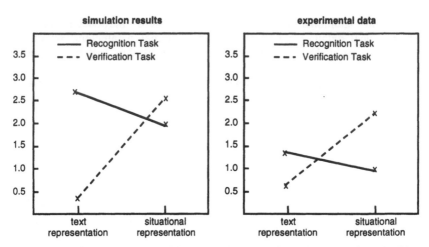

FIG. 7.7. A comparison between the representation strengths as they were determined by the computer simulation when a verification task is used instead of a recognition task. The experimental data for the verification task are taken from Schmalhofer (1986a; Fig. 3, asymptotic values). The predictions show how the model can be applied to unify empirical results from different experimental paradigms.

7.7 Summary

The prediction of the KIWi model that knowledge acquisition is driven by the goal of solving future tasks was tested in three experiments. Reading times, memory measures, and speed–accuracy trade off functions were empirically determined and compared to the model predictions. The model predictions were at first derived from the knowledge-level description and the experimental results were found to confirm these predictions. Furthermore, we applied the symbol-level processing specification of the model (i.e., the computer simulation) to the specific learning and test materials that were used in the three experiments. Although no parameters were estimated from the data, there was a very close correspondence between the model predictions and the experimental data. In contrast to a frequently used mathematical model that lumps the cognitive processes of the study and the test phases into a single measure, the KIWi model could be shown to use ontological primitives that are well suited for jointly describing the empirical results from different experimental paradigms by a uniform set of representation and processing constructs. Predictions for different types of test tasks could thus be derived without making any additional assumptions in the model. In the following chapter, it is experimentally evaluated how well the model predicted the acquisition of knowledge from different types of study materials such as text and examples.

Acknowledgment

The description of the experimental work which is reported in this chapter is based on a paper that appeared in the *Journal of Memory and Language* (Schmalhofer & Glavanov, 1986).

8

The Acquisition of Equivalent Knowledge From Different Types of Study Materials

When the KIWi model is applied to different types of learning materials, such as text and examples, the model's vantage for unifying different experimental paradigms can be quite directly appreciated. We applied the construction processes of the model to a text and observed which essential situational units were thereby constructed. Secondly, the model was applied to a sequence of examples and these examples were then iteratively modified until the KIWi model would construct the same essential situational units. For learning materials that are developed in this specific manner, the KIWi model thus predicts that the same essential situation knowledge would be acquired from either one of the two different types of materials. The construction processes that operate on the text are thus predicted to construct situational units, and links among these situational units that are also formed by the construction processes that operate on the examples. Given that the learners pursue the same processing goal in the two learning conditions, the integration processes will also yield the same circumscription at the situational level. Because the construction processes operate on different materials, the construction processes themselves as well as the intermediate knowledge representations are, however, predicted to be quite different between the two experimental conditions. The KIWi model thus predicts that the same situation knowledge will be acquired from the two types of materials, but that there are clear differences between the text and template base and that the construction processes themselves are also quite different.

These predictions are by no means trivial, and previous research has indeed emphasized the specific advantages of pictures, graphs, and examples in text rather than equating learning materials for their situational contents. Glenberg and Langston (1992) found that in learning a four-step procedure, subjects would mentally represent the procedure when the text was accompanied by pictures. On the other hand, when the text was presented alone, subjects tended to mentally represent the text. They interpreted their results as evidence that pictures help to build a situation model of what the text is about. Hegarty and Just (1993) had subjects learn about simple machines by presenting them with text and diagrams while monitoring their eye-movements. They found that the combination of text and diagrams particularly facilitated the understanding of the machine. The eye-fixation data indicated that the subjects integrated the information from the text and the diagram at the level of individual machine components. Anderson and Fincham (1994) argued that the initial use of examples would be restricted to analogical reasoning and that only later would rules be compiled that summarize the analogy process.

Several of these studies have, however, not controlled for the available study time and the subjects who studied two materials spent generally more time learning than the subjects who studied only one material (cf. Glenberg & Langston, 1992; Hegarty & Just, 1993). The comprehension advantage of studying two materials could thus simply be due to the longer study time. For the more controlled experimental conditions where the same study time is available in all conditions and where the learning materials are equated for situational contents, the KIWi model, on the other hand, predicts that the same situation knowledge will be acquired from text or examples as well as from the combination of the two materials.

A "three-pronged" approach has recently been advocated for empirically testing the more or less controversial assumptions about human text comprehension (Graesser et al., 1994). Three steps are involved in this approach: (a) A theoretical model is employed for deriving predictions about the experimental results. (b) Behavioral data are collected for evaluating the empirical predictions. (c) Verbal protocol data are collected to obtain additional converging evidence for a subject's cognitive processes during reading. With the KIWi model we have already presented such a theoretical model. In the first experiment of this chapter, traditional behavioral data are collected. In the other experiment, verbal protocol data are collected for an additional empirical evaluation.

8.1 Experiment 4

This experiment investigated whether subjects would indeed acquire the same situation knowledge from a text as they would acquire from informationally equivalent examples. Text and examples are considered informationally equivalent when the KIWi model constructs the same situation knowledge from either one of the two materials. In particular, the examples were constructed so that the KIWi model would learn the following facts about a LISP function: function name, type of arguments, number of arguments, and input-output relation. These facts were explicitly stated in the text condition. In the three conditions of this experiment, subjects learned the LISP functions a text, from examples, or both. In order to eliminate differences that are only due to differences in the learner's time allocation to the learning materials and the resulting memory differences, all subjects studied the learning materials for an equally long time period. The total study time sufficed to study the materials approximately twice. Thus, the subjects did not study under any time pressure.

By running the KIWi model with the two different study materials, it was predicted that the subjects of all three conditions would form approximately the same situation model. Because of this informational equivalence and the controlled study time, even the subjects who studied both text and examples should not form a better situation model than the other subjects. Text representation and template base on the other hand, will only be constructed when a text or examples, respectively, are studied. With respect to textbase and template base, differences are thus predicted among the three experimental groups. A preliminary report of the experimental data was presented by Schmalhofer, Boschert and Kühn (1990).

Method

Subjects. Eighty students from the University of Freiburg who did not have any knowledge about LISP participated in the experiment. They were paid for their participation.

Design. The experiment consisted of two learning phases, each of which was followed by a test phase. The first learning phase and the two test phases were identical for all subjects. In the second learning phase, the subjects were randomly assigned to one of the three experimental conditions. There were 26 subjects in the combination learning condition, whereas in the text and example conditions, there were 27 subjects each.

Materials. Learning Materials. The prerequisite LISP material was presented in the first learning phase. This material was identical for all three conditions, and explained the building blocks of LISP (i.e., atoms and lists). It was thus similar to the experimental materials that were used in the experiments of chapter 7. The second learning phase introduced the four LISP functions.

The *material of the text condition* consisted of 39 sentences, which were organized into 6 paragraphs of 3 to 13 sentences. The first paragraph explained the correct syntax of LISP function calls. The next four paragraphs explained the four LISP functions. The last paragraph discussed the argument specification and how nested function calls can be constructed. The upper part of Table 8.1 shows a typical paragraph of the text. All the sample materials shown in the Tables have been translated from German into English.

The *material of the example condition* consisted of 17 instruction sentences and 56 examples organized into 5 blocks. The first four blocks consisted of three organizing sentences and 12 examples for the four LISP functions. For each function, seven examples contained correct inputs to the LISP system and the result that was returned by the system was shown next to the input separated by an arrow. The other five examples showed syntactically incorrect inputs and the result "ERROR." The fifth block contained five instruction sentences and 8 examples of nested function calls. A typical block of the example material is shown in the lower part of Table 8.1.

TABLE 8.1

Typical Segments of the Learning Materials for the Text and the Example Conditions

Material for the LISP Function FIRST	
Text Defining the Function	*Examples Demonstrating the Function*
The function FIRST is used to extract the first s-expression from a composite s-expression. The function FIRST requires exactly one argument. The argument to the function FIRST must be a composite s-expression. The value returned by the function FIRST is the first s-expression of the given argument.	Next, the function FIRST will be discussed. The following examples illustrate how the function FIRST is to be used. Notice the quotes! The possible inputs to the LISP system are shown on the left side and the returned results are shown on the right side of one line.

(FIRST '(A B))	->	A
(FIRST '(A (B C)))	->	A
(FIRST '(A))	->	A
(FIRST (FIRST '((A B) C)))	->	A
(FIRST '((A B) C))	->	(A B)
(FIRST '((A B) (C D)))	->	(A B)
(FIRST '(FIRST ((A B) C)))	->	FIRST
(FIRST 'A 'B)	->	ERROR
FIRST '(A B)	->	ERROR
(FIRST (A B))	->	ERROR
(FIRST 'A)	->	ERROR
(FIRST (A 'B))	->	ERROR

Test Materials. The material of the first test phase consisted of 15 correct and 5 incorrect sentences about the building blocks of the programming language LISP. For the second test phase, 16 sentences and 40 examples were constructed. For each of the four functions one test sentence of each of the following four types was used: Original sentences (O-sentences) were taken directly from the text learning material. Paraphrased sentences (P-sentences) had no verbatim correspondence in the material but matched sentences of the text on a propositional level. Meaning-changed sentences (M-sentences) consisted of inferences that were implied by the text, such as statements that can be inferred from a correct situation model. Correctness-changed sentences (C-sentences) made an incorrect statement about LISP. The sentences were constructed in the same fashion as the test sentences of Experiments 2 and 3. Again, representational strengths for verbatim, propositional, and situational memory traces could thus be calculated from the subjects' responses to the different sentence foils. More specifically, the difference between O- and M- sentences can be used to measure the strength of a text representation, for example the combination of verbatim and propositional representation.

TABLE 8.2

A Sample of the Test Materials for the Sentence and Example Verification Tasks

---

Sentence verification tasks

Original:

The argument to the function FIRST must be a composite s-expression.

Paraphrase:

In order to extract the first s-expression from a composite s-expression, the function FIRST can be used.

Correctness-Changed:

The argument to the function FIRST may contain five or even more s-expressions.

Meaning-Changed:

The value returned by the function FIRST is always a composite s-expression.

| Example verification tasks | |
Correct	*Incorrect*
Simple examples:	
(LIST 'KARL 'MAY)	(FIRST '(GAR TEN SCHLAUCH))
--> (KARL MAY)	--> (TEN SCHLAUCH)
Function combinations:	
(LIST (LIST (LIST 'A 'B) 'C) 'D)	(FIRST '(FIRST (FIRST '(((X Y) Z) A))))
--> (((A B) C) D)	--> X

The 40 test examples consisted of 20 correct and 20 incorrect examples. Four simple examples (S-examples), one for each function, were the initial examples. Eight function combination or FC-examples contained function combinations where the same function was concatenated three times. Because the inputs of the S-examples matched at least one of the templates that, according to the computer simulation, were built by the learner in the learning phase, whereas the FC-examples did not match any of the templates, response differences between these examples constitute a measure for the strength of the template base. In addition, there were four other types of examples: four IO-examples tested the knowledge about the input–output relations, eight L-examples tested the knowledge about list structures, eight Q-examples tested the knowledge about the quote, and eight

D-examples tested the knowledge about function combinations with different functions. For all example types, half of the examples were correct examples and the other half were incorrect examples. A typical block of the test material is shown in Table 8. 2.

Apparatus. The experiment was run on IBM-PC/AT personal computers to which CMU button boxes with three buttons and a sound generator were connected. A more detailed description of this piece of equipment is given in Schmalhofer, Schlei and Farin (1986).

Procedure. Before the experiment, a brief introduction and practice with material unrelated to programming was performed by the subjects to make sure that they had understood the various experimental procedures. The first learning and test phases of the experiment, which were identical for all three conditions, were then performed. In the second learning phase, the subjects learned about the elementary LISP functions FIRST, REST, EQUAL, and LIST from text, examples, or text and examples. For both learning phases, the subjects were instructed to study the learning materials as if they were studying for a mid-term exam. Thereafter the sentence verification tasks were performed, followed by the example verification tasks. Because the procedure for the first learning and test phase did not differ from the second learning and test phase, only the latter is described in the following section.

Learning Phases. In the second learning phase, the learning materials were shown in two windows (a text window and an example window) in a way that the subjects could move freely between items and paragraphs using the buttons of the button box. At each time they could study only one item (i.e., a sentence or an example), but subjects were free in how they were able to allocate the total study time of 30 minutes to the different items.

Test Phases. In the test that immediately followed the second learning phase, the subjects had to judge the correctness of 16 test sentences and 40 examples.

In order to obtain information about the time course of knowledge utilization, a tapping speed–accuracy trade-off method was again employed that was quite similar to the one of experiment 3. With this response method, the subjects had to give 5 responses to each sentence or example. The first response was a pure guess that the subject had to make even before the test item had been presented. After 0.75 sec. (sentences) or 2 sec. (examples) the sentence or the example was presented on the screen. The following four responses were probed by response signals (tones) that occurred 1.5 sec. (sentences) or 4 sec. (examples) apart from each other.[3] To summarize, the 5 responses for each item consisted of one "guess" and four "fast" responses. Subjects thus had to give their consecutive

---

[3]Pretests showed that subjects took much more time to reach a response asymptote for the example verification tasks than for the sentence verification tasks. In order to obtain information about the critical changes in the time course of the responses, the time intervals between the responses were longer for test examples than for sentences.

responses at predetermined points in time, which were additionally indicated by response signals. Because the subjects had practiced this response method in the practice phase, they were highly reliable in producing the fast consecutive responses as well as in indicating the confidence of the response (i.e., the duration of the button press). The 16 test sentences were presented individually in random order. After these sentences, the four simple examples (S-examples) were presented. The remaining 36 examples were then presented in random order. For each button press, the subjects were asked to indicate the confidence in their decision by the duration of the button press, short durations indicating low confidence and long durations indicating high confidence.

Results

The results are reported in two sections. The first section concerns analyses of the knowledge representations after learning from text and examples. Because the last of the subjects' five responses are best suited for indicating the final strength of a knowledge representation, the early responses that indicate speed–accuracy relations were therefore excluded from these initial analyses. In the second section, analyses for the time course characteristics of the subjects' responses are presented. For these analyses, all responses were included. These analyses were employed to test hypotheses about the onsets of the various contributions from the different knowledge representations (textbase, template base, situation model).

TABLE 8.3

Relative Frequencies of "YES" Responses for the Three Learning Conditions, the Four Types of Test Sentences, and the Two Types of Test Examples

	Type of Test Sentence				Type of Test Example	
	Original	Paraphrased	Meaning-changed	Correctness changed	Simple	Function combination[4]
Condition						
Text	0.92	0.90	0.70	0.29	0.85	0.57
Example	0.76	0.82	0.78	0.32	0.94	0.61
Combination	0.82	0.87	0.69	0.43	0.93	0.62

Asymptotic Representation Strengths. Relative frequencies of "yes" responses were calculated for the responses at 5 seconds after the presentation of a

---

[4]These data show that the FC-examples were very difficult for all subjects. The same is true for the other example types (L-, Q-, and D-examples) where the relative frequencies of correct solutions for the three subject groups ranged between 0.50 and 0.74 with a mean of 0.61, respectively.

test sentence, and for the responses at 12 seconds after the presentation of a test example. The results are shown in Table 8.3.

D' scores were calculated for every subject for each of the three cognitive representations. The mean d' scores of the text representation (O- vs. M-sentences),[5] the template base (S- vs. FC-examples), and the situation model (M- vs. C-sentences) obtained for the three conditions are shown in Table 8.4.

TABLE 8.4

d'-Values for the Text Representation, the Template Base and the Situation Model for the Three Conditions (Correctness Ratings in Parentheses)

		Knowledge Representation	
	Text Representation	Situation Model	Template Base
Condition			
Text condition	0.53 (3.15)	1.03 (6.27)	0.69 (3.07)
Example condition	-0.06 (-0.26)	1.18 (6.80)	0.79 (4.64)
Combination condition	0.31 (1.91)	0.66 (3.72)	0.73 (4.42)

A 3 × 3 ANOVA with the factors learning condition (text, examples, both materials) and memory representation (text representation, template base, and situation model) revealed differences among the cognitive representations, $F(2,154) = 15.29$; $MS_e = 0.67$; $p < .001$, but not among the conditions. The text representation was weaker than the template base, which in turn was weaker than the situational representation. The interaction between the two factors was also significant, $F(4,154) = 2,71$; $MS_e = 0.67$; $p < .05$). This is due to the fact that for the example condition the text representation was not existent but the template base was strong, whereas for the text condition, the text representation was strong and the template base was comparably weak.

The most interesting result of this analysis is the absence of differences in the situational representation among the three conditions. Even subjects who studied text as well as examples did not form a stronger situation model than the subjects who studied only one material. This is exactly the result predicted by the model — that all conditions form an equivalent situation model. The instructional materials that were constructed to be informationally equivalent with the assistance of the computer simulation were indeed informationally equivalent for the particular subjects of this experiment.

---

[5]The measure for the strength of the text representation (O- vs. M-sentences) may be thought of as the sum of a verbatim representation (O- vs. P-sentences) and a propositional representation (P- vs. M-sentences). Because the d' scores for the verbatim representation are practically zero (0.03 for the text condition, -0.15 for the example condition, and -0.14 for the combination condition) the strength of the text representation is basically identical to the propositional representation.

Another prediction from the model was also confirmed: Only subjects who studied text or both materials formed a text representation. Contrary to our expectations, even the subjects who studied text built a template base. A possible explanations for this unexpected finding could be that the subjects formed a template base while working through the test examples. The result could also be explained by a difference in difficulty between the two groups of test examples that were used to measure the strength of the template base. For this reason, the function combination examples, which were quite difficult to verify correctly, were replaced by easier examples in the later experiments that investigated expertise differences (see chapter 10).

Correctness Ratings. The experimental procedure as well as the calculation of the correctness ratings is a refinement of the previously used response method (see chapter 7). Because it is assumed that the confidence in a decision constitutes another important component for measuring the strength of the subjects' cognitive representations, correctness ratings were computed from the subjects' responses and from the confidence ratings that were calculated from the durations of the button presses. Remember that the subjects had been instructed to indicate confidence in their decisions by the duration of their button press. For each subject and for both types of verification tasks, all durations were divided into 9 categories of equal frequency. The values 1 to 9 were assigned to the 9 categories of response durations that were thus obtained. These numbers are the confidence ratings obtained for a response. The number 1 indicated the category with the shortest durations (low confidence) and the number 9 indicated the category with the longest durations (high confidence). For those responses, where the subject had pressed the "no" button, the values were then multiplied by -1. Thus, for each button press of each subject, a *correctness rating* was obtained, which had a value either between -9 and -1 or between +1 and +9. This correctness rating is a compound measure that contains the correctness of the answer in combination with the confidence of the subject in the decision. This response scaling technique has a number of similarities with the rating-scale model of signal detection (cf. Baird & Noma, 1978).

For all further analyses, these *correctness ratings* were taken as the dependent measure. But basically the same results were obtained with a d' analysis (see Table 8.3). Using the correctness ratings instead of the d' values has the advantage that no familiarity with signal detection analysis is required for understanding how the dependent measures were calculated that indicate the various representation strengths.

Differences of the correctness ratings between O- and M-sentences constitute a measure for the strength of the text representation. The differences between the correctness ratings of the S- and FC-examples and the M- and C-sentences yielded the respective measures for the template base and the situation model. A 3 × 3 ANOVA with the factors learning condition and type of representation yielded the same results as the previously reported analysis with the d' scores as dependent measure. Our experimental findings are thus not dependent on the specific scaling method applied.[6]

The Time Course of Knowledge Utilization.   The tapping speed–accuracy trade-off method yielded responses at different points in time. The collected data can thus be employed for investigating the time course of knowledge utilization in verification tasks. The indicators for textbase, template base, and situation model were calculated as the difference of correctness ratings, according to the description that was given in the method section. The resulting time-course characteristics for the three experimental conditions and the three cognitive representations are shown in Fig. 8.1. Because the overall effects of the different learning conditions were reported by the previous analyses, only the effects involving the factor processing time are presented in the analyses of this section.

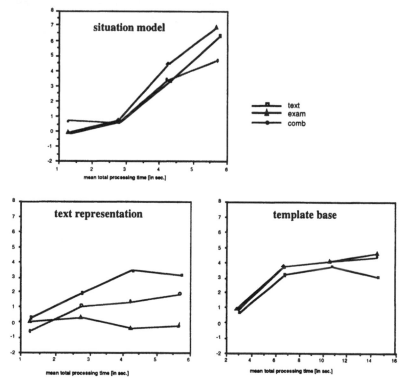

FIG. 8.1.   Time-course of the activated strength of text, template, and the situation representation in the three learning conditions.

---

[6]The correlation between d' scores and the respective correctness rating differences was 0.92 for the text representation, 0.84 for the template base, and 0.92 for the situation model.

Text Representation. A 3 × 4 ANOVA with the factors learning condition and processing time for the correctness rating differences (i.e., the indicator for the strength of the text representation) showed differences for processing time, $F(3,231) = 5.38$; $MS_e = 8.84$; $p < .005$, as well as for the interaction of processing time and condition factors, $F(6,231) = 2.33$; $MS_e = 8.84$; $p < .05$. These statistical results are interpreted in the following way: In the text and combination conditions, there was an increase in the strength of the text representation in the first three seconds. At this point an asymptote was reached. In the example condition, on the other hand, there was no change at all, which resulted in the significant interaction.

Template Base. A 3 × 4 ANOVA with the factors learning condition and processing time for the correctness rating differences (i.e., the indicator for the strength of the template representation) revealed only differences for processing time, $F(3,231) = 30.20$; $MS_e = 6.03$; $p < .001$. This difference was due to a strong increase in the first eight seconds for all conditions.

Situation Model. A 3 × 4 ANOVA with the factors learning condition and processing time for the correctness rating differences (i.e., the indicator for the strength of the situation representation) revealed only differences for processing time, $F(3,231) = 47.71$; $MS_e = 11.24$; $p < .001$. This is interpreted in the following way: There was a steady increase for all conditions after three seconds of processing time until the last decision.

TABLE 8.5

Parameter Estimates for the Approximation of the d' Values for the Text Representation, the Template Base, and the Situation Model for the Three Learning Conditions

	Knowledge Representation								
	Text Representation			Situation Model			Template Base		
	δ	β	λ	δ	β	λ	δ	β	λ
Condition									
Text	1.17	0.56	3.65	3.25	0.32	11.42	2.72	0.77	3.42
Example			0.00	2.53	0.24	13.12	2.33	0.40	4.51
Combination	1.25	0.41	2.17	2.56	0.54	5.79	2.22	0.41	4.36

In summary, these analyses show that the text representation was activated more rapidly than the situation representation. The asymptote of the contribution of the text representation was reached after about three seconds, and the asymptote of the situational representation was not reached during the first four responses at all. The onset of the contribution of each of the knowledge representations was determined by an approximation of the d' scores observed at different processing times t by the function which was presented in equation 1 in chapter 7. Table 8.5 shows the values of the three parameters (λ, β, δ) for the three conditions and the three knowledge representations, which were obtained with the calculation procedure described in chapter 7. There were some occasions where, due to the limited number of data points, unrealistic parameter estimates were obtained. On such occasions, the parameter search space was restricted to a more reasonable subsection.

Remember that the parameter δ specifies the onset of the contribution from each representation. From the values of Table 8.5 it can be seen that the onset of the peripheral representations (i.e., the text representation and the template base) occurs earlier than the onset of the situation model. This result is thus quite different from the result, obtained in experiment 3. In particular, these results are in good agreement with the predictions of the C–I theory. The C–I theory assumes that the various nodes are activated in a bottom-up fashion. Text-base and template-base would therefore become activated before the situation model. The estimates for the δ–parameters show this prediction quite clearly, specifically in the relation between textbase and situation model.[7]

The β–parameter shows the rate of change in the representational strengths after its onset at time δ. In relation to the C–I theory, this parameter can be identified with the change of activation in the respective nodes, which occurs when activation is spread through the network. Because we have, however, not obtained any detailed a priori predictions, we will restrain from interpreting these parameters any further.

Discussion

In the current experiment it was shown how the representational strengths of textbase, template base, and situation model can be determined by using a process dissociation procedure on the response frequencies to sentence verification tasks. Text and examples were constructed so that according to the KIWi model, human learners should acquire the same situation knowledge from each. The strengths of the peripheral representations (textbase and template base), which are formed en route to the construction of a situation model, on the other hand, would be different between the two learning conditions. These predictions were clearly supported by the experimental outcomes. The measures for the textbase and template base behaved exactly in the predicted manner. One exception may be the situational indicator in the combined learning condition, which is somewhat lower, although not statistically significant, than in the other two learning conditions. A possible explanation is that some learners may have studied the examples before the text, yielding some incorrect hypotheses that then interfered with the statements presented in the text.

Now that the present experiment has established how equivalent situation knowledge is acquired from different learning materials, the processes of learning from text and examples will be further investigated by a think-aloud investigation. Think-aloud protocols are intricate data that may lead to detailed

---

[7] The results obtained for the text representation in the example conditions were artificial and are therefore not shown in Table 8.5. Because the text representation does not really exist in the example condition, no meaningful estimates were obtained from the random fluctuations among the various data points.

insights into comprehension processes. An objective and fruitful analysis of such data requires constraints that reduce the arbitrariness of otherwise only exploratory protocol interpretations. In order to analyze the verbal protocols from text understanding and learning from situation examples, the KIWi model, whose empirical validity was thereby further assessed, served as such a constraint in the protocol analysis procedure. In experiment 5, all subjects had the same very general comprehension goal while acquiring some basic knowledge of a programming language (LISP) by studying text and/or programming examples.

8.2 Experiment 5

In empirically determining the functional characteristics and qualities of different online comprehension processes, verbal protocols may provide additional insights into the qualities of learning from text and examples. Verbal or think-aloud protocols are data that consist of a sequence of written natural language expressions, as well as marks that divide a protocol into a number of episodes. These episodes may consist of one or several words, phrases, sentences, a paragraph of any length, or simply of no verbalizations at all. They are obtained by transcribing a person's utterances in some task under well-defined instructions, followed by applying rules for segmenting the protocol thereafter. Unlike response times that solely reflect the duration of some information processes, protocols also show which information was processed and in which sequence. Verbal protocols thus present a detailed on line trace of human information processing. Because a person's utterances can be directly recorded and transcribed, verbal protocols have recently been viewed as objective data, that can be scientifically analyzed.

Ericsson and Simon's (1984) analysis of a large body of think-aloud data revealed the conditions under which verbal data provide an authentic trace of the task-related processes, and which conditions produce interference and incomplete protocols or epiphenomenal data. Based on the type and number of intervening cognitive processes resulting from concurrent think aloud instructions, Ericsson and Simon distinguished three kinds of verbalizations: (a) When information is encoded verbatim or propositionally, it is basically verbalized in the form in which it is heeded in working memory during the performance of the task. (b) Heeded information that is represented in a nonverbal form (e.g., images or templates) must be cognitively translated into a verbal form in order to be verbalized. (c) Verbalizations where a subject is required to report selectively or to explicitly attend to information that would not be heeded otherwise during the regular task performance, on the other hand, involves a number of mediating processes and may produce epiphenomenal data.

These results were obtained through the application of a relatively general information processing model, which Ericsson and Simon extracted from the large body of memory and cognitive science research so that it was equally valid for the different areas of cognition such as concept formation, problem solving, numerical calculations, and other areas. Their success is mainly due to the application of that model, which allowed them to determine the significance of different verbalizations so that the arbitrariness of otherwise only exploratory protocol analyses was greatly reduced. Their work makes it quite clear that the more specific and correct the model one applies, the more objective and fruitful the analyses of the think-aloud utterances will be. When one concerns oneself only with a subdomain of cognition such as text comprehension and learning from examples, the C–I theory and the KIWi model can be applied as a more specific model for analyzing respective verbal protocols. On this basis a number of processes can be distinguished (see Fig. 6.1) and the various episodes in the verbal protocols can be classified according to which of the processes they indicate. In the next two sections, the different processes that occur in learning from text and in learning from examples are stated once more, so that they can then be applied as a basis for analyzing the verbal protocols. The various processing components are denoted by letters (for knowledge acquisition from text) and numbers (for discovery learning from example situations).

Knowledge Acquisition From Text. On the basis of the C–I theory, a number of processes can be distinguished. As previous research shows, propositional text representations are constructed from the sentences of a text in working memory by a cyclical process (a). After the instantiation of the relevant prior domain knowledge (b), which may be stored in the form of a schema, a general situational representation of the domain is formed, for instance by filling the slots of the instantiated schema (c). From technical texts such as a text about a programming language, templates, which represent the form of correctly built program examples, may be constructed in a fourth step (d). From such templates specific examples may be easily generated (Anderson et al., 1984).

Discovery Learning From Example Situations. Example situations, on the other hand, are used to construct templates (1), from which a general situational representation can be inferred (2). By additional organizational and transformational processing, fragments of a propositional text representation my then be formed (3). In the present study the think-aloud method is applied to investigate the characteristics of the described text comprehension processes (a–d) in relation to the discovery learning and problem solving processes (1–3) that occur in the learning from situation examples.

With the exception of applying the think-aloud method, the experiment was identical to experiment 4 and consisted of two knowledge acquisition phases. The first knowledge acquisition phase which was identical for the three experimental conditions, was used to induce similar background knowledge that was needed to understand the secondly presented materials. In the three conditions of the second learning phase, subjects studied text, examples, or text and examples while their verbalized thoughts were recorded (see also Schmalhofer & Boschert, 1988).

Method

Subjects. Eighteen psychology students from the University of Freiburg participated in this study and were paid for their participation.

Materials and Apparatus. The same materials and apparatus were used as in experiment 4. In addition, a dictaphone was used to record the subjects' verbalizations.

Procedure. The 18 subjects were randomly assigned to the three conditions of the experiment. The subjects were instructed to study the material as if they were studying for an exam in a programming course. The subjects were instructed to speak out loud every thought that went through their head. In a preceding practice phase, the vocalization of thoughts was first exercised with number multiplication and memory retrieval tasks.

TABLE 8.6

Relative Frequencies of 5 Types of Transitions Between the Items of the Learning Materials for the Three Experimental Conditions

	Between Materials		Within One Material		
	From Sentence to Example	From Example to Sentence	Regression	Next Item	Skip
Text condition			.08	.89	.03
Example condition			.04	.90	.06
Combination	.03	.02	.02	.87	.06

Results

As can be seen from Table 8.6, the 6 subjects of each condition studied the sentences and examples pretty much in the indicated sequential order, without skipping many items or frequently regressing to previous items. In the combination condition, subjects only rarely switched between studying text and examples. Because the analysis of verbal protocols is very time consuming, it was decided to analyze only two subjects of each condition. The protocols of the first knowledge acquisition phase, which was identical in the three conditions and thus without particular interest in the study, were used to select 2 subjects from each condition. Because the two subjects with the most explicit verbalizations were selected from each condition, these selected subjects were matched across the three conditions. For the 6 selected subjects the recorded verbalizations of the second knowledge acquisition phase were transcribed and the resulting protocols were further analyzed.

Segmentation of Protocols. Because in the present study, sentences and examples were presented one after the other, the transition from one item to the next constituted a natural segmentation of the think-aloud protocols. Each segment was assumed to be an episode unless a segment contained verbalizations pertaining to different topics. In such cases, each new topic defined a new episode. The number of episodes per item thus obtained ranged from 1 to 12 with an average of 1.38 in the text, 1.96 in the example, and 2.10 in the combination condition.

TABLE 8.7

Typical Verbalizations for the Different Model Categories

Category	Verbalization
Input rehearsal (**R**) :	"Der Wert der Funktion ist der erste S-Term des Arguments."
	[The value of the function is the first s-expression of the argument]
	(when reading the respective sentence)
Activation of related	"Also zwei Funktionen hintereinander, wie f von g von x." domain
knowledge (**DK**):	[So, two functions, concatenated, like f(g(x))]
	(when reading a sentence about function combination)
Recently acquired LISP	"Dies eine Argument auch ein zusammengesetzter S-Term, alles
knowledge (**LK**):	wie bei FIRST, ... ähnlich." [One argument, and it is also a composite
	s- expression, just like with FIRST ... similar]
	(when reading about REST after having studied FIRST)
Activation of general concept	"Das Wort equal heißt gleich, das kenn' ich also schon." [The word
knowledge (**CK**):	equal means the same, something I know already]
	(when reading the first sentence about EQUAL)
Example construction (**EC**):	"Also wenn sie nicht gleich sind, AB und CD, dann krieg ich NIL
	raus durch EQUAL." [So, if they are not identical, like AB and CD,
EQUAL)	then EQUAL returns NIL]. *(when reading a sentence about*
Output prediction (**PO**):	"Das müßte Klammer auf A B Klammer zu geben." [This should
	result in (A B)" *(when studying (LIST 'A 'B) -->)*
Test of prediction (**PT**):	"Ja stimmt." [That's right] *(when (A B) is seen)*
Generalisation (**G**):	"Zu jedem Atom und zu jedem Term gehört ein Strich. Und
	außenrum die Klammern." [There must be a quote before each atom
	or expression, and around it parentheses] *(after having studied 10*
	LIST-examples)
Generalisation and	"LIST, da werden also die einzelnen Elemente zusammengesetzt.
organisation (**GO**):	FIRST, da wird das erste genommen. Bei REST werden die
	übriggebliebenen Elemente genommen. Bei EQUAL gleiche
	Elemente oder Atome sind T. Und wenn sie verschieden sind. NIL,
	nicht identisch." [LIST puts single elements together. FIRST takes
	the first. REST takes the remaining elements. With EQUAL, identical
	elements are T and if they are different, NIL, not identical] *(after*
	having studied all examples of LIST, FIRST, REST and EQUAL)

Definition of Categories. In the second step of the analysis, the outlined processes, that were denoted a, b, c, d, and 1, 2, 3, respectively, were used to derive the verbalization categories which should occur according to the model. The construction of a textbase from propositions (a) and entering propositions into the slots of an instantiated schema (c) require those propositions to be heeded in working memory. Textbase construction and/or slotfilling may thus occur when a learner re-reads (parts of) a sentence. This category that did not include the first reading of an input was called input rehearsal (R). The first reading was not analyzed at all because it occurred quite regularly when an item was first inspected. To find an appropriate schema (b) and to form a general situational representation, previously acquired related domain knowledge (DK) or more recently acquired LISP knowledge (LK) may be activated. In some cases general concept knowledge (CK) may also be required for constructing a situational representation. The operationalization of the general situational information (d) should be reflected in the verbal protocols by the construction of partial or complete examples (EC).

In the example condition, input rehearsal should also reflect the information in working memory that may be used for constructing a template (1). After a template is constructed, it can be applied for predicting the yet unseen output from the input of an example (PO). Consequently such predictions may be tested by comparing them to the presented output (PT). From templates, general situational statements (G) may also be derived (2). By organizing a number of those general statements (3), a text representation may emerge (GO). For each process postulated by the model, corresponding verbalizations are thus defined as the traces that may be observed when that process is executed. For each episode of the protocols it could consequently be decided whether it reflected some comprehension process. As seen in table 8.7, the protocol contained indications for all processes.

Assessment of Individual and Condition Differences.   Furthermore, the frequencies with which the different verbalizations occurred were determined. In order to investigate differences in the individual verbalization patterns in relation to the differences between the three experimental conditions, the frequencies of the different verbalization episodes were correlated for all 15 subject pairs. Whereas the correlation between the subjects within one condition is a measure for the individual similarity of these two subjects, a null or negative correlation between subjects of different conditions reflects condition differences in addition to the individual differences. The correlations for within-condition subject pairs ranged from .95 to .97. The correlation between the subjects of the text and the example condition ranged from -.02 to -.09. In this model-based protocol analysis, interindividual differences were obviously quite negligible. The absence of a correlation between the subjects of the text and example condition clearly indicated differences between the text and example encoding processes.

TABLE 8.8

Some Descriptive Statistics of the Verbalization Protocols in the Three Conditions

	Text	*Combination*	*Examples*
Number of episodes (per subject)	116	162	162
Number of repeated words (per subject)	1660	1410	1262
Number of new words (per subject)	1101	2124	1753
average study time in min. (per subject)	28	49	33
Percentage of model-based verbalisations	57	47	76

Because encoding processes are shared between the combination condition and the two other conditions, the verbalizations of the subjects of these conditions should be correlated. The correlation between the subjects of the text and combination condition ranged between .44 and .47. The correlation between the subjects of the example and combination condition ranged between .75 and .86. All correlations above .79 are significant at the .01 level. The protocols thus highlight differences in the comprehension processes for text and example situations.

TABLE 8.9

Relative Frequencies for the Different Types of Verbalization Episodes

	Text	*Combination*	*Examples*
Input rehearsal (1, a, c)[*] [R][+]	.52	.35	.11
Activation of knowledge (1, b)[*] [DK, CK][+]	.05	.02	.01
Retrieval of LISP knowledge (1, b)[*] [LK][+]	.32	.08	.11
Example construction (d)[*] [EC][+]	.09	.00	.00
Output prediction (result of 1)[*] [PO][+]	.02	.40	.51
Test of prediction (result of 1)[*] [PT][+]	.00	.10	.18
Generalization and organization (2, 3)[*] [G, GO][+]	.00	.04	.08

[*]Digits and letters in round parentheses refer to the steps of constructing a text or situation representation as described in the text and depicted in Fig. 6.1.
[+]Letters in brackets refer to the categories in Table 8.7.

Table 8.8 shows some general statistics of the verbalization protocols in the three conditions. Table 8.9, which shows the relative frequencies of verbalizations for the different (in some cases pooled) categories for the text, example, and combination condition, substantiates the differences in the knowledge acquisition from text and examples. Verbalizations for input rehearsal are more frequently observed in the text than in the example condition. Also, more prior knowledge is verbalized in text comprehension than in discovery learning from examples. This may possibly mean that under the given experimental conditions, text comprehension was more knowledge-driven whereas the examples were processed by general discovery heuristics (Langley, Simon, & Bradshaw, 1983). The majority of verbalizations in the example condition consist of the prediction of an output during the studying of an input of an example with a frequent subsequent test of this prediction. From Table 8.9 it can furthermore be calculated that only 40% of the episodes did not indicate any of the described processes.

Transition Between Verbalization Episodes. The sequence of verbalization episodes was assessed by calculating relative transition frequencies separately for the text and example condition. By definition, for each category the sum of the relative transition frequencies is equal to one. For each of the categories with more than 12 verbalizations the three highest transition frequencies, q_t and q_e, will be reported for the text and example condition. After rehearsing a text input, subjects most frequently continued to rehearse q_t (R/R) = .53, activated prior LISP knowledge q_t (LK/R) = .30, or constructed an example q_t (EC/R) = .11. After rehearsing an example input, subjects most frequently predicted an output q_e (PO/R) = .50, continued rehearsing q_e (R/R) = .30, or activated prior LISP knowledge q_e (LK/R) = .13. After having activated prior LISP knowledge in the text condition, subjects most frequently rehearsed the input q_t (R/LK) = .55, activated more LISP knowledge q_t (LK/LK) = .36, or activated related domain knowledge q_t (DK/LK) = .05. In the example condition, subjects most frequently predicted an output q_e (PO/LK) = .50, generalized the example q_e (G/LK) = .19, or rehearsed the input q_e (R/LK) = .19. After having constructed an example in the text condition, subjects most frequently rehearsed the input q_t (R/EC) = .42, activated more LISP knowledge q_t (LK/EC) = .33, or constructed another example q_t (EC/EC) = .25.

With only one exception, the PO, PT, and G categories occurred only in the example condition. After having predicted an output, subjects most frequently predicted another output q_e (PO/PO) = .43, tested the prediction q_e (PT/PO) = .36, or rehearsed the input q_e (R/PO) = .09. After the test of an output, subjects most frequently predicted another output q_e (PO/PT) = .76, generalized q_e (G/PT) = .09, or activated LISP knowledge q_e (LK/PT) = .09. After a generalization, an output is predicted q_e (PO/G) = .79, or prior LISP knowledge is activated q_e (LK/G) = .11. These transition frequencies, which are graphically represented in Fig. 8.2 seem to indicate that the traced comprehension processes are interleaved and do not occur in a strict sequence. From these sequences, the particular ordering of the various component processes can be further assessed.

The remaining episodes were also analyzed and categorized into six classes. These verbalizations reflected cognitive processes which are not part of the model. There were statements of comprehension, non-comprehension, and questions with a frequency of .14, .20 and .11 in the text, combination, and example condition, respectively. These statements indicate the online monitoring of the comprehension processes. With a frequency of .01, the goal statements appeared equally often in the three conditions. Such goal statements can be taken as an indication of problem solving which occurred in discovery learning as well as in text comprehension. Action descriptions and fillers that occurred on average of .17 are simply verbalizations of what the subject is currently doing. 3% of the statements could not be clearly categorized and were therefore labelled as vague statements. For 5% of the items, the subjects did not make any remarks. By analyzing the similarities or differences among the conditions for these additional categories it was furthermore found that problem solving processes and meta cognitive processes, such as monitoring knowledge acquisition, occurred in discovery learning as well as in the comprehension of technical texts. Differences between the experimental conditions thus occur with respect to the predicted processing but not for the other comprehension processes.

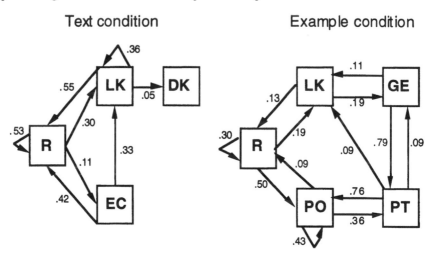

FIG. 8.2. Conditional transition frequencies between the various verbalization categories of the two experimental conditions.

8.3 Summary

Whereas one of the fundamental assumptions of processing goals and cognitive representations was already confirmed by the experiments of the previous chapter, in this chapter we have applied the KIWi model for designing the experimental learning materials. More specifically, situational examples of programming constructs (LISP examples) and an expository text about LISP were developed, so that the KIWi simulation would construct the same situation model from either learning material. It was consequently predicted that human learners would acquire the same situation knowledge from either one of the learning materials (situation examples or text). Because the learning processes that construct the situation representations differ for the two learning materials, it was furthermore expected that verbatim and propositional text representations would be formed in learning from text but not in learning from examples. Instead of the recognition task that was used in the previous chapter, sentence verification instructions were now employed for the following reasons: When the surface appearance of the learning materials is so different between text and situation examples, it would make little sense to ask subjects whether they recognize a particular item because the surface appearance of the test item would often suffice for making the decision; a verification task, on the other hand, asks a learner whether a sentence is true with respect to the subject domain; and because the same process dissociation procedure can be applied equally well to the responses of either task (Schmalhofer, 1986a), the verification task was well suited for testing the specific model predictions. In the three conditions of experiment 4, subjects studied a text or examples that – according to the KIWi model – were informationally equivalent to the text, or the text as well as the examples could be studied. The same amount of study time was available and used in all three conditions. The process dissociation procedure of the sentence verification responses confirmed the predictions: Although there was no significant difference in the situational representation, only the subjects who studied a text had acquired a propositional representation of the text.

The same experimental materials were used in experiment 5 for investigating the processes of learning from examples and learning from text by a think-aloud method. This study showed that the learners read the materials almost completely sequentially with only few regressions and look-aheads. The model-guided analyses of the think-aloud protocols revealed that related domain knowledge (LISP and commonsense knowledge) is indeed heeded in learning from text as well as in learning from examples. This finding provides some direct evidence for the use of associative knowledge from long-term memory during the construction phase of learning, as has been postulated by the construction–integration theory and by the KIWi model. More importantly, there was also evidence that the text learners operationalized the information of the text by attempting to construct examples, and the example learners performed generalization and abstraction processes. Therefore, the subjects did not simply memorize the examples as would be predicted by instance-based theories but did indeed construct general knowledge from the examples and thereby integrated the examples with their prior knowledge (cf. chapter 5; Anderson & Fincham, 1994; Heit, 1994).

Although the verbal protocols were too sparse to reconstruct a complete trace of the various cognitive processes, they still provided evidence for the psychological reality of the postulated processes: Whereas the activation of domain knowledge (LISP and commonsense knowledge) was more visible in learning from text, generalization processes were only found in learning from examples and in the combination condition. This is in agreement with the abstraction processes of the KIWi model that are part of the knowledge construction that occurs in learning from examples. In learning from text, on the other hand, the activation of domain knowledge from long-term memory is a more integral part of the construction processes. Finally, the observed "generalization and organization" verbalizations may be interpreted as some evidence for the postulated integration processes. Although the verbal protocols did not give us a fine-grained trace of the postulated learning processes, they nevertheless provided clear indicators for the types of processes postulated by the model. In addition, there were verbalizations that indicated different processes such as comprehension monitoring. Such metacognitive processes are not (or are not yet) part of the model.

9

Material Transformation

Learning from text as well as learning from examples can be described by knowledge construction and knowledge integration episodes. The specific knowledge construction processes that operate on examples are, however, quite different from the specific knowledge construction processes that operate on the sentences of a text. In learning from text, elaborative and deductive processes are important, and in learning from examples, inductive and abductive inferences are important. Despite these differences, essentially the same situation knowledge can be acquired from either one of the two materials. The experiments of the previous chapter confirmed these predictions in different ways. More specifically, it was shown that identical learning results can, indeed, be obtained by diverse knowledge construction processes, when the learners have an identical learning goal and the learning materials have been developed to be informationally equivalent, according to the assumptions of the KIWi model.

Human learners are thus quite flexible, in that they can achieve an essentially identical learning result from quite different information sources. In this chapter, we further analyze the relation between the general or abstract information that is typically presented by the sentences of a text and the more specific information that is typically presented by a case or example. In two experiments, it was investigated how subjects would operationalize the information of a text by generating examples and how subjects can gain abstract knowledge from examples and generate abstract sentences. In these experiments, subjects had to construct examples from sentences and vice versa. Whereas experiment 6 used a think-aloud method with a small number of subjects, a large number of subjects was employed in experiment 7 and the performance data were analyzed so that individual differences could be assessed. More specifically, the errors that arise when subjects generate examples are qualitatively assessed by applying the KIWi model as a tool for analyzing the subjects' individual responses. Thereby, it is shown how the KIWi model could possibly be applied for the diagnosis of knowledge.

The current literature on cognitive modeling distinguishes relatively strictly between case-based and rule-based reasoning. Kolodner (1993, p.93) depicted the most important differences between the two approaches: Whereas the research on rule-based reasoning has emphasized the mechanisms of reasoning and the form of knowledge, case-based reasoning assumes that the episodes, which occurred in real-life, should be stored as knowledge with all their interrelatedness and redundancies. Such stored episodes are then called cases. Whereas *rules* are small and ideally independent but consistent pieces of knowledge, *cases* are large knowledge chunks that are partially redundant with other cases.

The information that is presented by the sentences of a text is actually quite similar to the small and ideally independent pieces of knowledge that are coded by the rules of a traditional knowledge-based system. In particular, each sentence of an expository text usually presents some new information that is consistent with the previously stated sentences. In the LISP examples, on the other hand, several rules of the LISP syntax and the properties of functions and function combinations are jointly instantiated and realized in the example. A LISP example thus embraces several different rules that have been compiled and instantiated for a specific purpose (like a particular programming goal) and form a case.

In the two experiments of this chapter, subjects had to construct cases (i.e., LISP examples) from a set of general rules (presented by sentences) and they had to generate general rules (i.e., sentences) from a set of cases (i.e., LISP examples). Before performing these tasks, all subjects had acquired the prerequisite domain knowledge in the first part of each experiment. The think aloud method was employed to obtain evidence for the various component processes in this transformation task. From the KIWi model, it was predicted that the same component processes would be observed as in experiment 5, but with somewhat different frequencies. Experiment 7 was performed so that individual differences could be qualitatively assessed, and so that the various errors that may occur in the transformation processes could also be identified.

9.1 Experiment 6

The subjects studied a selection of the text materials that were already used in experiments 4 and 5. Exactly those sentences were used that according to the KIWi model would allow the construction of examples. Similarly, a sequence of examples was selected that would allow for the construction of general sentences about the arguments and the input–output relation of a function. These materials were selected for the functions FIRST and LIST.

Method

Subjects. Four students from the University of Freiburg who were paid 20DM participated in this study.

Materials. All subjects studied the material about data representations in LISP (which was already used in experiments 4 and 5). The subjects then had to perform the material transformation tasks. From the sentences that are shown in Table 9.1, five examples for the function FIRST had to be generated, and from the examples shown in Table 9.2, general sentences about the function LIST had to be generated. The 9 sentences and the 7 examples were selected so that they could be used by the KIWi model to construct the predicted sentences and examples that are shown in Table 9.3.

TABLE 9.1

English Translation of the Instructions for Building Examples From Text

Sentences 1-9 give a description of the function FIRST. Please study the sentences carefully and use your previously acquired knowledge (i.e., the knowledge you acquired in the first learning phase as well as the information given in sentences 1–9) to build 5 correct examples with the function FIRST. An example consists of an input to the LISP system and the corresponding output (the value of the function). The input and output should be separated by an arrow.

Please construct the five examples now.

1) An input to the LISP system starts with an opening parenthesis, i.e., (.
2) The next element is the function name.
3) After the function name follows the argument.
4) The input to the LISP system ends with a closing parenthesis, i.e.,) .
5) The function FIRST extracts the first s-expression out of a composite s-expression.
6) The function FIRST has precisely one argument.
7) This argument must be a composite s-expression.
8) The value of the function FIRST is the first s-expression of its argument.
9) If an s-expression is used as an argument, then there has to be a quote in front of this s-expression.

Procedure. Again each subject first practiced thinking aloud while performing a multiplication and a memory retrieval task, and read the text about data representations in LISP. For two subjects, the LIST examples were presented and they had to construct five general sentences about this function while thinking aloud. Thereafter the sentences about the function FIRST were presented and they had to generate five examples and think out loud. The examples as well as the sentences were presented on one sheet of paper. For the other two subjects the two tasks were presented in the reversed order.

TABLE 9.2

English Translation of the Instructions for Deriving Sentences From Examples

Examples 1-7 give a description of the function LIST. Please study the examples carefully and use your previously acquired knowledge (i.e., the knowledge you acquired in the first learning phase as well as the information given in the examples 1-7) to make 5 correct statements about the arguments of the function LIST. Please build grammatically complete sentences.

1)	(LIST 'A 'B 'C)	-->	(A B C)
2)	(LIST 'A 'B)	-->	(A B)
3)	(LIST '(A B) 'C '(D E))	-->	((A B) C (D E))
4)	(LIST '((A B) C) 'D)	-->	(((A B) C) D)
5)	(LIST 'A B)	-->	ERROR
6)	(LIST A B)	-->	ERROR
7)	(LIST '(A B) C)	-->	ERROR

Results

It was first determined whether the subjects actually generated examples and sentences similar to those predicted by the model. From the examples that were generated by the subjects, the best fitting example was selected for each predicted example. Table 9.3 shows that close matches could be found for 3 of the 4 predicted examples. Whereas the second example matched character by character, the inputs of example 1 and 3 still showed an identical structure but the individual elements differed. These differences are quite irrelevant with respect to the subject domain of LISP. The differences on the output side, on the other hand, yield an erroneous LISP example and are therefore substantial.

TABLE 9.3

Predicted and Observed Examples

	Predicted			Observed		
1)	(FIRST '(A B))	->	A	(FIRST '(B 519))	->	(B)[*]
2)	(FIRST '((A B) C))	->	(A B)	(FIRST '((A B) C))	->	(A B)
3)	(FIRST '((A B)(C D)))	->	(A B)	(FIRST '(A B (C D)))	->	(A B)[*]
4)	(FIRST '(A))	->	A		---	

[*]Although the input side agrees with the predicted examples, the output side of these examples are actually incorrect.

The sentences that most closely matched the 3 predicted sentences are shown in Table 9.4. As could be expected, the inferred sentences did not match literally but only with respect to the meaning of the sentences. Although the sentences shown in Table 9.4 are correct, subjects also generated sentences that were incorrect with respect to LISP. Whereas 65% correct sentences were inferred from the examples, only 5% of the generated examples were completely correct. These results indicate that although the cognitive processes for constructing examples from text and deriving general sentences from examples are differentially error-prone, both transformations may in principle be correctly performed by human subjects.

TABLE 9.4

Predicted and Observed Sentences

Predicted	Observed
1) The function LIST has two or more arguments.	---
2) The arguments of the function LIST may be either LISP atoms or composite s-expressions.	Funktionsargumente können S-Atome oder/und S-Terme sein. [The arguments of the function may be atoms and/or s-expressions]
3) If an s-expression is used as an argument, then there has to be a quote in front of this s-expression.	Zur Bezeichnung der Argumente muß jeweils bei jedem einzelnen Argument das Anführungszeichen stehen. [In order to mark the arguments there must be a quote before each argument]

Table 9.5 shows some descriptive statistics of the verbalization protocols. As can be seen from this table, subjects required about the same time for the two different transformations but vocalized more words when examples were to be constructed.

TABLE 9.5

Some Descriptive Statistics of the Verbalization Protocols in the Material Transformation Tasks

	From Text to Examples	From Examples to Text
Number of episodes (per subject)	57	26
Number of repeated words (per subject)	359	136
Number of new words (per subject)	558	424
average study time in min. (per subject)	14	13
Percentage of model based verbalizations	73	65

The think-aloud protocols were also used for a more detailed analysis of the cognitive transformation processes. As in the previous experiment, the protocols were first segmented into episodes. Then the relative frequencies of different types of verbalizations were determined with the previously established categories (see

Table 8.7). In comparison to the previous experiment (experiment 5), about 10% more verbalizations fell into the model categories. Table 9.6 shows the relative frequencies of the different model verbalizations. In both conditions, input rehearsal occurred most frequently and retrieval of LISP knowledge also played a major role. Whereas in the text-to-example condition, subjects engaged in example construction and output prediction, generalization and organization processes only occurred in the example-to-text condition. The specific goal of generating examples or sentences, which was more definite than the general knowledge-acquisition goal of experiment 5, more frequently generated the predicted verbalizations. Also, conditional transition frequencies were calculated in the same way. Figure 9.1 shows these transition frequencies.

TABLE 9.6

Relative Frequencies of the Different Model Verbalizations

	From Text to Examples	*From Examples to Text*
Input rehearsal (1, a, c)[*] [R][+]	.45	.47
Activation of knowledge (1, b)[*] [DK, CK][+]	.00	.00
Retrieval of LISP knowledge (1, b)[*][LK][+]	.08	.14
Example construction (d)[*] [EC][+]	.31	.00
Output prediction (result of 1)[*] [PO][+]	.16	.00
Generalisation and organisation (2, 3)[*][G, GO][+]	.00	.39

[*]Digits and letters in round parentheses refer to the steps of constructing a text or situation representation as described in chapter 8 and graphically shown in Fig. 6.1.
[+]Letters in brackets refer to the categories in Table 8.7.

Discussion

This experiment demonstrated that subjects are quite capable of generating examples from sentences that describe isolated rules and vice versa. More specifically, the subjects generated the examples and sentences that were predicted by the model. Moreover, the verbal protocols provided further evidence for the subprocesses, which were postulated to occur in these material transformation tasks. The experiment also showed that subjects make a variety of errors, which are not described by the KIWi model. The model only describes the correct performance.

In order to further investigate the different types of errors that may occur and also to obtain some appreciation for the individual differences that may exist among various learners, an additional experiment with a larger number of subjects was performed. Instead of collecting verbal protocols, a large number of generated examples and sentences were analyzed in this experiment. Also, a more sophisticated counterbalancing scheme was used, but in all other respects the experiment was identical to the previous one.

From text to examples   From examples to text

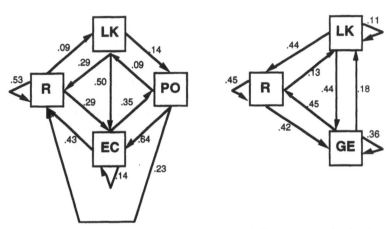

FIG. 9.1. Conditional transition frequencies between verbalization categories in the two material transformation tasks.

9.2 Experiment 7

This experiment was identical to experiment 6, except that no think-aloud instructions were given and that a larger number of subjects was run.

Method

Subjects. Ninety-five students from the University of Freiburg were paid to participate in the experiment.

Procedure. The study was performed as a group experiment with up to 20 subjects per session. Each subject had to perform a sentences-to-examples and an examples-to-sentences transformation task. Two different LISP functions (FIRST and LIST) were employed. The LISP functions (FIRSTor LIST), the particular tasks, and the order of presentations were counterbalanced across subjects. Constrained by these restrictions, each subject was randomly assigned to one of four conditions.

Results

The collected data were analyzed in several different ways. First, the relative frequencies of correctly generated items (sentences or examples) is reported. The quality of the generated sentences was then assessed by distinguishing between abstract statements that described a general characteristic of a LISP function (e.g., the number or type of arguments) and purely descriptive statements about a specific LISP example. Finally, for each subject, the KIWi model was applied to the examples that were generated by this subject. Thereby, it could be diagnosed which template a subject had generated from the text and what the specific difficulties were in understanding the text.

The correctness of the generated examples and sentences was scored in the following way. Each example was submitted to the LISP system. An example was then scored to be correct when its input was syntactically correct as determined by a LISP interpreter and its output was identical to the respective output of the LISP interpreter (i.e., the example was also semantically correct). A generated sentence was considered correct when the sentence made a true statement about the particular LISP function and stated a characteristic of the LISP function or when it just described the particular example.

TABLE 9.7

Relative Frequencies of the Different Types of Sentences and Examples That Were Generated in the Two Transformation Tasks for Two LISP Functions

	Generated Items					
	Sentences				Examples	
	Abstract Correct	Abstract Wrong	Specific Correct	Specific Wrong	Completely Correct	Only Input Correct
FIRST	.59	.20	.12	.04	.31	.14
LIST	.65	.15	.04	.07	.19	.04

Note. There were examples and sentences that could not be clearly classified. These items account for the fact that the sum of the relative frequencies is less than 1.

Two separate 2×2 ANOVAs with the factors "task demand" (generalizing specific examples vs. instantiating general statements) and "presentation order" (initially generalizing specific examples vs. initially instantiating general statements) and the correctness of the generated item as a dependent measure showed that generating examples was more difficult than generating sentences (for the function FIRST: $F(1,91) = 14.44$, $MS_e = 1.01$, $p < .0001$; for the function LIST: $F(1,91) = 51.17$, $MS_e = .87$, $p < .0001$), whereas neither "presentation order" nor the interaction effect were significant ($F < 1$). It is suspected that for solving the more difficult task of generating examples, prior domain knowledge may play a more important role. This hypothesis was hinted at by several analyses in which the very limited computer experience (some word processing) that some subjects had was used to differentiate the subjects with computer experience from the subjects without any prior computer experience.

For the generated sentences, it was then determined which sentences made a statement about a LISP function in general (i.e., abstract statements) and which sentences simply described some aspect of a specific LISP example. Respective relative frequencies were then calculated. The results are shown in Table 9.7. From this table, it can be seen that all relative frequencies clearly differ from 0. Therefore it may again be concluded that specific examples can be correctly derived from general statements and general statements can be correctly inferred from a sequence of specific examples. The subjects were thus capable of performing the transformation processes that were postulated by the KIWi model when they were explicitly instructed to do so.

The results of Table 9.7 also show that subjects made many mistakes and that they are by no means as perfect as the computer runs of the KIWi model. The examples and sentences of the study were designed so that the subjects would infer specific sentences and examples. Overall, none of the general correct sentences was verbatim identical to the predicted sentences, but about 10% carried the same meaning as the predicted sentences. We have thus shown that we can specify a list of examples so that some predetermined sentence can be derived from it by subjects with some given prior domain knowledge. Similarly, a list of sentences can be constructed so that some predetermined examples can be derived from it.

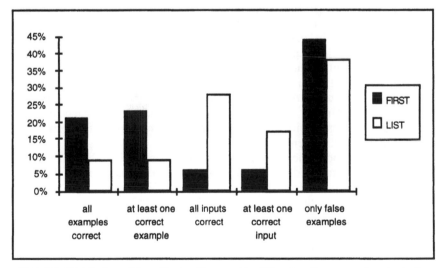

FIG. 9.2. Distribution of the subjects with respect to different performance categories in the example generation task.

In order to analyze how well individual subjects were able to operationalize the information that was presented by the sentences, we submitted the set of up to 5 examples that were generated by a subject to the KIWi program and determined the template that the subject had supposedly formed. For 65% of the subjects, a single template was sufficient to subsume all the examples they had generated. The other 35 % of the subjects generated a larger variety of examples and two different templates were required to characterize the set of generated examples. For the function FIRST, 52 different templates were obtained. Because there were approximately 220 examples generated, the KIWi model allowed us to qualitatively characterize the subjects by classifying each subject into a category. The subjects were then further grouped into the following five categories: (a) Subjects who generated only correct examples, (b) subjects who generated at least one completely correct example, (c) subjects whose generated input to the LISP interpreter were all correct, but the output was erroneous, (d) subjects who generated at least one correct input to the LISP interpreter, and (e) subjects whose generated inputs were all incorrect. Figure 9.2 shows how the subjects were distributed across these five different categories for the two LISP functions FIRST and LIST.

Discussion

The examples and the sentences were constructed so that, with the knowledge obtained from the preceding learning material, the simulation program could construct the specific examples from the sentences and vice versa. Subjects were then similarly asked to generate sentences from examples as well as to generate examples form sentences. The experimental results showed that some subjects were quite successful in generating the predicted sentences and the predicted examples. These subjects performed transformation processes whose results correspond to the result of the transformation processes of the simulation model. It was also found that there are many possibilities for making mistakes in this transformation task and there were large differences in the performance of the various subjects. Unlike the simulation program, which executes the transformation processes reliably, subjects made several types of mistakes — errors in syntax as well as semantic errors.

Concerning methodological issues, it was furthermore shown how the KIWi model may be employed for assessing an individual's capability of operationalizing abstract information. By using the KIWi model as a tool for analyzing the examples that were generated by an individual, each individual could be grouped into one of several categories. Supposedly, each category corresponds to a certain configuration of capabilities. Further research would be required for determining the reliability and validity of this assessment procedure.

9.3 General Discussion

Somewhat similar to our juxtaposition of a set of sentences and a set of examples, Larkin and Simon (1987) distinguished between *sentential* and *diagrammatic* representations of information. Their sentential representation corresponds to the sentences of a natural language description. Their diagrammatic representation corresponds to the components of a diagram. They also developed respective models of information-processing systems that were denoted as sentential and diagrammatic. These systems consisted of the particular representation together with the programs that operated on them to make new inferences. Larkin and Simon designed their two information-processing systems to be *informationally equivalent*, in the sense that everything that was explicitly or implicitly contained in the one system was also explicitly or implicitly contained in the other system. The essential difference between the two systems was what exactly was explicit in a representation and what had to be inferred by the programs (i.e., what was only implicitly contained in the representation).

The two systems (sentential and diagrammatic) were therefore only notational variants of the same knowledge. Sentences and diagrams are thus viewed as denoting the same reality, using different notations. A simple example may clarify this assessment. Assume that you wanted to express the knowledge about two facts a and b. In one system, you would explicitly represent a, together with a program that will infer b from a (i. e., by: $a \rightarrow b$). In the other system, you would explicitly represent b, together with a program that will infer a from b (i.e., $b \rightarrow a$). Both systems are informationally equivalent. Because of the notational differences, the first system provides an easier access to a, whereas b has to be inferred. For the second system, it is the other way around.

In the very same manner, Larkin and Simon showed that in diagrammatic representations the needed information is often explicit at a single location. Therefore, a diagram is (sometimes) worth 10,000 words. Representational formats (such as sentential and diagrammatic representations) thus differ in what is explicitly stated by them and what remains implicit. A "diagrammatic representation preserves explicitly the information about the topological and geometric relations among the components of the problem, while the sentential representation does not." (Larkin & Simon, 1987, p. 66).

Larkin and Simon's analyses were strictly guided by the representational view of knowledge and the strong version of the physical symbol system hypothesis (cf. section 1.1). They could consequently only deal with closed and firmly represented segments of reality, which do not leave any room for creative knowledge-acquisition processes. In Larkin and Simon's systems, everything that can possibly be known must already be explicitly or implicitly contained in the diagram or the sentences. In the KIWi model, knowledge acquisition is not only the storage of information. The representational view of knowledge may be appropriate as far as the material-related knowledge representations, namely the textbase and template base, are concerned. At least at the situational level, knowledge acquisition is viewed as a creative process in the KIWi model. We have therefore used the situation model as a criterion for the equivalence between different learning materials. A situation model is the product of creative knowledge-construction processes. These construction processes exploit environmental affordances and make circumstantial inferences that are implicitly present in the given learning situation. By a context-sensitive constraint-satisfaction process, a person's prior knowledge is attuned to the newly constructed knowledge rather than giving precedence to the more formal principles of inference generation. A situation model is thereby formed as the goal driven attunement of the learner's prior knowledge and the learning materials.

9.4 Summary

In this chapter we have continued our investigations of the knowledge construction processes that operate on different learning materials. Whereas the experiments of the previous chapter had subjects acquire knowledge from the different materials, the current experiments required subjects to derive specific examples from the general statements of a text and to infer general sentences from specific examples. In one condition, subjects were presented with exactly those sentences that according to the model, were sufficient for generating specific examples. In the other condition, subjects were presented with a selection of examples that, according to the model, were sufficient for generating the general statements. These two experimental conditions were used in both experiments of this chapter. Experiment 6 employed a think-aloud method. It was predicted that the same type of verbalizations and transitions would be obtained in this transformation task as in the knowledge acquisition task that was studied in the previous chapter. Although there were some differences in detail, the observed verbalizations were, in general, consistent with the experimental predictions. Our analysis of the verbalizations also demonstrated which knowledge construction processes are performed under the two different task demands. Experiment 7 used a larger sample of subjects for the same tasks but did not employ a think-aloud method. A larger sample of generated sentences and examples could thus be analyzed. Thereby it was found that subjects make a variety of creative errors in these tasks and that there are systematic interindividual differences. Furthermore, it was demonstrated how the KIWi model can be applied to assess a person's capability of operationalizing abstract information for specific circumstances. In the general discussion, it was pointed out how the present definition of informational equivalence differs from a previously used definition. In the next chapter it is be researched how prior domain knowledge affects the acquisition of knowledge from different types and different combinations of learning materials.

10

The Effect of Prior Knowledge on Learning From Different Types of Materials

---

In order to develop and experimentally evaluate the KIWi model, we applied the levels approach towards cognitive modelling that was introduced in chapter 3. Following this approach, we first identified the central properties of the model (a kind of signature of the model in terms of a knowledge-level description) and subsequently tailored experimental designs so that these experiments would quite directly assess each of these *signature assumptions* as well as their relation to one another. Thereby, we also employed *symbol-level* descriptions that reified and refined the characterization at the knowledge level in the form of information-processing mechanisms.

Of course, one could conceive many other independent variables, measures, and designs that could somehow be related to the KIWi model and could therefore also be used to empirically test the model (especially when additional theoretical or technical assumptions are independently introduced for different experiments, as is often done in experimental psychology). According to traditional views of experimental psychology, such experiments are similarly valuable for testing a theory or model. Indeed, in experimental psychology, there are often discussions about subordinate technical issues, such as whether *independent free associations* to several key words or *association chains* from a single key word, would be the correct technique to empirically determine a subject's memory structure (cf. McNamara, 1994) when *spreading activation theories* (Anderson, 1983) are empirically tested against their competitors such as *compound cue theories* (Ratcliff & McKoon, 1988, 1994).

We believe that jumbling different levels of granularity and mixing technicalities with fundamental issues is a counterproductive research methodology for experimental psychology, especially when a competitive comparison of different theories is conducted. The levels approach towards cognitive modelling is basically the proposal of introducing more systematicity in developing, testing, and unifying theories of cognition. By introducing different levels of concern, the theoretical constructs as well as the empirical variables are ordered according to their significance for the development and evaluation of models of cognition (see Fig. 3.2). With the levels approach towards cognitive modelling, we are, a priori, explicit about which variables are of a more fundamental concern when testing the model, and that all other variables will be assigned a subordinate status. The subordinate variables are only used to empirically examine refinements of the signature assumptions (rather than as a means for testing and empirically rejecting the signature assumptions themselves). These methodological issues are further discussed in chapters 12 and 13.

Using the knowledge-level description of the KIWi model (i.e., the C–I theory), *processing goals, learning materials*, and *prior knowledge*, as well as the *construction and integration skills* that yield *pluralistic views* and *situation oriented circumscriptions* in the form of *multilevel representations* were identified as the *signature assumptions* of the model (see Fig. 4.2). The experiments that were reported in chapters 7, 8, and 9 confirmed the signature assumptions concerning processing goals, learning materials, multilevel representations, and how they become related by the construction and integration skills, as well as several subordinate refinements of the model. In the present chapter we turn to the remaining central issue of the model, namely the effect of prior knowledge on knowledge acquisition and its relation to the different types of learning materials (learning from text, from examples, and by exploration).

Previous research on the effect of prior knowledge was mostly concerned with the investigation of memory and performance. This research on expert–novice differences has generally shown that experts possess a large body of domain-specific knowledge that functions as an encoding and retrieval structure for memorizing (Chase & Simon, 1973; Ericsson & Chase, 1982; Schneider, Körkel, & Weinert, 1989) and for solving the problems that are typical for the particular subject domain (e.g., Novick, 1988; Novick & Holyoak, 1991). Expert memory and expert performance was thus explained by postulating that experts have acquired a large vocabulary of domain-specific schemata, which would impose the right structure for encoding and remembering information as well as for decomposing and solving problems. Expertise was also assumed to be quite specific to the particular experiences of the expert. Whereas both adolescent and adult chess experts have an excellent memory for chess-board constellations from real games, their memory for random chess-board constellations is much closer to the memory of novices (Ericsson & Kintsch, 1995; Schneider, Gruber, Gold, & Opwis, 1993).

In this research we are interested in knowledge acquisition. We are, therefore, not so much concerned about how subjects encode and remember specific instances (e.g., a particular chess-board constellation or a particular computer program), but instead we are more interested in how subjects acquire knowledge and competence in a new domain (e.g., how they learn a new programming language). The expert subjects of the experiments that are reported in this chapter are therefore a priori not at all knowledgeable about the specific programming language (i.e., LISP), but have previously worked with computers and other programming languages (such as PASCAL, BASIC, and FORTRAN). The expert subjects therefore are also called computer users, and the other subjects who have not had any experiences with computers are called novices. Because LISP differs from these other programming languages by its programming style (a functional versus an imperative programming style), the underlying programming structures are quite different. Indeed, it is often believed that knowledge of one of these traditional programming languages (PASCAL, BASIC, or FORTRAN) would hinder the learning of LISP (cf. Winston, 1984). Any advantages that computer users may have in learning LISP cannot therefore simply be explained by assuming that they would possess a certain schema that facilitates the structuring and encoding of the new programming constructs. Instead, we postulate that the computer users possess domain-related knowledge construction processes that together with the integration processes, yield an appropriate domain-specific model of the new subject domain. Therefore, domain-specific schemata do not preexist in memory, but such structures are dynamically formed by domain-related knowledge-construction and integration processes.

In the area of text comprehension, it has recently been debated how much inferencing and knowledge construction is being performed during knowledge acquisition. According to the *minimalist position* (McKoon & Ratcliff, 1992), the only tinferences are assumed to be routinely generated during reading are those that are based on information that is quickly and easily available, and those that are required to make a propositional textbasc locally coherent. The *constructionist position* (Graesser, Singer, & Trabasso, 1994), on the other hand, emphasizes that readers would often perform global inferences and establish a referential situation model of what the text is about. For the purpose of the current chapter, we propose a unification of these two controversial positions by assuming that whether or not subjects are minimalist or constructionist depends on whether or not sufficient prior domain knowledge is easily available to the reader. In general terms, we would thus predict that the novices behave more according to the minimalist position and the computer users behave more according to the constructionist position.

This general prediction and related predictions were tested in three experiments in which novices and computer users acquired knowledge about a new programming language (i.e., LISP) from different types of learning materials. In experiment 8, the subjects acquired knowledge either from text or from examples. In experiment 9, the subjects acquired knowledge from a combination of text and examples, and the order of presentation was manipulated. The text was either presented before the examples or the examples were presented before the text. In experiment 10, learning from examples was compared to learning by exploration. By a combined consideration of the three experiments we can thus evaluate the effect of prior knowledge on the three types of learning situations, as well as on their combination (text and examples). The experimental procedures were identical to the procedures used in previous experiments (cf. experiment 4) and time-course characteristics were collected. The particular process dissociation method was again employed so that the memory strength of textbase, template base, and situation model could be separately assessed. For selected test items, the verification latencies of expert and novice subjects were also compared to one another. Thereby, the relative amount of processing at study and at test time could be compared between the expert and the novice subjects.

The following predictions were derived from the KIWi model. In learning from text as well as in learning from examples, the expert subjects will be more successful in developing a situation model, but there will be no substantial differences in the formation of textbase and template base. Whereas learning by exploration will yield better learning results in expert subjects, learning from demonstrations will be better suited to novices. Because the material-appropriate construction processes (cf. McDaniel, Einstein, Dunay, & Cobb, 1986) of text and examples supplement each other, the combination of text and examples may at least (partially) compensate for the lack of prior domain knowledge. It is therefore predicted that the expert–novice differences that are predicted for the acquisition of knowledge from a single learning material (text or example) will be quite diminished when a combination of text and examples is employed.

10.1 Experiment 8

This experiment examined the effect of prior domain knowledge on the formation of text representation, template base, and situation model when either a text or examples were used as learning materials. The same learning materials were used as in experiment 4, except that the description of the function schema was eliminated. Thereby, the effect of prior domain knowledge could be examined. Unlike the novices, subjects with prior programming experience already possess domain-related knowledge and would therefore execute more situation-adequate knowledge-construction processes during learning. Leaving out the description of the function schema from the learning materials should therefore hardly affect the learning of the computer users. They should still be able to form an adequate situation model from text as well as from examples.

The novices, on the other hand, should show a clear deterioration in the formation of a situation model, because they now lack some prerequisite knowledge for building the situation model. Text representation and template base, on the other hand, should be about equally well-constructed by all subjects. In this experiment, there was no combination condition. Subjects acquired knowledge about the four LISP functions either from a text or from examples.

Method

Subjects. 79 students of the University of Freiburg who did not have any knowledge about LISP participated in this study and were paid for their participation. 40 students who are subsequently called "novices" had no previous programming experience at all. The remaining 39 students, who are subsequently called computer users, had about 1.5 years of programming experience in programming languages other than LISP (e.g., PASCAL, COBOL, BASIC, etc.).

Design. As in experiment 4, each of the two learning phases was followed by a test phase. In the second learning phase, the 40 novices and the 39 computer users were randomly assigned to one of the two experimental conditions. A 2×2 between-subject group design was used with the factors learning condition (text or examples) and prior knowledge (novices or computer users). There were 19 computer users in the text-learning condition, whereas the remaining three subject groups consisted of 20 students each.

TABLE 10.1

Presentation Order of the Examples That was Determined by the KIWi Model to be Optimal for Avoiding Over-Generalizations in Novices

(FIRST '(A B))	->	A
(FIRST '((A B) C))	->	(A B)
(FIRST 'A 'B)	->	ERROR
FIRST '(A B)	->	ERROR
(FIRST '(A (B C)))	->	A
(FIRST (A B))	->	ERROR
(FIRST '((A B) (C D)))	->	(A B)
(FIRST 'A)	->	ERROR
(FIRST '(A))	->	A
(FIRST (A 'B))	->	ERROR
(FIRST (FIRST '((A B) C)))	->	A
(FIRST '(FIRST ((A B) C)))	->	FIRST

Materials. The same materials were used as in experiment 4 with the following exceptions: (a) In the first learning phase, the paragraph that induced the function schema was omitted in order to test the influence of prior knowledge; (b) In the text of the second learning phase, the paragraph that explained the quote was shown before the paragraphs about the four functions; (c) In order to avoid overgeneralizations of the templates built by the subjects, the positive and negative examples were presented in an order determined by the KIWi model to be optimal for novices (see Table 10.1); (d) Because the test examples in experiment 4 had been too difficult for all subjects, the FC-, Q-, and D-examples were simplified, and four IO-examples and four L- examples were added.

Procedure. The same procedure was used as in experiment 4 with the following exceptions: (a) In this experiment, the materials were shown item (sentence or example) by item and each item could only be studied once, but for as long as the students wished. Unlike experiment 4, reading time was therefore not a controlled but a dependent measure. (b) In the sentence and example verification tasks of the second test phase, the same tapping speed–accuracy trade-off method was used, except that for each item an additional response was required. This was achieved by adding a double tone as an additional response signal to the end of the previously used response signals. The subjects were instructed that after this double tone, they had as much time available as they wanted for one final decision about the correctness of the presented item. There was consequently no time pressure for this last response and the respective response latencies may therefore be quite informative. In summary, the subjects thus judged each item 6 times in a row: one guess, four fast responses, and one final response without time pressure. The responses, their latencies, and the confidence ratings (which the subjects expressed by the duration of their button presses) were collected as dependent measures.

Results[8]

In reporting the experimental results, we proceed from presenting summary results to analyses that are directly motivated by the assumptions of the KIWi model and by more specific research questions. An analysis of the study times showed that the examples were studied longer than the text, $F(1,75) = 73.75$; $MS_e = 68735$; $p < .001$. Although computer users studied somewhat faster (5.55 min. for text and 14.41 min. for examples) than novices (8.04 min. for text and 16.15 min. for examples), this effect was only marginally significant, $F(1,75) = 3.17$; $MS_e = 68735$; $p < .10$. There was no interaction.

Table 10.2 shows the various descriptive statistics for the final responses to each test item (i.e., the responses that were probed by the double tone) from the sentence verification tasks. For the different experimental conditions and the four different types of test sentences (O-, P-, M-, and C- sentences), the relative frequency of correct responses, the average confidence ratings, the average correctness rating, and the average response latencies are shown. The correctness ratings were calculated in exactly the same manner as in experiment 4 (see section 8.1). As the reader may remember, the correctness ratings are obtained by a well-motivated concatenation of the subjects' yes/no responses with the corresponding confidence rating.

In addition to the four different types of test sentences, the dependent measures were calculated for those test sentences, that were presented at the very beginning of the sentence verification tasks. These sentences are the least influenced by additional learning processes that could occur during the test phase. Later on, we

---

[8] In all statistical analyses, Greenhouse-Geisser adjusted-alpha levels are reported whenever a nonhomogeneity of variances is detected.

use the response latencies to these initial test items to determine whether the different learning conditions and the two subject groups are differentially prepared for the sentence and example verification tasks.

TABLE 10.2

Four Performance Measures for the Two Learning Conditions, the Two Subject Groups, and for the Four Sentence Types, as Well as the Initial Test Sentences

			Sentence Type		
Condition	Initial	Original	Paraphrased	Meaning-changed	Correctness-changed
Relative Frequencies of Correct Responses					
Text					
Novices	0.70	0.94	0.81	0.72	0.47
Computer users	0.82	0.93	0.89	0.83	0.70
Examples					
Novices	0.65	0.71	0.72	0.74	0.52
Computer users	0.76	0.77	0.89	0.75	0.67
Average Confidence Ratings					
Text					
Novices	7.02	7.71	7.45	7.11	6.86
Computer users	7.37	7.46	7.16	7.00	7.30
Examples					
Novices	6.77	6.60	6.63	6.90	7.45
Computer users	7.42	7.41	7.13	6.95	7.36
Average Correctness Ratings					
Text					
Novices	2.90	6.46	4.22	2.56	0.11
Computer users	4.63	6.38	5.87	4.61	-2.80
Examples					
Novices	2.63	3.27	3.05	2.97	-0.63
Computer users	3.35	3.84	5.32	3.15	-2.06
Average Latencies in sec.					
Text					
Novices	10.92	10.01	10.65	11.42	10.06
Computer users	9.77	9.38	11.26	12.14	10.36
Examples					
Novices	15.81	14.70	13.81	14.48	12.45
Computer users	12.21	12.15	11.54	11.53	10.88

Note: The response latencies were measured from the onset of the test item and are therefore relatively long.

From the mean correctness ratings for the novices (3.28 in text condition, 2.48 in example condition) and the computer users (4.91 in text condition, 3.59 in example condition), it can be seen that the text condition performed better than the example condition and that the computer users performed better than the novices. A 2 × 2 ANOVA confirmed this observation. There were significant main effects for the learning condition, $F(1,75) = 6.20$; $MS_e = 3.45$; $p < .05$, and for prior knowledge, $F(1,75) = 10.50$; $MS_e = 3.45$; $p < .01$. The interaction was not significant. The better performance for the subjects of the text condition is explained by the model predictions: Subjects who studied text can utilize the situation model as well as the text representation for sentence verification, whereas the subjects of the example condition can at best utilize the situation model. In general, the results of the sentence verification tasks thus show that the computer users performed better than the novices and that subjects who learned from text performed better than the subjects who learned from examples. It can thus be concluded that prior programming knowledge was indeed helpful for learning LISP, even though the programming constructs of LISP are quite different from the programming constructs of the traditional languages that the computer users had previously learned.

Table 10.3 shows the respective measures for the example verification tasks. From the mean correctness ratings for the novices (2.67 in text condition, 2.80 in example condition) and the computer users (2.86 in text condition, 3.91 in example condition), it can be seen that again the congruent learning condition (learning from examples) performed (somewhat) better than the incongruent learning condition (learning from text), although, in this case, the learning condition failed to yield a significant result, $F(1,75) = 3.59$; $MS_e = 1.94$; $p < .10$. In general, the results are, however, quite similar to the sentence verification tasks where learning from text had been the congruent learning condition and learning from examples the incongruent learning condition. This congruency effect needs to be explained. The KIWi model accounts for the congruency effect quite nicely by the material-specific contributions of the intermediate knowledge representations (textbase and template base, respectively). And again, the computer users performed better than the novices, $F(1,75) = 4.46$; $MS_e = 1.94$; $p < .05$. There was no interaction effect.

In order to assess the strengths of the various knowledge representations and to thereby test the predictions of the KIWi model more directly, further analyses were performed that are reported in the following three subsections. We proceed in the same manner as in chapter 8. In the subsection on *asymptotic representation strengths*, the process dissociation procedures are applied to the final decisions (i.e., the ones that were probed by the double tone) and the asymptotic representation strengths of text representation (verbatim and propositional combined), situation model and template base will thereby be determined. In the subsection on the *time course of knowledge utilization,* we perform more detailed analyses of the complete speed–accuracy trade-off functions. In the subsection on the *processing times for the initial items*, an analysis of how much relevant preprocessing of possible test items may already have occurred in the knowledge acquisition phase is performed.

TABLE 10.3

Four Performance Measures for the Two Learning Conditions, the Two Subject Groups, for the Four Example Types, and the Initial Examples.

Condition	Example Type				
	Initial Example	Basic I/O-Relation	Argument Structure	Argument specification	Function combination
Relative Frequencies of Correct Responses					
Text					
Novices	0.75	0.86	0.55	0.62	0.72
Computer users	0.86	0.94	0.61	0.56	0.79
Examples					
Novices	0.84	0.90	0.58	0.63	0.77
Computer users	0.90	0.92	0.72	0.68	0.86
Average Confidence Ratings					
Text					
Novices	6.19	7.39	6.37	6.94	6.77
Computer users	5.99	6.61	5.92	5.88	5.97
Examples					
Novices	6.51	6.23	6.04	5.81	5.77
Computer users	6.45	6.75	6.32	6.54	6.27
Average Correctness Ratings					
Text					
Novices	3.29	5.63	0.52	1.47	3.06
Computer users	4.78	5.99	1.55	0.12	3.76
Examples					
Novices	4.34	5.02	1.16	1.86	3.17
Computer users	5.27	5.67	2.88	2.37	4.72
Average Latencies in sec.					
Text					
Novices	25.42	19.51	22.88	23.93	23.65
Computer users	21.85	19.75	23.20	24.32	26.21
Examples					
Novices	21.96	19.63	21.93	21.48	22.20
Computer users	20.49	20.06	24.42	22.55	23.09

Asymptotic Representation Strengths. The final decisions were used for determining the asymptotic representation strengths. From the pairs of correctness ratings of the O- and M-sentences, the M- and C-sentences, and the S- and FC-examples, measures for the strength of the text representation, template base, and the situation model were calculated in exactly the same way that was previously described. The measure for the template base was computed from the difference between the S-examples (which were identical to the S-examples in experiment 4) and the FC-examples (which were examples with function combinations of two different, rather than three identical, functions). The resulting representation strengths are shown in Fig. 10.1 as the rightmost data points of the time-course characteristics. A $2 \times 2 \times 3$ ANOVA with the factors learning condition, prior knowledge, and type of representation showed differences for prior knowledge, $F(1,75) = 6.27$; $MS_e = 13.52$; $p < .05$, as well as differences for the type of representation, $F(2,150) = 9.43$; $MS_e = 20.37$; $p < .001$. The interaction between prior knowledge and representation type, $F(2,150) = 4.15$; $MS_e = 20.37$; $p = .025$, was also significant, whereas the interaction between the learning condition and the representation type $F(2,150) = 3.03$; $MS_e = 20.37$; $p < .10$, was only marginally significant.

An important result from this analysis is that the computer users have a stronger situation model than the novices. The situation model and the template base were stronger than the text representation. The interaction between prior knowledge and representation is due to the computer users' stronger situation model. There is no substantial difference between novices and computer users in the strengths of the text representation and the template base. Finally, the interaction between learning condition and representation type is explained in a straightforward manner by the stronger text representation that results in learning from text, whereas there is no difference in the strengths of the templatebase and the situation model between text and example condition.

Prior domain knowledge is thus most important for the formation of the situation model and textbase and template base are hardly affected by a lack of prior knowledge. Although novices and computer users build the more peripheral representations about equally well, there are clear differences in the situation model. In other words, the novices represent more at the material-related levels, and the representation of the computer users is dominated by the situation model. A somewhat surprising but interesting result is that the computer programmers who studied text showed almost as strong a template base as the subjects (novices and computer users) who studied examples. This finding indicates that computer users may already prepare for writing computer programs when they study a text and thus already form a (partial) template base, whereas the novices who study text do not prepare in this manner for possible future tasks.

Time Course of Knowledge Utilization. The data from the tapping speed–accuracy trade-off method provides information about the degree to which a specific representation became involved during the different phases of the verification process. From the point of view of the C–I theory and the KIWi model, these data can tell us what the results of the integration process are at different processing stages. The various representation strengths were therefore also computed for the different processing times. The results are shown in Fig. 10.1. Because statistical analyses of the effects of the learning conditions and the learner's prior knowledge reported in the previous section, we now only report the statistical results that involve the factor of processing time.

Text Representation. A $2 \times 2 \times 5$ ANOVA of the strength values for the textbase with the factors learning condition, prior knowledge, and processing time revealed only the processing time to be significant, $F(4,296) = 8.36$; $MS_e = 7.26$; $p < .001$. In all conditions, there was some increase in the strength of the text representation during the first five seconds, and an asymptote was reached at a relatively low level.

Template Base. A $2 \times 2 \times 5$ ANOVA of the strength values for the template base with the factors learning condition, prior knowledge, and processing times showed also a significant effect of processing time, $F(4,300) = 15.02$; $MS_e = 6.08$; $p < .001$. For the template base, there was a relatively steady increase of the strength values up to the last response.

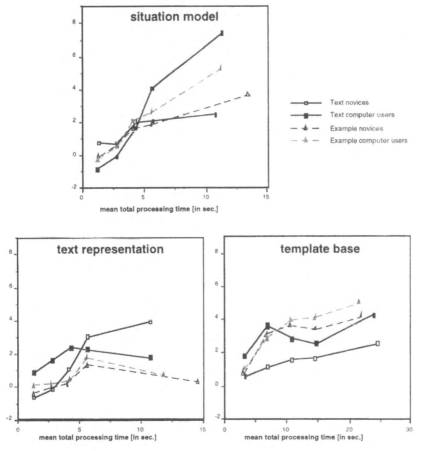

FIG. 10.1. Utilized memory strengths of the three different representations for the two different learning conditions and the two subject groups.

Situation model: A $2 \times 2 \times 5$ ANOVA of the strength values for the situation model revealed a difference for processing time, $F(4,296) = 28.22$; $MS_e = 9.71$; $p < .001$, and a prior knowledge by processing time interaction, $F(4,296)$

$= 5.44$; $MS_e = 9.71$; $p < .005$. For the situation model, there was a steady increase of the strength values until the last decision. In relation to the novices, the rate of the increase was much greater toward the end for the computer users, thus yielding a significant interaction.

The time-course characteristics that are shown in Fig. 10.1 can be quite directly interpreted in terms of the spreading activation process of the model. For the computer users the activation spreads rather quickly through the text representation and finally settles on the situation model. For the novices, on the other hand, the activation spreads much slower at the text representation and it remains more in the text representation and there is only little spread to the situation level. For the template base, activation spreads quite early for all conditions, except for the novices who learned from text. Their increase of activation is quite slow and the activation stays mostly at the level of the text representation.

Processing Times of the Initial Test Items. An interesting result that confirms the processing assumptions of the KIWi model was obtained for the four initial sentences of the sentence verification task. According to the model, the subjects who learned from examples have no text representation available and must therefore derive from the situation model whether or not a test sentence is correct, which requires additional processing time. Subjects who learned from text, on the other hand, may match a test sentence to their textbase and thus require less time. An even stronger prediction may be obtained for the processing of the first four examples in the example verification task. For the subjects who learned from examples, these examples are redundant because similar examples have been presented in their learning phase. In the text condition, on the other hand, these are the first examples that are presented. The subjects of the text condition must therefore construct templates from these examples and would consequently take longer than the subjects of the example condition who can utilize the previously constructed templates. By assuming that the expert subjects would be better able to operationalize the newly acquired knowledge for the anticipated test tasks during knowledge acquisition, we furthermore predict that this congruency effect between learning and test materials would be smaller for the expert subjects. The mean latencies for the last decision for the verification of the initial sentences and examples (as measured from the double tone) are shown in Fig. 10.2.

A $2 \times 2 \times 2$ ANOVA with the factors learning condition, prior knowledge, and type of test item (sentence or example verification) revealed differences for prior knowledge, $F(1,75) = 7.79$; $MS_e = 30.22$; $p < .01$, type of test item, $F(1,75) = 3.99$; $MS_e = 10.28$; $p < .05$, and a highly significant learning condition by test item interaction, $F(1,75) = 35.86$; $MS_e = 10.28$; $p < .001$. The three-way interaction was also significant, $F(1,75) = 4.96$; $MS_e = 10.28$; $p < .05$. These results clearly confirm the predictions from the model. The congruency effect is clearly supported by the learning condition by test item interaction. Because there was no overall effect of learning condition, it is clear that each learning condition prepares specifically for one type of test task. The overall effect of prior knowledge shows again that the computer users performed better than the novices. The three-way interaction confirmed that the congruency effect is smaller for the expert subjects than for the novices. Expert subjects are thus less dependent on the specific study material than are novices.

The same analyses were performed for the correctness ratings. Here, the observed interaction between learning condition and type of test item vanished, leaving only an effect of prior knowledge, $F(1,75) = 4.48$; $MS_e = 13.02$; $p <$ .05, and type of test task, $F(1,75) = 4.48$; $MS_e = 9.79$; $p < .05$ (examples being easier to verify than sentences). A simple trade-off between allocated processing time and correctness of the response can therefore be excluded in our interpretation of the latency data.

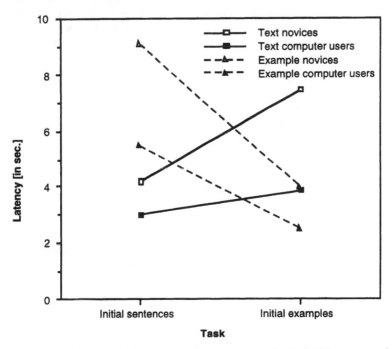

FIG. 10.2. Response latencies of the novices and computer users for the initial sentence and example verification tasks and the two learning conditions.

Discussion

The experimental results confirmed the predictions of the KIWi model in several different ways. It was shown that prior knowledge about a related but different subject domain (e.g., a different type of programming language) is quite useful when learning a new subject domain (e.g., the programming language LISP) even when there are no fixed schemata that could be directly used for encoding the new knowledge. Such prior knowledge yields additional knowledge-construction processes that help to form an appropriate situation model. The knowledge representations of the computer users are thus quite adequately described by the constructionist position, where the learners are assumed to establish a referential situation model that requires global inferences. The analysis of response latencies furthermore showed that the expert subjects would establish such global inferences at the time of knowledge acquisition rather than at test time. The knowledge representations of the novices, on the other hand, may be closer to the assumptions of a minimalist position. They built a coherent text representation but failed to perform more global inferences and establish an appropriate situation model. When more constructive inferences were required at test time, they performed such constructive processes, as indicated by longer response latencies. Due to their prior knowledge, expert subjects are thus more successful in preparing for future unknown test tasks than novice subjects. The time-course characteristics of the verification tasks furthermore showed how activation spreads differently among text and situation nodes in computer users and novices.

10.2 Experiment 9

This experiment investigated whether and to what degree additional examples (after studying the text) and additional text (after studying examples) can improve the formation of a situation model in novices and computer users. In all other respects, the experiment was completely identical to the previous one. The same experimental procedures were used and the data were analyzed in exactly the same way as in the previous experiment. Because text and examples have different levels of specificity, their combination may provide a richer set of constraints that may assist the novices in constructing global inferences so that an appropriate situation model could be formed. To a certain degree, the second learning material may thus be a substitute for the prior domain knowledge that is missing in novices.

Method

Subjects and Design. Eighty students were recruited from the same subject populations as in the previous experiment. No subject had had any prior knowledge of LISP. For their participation, subjects received monetary compensation. Half of the subjects were novices and did not have any prior programming experience. The other 40 subjects were computer users and had had about 1.5 years of programming experience. There were two different learning conditions with 20 computer users and 20 novices in each condition: In the first condition, subjects studied text before the examples, whereas in the other condition the order of the materials was reversed.

Materials. The materials in this experiment were identical to the materials of the previous experiment except that in the second learning phase, both the text and the examples were presented for each function. In the text–example condition, the text was presented before the block with the respective examples (see Table 10.1). In the example–text condition, the block of examples was presented before the text.

Results

The examples were again studied for a longer time period than the text. However, neither the subjects' prior knowledge nor the learning condition yielded any significant reading time differences. Quite interesting results were obtained, once we started to use the KIWi model to guide our statistical analyses of the reading times (cf. section 3.2). According to the KIWi model, the sequence of the already presented examples and the knowledge thereby acquired have a definite influence on the knowledge construction processes that are subsequently performed, and on how much new knowledge is thereby constructed. By running the sequence of examples through the knowledge-construction processes of the KIWi model (see Schmalhofer, 1986b), we could thus classify each example on the basis of how much new knowledge may be acquired from it. Thereby, four types of examples were distinguished: new, partially new, redundant, and negative examples.

Because the number of characters differed among the four types of examples, a partial correlation with the number of characters as the independent variable was separately calculated for each example and each subject. The reading-time residuals that were thus obtained were then further analyzed. Figure 10.3 shows the average reading-time residuals for the different experimental conditions and the four types of examples. A subject group-by-learning condition-by-example type ANOVA of the reading time residuals showed a significant difference of the example type, $F(3,228) = 83.32$; $MS_e = 14.76$; $p < .001$, and a significant interaction of example type and learning condition, $F(3,228) = 3.89$; $MS_e = 14.76$; $p < .05$.

Both of these effects were predicted by the model: Because the amount of knowledge construction decreases with the amount of redundancy of an example, the study times should decrease accordingly. When a text is studied in depth so that a situation model is constructed before the examples are presented (as in the computer users), the new examples can also be processed more deeply, yielding longer study times. For those subjects, the partially new examples do not provide any new information and are therefore processed as fast as the redundant examples. For the subjects who have not read any text before the examples, the partially new examples still yield some new information and require longer reading times.

Table 10.4 shows the relative frequencies of correct responses, the average confidence ratings, the average correctness ratings, and the average response latencies for the final responses in the sentence verification tasks. From the mean correctness ratings for the novices (3.52 in the text–example condition, 3.60 in the example–text condition) and the computer users (4.88 in the text–example

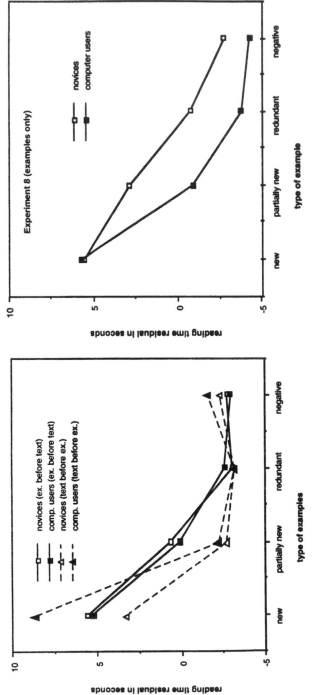

FIG. 10.3. Average reading time residuals for the different types of examples that were defined by simulation runs of the KIWi model and the four different experimental conditions.

condition, 3.50 in the example–text condition) it can be seen that both conditions and both subject groups performed about equally well. This result was also confirmed by a 2 × 2 ANOVA with the factors learning condition and subject group. The interaction effect was not significant.

TABLE 10.4

Four Performance Measures for the Different Experimental Conditions, the Four Sentence Types, and the Initial Sentences

	Sentence Type				
	Initial	Original	Paraphrased	Meaning-changed	Correctness-changed
Condition					
Relative Frequencies of Correct Responses					
Text-Example					
Novices	0.70	0.85	0.80	0.74	0.51
Computer users	0.79	0.94	0.92	0.84	0.67
Example-Text					
Novices	0.71	0.82	0.82	0.70	0.56
Computer users	0.64	0.81	0.84	0.75	0.60
Average Confidence Ratings					
Text-Example					
Novices	7.29	7.67	7.86	7.55	7.77
Computer users	7.05	7.11	7.39	7.26	6.91
Example-Text					
Novices	7.36	7.79	8.10	7.15	7.63
Computer users	7.52	7.02	6.92	6.96	6.84
Average Correctness Ratings					
Text-Example					
Novices	2.79	5.17	4.59	3.77	-0.55
Computer users	4.07	6.26	6.16	4.71	-2.39
Example-Text					
Novices	3.41	5.04	5.32	2.75	-1.30
Computer users	2.05	4.05	4.70	3.41	-1.84
Average Latencies in sec.					
Text-Example					
Novices	12.16	11.90	11.55	11.94	12.13
Computer users	12.25	10.47	10.59	11.36	12.27
Example-Text					
Novices	12.04	11.17	12.04	11.15	12.37
Computer users	12.10	12.06	11.67	12.01	11.93

Table 10.5 shows the respective measures for the example verification tasks. From the mean correctness ratings for the novices (2.75 in the text–example condition, 3.30 in the example–text condition) and the computer users (3.39 in the text–example condition, 3.88 in the example–text condition) it can be seen that again both conditions and both subject groups performed about equally well. A 2 × 2 ANOVA with the factors learning condition and subject group confirmed this observation. The interaction effect was not significant. At this global level,

the results show that being presented with text and examples helps the novices to perform about as well as the computer programmers. For the computer programmers, the second type of material does not yield any further improvement. For them, text by itself or examples by themselves are sufficient for acquiring all the knowledge that is needed. This interpretation can be further tested by the following, more detailed, model-oriented analyses.

TABLE 10.5

Four Performance Measures for the Two Learning Conditions, the Two Subject Groups, the Four Example Types, and the Initial Examples

Condition	Example Type				
	Initial I/O-Relation	Basic Structure	Argument specification	Argument combination	Function
Relative Frequencies of Correct Responses					
Text-Example					
Novices	0.81	0.88	0.60	0.61	0.70
Computer users	0.92	0.96	0.68	0.71	0.86
Example-Text					
Novices	0.86	0.92	0.57	0.67	0.75
Computer users	0.89	0.93	0.71	0.77	0.85
Confidence Ratings					
Text-Example					
Novices	7.51	7.37	6.94	6.94	6.76
Computer users	5.70	5.75	5.56	5.91	5.44
Example-Text					
Novices	6.91	7.25	6.63	6.56	6.39
Computer users	5.90	6.84	5.29	5.77	5.72
Correctness Ratings					
Text-Example					
Novices	4.51	5.47	1.49	1.39	2.63
Computer users	4.85	5.29	2.04	2.51	3.74
Example-Text					
Novices	5.19	6.30	1.18	2.33	3.37
Computer users	4.70	5.97	2.49	3.17	3.89
Latencies in sec.					
Text-Example					
Novices	21.51	19.14	22.01	22.21	23.04
Computer users	21.82	19.29	24.88	23.60	23.10
Example-Text					
Novices	22.80	19.33	22.02	21.56	22.92
Computer users	21.90	19.62	25.68	23.29	23.84

Asymptotic Representation Strengths. The correctness ratings of the final decisions were again used to determine the asymptotic representation strengths of textbase, template base, and situation model. A $2 \times 2 \times 3$ ANOVA with the factors learning condition, prior knowledge, and representation did not show any significant differences except for differences among the three representations,

$F(1,76) = 15.07$; $MS_e = 22.38$; $p < .001$. In all four experimental conditions, the situation model and template base were quite strong and the textbase was relatively weak.

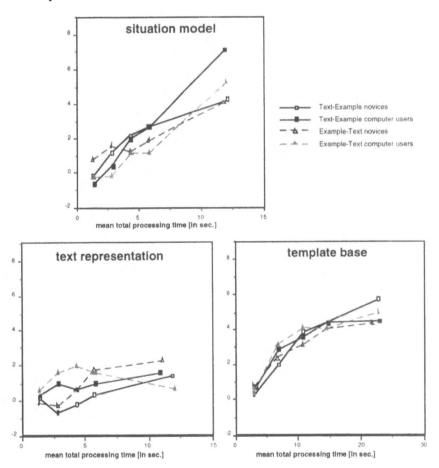

FIG. 10.4. Accuracy scores at different processing times for the three memory representations, the two learning conditions, and the two subject groups.

This result confirms that by being presented with both types of learning materials, even the novices succeeded in forming an appropriate situation model, whereas the computer users could not further improve their situation model by studying a second type of material. Because for the computer users, the two materials were *informationally equivalent*, studying both materials does not yield any further knowledge (cf. combination condition of experiment 4). Because of their lack of prior knowledge, for the novices, the two materials are <u>not</u> *informationally equivalent* . Therefore, the knowledge construction processes that are performed for the text supplement the knowledge construction processes that are performed for the examples. Appropriate and sufficiently many constraints are thus provided for the integration processes to build an adequate situation model.

Time Course of Knowledge Utilization and Processing Times of Initial Test Items. Beause the second learning material was predicted to compensate for the lack of prior knowledge in the novice subjects, and no further improvement is to be expected in the computer users, the various differences that were found in experiment 8 were now expected to be strongly diminished or have vanished altogether. The statistical analyses of the time course of knowledge utilization confirmed these predictions. For the textbase and the template base only the processing time yielded significant differences. For the situation model there was a significant effect of processing time as well as a processing time by prior knowledge interaction, $F(4,304) = 2.33$; $MS_e = 10.02$; $p < .05$.

This interaction effect is due to the computer users showing a larger situational contribution at later processing times and novices showing a comparably large contribution at earlier processing times. Figure 10.4 shows the time-course characteristics for textbase, template base, and situation model. These time-course characteristics may again be used to assess how the specific differences of the multilevel representation network of expert and novice subjects influences the spreading activation in verification tasks at different processing stages.

As expected, the time differences in determining the correctness of the initial examples and sentences also vanished. Because subjects had already studied both materials, there was no difference in the amount of knowledge construction during the test phase. There was no significant difference except for the type of test task, $F(1,76) = 12.94$; $MS_e = 5.88$; $p < .001$.

10.3 Experiment 10

It is well known that more effective learning can be achieved by tailoring the learning episodes to the particular needs of an individual rather than presenting the same sequence of examples to all learners. One way to achieve such an individualization is to simply allow the learners themselves to determine the learning episodes. This can be achieved by having the learners learn by exploration: The learners themselves set their own learning goals according to their specific interests. The advantages of learning by exploration may be due to a number of different factors. Learners can selectively acquire the knowledge that they consider most important. They can be more active and set their own learning goals. In order to achieve their learning goals, they can engage in problem solving. This may lead to procedural and problem-solving oriented knowledge representations that are better suited for solving programming tasks. Successfully solving these problems may be quite motivating for the learner. Because learning by exploration originates from the student's own domain knowledge, the newly acquired knowledge becomes inherently connected and interwoven with the prior knowledge. Because of a kind of generation effect (McDaniel & Waddill, 1990; Slamecka & Graf, 1978), it may therefore be better remembered.

However, each of these advantages may also turn into a disadvantage. A student could have insufficient domain knowledge to set appropriate learning goals. Because of insufficient domain knowledge the students may not be able to determine which knowledge is really important. They may acquire suboptimal procedures for achieving their goals or, in the extreme case may develop no successful procedures at all. Problem solving processes may not always be successfully completed and can be more time consuming than is learning from instructions. This causes frustration for the learner. A student's lack of domain knowledge can thus put severe limitations on what can be learned by exploration.

Although learning by exploration and learning from examples differ in a number of interrelated ways, one difference appears to be most fundamental. Whereas instructional materials such as sequences of examples are determined by the teacher, who is very knowledgeable of the domain, in exploration the learning episodes are generated by the students who know about their particular knowledge desires. The advantages and disadvantages of learner versus teacher-generated learning episodes were investigated in an experiment with 40 computer users and 40 novices.

Method

Subjects. Forty computer users and forty novices were recruited from the same subject populations as in the previous two experiments.

Procedure and Materials. As in the two previous experiments, all subjects were first instructed about the fundamental LISP concepts (atoms and lists). Then they acquired additional knowledge about some simple LISP functions either by exploration or by learning from demonstration examples. In particular, the function FIRST, which extracts the first element from a list, and the function SET, which binds a LISP expression to some symbol, were learned. Simple LISP functions were again used as the learning domain because modularity is a prerequisite for the explorability of a subject domain, and the LISP functions satisfy this requirement.

Exploration Condition. In the exploration condition, the learners could enter LISP expressions with an editor providing help for generating syntactically correct inputs. A specifically designed LISP interpreter (Kühn, 1987; Kühn & Schmalhofer, 1987) evaluated these expressions and gave appropriate feedback. The exploration condition was divided into three blocks. In each block, the subjects were to attend to a different function. In the first and second block, the subjects generated 8 inputs, in the third block they generated 16 inputs. At the beginning of each block, one or two simple meaningful inputs to the LISP system were presented, namely 1. "(FIRST '(A B))", 2. "(FIRST (FIRST '((A B) C)))", 3. "(SET 'FRIENDS '(JACK JOHN)), (FIRST FRIENDS)".

Example Condition. In the example condition, 32 appropriately selected examples were presented. Each block started with the same example that was presented in the exploration condition. In the exploration and example conditions, 32 examples were thus generated or presented. The exploration subjects, who entered the presented inputs, had to create another 28 inputs on their own, whereas the subjects in the example condition were presented with 32 examples and could not generate any examples by themselves.

Programming and Evaluation Tasks. The acquired knowledge of each learner was tested by 10 programming tasks in which the subject had to generate an input to the LISP system in order to obtain some prespecified result. The inputs were evaluated by the LISP interpreter and the result was shown to the subject. If the result of the subject's input was not the result that was to be achieved, the subject was given two more trials to achieve the correct result. (No help information was provided). Thereafter, the subject's knowledge about the LISP system was examined by evaluation tasks, in which inputs to the LISP system were presented, and the subject, rather than the LISP interpreter, had to generate the results. The whole experiment took between 1.25 and 3 hours. A preliminary report of this experiment was presented by Schmalhofer and Kühn (1988).

Results and Discussion

For the novices and the computer users, the relative frequencies of correct solutions in the programming and the evaluation tasks as a function of instruction method are shown in Fig. 10.5. A $2 \times 2 \times 2$ ANOVA with the factors prior knowledge, instruction method, and test task showed that overall the two tasks were about equally difficult, $F(1,76) = 0.31$, and that computer users performed better, $F(1,76) = 21.6$, $MS_e = 0.35$, $p < .001$. More interestingly, novices performed better in the evaluation tasks and computer users performed better in the programming tasks, resulting in a prior knowledge-by-test task interaction, $F(1,76) = 20.5$, $MS_e = 0.14$, $p < .001$. In addition, learning from examples was more useful for correctly solving the evaluation tasks and learning by exploration was more effective for the programming tasks, resulting in an instruction method-by-test task interaction, $F(1,76) = 5.13$, $MS_e = 0.14$, $p < .05$. Supposedly, in the exploration condition the generation of inputs was trained, which is an important component for successfully solving programming tasks. The demonstration groups had some advantage in the evaluation tasks, possibly because the self-generated learning examples provided less complete information about the system than the examples selected by a teacher. This effect was largely due to the computer users.

In order to analyze the relation between the subjects' (programming and evaluation) performance and the studied examples, the training examples generated by the subjects in the exploration condition, as well as the training examples presented in the example condition (learning from demonstrations) were classified as belonging to one of four categories which were defined as follows: (a) positive examples that contain new information about the system, (b) redundant positive examples, (c) "near misses" (Winston, 1984; i.e., negative examples that are very similar to positive examples and thus convey information about the system), and (d) all other inputs (classified as "far misses"). This classification was again performed by the knowledge construction component of the KIWi model (see Schmalhofer, 1986b).

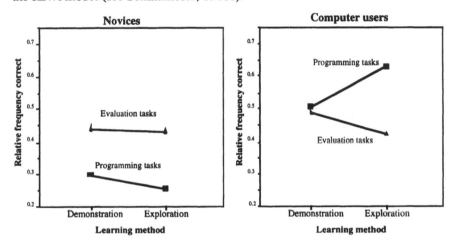

FIG. 10.5. Proportions of correctly solved test tasks as a function of learning from examples (demonstration condition) and learning by exploration.

TABLE 10.6

Proportions of Four Types of Training Examples as Generated by Novices, and Computer Users, or Presented in the Instruction Condition

Type of example	Novices	Computer users	Demonstration
positive new	0.22	0.31	0.38
positive redundant	0.28	0.31	0.12
"near misses"	0.24	0.19	0.50
"far misses"	0.26	0.19	0.00

Table 10.6 shows the relative frequencies of the four types of examples generated by the novices, the computer users, and the examples presented in the demonstration condition (learning from examples). It can be seen that both novices and computer users generated more redundant inputs than were presented in the instruction condition. Also, computer users generated more positive new examples than novices, $t(38) = 2.45$, $p < .05$. Furthermore, a considerable

proportion of the generated inputs in the exploration condition were far misses that cannot provide any useful new insights.

Although the training examples generated in the exploration condition were of poorer quality than those presented in the demonstration condition, the computer users of the exploration condition performed better in the programming tasks than the computer users of the demonstration condition. For the programming tasks, the advantage of generating training examples apparently can outweigh the disadvantage due to the usually poorer quality of self-generated training examples.

Thus, the knowledge that can be acquired by exploration depends on the quality of the generated training examples, which itself depends on the subjects' prior knowledge. Two multiple regression analyses were conducted for the proportions of correctly solved programming and evaluation tasks with the proportions of the first three types of training examples (positive new, positive redundant, and near misses) and prior knowledge (with the dummy coding 0 for novices and 1 for computer users) as predictors. Initially, all four predictors were entered into the regression equation and insignificant predictors were then stepwise removed. The results of these analyses are shown in Table 10.7.

It can be seen that the proportion of positive new training examples is a good predictor of the performance in the two tasks, even after the effect due to differences in prior knowledge has been taken into account. The results furthermore show that as more redundant training examples were generated, fewer programming tasks could be solved in the test phase. The results demonstrate that the effectiveness of learning by exploration depends on the learners' domain knowledge and their ability to generate appropriate training examples.

TABLE 10.7

Prediction of Correctly Solved Tasks From Prior Knowledge and Three Types of Generated Training Examples in the Exploration Condition

	programming tasks ß-weight	correlation	evaluation tasks ß-weight	correlation
prior knowledge	0.290***	0.605***	0.104*	0.457**
positive new	1.328***	0.621***	0.399*	0.433*
positive redundant	-0.421+	-0.038		

***p < .001; ** p < .01; *p < .05; +p < .10

Figure 10.6 presents an overview of how the subjects allocated their time in learning from examples and in learning by exploration. Because in the exploration condition, the analysis of the input also included the typing of the input, this phase required substantially more time in the exploration condition. The analysis of the complete example also required substantially more time in the exploration condition, because it possibly also included the conception of the next example, which was already provided in the example condition. We can thus see that the subjects in the exploration condition performed many more processes that are also relevant for solving programming tasks. Because the computer users acquired procedural knowledge from performing these processes, they were better able to solve programming tasks after learning from exploration than after learning from examples. Because the novices could not produce sufficiently informative examples, they were better off when learning from examples.

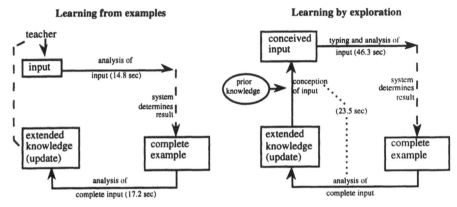

FIG. 10.6. How the learners allocated the time for the various subprocesses in learning by exploration or by demonstration.

10.4 General Discussion

From the C–I theory and the KIWi model, we had predicted that a learner's prior domain knowledge would improve learning from text, learning from examples, and learning by exploration in that the knowledge construction processes that are performed during learning will generate a richer set of situational units than the knowledge-construction processes of novices. When the prior domain knowledge is inherently related to the new subject domain (such as the knowledge about different programming languages), the constructed situational units will be related to one another in many aspects. The integration processes will therefore yield a coherent situational representation of the new subject domain in the form of an appropriate situation model. For novices, on the other hand, the constructed situational units are fewer and far less coherent. The knowledge units that are constructed by the novices cohere only at the material-related levels and the integration processes therefore form a representation that is more centered around the textbase or the template base. Knowledge of a related domain thus facilitates the acquisition of new knowledge, even when there is no common schema structure that could be transferred from the old to the new domain, as it has been investigated in previous research (e.g., Chase & Simon, 1973; Krems & Pfeiffer, 1992; Schneider et al., 1993).

Similar to the simulation runs reported in chapter 7, we could furthermore support this explanation by applying the simulation model to the various experimental conditions of the three reported experiments.

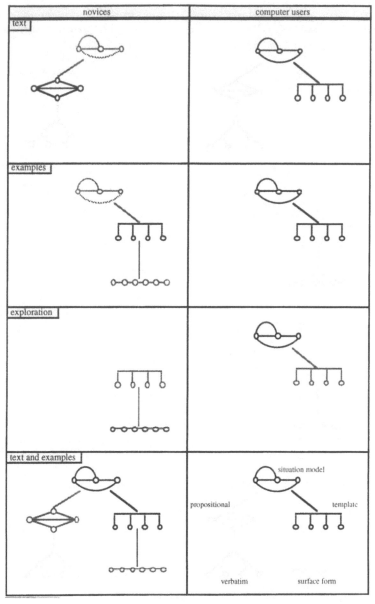

FIG. 10.7. The relative strengths of the five different levels of representation for novice and expert subjects (computer users) and the different learning conditions. The degree of darkness indicates the strength of a representation. As can be seen in the lower right panel, the six different symbols stand for the verbatim and propositional text representation, the situation model, the template base, and the surface form of the examples.

Because of the large number of different experimental conditions (which is a consequence of the fact that we are empirically evaluating a unifying theory), it would be quite unreasonable to present the complete knowledge nets for the various conditions (as we did in Figs. 7.4 and 7.5). Instead of such an explicit, space-consuming presentation, Fig. 10.7 only shows a comprehensive summary of what would be obtained from such simulation results. These results are consistent with the experimental data that are reported in this chapter.

Figure 10.7 shows the strengths of five different levels of representations for the novice and expert (computer users) subjects and the different learning situations that were investigated in the three experiments. The different levels are symbolized by different structures, which stand for the verbatim text, the propositional textbase, the situation model, the template base, and the example surface form. The degree of darkness represents the relative strength of the respective representation.

The comprehensive overview of the experimental results that is presented in Fig. 10.7 clearly shows that in all conditions in which only one learning material was presented, the novices' representations are centered around the textbase or the template base, whereas the experts' representations are centered around the situation model. When two learning materials are studied, the novices' representations also become centered around the situation model. The second type of material yielded additional construction processes for situational knowledge and thus functioned similar to the prior knowledge that can be employed by the expert subjects. Because for the experts, the second type of material yielded only redundant information, the second type of material does not change much for the expert subjects. This interpretation was furthermore supported by the analyses of the verification latencies (see Fig. 10.2) and the reading times (see Fig. 10.3).

With domain knowledge (prior knowledge or knowledge recently acquired from text), much more knowledge can be constructed from the very first example. This additional processing yields longer study times than the study times of subjects without domain knowledge who process the first example only shallowly. The deeper processing of the first example results in the subsequent examples being redundant.

The subsequent examples are therefore studied longer by subjects without domain knowledge who still acquire new knowledge from these examples. The processing time of the initial test items similarly showed that the expert subjects were better prepared for the different kinds of test tasks, because they had performed more thorough knowledge acquisition processes than the novices.

The presented explanation is in good agreement with similar theoretical accounts and various experimental results (cf. Allwood, 1986). As previously mentioned, assuming that novice subjects perform minimalist knowledge-construction processes and expert subjects perform constructionist knowledge-construction processes fits together quite well with the constructionist position (Graesser et al., 1994) and reasonably well with the minimalist position (McKoon & Ratcliff, 1992). The results and the proposed explanation are also in good accord with Gernsbacher's (1990) structure-building framework, in that we are also proposing that coherence relations at different levels determine an important part of which structures of a representation emerge during learning. Einstein and McDaniel's material-appropriate processing framework (Einstein, McDaniel, Owen & Coté, 1990) also emphasizeed that processing activities have different effects across different learning materials. This framework gives a similar account of how explicit processing goals and the processes that are typically performed on some material (such as different genres of text, examples, etc.) are combined. McNamara et al (in press) have also shown how the organization of the study material and prior knowledge interact in determining which memorizing and knowledge construction processes are performed. Similar to the present investigation of knowledge integration from text and examples, Hegarty and Just (1993) researched how text and diagrams are integratively processed, and obtained quite similar results.

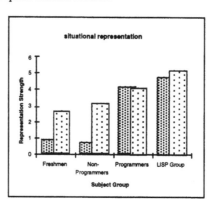

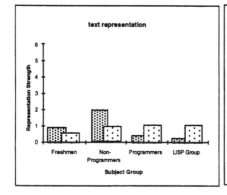
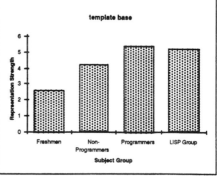

FIG. 10.8. Representation strengths of text representation, situational representation and template base, for two texts (LISP and Greek mythology) and four subjects groups, where only the programmers and LISP group have prior programming experience (adapted from Schmalhofer, 1983).

Obviously, from the point of view of an individual difference account one may pose the questioned whether the observed differences between the novice and the expert subjects are indeed due to differences in prior domain knowledge or whether they are possibly due to some other individual skill or aptitude. Schmalhofer (1983) addressed this question by having all subjects study a second text from a different subject domain (Greek mythology) where the prior knowledge differences should not have any influence. There were also an additional two subject groups in that study. A group of subjects who were three years less advanced in their college education (called *freshmen*) and a group of subjects who already knew LISP.

Figure 10.8 presents the asymptotic values of the representational strengths for text representation, situation model and template base. These results show that the individual performance differences are indeed due to prior domain knowledge: Although the situational representation for the LISP and mythology text clearly differ for the freshmen and the nonprogrammers, this difference does not exist for programmers or for the LISP group. Schneider et al. (1989) similarly found that even in children, performance differences are due to domain knowledge rather than some general aptitude.

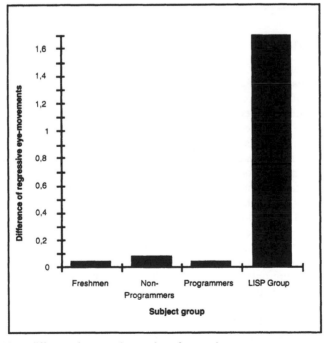

FIG. 10.9. Mean difference between the number of regressive eye movements per sentence in the LISP and mythology texts (from Schmalhofer, 1983).

The experiment by Schmalhofer (1983) also collected eye-monitoring data during the study phase, and the average number of regressive eye movements was determined for each subject and each text. These data provide an additional opportunity to examine our theoretical account for expertise differences on knowledge acquisition. If it is indeed true that the programmers did not employ a schema for encoding the new learning material, their number of regressive eye movements should not differ between the two texts. The LISP group, on the other hand, would employ a schema structure for a top–down encoding of the learning material and should therefore show significantly more regressive eye movements on the mythology text than on the LISP text. Figure 10.9 shows the average difference in regressive eye movements per sentence between the mythology and the LISP texts. These results clearly confirm that only the subjects who already knew LISP used top-down encoding with the assistance of a schema whereas the programmers used the same bottom-up knowledge-construction processes as the two novice subject groups. But due to their prior domain knowledge, the knowledge-construction processes of the programmers yielded better results. According to the objectives of a unifying theory, we have thus supported our theoretical explanation of expertise differences on the acquisition of knowledge by a large variety of different experimental designs and experimental measures.

10.5 Summary

It was investigated how prior knowledge about computer programming would influence the learning of a new programming language. In three experiments, the knowledge acquisition of learners with prior programming experience was compared to the knowledge acquisition of novices. The process dissociation procedure of the responses to sentence and example verification tasks, which had been used in the previous experiments, was again applied in experiments 8 and 9. Experiment 10 investigated how learners with different prior knowledge would solve programming tasks and evaluate existing programs after they had either learned from examples or by exploring a programming language on their own.

The results showed that when only one type of learning material was studied, the formation of a situation model mostly depended on the learners' prior domain knowledge. Here, novices did not have the domain knowledge available that is needed for constructing an appropriate situation model. The text and template bases, on the other hand, were relatively independent of the learners' prior knowledge and were only influenced by the particular learning material. Because textbase and template base are formed by general heuristic processes, they can be equally well formed by novices and computer users.

Because text and examples most likely activate different but related knowledge in long-term memory and this activated knowledge becomes coordinated by the integration processes, the novices were better able to form an appropriate situation model when both materials were studied than when only one was. Deficits in a learner's prior knowledge can thus be (at least partially) compensated by studying two types of materials: text and examples.

In learning by exploration, computer users are better able to construct informative new inputs than novices and consequently also acquire more appropriate knowledge from their explorations. Novices were therefore better off learning from examples that were supplied by a teacher (demonstration condition), whereas computer users were more likely to write correct computer programs when they had learned by exploration instead of learning from demonstrations. Although the activity of generating inputs to the system has thus helped the computer users to better prepare themselves for the programming tasks, the novices did not benefit from this exercise but were better off when learning from the examples provided by the teacher.

In good agreement with the predictions of the C–I theory and the KIWi model, it was thus found that even when there is no schema structure that can be directly employed for encoding the new learning material, prior domain knowledge will facilitate knowledge acquisition. The more powerful knowledge-construction processes of expert subjects yield a variety of situational units that are then serependitously coordinated by the knowledge-integration processes in a context-sensitive way to yield an appropriate situational model. This theoretical explanation was well supported by the different analyses that are reported in this chapter, which concludes our systematic experimental evaluation of the signature assumptions of the model. In the next chapter we perform a more competitive evaluation by comparing the knowledge-integration predictions of comprehension-based theories with some competing assumptions of case-based theories.

11

An Experimental Comparison
of the Integrated Knowledge
Acquisition and the Example
Dominance Hypotheses

The previously reported experiments showed that knowledge can obviously be acquired from text, examples, and a combination of text and examples. The research on text comprehension indicates that texts can only play an important role for acquiring knowledge when the readers engage in strategic inferences for constructing a *situation model* (Graesser, Singer, & Trabasso, 1994; Graesser & Zwaan, 1995). This requires that a reader possess prior domain knowledge that is easily available (McKoon & Ratcliff, 1995). The studies on learning from examples, on the other hand, show that from examples, practically useful knowledge can be acquired with or without prior domain knowledge (cf. Anderson & Fincham, 1994). With prior knowledge a situation model may be formed, whereas without any prior knowledge one may still build a practically useful template base. It may thus appear that for learners without prior domain knowledge texts, are relatively unimportant.

Whereas theories of case-based reasoning stress that the storage of cases (or examples) would allow a person to propose solutions to new problems quickly and thus save time (e.g., Kolodner, 1993), comprehension-based theories postulate that subjects would indeed construct a deeper level of knowledge by integrating the various sources of information and thus require more time during learning. In this chapter, we perform a competitive evaluation of comprehension-based theories against this key assumption of case-based learning (cf. section 2.3 and Fig. 2.4). More specifically, we experimentally test the *integrated knowledge-acquisition* hypothesis of comprehension-based learning against the *example-dominance* hypothesis of case-based theories of learning.

11.1 Competitive Assumptions

In a sequence of six experiments, LeFevre and Dixon (1986) compared the relative efficacy of the two learning materials. They had subjects study a text together with an example. The text described one procedure and the example demonstrated another clearly distinct procedure. After the subjects had read these conflicting materials, they had to perform the procedure that they believed had been presented by the learning material. Several control measures indicated that the subjects did not notice that the information from the text was in conflict with the information provided by the examples. Because most subjects consistently used the information from the examples and disregarded the text, LeFevre and Dixon concluded that learners would process a text only superficially when there are other sources of information, such as examples, available.

Example-Dominance Hypothesis

In terms of current theories of text processing, it may be postulated that learners do not perform strategic inferencing when reading a text in combination with examples: Only automatic inferencing is performed (McKoon & Ratcliff, 1992) and a *textbase* is formed. From the examples, a template base and a (partial) situation model are constructed. However, no attempts are made to integrate the situation model with the textbase or template base. The textbase on the one hand, and the template base and situation model on the other hand, exist in memory completely independent from one another. When the subjects are subsequently tested, they will either retrieve information from the textbase or utilize the template base and situation model. Test performance that relies on the situation model and the template base therefore does not depend on the studied text; and test performance that relies on the textbase does not depend on the studied examples. The subjects would consequently not even notice when text and examples contradicted each other.

This explanation rests on three assumptions: (a) the encoding of a text is independent of the encoding of examples, (b) there is only a shallow processing of the text, and (c) examples may be understood at a deeper level. Because the examples are viewed as the most important part of the instruction materials, the combination of the three assumptions is termed the *example-dominance* hypothesis. LeFevre and Dixon concluded from their experiments, which supported this hypothesis, that their results would paradoxically recommend against the use of examples in texts. Because readers are inclined to process a text only shallowly when examples are present, examples would prevent a deep-level understanding of the text so that the text becomes completely useless for acquiring new domain knowledge.

Integrated Knowledge-Acquisition Hypothesis

Given that in real life learning materials, examples are frequently presented together with text and seem to play an important role in acquiring new knowledge, something appears to be fundamentally wrong with LeFevre and Dixon's recommendations. Although the use of contradictory information allowed LeFevre and Dixon to decide which material dominated the other, it must be noted that such learning materials are quite unnatural. Rather than presenting conflicting or competing information, text and examples should provide consistent and supplementary information (cf. Grice, 1967). It is therefore questionable whether the example-dominance hypothesis would hold for more natural learning materials, where text and examples are consistent and supplement each other.

An alternative to the example-dominance hypotheses is the integrated knowledge-acquisition hypothesis. This hypothesis can be derived from the KIWi model. According to this hypothesis, subjects may very well perform strategic inferencing when studying a text. Next to the textbase, the learners will therefore also construct a more or less complete situation model. The completeness of the situation model depends on the information provided by the text and the learner's prior domain knowledge. When studying subsequent examples, the partially constructed situation model can assist in forming a template base. The (partial) situation model may simultaneously be augmented by abstract hypotheses, which are obtained by interpreting the studied examples in terms of the situation model. In the situation model, the knowledge acquired from the text is thus integrated with the information provided by the examples.

How much new knowledge can or needs to be acquired from the examples depends on the completeness of the information provided by the text. When the text contains sufficient information, the presented examples can be completely explained with the knowledge acquired from the text (Mitchell, Keller, & Kedar-Cabelli, 1986). When some information is deleted from the text, questions are generated (Graesser & McMahen, 1993) and common sense is used to extract the required situation knowledge from the examples. When no text is presented, only the examples are available from which a (partial) situation model can be constructed by commonsense considerations (Lewis, 1988). For test tasks that query the text, the text representations and the situation model will be utilized. For test tasks that are oriented toward the examples, the situation model will be utilized together with the template base. According to the integrated knowledge acquisition-hypothesis, the performance in the different test tasks would thus depend on the studied examples as well as the amount of text information that had been presented.

Experimental Predictions

An experiment was performed in which the predictions of the example-dominance hypothesis could be compared to the integrated knowledge-acquisition hypothesis in a more natural learning situation. The amount of text information about the concept of a programming language (LISP) was systematically manipulated. In three experimental conditions (complete-text, partial-text, and no-text conditions) a LISP function was (a) completely described, (b) partially described, or (c) no text at all was presented. Under all three conditions more knowledge about the same LISP function could then be acquired from examples.

The subjects' acquired knowledge was tested by sentence and example verification tasks. In order to avoid possible problems in interpreting the experimental results due to trade-offs between the speed and the accuracy of the responses in the different experimental conditions, speed–accuracy trade-off functions were again collected with a tapping procedure. The subjects again gave a confidence rating for every response by the duration of the button press. As a baseline control, a LISP function that was not presented during the study phase at all was also tested with a corresponding set of sentences and examples.

For the sentence verification tasks the following predictions are derived from the two competing hypotheses. The example-dominance hypothesis assumes that independent structures are formed when studying text (textbase) and examples (template base and situation model). Because the test sentences are only compared to the textbase, the knowledge acquired from examples would not have any effect on the performance in the sentence verification task. The complete-text condition, would consequently perform better than the partial-text condition, which would in turn perform better than the no-text condition. Because the textbase remains unrelated to the information acquired from the examples, the no-text condition is predicted to perform at the level of the baseline control. The integrated knowledge-acquisition hypothesis on the other hand assumes that textbase, situation model, and template base form one integrated structure with three representations. For verifying sentences, the textbase and the situation model can be used. The knowledge acquired from examples will thus also assist in verifying sentences. The no-text condition is therefore predicted to perform clearly better than the baseline control.

For the example verification task, the following predictions are derived. The example-dominance hypothesis assumes that the test examples are only compared to the template base and the situation model without utilizing any text information. When there are no differences in the examples that were studied, the complete-text condition, the partial-text condition, and the no-text condition should perform equally well and clearly better than the baseline control. The integrated knowledge-acquisition hypothesis, on the other hand, assumes that the text information is used for better understanding the examples. The knowledge acquired from text will thus also assist in verifying examples, and the more text that is presented, the better the performance will be in the example verification tasks.

11.2 Experiment 11

Method

A 3 × 3 × 3 Greco-Latin square design was used to counterbalance the
experimental manipulation, that is, the complete-text, partial-text, and no-text
conditions with the specific LISP functions (i.e., FIRST, EQUAL, LIST), and
the order in which these functions were studied. In this within-subjects design, a
subject learned one function from a complete text with examples, another
function from a partial text with examples and a third function from examples
alone. A fourth function (i.e., REST) was tested but never studied.

Subjects. Fifty-four students of the University of Colorado, who did not have
any prior knowledge about computer programming completed the experiment
successfully. An additional six subjects failed to pass a criterion test task six
times in a row (administered after the first learning phase) and therefore did not
participate any further.

Materials. The learning materials again consisted of the learning materials
that were a prerequisite for understanding the experimental learning materials, and
the experimental learning materials, in which three specific LISP functions were
explained (FIRST, EQUAL, LIST).

The prerequisite learning materials consisted of 16 paragraphs with two to
four sentences per paragraph. The introduction consisted of a motivating
paragraph. The main topics were: (a) how a user interacts with the LISP System,
(b) data representations (atoms and lists) in LISP, (c) the evaluation of terms in
LISP, and (d) how functions are defined, namely that a function is defined by
three specifications: the number of arguments, the type of argument, and the
input–output relation. In the last paragraph, the presented material was
summarized.

The prerequisite learning material consisted of text with some examples and
was sufficient for adequately understanding the specific LISP functions to be
learned from the experimental learning materials. This sufficiency was
demonstrated by running the KIWi model on a formalization of the learning
materials: With the content sentences from the prerequisite learning materials, the
KIWi model could construct a situational representation of a specific LISP
function from the complete description of the function (text) as well as from the
sequence of examples that were used as part of the experimental learning
materials. In a previous experiment (see chapter 8), it was shown that text and
examples that were constructed according to this sufficiency criterion did indeed
yield an equivalent situation model when the learners were provided with long
study phases.

The experimental learning materials described three specific LISP functions.
For each function the materials consisted of an introductory sentence together
with zero, two, or four content sentences (depending on the experimental

condition) followed by two transition sentences and four specific examples. The examples varied with respect to their incidental structure, so that when given unlimited processing resources, the KIWi model constructed a correct representation of the situation model under all three experimental conditions. A sample learning material for the function FIRST in the complete-text condition is shown in Table 11.1. In the partial-text condition the same material was used, except that the sentences marked with a * were missing. In the no-text condition the sentences marked with # were also missing.

TABLE 11.1

A Sample of the Learning Materials

Now we will introduce the function FIRST.

* The function FIRST is used to select an s-expression from a list.

The function FIRST requires exactly one argument.

The argument of the function FIRST must be a list.

* The function FIRST returns the first s-expression of the given argument.

The following examples illustrate how the function FIRST is to be used.

The inputs to the LISP System are shown on the left side and the results returned by the system are shown on the right side on the same line after an arrow.

(FIRST '(A B C D))	-->	A
(FIRST '(H (L (P Y))))	-->	H
(FIRST '((Z Q T) (J)))	-->	(Z Q T)
(FIRST '((M E) (I R)))	-->	(M E)

The test materials consisted of 24 test sentences and 16 examples. For each of four LISP functions (FIRST, EQUAL, LIST, and REST) six test sentences were constructed. The six sentences of a function consisted of three correct and three incorrect test sentences addressing the number of arguments, the type of argument, and the input–output relation of the function. The correct sentences were taken directly from the experimental learning material.[9] The incorrect sentences were obtained by exchanging corresponding properties between different functions.

There were four test examples for each function. The two correct examples were directly taken from the learning material. Two incorrect examples were constructed by employing an argument specification or an input–output relation from a different function or function combination. The test materials for the function FIRST are shown in Table 11.2.

---

[9] Because the function REST was used as a baseline control, the text and the examples for the function REST were not used as learning material.

TABLE 11.2

A Sample of the Test Materials

Correct	Incorrect
Sentences	
The function FIRST requires exactly one argument.	The function FIRST can be given any number of arguments.
The argument of the function FIRST must be a list.	The argument to the function FIRST can be an atom and/or a list.
The function FIRST returns the first s-expression of the given argument.	The function FIRST returns a list of all the s-expressions which were given as arguments.
Examples	
(FIRST '((Z Q T) (J))) --> (Z Q T) (FIRST '((M E) (I R))) --> (M E)	(FIRST '(Z Q T) '(J)) --> (Z Q T) (FIRST '((M E) (I R))) --> M

Procedure. The experiment was again run on two IBM-PC/AT personal computers, to which a box with three buttons and a sound generator were connected. Headphones were used for presenting the response signals in the sentence and example verification tasks. In a practice session with unrelated materials, the subjects were trained to study learning materials on the computer screen and to respond according to the requirements of the tapping speed–accuracy trade-off method in the verification tasks.

In the first learning phase, the subjects acquired basic knowledge about data representations (atoms and lists) in LISP, the evaluation of terms in LISP, and how functions are defined. The subjects were instructed to study all learning materials as if they were preparing for an exam in one of their classes. The learning materials were shown in a window on the screen. Unlike the second learning phase, the subjects could move freely here between the paragraphs using the buttons of the button box. However, they could only study one paragraph at a time. The subjects were free to study the material as long as they wanted. The first learning phase was repeated until a subject correctly solved 80% of the items of a following test task or had failed this test six times in a row, which terminated the experiment.

In the second learning phase, the subjects learned about the three specific LISP functions — FIRST, LIST, and EQUAL. Every subject had to learn each function and was presented with one complete text followed by examples, one partial text followed by examples and one only with examples. The sentences and examples were presented item by item. After they had finished reading an item, subjects pushed a button and the next item was shown. Reading times were recorded for each sentence and for each example.

In the test phase, which followed the second learning phase, the subjects had to perform the sentence and example verification tasks. The 24 test sentences were presented individually in random order followed by the also randomly presented 16 examples. In order to obtain information about the time course of knowledge utilization and in order to control possible trade-off effects of response time and response accuracy, a tapping speed–accuracy trade-off paradigm was used: The subjects had to give six responses to each sentence or example. The subjects made the first response 0.75 s before the test sentence or the test example was presented on the screen. Here, the subjects could only guess but in following responses they had increasingly more time to fully process the test sentence or test example. The following five responses were probed by response signals (tones) which occurred 2 s apart from each other. Again, the last response signal differed from the previous ones, indicating that there was no time pressure for the final response. For each button press, the subjects were asked to indicate the confidence in their decision by the duration of the button press, short duration indicating low confidence and long duration indicating high confidence.

Results

A reading times-analysis of the individual sentences and examples showed that there was no difference among the three experimental conditions and that the reading times decreased from the first to the last presented LISP function. Similar position effects were also found in the analysis of the sentence and example verification tasks. For instance, in the sentence verification tasks, differences among the three experimental conditions were more clearly visible for the first than for the last studied LISP function. For the third presented LISP function, subjects may have utilized analogies (Anderson et al., 1984; Novick & Holyoak, 1991) to the previous LISP functions, and thereby improved their performance. Such effects are, however, not suited for differentiating between the example-dominance and integrated knowledge-acquisition hypotheses. Because the counterbalancing scheme was only used to control the effects of the specific LISP functions and their position in the learning material, these particular effects need not be reported here. Instead they are treated as part of the error variance, against which the systematic influence of the amount of learning material is tested.

Sentence verification. The speed–accuracy trade-off functions of Fig. 11.1 show the relative frequencies of correct responses for the different processing times in the sentence verification task. These results show that the available processing time, $F(4,212) = 16.48$, $MS_e = .02$, $p < .001$, and the amount of learning material (complete-text, partial-text, no-text conditions, and baseline control) that was studied, $F(3,159) = 26.93$, $MS_e = .16$, $p < .001$ affected the correctness of a response. In addition, there was a significant interaction, $F(12,636) = 10.26$, $MS_e = .02$, $p < .001$.

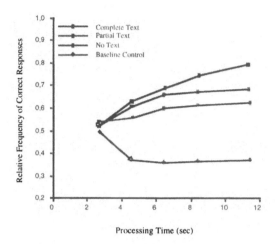

FIG. 11.1. The relative frequency of correct responses for the pooled test sentences as a function of different amounts of learning materials and at different processing times.

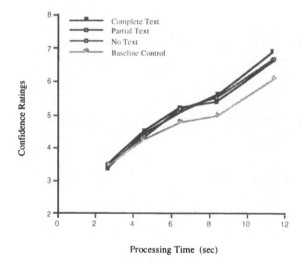

FIG. 11.2. The average confidence ratings in a response for the pooled test sentences as a function of different amounts of learning materials at different processing times.

At the asymptote of the speed–accuracy trade-off function (i.e., the subjects' responses, which occurred approximately 11 seconds after the presentation of the sentence) the test sentences were verified significantly better in the complete-text condition than in the partial-text condition, $F(1,53) = 5.72$, $MS_e = .06$, $p < .05$.

The partial-text condition was better than the no-text condition, $F(1,53) = 6.83$, $MS_e = .07$, $p < .05$, which in turn was better than the baseline control, $F(1,53) = 107.33$, $MS_e = .04$, $p < .001$, where no learning material at all had been presented. Correct knowledge was generally acquired from the three types of learning materials (complete-text, partial-text, no-text conditions). For the baseline control, where subjects had not received any learning materials at all, they did not respond at chance but frequently made incorrect inferences when they were tested.

The duration of the subjects' button presses, which indicated the confidence in the specific response, were scaled according to the previously used procedure (cf. section 8.1). This scaling procedure yields confidence ratings that range between one and nine. The confidence ratings for the responses are shown in Fig. 11.2. Amount of learning materials, $F(3,159) = 3.03$, $MS_e = 2.98$, $p < .05$, and the available processing time, $F(4,212) = 92.69$, $MS_e = 3.14$, $p < .001$, significantly influenced the subjects' confidence in their responses. In addition, there was a significant interaction effect, $F(12,636) = 2.26$, $MS_e = .60$, $p < .05$. When no learning material was studied (baseline control), the subjects' confidence was significantly lower than when only examples were presented (no-text condition), $F(1,53) = 11.27$, $MS_e = 1.67$, $p < .001$. For the three experimental conditions, on the other hand, the subjects' confidence was about equal.

Depending on the experimental condition, a test sentence may have been explicitly presented or had to be inferred from the examples in combination with the basic LISP knowledge. In order to analyze which inferences were made in the different experimental conditions, the two sentences addressing the input–output relation of a LISP function (explicitly presented only in the complete-text condition) and the two sentences addressing the argument specification of a LISP function (explicitly presented in the complete- and partial-text conditions) were separately analyzed. The results for the input–output sentences are shown in Fig. 11.3. Again, the correctness of a response increased with the amount of learning materials, $F(3,159) = 6.17$, $MS_e = .22$, $p < .05$, and the available processing time, $F(4,212) = 40.21$, $MS_e = .07$, $p < .001$ and there was also a significant interaction, $F(12,636) = 4.01$, $MS_e = .06$, $p < .001$. For the subjects' responses that occurred approximately 11 seconds after the presentation of the sentences, the no-text condition performed better than the baseline control, $F(1,53) = 19.09$, $MS_e = .12$, $p < .001$, and there was no significant difference among the three experimental conditions.

For the no-text and partial-text conditions subjects thus correctly inferred the input–output relation from the studied examples. In the complete-text condition, where the input–output relation had been explicitly stated, the input–output test sentences were correctly verified more often, although this difference did not turn out to be statistically significant. In the baseline control condition, the subjects performed at about chance level. The analysis of the confidence ratings showed the same results as the analysis of the pooled test sentences.

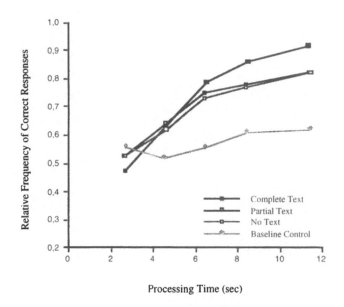

FIG. 11.3. The relative frequencies of correct responses for the input–output sentences as a function of different amounts of learning materials at different processing times.

The results for the sentences addressing the argument specifications, which are shown in Fig. 11.4, indicate once more that the amount of the studied learning material, $F(3,159) = 20.68$, $MS_e = .30$, $p < .001$, affected the correctness of a response. Although the available processing time was not significant, there was a significant interaction effect, $F(12,636) = 7.07$, $MS_e = .04$, $p < .001$. This is explained by the baseline control yielding mostly incorrect answers and the three experimental conditions yielding mostly correct answers. For the subjects' last responses, there was no significant difference ($F < 1$) between the complete-text condition and the partial-text condition. The partial-text condition was better than the no-text condition, $F(1,53) = 5.68$, $MS_e = .13$, $p < .05$, which in turn was clearly better than the baseline control, $F(1,53) = 92.65$, $MS_e = .06$, $p < .001$.

In the complete-text and partial-text conditions, where the argument specifications had been explicitly stated, the particular test sentences were correctly verified about equally well. In the no-text condition, the subjects performed at about chance level. The argument specifications were thus only inferred from the studied examples when at least the input–output specification had been presented as part of the text (i.e., the complete and partial-text conditions). Without any learning materials, mostly incorrect inferences were made at the time when the subjects were tested. The analysis of the confidence ratings again showed the same results as the analysis of the pooled test sentences.

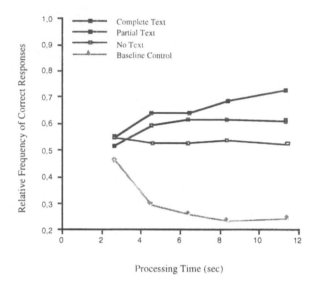

FIG. 11.4. The relative frequencies of correct responses for the argument specification sentences as a function of different amounts of learning materials at different processing times.

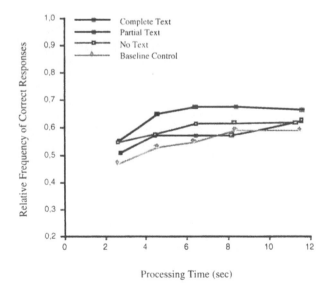

FIG. 11.5. The relative frequencies of correct responses for the pooled test examples as a function of different amounts of learning materials at different processing times.

Example verification. Figure 11.5 shows the relative frequencies of correct responses for the different processing times in the example verification task. The available processing time, $F(4,212) = 16.36$, $MS_e = .02$, $p < .001$, and the amount of learning material, $F(3,159) = 3.70$, $MS_e = .13$, $p < .05$, affected the correctness of a response and there was no significant interaction ($F < 2$). The complete-text condition performed better than the partial-text condition for the two responses in the processing interval between six and ten seconds, $F(1,53) = 5.92$, $MS_e = .05$, $p < .05$, and, $F(1,53) = 5.10$, $MS_e = .05$, $p < .05$. The no-text condition performed better than the baseline control for the response given about six seconds after the presentation of the example, $F(1,53) = 4.80$, $MS_e = .05$, $p < .05$. The information acquired from text thus also affected the performance in the verification of the example tasks.

Discussion

In general, the example-dominance hypothesis is supported by results that show that the performance in the sentence verification task depends only on the studied text and the performance in the example verification task depends only on the studied examples. The integrated knowledge-acquisition hypothesis, on the other hand, is supported by results that show that the performance in the sentence verification task also depends on the studied examples and the performance in the example verification task also depends on the studied sentences.

The analysis of the sentence verification tasks showed the following response patterns: (a) Statements that were explicitly presented in a condition could be better verified than test sentences that had to be inferred. This result shows that the text had at least been superficially processed and does not discriminate between the two competing hypotheses. (b) Test sentences that were not explicitly presented in the text were better inferred when examples had been presented than when only the general background knowledge had been acquired. Actually, with the presented examples, such test sentences were quite often correctly inferred. For instance, there were approximately 80% versus 60% correct responses for the input–output sentences. For the argument specifications, there was a difference of approximately 25% between the two conditions. Information acquired from examples was thus utilized for verifying the test sentences.

The analysis of the example verification tasks showed that the amount of text information influenced the overall performance in the example verification task. This result contradicts the assumption that texts would be encoded only superficially and that examples would be the most important part of the learning material. Some text information was obviously integrated with the information from examples. The results thus contradict the example-dominance hypothesis and support the integrated knowledge-acquisition hypothesis. In an additional experiment (see Schmalhofer, 1995), it was furthermore shown that information is integrated between learning from text and learning by exploration.

Because the amount of text information differentially influenced the verification of examples at different processing times, it was of particular interest to analyze differences in the time course. With complete-text information, the verification performance improved faster in early stages of the processing than when the text had been only partially presented. The integration of the complete-text information with the examples may have yielded a consistent structure that facilitated an early utilization of the knowledge for verifying examples. Some incorrect inferences were drawn in the partial-text condition. Because of the resulting interference effects, the examples were therefore not verified as easily. The no-text condition, on the other hand, only relied on the template base, which is particularly useful for verifying examples, thereby avoiding an interference effect and performing at least as well as the partial-text condition. The relatively good performance of the baseline control is explained by learning from analogy in combination with the various sentences presented in the preceding sentence verification task. The analysis of the subjects' confidence ratings finally showed that the confidence in a response did not depend on whether the utilized knowledge had been acquired from text or from examples.

11.3 Summary

We performed a competitive evaluation of comprehension-based theories of learning against the assumptions of a simple case-based reasoner that would only focus on the examples and ignore the text. The example-dominance hypothesis (which is based on the assumptions of case-based reasoning) assumes an independent processing of text and examples, only shallow processing of the text, and a deeper understanding of the examples. The integrated knowledge-acquisition hypothesis (which is based on comprehension-based theories of learning), on the other hand, postulates that information acquired from examples can supplement the text information, and that text facilitates the understanding of examples (by integrating the information from text and template base into a situation-oriented abstraction).

The experimental results showed that incomplete text information was supplemented with the information that was extracted from the studied examples: Sentences that were not explicitly presented in the text were nevertheless correctly verified when examples had been studied. Examples were better understood when additional text information had been presented. The more text that had been studied, the better was the verification of the examples.

Given the present results, one can no longer simply say that psychological experiments would "recommend against the frequent use of examples in instruction sets" and that "readers are inclined to process written instructions shallowly when other sources of information are available" (LeFevre & Dixon, 1986, p. 29). The present experiments show quite to the contrary, that information from text and examples was processed at a deeper level and that the two sources of information were integrated. Because the subjects did not have any previous programming experience, this claim can even be made for learners with little prior domain knowledge. Learning materials with text and supplementary examples can therefore be quite effective, especially for novices. Catrambone (1995) showed that learning from examples can be improved when information relating the decomposition into subgoals is presented with the example.

In a competitive evaluation of the KIWi model, we have thus shown that learners acquire new knowledge by comprehending knowledge assets from different types of intermediate representations into an integrated and more abstract circumscription rather than only storing specific experiences in the form of cases, as proposed by case-based reasoning. We have thus completed the empirical evaluation of the KIWi model and now turn to discussing how the present research results may possibly be employed in developing modern instructional technologies and expert systems.

Acknowledgment

This chapter is based on a previous report that has been published in an edited volume by Lawrence Erlbaum Associates (Schmalhofer, 1995).

Part III

Application, Discussion, and Prospects

12

Instructional Technology
and Expert Systems

In Part II of this book, we presented experimental psychology research that addressed the question of how subjects would acquire knowledge in a new subject domain. The conducted experiments were guided by a general theory, namely the C–I theory that is described in Part I of the book. For presenting this theory as well as for its experimental evaluation, we applied the levels approach towars cognitive modeling. We have thereby obtained a thoroughly tested and *unified theory* of knowledge acquisition. By using the levels approach as a research methodology, we particularly wanted to facilitate the utilization of research results from experimental psychology into other areas of psychology, other disciplines outside of psychology, as well as its utilization for practical applictions in real-life situations.

Because traditional research in experimental psychology has yielded a large number of different paradigms with numerous fine-grained and increasingly differentiated research findings, it has became increasingly difficult to utilize these results outside the particular area of specialization. The levels approach toward cognitive modeling, on the other hand, yielded a unified theory that spans several different paradigms. The various details (which are only sometimes important) are viewed as specializations of the more important general postulates and are hidden at a lower level of description. The highest level of description, the knowledge level, was furthermore established from an evolutionary perspective, namely that the human cognitive system and its environment have evolved together. The levels approach toward cognitive modeling thus provides a method for separating the different levels of concern, while maintaining a consistent account across a

245

larger realm of experimental phenomena. Without such a unified theory, it would be extremely difficult if not impossible to decide which one of the many different experimental effects that have been found in psychological laboratories would be relevant for the various practical applications.

Obviously, we must now address the question of how our research findings can possibly be applied in the described manner. We consider the areas of instructional psychology, education, the development of expert systems as a subarea of computer science, and the utilization of such systems in application domains such as mechanical engineering and quality assurance in the pharmaceutical industry. More specifically, we consider how the present research results could be useful for developing various instruction materials and tools (instructional technology) and how the research findings could be used for designing expert and knowledge-based systems for different application domains (expert system development).

As it turns out, in both areas — instructional technology and expert systems — there are basically two different ways of applying our research results: One way is guided by the *worldview of symbolic cognition* and the other way is guided by the *worldview of situated cognition* in combination with the postulates of an evolutionary psychology. In chapter 3, we pointed out that the worldview of symbolic cognition and the woldview of situated cognition are both equally valuable. This is true despite the current controversies between the two camps of symbolic and situated cogntion. More specifically, as was explained in chapter 3, the worldview of situated cognition must not be taken as an argument for throwing out the sophisticated computer simulation techniques that have been developed over the last 30 years (see Hayes, Ford, & Agnew, 1994). From the point of view of situated cognition, computer simulations should simply be seen as descriptive simulations (Greeno & Moore, 1993) where the target system is only assumed to have those properties that are described by the symbolic system (rather than saying that the target system has the same properties as the symbolic system). Even for situated cognition, computer simulation techniques are very important as external representations that facilitate human learning and communication (see Lajoie & Lesgold, 1989).

12.1 Instructional Technology

According to a purist's view of symbolic cognition, the KIWi model would be interpreted as a complete explication of how humans acquire knowledge. In order to improve and optimize human learning, we could therefore feed a variety of different learning materials and different sequences of learning materials into the model. For each instructional set, we may then inspect the representational content of the knowledge that the model acquired from the different instructional sets. We can thus select the instructional set that yielded the desired representational content with the shortest study time. Because the model is assumed to be a complete explication of how humans acquire knowledge, the human learners are expected to behave in exactly the same way as the model and we can thus present the best possible learning material to the learner. Kühn

(1987) applied the model in this manner to determine an optimal sequence of instructional examples. He then presented some learners with the optimal sequence and other learners with a sequence that had been used in a published programmer's manual. His results showed that the sequence that was optimal according to the model was indeed better than the traditionally used sequence. Whereas the traditional sequence yielded inferences that were overgeneralizations and therefore incorrect, the sequence that was determined by the model did not yield such incorrect inferences and therefore produced better results. For word processing skills, Schmalhofer (1987a) similarly determined the efficacy of how-it-works and how-to-do-it instructions. The model can thus be employed as a tool for developing instructional materials that are effective with respect to a particular learning goal.

Such a model-guided design of instructional materials may be of particular importance for the development of (off-line as well as on-line) computer manuals and for instructions on how to use a complex computer system for performing specific tasks (see Gong & Elkerton, 1990). It is a well-documented fact that such manuals are often quite insufficient and thus limit the productivity of computer users (Nelson, Whitener, & Philcox, 1995). One may even go one step further and utilize a cognitive model for developing a computer system (e.g., a word processor) so that it would be easy to learn and easy to use. Computer systems and programming environments may thereby turn into environments for designing processes and products in specific application domains (Winograd, 1995). Such an improvement of computer systems may be performed with completely formalized models (e.g., Kieras & Polson, 1985) as well as with informal knowledge-level descriptions. For many practical applications it is often too expensive to develop a completely formalized model so that preference is often given to less formal approaches (cf. Lewis, Polson, Wharton, & Rieman, 1990).

When we develop an instructional set in this manner, we obviously need to specify a learner's prior knowledge in the model. Because of individual differences and the general problem of diagnosing a person's knowledge (cf. Lukas & Albert, 1993), this may be quite difficult or even prohibitively expensive. The problems that result from individual differences and the resources that are required for diagnosing an individual's prior knowledge can be at least partially resolved by employing intelligent tutoring systems (ITSs), where a learner's knowledge is dynamically diagnosed during the course of learning (Anderson, Boyle, Corbett, & Lewis, 1990). By the *model-tracing (or knowledge-tracking) technique* that has been developed and popularized by Anderson and his colleagues, a model of a learner's knowledge is continuously updated according to the learner's past activities during problem solving and learning. Appropriate advice can then be given to the student on the basis of the constructed model trace. Such intelligent tutoring systems have proven to be quite effective and have been successfully applied in teaching computer programming at the university and the high-school levels (cf. Anderson & Skwarecki, 1986; Weber, 1994). For specific subject domains, Anderson and his colleagues have shown that such ITSs are almost as effective as human tutors and much more effective than classroom instructions. Similarly, when we want to develop a computer system (e.g., a travel advisor that can competently book hotel reservations) on the basis of a cognitive model, a user's knowledge and how it changes over time must be similarly diagnosed. The techniques that are used in this area of user modeling (e.g., Kobsa & Wahlster, 1989) are quite similar to the techniques that are employed in ITSs.

The model-tracing technique is closely tied to the world view of symbolic cognition. In the ITS, the system developers must therefore represent a) the subject domain that is to be learned by the student (e.g., the programming language LISP, or geometry), b) the students' prior knowledge and their learning mechanisms in the form of a *cognitive model*, and c) the instructional materials and how they need to be presented so that the student would achieve a certain knowledge state. Most of these entities are represented in some canonical form, so that the various instantiations that are specifically needed in a given course of tutoring can always be dynamically generated. As long as the assumptions of symbolic cognition are approximately appropriate for a given subject domain, the model tracing techniques and the ITSs can be very useful and effective. ITSs are therefore very good instructional devices when the developers, teachers, or educators are indeed able to look far enough into the future to determine which basic skills the student should acquire to be optimally prepared for life. ITSs are also very good instructional devices when the subject domain is so small and self-contained that the developers, teachers, or educators do indeed know what the student needs to know for being successful (for example to pass a specific examination). In other words, ITSs and the worldview of symbolic cognition are appropriate and useful whenever we are dealing with a stable and closed world where nothing intrudes from the outside and no changes emerge from within. Mathematical and technical domains such as geometry and computer programming are probably the subject domains that come the closest to this ideal.

The assumption that everything that will be relevant in the future can be foreseen by the system developers remains a crude approximation, even in these relatively small task domains. But even for these domains, the development of a full-blown ITS is quite expensive. We had already mentioned that Anderson's tutor was very effective in teaching students to write computer programs. On the other hand, there may still be some drawbacks, even in such successful systems. For example, Schooler and Anderson (1990) showed that students who learned computer programming by the immediate feedback of a tutor showed deficiencies in their ability to debug programs. Because the tutor told the students immediately how to develop the program correctly, they did not acquire any skills in diagnosing and fixing deficient programs. The tutor obviously trained the skills of coding programs at the expense of practicing the debugging of programs. As every programmer knows, computer programming is an iterative process in which both testing and debugging play an important part. This example demonstrates that even for such a well-structured domain as computer programming it is quite difficult to determine the set of basic skills that should be trained by a tutoring system so that the student can be optimally successful in the respective real-life situation.

Because even application fields like programming change and evolve over time, and because such changes occur increasingly rapidly, it may often be difficult to determine which target knowledge or basic skills a student needs to acquire. Can a system developer, teacher, educator, or anybody else really know in every detail which skills and knowledge need to be acquired to be well prepared for the future? Should a tutoring system therefore really lead a student along preconceptualized paths of reasoning? With respect to the preconceptualized paths of guidance, many ITSs are quite analogous to the programmed learning lessons that were developed on the basis of behavioristic learning theories. Whereas in programmed learning, the paths through a lesson were defined in terms of which tasks were presented and solved by the student, the paths in an ITS are defined in terms of the thoughts (e.g., as they are represented by production rules) and the knowledge that was thereby acquired (e.g., as it is represented by schemata or schema instantiations). ITSs can thus be understood as programmed lessons in which the terminology of surface-oriented descriptions has been replaced by a terminology for representing deep knowledge. No doubt about it, this is a very significant progress that required several decades of research, but we should also be aware of the properties that remained unchanged in the transition from behavioristic to cognitive learning theories.

If we believe that students should be allowed to try out novel approaches for tackling a given problem (e.g., writing a computer program, designing a building, etc.) and that they may even come up with some solutions that were not thought of by the developers of the tutoring system, we need a different approach tutoring. As we have already shown, the C–I theory with its construction and integration phases describes cognitive processes that allow for what Boden (1991) called *impossibilist creative acts* (see section 1.2). The construction phase yields knowledge snippets that are derived from separate and independent representational spaces (such as a specific programming language, mathematical knowledge, commonsense knowledge, etc.). During the construction phase, these knowledge snippets may become related to one another for the first time ever. The integration processes may then produce a consistent circumscription of a suitable selection of these knowledge snippets. The result of such comprehension processes may therefore be a creative product, quite similar to Kekule's merging of the representation space for the chemical structures of carbon hydrates with the representations (or images) of curled snakes (see section 1.2).

Because such creative acts are to a certain degree random events, it is certainly impossible to predict the respective cognitive processes in any detail. But one may nevertheless provide an environment where creative acts are more likely to occur than in other environments (cf. Weinert, 1993). If we want to encourage students to be creative, we should therefore avoid the *model tracing technique*. When we are concerned with knowledge acquisition as a creative process, the *world view of situated cognition* is much more valuable. Instead of trying to trace a learner's internal representations, we should build a learning environment where a student can construct and try out different interpretations of a given problem. Such a tutoring approach and a respective learning environment, called ANIMATE, has been developed by Nathan, Kintsch, and Young (1992). Their tutoring approach is based on the C–I theory (Kintsch, 1988). The learning environment ANIMATE was developed for algebra word problems.

The learning environment ANIMATE knows nothing of the problem at hand or the student's actions, but it encourages students to explicate their reasoning about the situations described in the algebra-word problems. Consider the following algebra word problem that was used by Nathan et al. (1992): "A plane leaves Denver and travels east at two hundred miles per hour. Three hours later, a second plane leaves Denver on a parallel course and travels east at two hundred fifty miles per hour. How long will it take the second plane to overtake the first plane?" (p. 333). By animating how the airplanes leave Denver according to the mathematical equations that were written by the student, ANIMATE gives a *situation-based meaning* to these mathematical equations. Thereby the students can more easily evaluate whether their equations are consistent with their understanding of the situation. In this manner, ANIMATE provides the possibility of establishing various links between the domain of formal algebra and the respective situation in the real world.

This tutoring approach thus stresses the importance of external representations and the establishment of links between different conceptual spaces. It is in good agreement with the assumption that thinking and problem solving are situated activities that occur within restricted portions of some environment. Rather than pushing a student along some more or less logical train of thought in some given conceptual space, this tutoring approach allows the students to actively perform interplays of formal descriptions and real world contents. By jointly generating relations in the domain of formal algebra and the real-world domain of planes leaving an airport, a student can build conceptual bridges that encompass both the world of mathematics and the real world. For a restricted portion of some environment, students can thus themselves perform dialectic processes among form, content, and context (cf. Falmagne & Gonsalves, 1995) and thereby create a consistent account of form and content. For instance, it may be discussed whether or not the speed of an airplane can be a negative number and what that would mean in the real world. In short, ANIMATE advocates a comprehension-based approach to tutoring. In this respect it is clearly different from model tracing or search-based approaches (cf. Anderson & Corbett, 1993), as well as from case-based approaches to tutoring (e.g., Puppe & Reinhardt, 1994; Weber, 1994).

For the first few hours of acquiring knowledge about the programming language LISP, Schmalhofer, Kühn, Charron, and Messamer (1990) developed an exploration environment with different tutoring strategies that were derived from the results of the previously reported experiments. On the basis of a comprehension-based theory of learning, it was then determined how effective different amounts of receptive and exploratory learning are, and it was shown that the advantages of learning by exploration and learning from instructions can be successfully combined (Schmalhofer, Kühn, Messamer, & Charron, 1990). Anderson and Corbett (1993) similarly showed that it is sometimes better to allow a student to explore rather than to employ tutorial assistance that pushes a student along some preconceptualized train of reasoning. We have now shown a few possibilities of how a unified theory of knowledge acquisition can be applied to develop instructional technologies that are based on research results rather than on some specific philosophy or mere conjectures.

Our discussion of instructional technology was quite brief. Obviously, we could therefore only scratch the surface of a quite large and important field where cognitive research may be successfully applied. Sandoval (1995) discussed more generally how cognitive psychology and teaching science are related to one another when curricula for the various subject matter areas are to be developed. Weinert and Helmke (1995) pointed out that teacher-controlled instruction may also yield active student learning and that self-directed instruction does also have its disadvantages. Although their analyses addressed more complex learning situations than our experimental investigations, their conclusions are in rather close agreement with the experimental results of chapter 10, where we demonstrated the advantages and drawbacks of different knowledge acquisition scenarios with respect to different groups of learners.

Kozma (1987, 1991) described the implications of cognitive psychology for computer based learning tools and multi-media systems. He portrayed learning with media as a complementary process within which representations are constructed, sometimes by the learner and sometimes by the medium. ITSs have traditionally been described as consisting of four components: the representation of expert knowledge, a student or learner, a modeling component, and components for tutorial planning and communication (see Mandl & Lesgold, 1988). In many respects, ITSs and expert systems are thus quite similar. Lesgold and Schmalhofer (1994) consequently attempted to characterize both types of systems as media for embodying and sharing knowledge. From the perspective of education, Snow and Swanson (1992), on the other hand, characterized ITSs as the microadaptation of instruction. These are just a few examples of a large body of research literature.

There is a quite general conclusion that can be drawn from this application-oriented research. Whenever different areas of research or practice, such as cognitive psychology, educational research, and classroom practice are to be related to one another, there is always some initial gap, that is caused by different terminologies and the different goals which traditionally existed in an area. Filling such gaps requires a dedicated effort from all sides that are involved. Weinert, Schrader, and Helmke (1990), for example, took such an effort in linking the cognitive research on expert–novice differences to the variables that are traditionally used in research on teaching. Without such additional bridge-building research, it will be extremely difficult to utilize the results from cognitive research for real-world teaching situations. The unified theory of knowledge acquisition may be used as one of the pillars on which this bridge-building research may rest.

12.2 Expert Systems

Before we describe how we utilized the results from our psychological research for the development of expert systems, we present a brief overview of expert systems. One of the first and best known expert systems is MYCIN (Shortliffe, 1976). MYCIN was used for the diagnosis and treatment of bacterial infections and is a typical example of a *first generation* expert system. It basically consists of an *inference mechanism* and a *rule base*. The inference mechanism uses backward chaining and a depth first search. The rule base consists of diagnosis rules where each rule has a certainty factor associated with it. For its small area of competence, MYCIN performed much better than the best human experts. In several ways, MYCIN is typical of a first generation expert system. It was developed by rapid prototyping for a specific domain of application (i.e., medical diagnosis of bacterial infections). Besides the user interface, the explanation component and the knowledge editor, which are the peripheral components of the system, MYCIN's architecture consists of two components: The domain-independent inference mechanism (or *engine*) that can supposedly be applied to any domain, and the domain-specific rule base that is assumed to operate together with the general *inference engine. The domain-specific rule base must be newly acquired for every application* domain.

Subsequent research has shown that such inference engines (that are developed by rapid prototyping) impose conceptualizations that are often inappropriate for the particular domain of application. It was therefore often quite difficult or even impossible to establish or extend a domain specific rule base so that the inference engine and rule base would together successfully perform the task at hand. Even within an application domain and a specific task, it was (almost) impossible to extend a rule base without deteriorating the previously achieved task performance of a system. In short, such systems are difficult to develop and maintain for larger fields of applications (see Clancey, 1983).

The *second generation* of expert systems has therefore emphasized that the construction of expert systems should be viewed as a model building process (Breuker & Wielinga, 1989; Clancey, 1985) where a domain-appropriate model has to be constructed, possibly by selecting, instantiating, and adjusting some interpretation model from a library of generic models (see Breuker & Van de Velde, 1994). Such models may be formally specified by specifically designed modelling languages (e.g., Angele, Fensel, Landes, & Studer, 1991; Wetter 1990). An example of such an expert system that was successfully used in practice is the FRAUDWATCH system (Killin, 1992). This system is used to screen financial transactions that are authorized by a credit-card number. The system then determines which transactions are possibly fraudulent. Such systems have proven to be very successful and have also shown high economic returns. Whereas the first generation systems contained knowledge that was rapidly compiled for rather specific tasks, the second generation of expert systems has been constructed by modelling deep knowledge (see Schmalhofer & van Elst, 1995), where a complete set of requirements are identified that are to be satisfied by the system. Both the expert systems of the first and the second generation are in close accord with the world view of symbolic cognition.

But let us now address the question of how one could utilize the results from our psychological research for developing an expert system in some field of application like mechanical engineering. This was the topic of a larger research project that was conducted from 1989 to 1993 by the *knowledge acquisition group* at the German Research Center for Artificial Intelligence (DFKI) in Kaiserslautern. This research yielded a general knowledge acquisition method, namely the *Integrated Knowledge Acquisition Method* (IKAM), for constructing expert systems, and a specific expert system, the *Case-Oriented Expert* or COEx-*system*, that can be used for production planning in mechanical engineering.

This knowledge engineering project was performed according to the following rationale. In the psychological research, we investigated how human learners acquire competence in some new area and how different learning materials and learning situations are thereby utilized. The results of this research were expressed in a precise and concise manner by a unified theory. If human knowledge acquisition is indeed well adapted to the specific requirements of the human environment (as we argued in chapter 3), it may also be quite beneficial to develop an expert system (or knowledge-based system) in the same manner as humans build up their knowledge-based system for a specific application domain.

For the purpose of developing the general knowledge acquisition method for expert systems (i.e., IKAM) as well as for building the expert system itself (i.e., the COEx-system), the following general conclusions were drawn from the previously reported psychological research. Because cognitive systems are well adapted to their environments, a thorough analysis of the application domain (in our case mechanical engineering) will yield important requirements that are to be met by the expert system. Similar to the humans' integrated knowledge acquisition from different sources (see chapter 11), the various information sources that are available and easily accessible in an application domain should be jointly used for developing the system. Just as human knowledge depends on the learner's prior knowledge, the development of an expert system should be guided by a so-called model of expertise (Breuker & Wielinga, 1989). Similar to the learning processes in the KIWi model, we furthermore distinguished between material-related representations that may be still informal and the completely formalized knowledge base that is no longer directly attached to the specific learning materials.

Analysis of the Application Domain of Mechanical Engineering

Similar to a rational analysis, the field of mechanical engineering was first analyzed. *H*istorical, *so*ciological and *co*gnitive factors were thereby taken into consideration, and the particular analysis was therefore termed HISOCO analysis. The results of the analysis showed that practical skills and theoretical knowledge are the two important types of expertise in mechanical engineering (Fandel, Dyckhoff, & Reese, 1990; Spur, 1979). It was then identified that there are three traces of expertise that can be used for building an expert system: (a) The general knowledge that renowned theoreticians accumulated in their research can be found in various textbooks. (b) The specific solutions that practitioners have found are stored in the filing cabinets or data bases of companies. (c) Through their possibly implicit expert memories, practitioners may in addition possess an expert classification for the various types of tasks. These expert memories may be tapped with appropriate knowledge-elicitation techniques. A more detailed description of the HISOCO analysis was given by Fischer and Schmalhofer (1990) and Schmalhofer, Bergmann, Kühn, and Schmidt (1991).

A Flexible Knowledge-Engineering Method

We have subsequently developed an integrated knowledge-acquisition method for constructing an expert system from these different sources of information (textbooks, previous solved cases, and expert memories). The development process was guided by a model of expertise (Breuker & Wielinga, 1989). Figure 12.1 presents an overview of the integrated knowledge-acquisition method. Whereas other approaches to knowledge engineering (i.e., the process of developing expert systems) have proposed specific process models (e.g., Neubert & Studer, 1992), the current approach specifies only a guideline and thus allows for more flexibility. As can be seen from Fig. 12.1, it determines four different episodes in which the information that is available in an application domain becomes increasingly more structured. Initially, relevant and sufficient information is selected from the available information sources. The consistency and redundancy of this information is then assessed and an early knowledge verification is thereby performed. After a step of possible knowledge extensions, the structured information is then translated into a formal representation. For example, the well-known description logics (Brachman & Schmolze, 1985; Hanschke, Abecker, & Drollinger, 1991) may be applied for this formalization (see Reinartz & Schmalhofer, 1994). For performing knowledge engineering with IKAM, a number of software tools have been developed. COKAM, CECoS and the KR-Tool are some of these tools whose area of application is also indicated in Fig. 12.1. A more detailed description of this method was presented by Schmalhofer, Kühn, and Schmidt (1991).

This method was then applied to the problem of production planning in mechanical engineering and the case-oriented expert system and COEx architecture were thereby developed. Depending on how closely some new planning problem is related to the previously solved problems, the COEx system will either retrieve a previous solution (and thereby present a case-based solution), retrieve a skeletal plan that can be instantiated for the specific problem, or retrieve an abstract plan schema that is then either automatically or interactively refined.

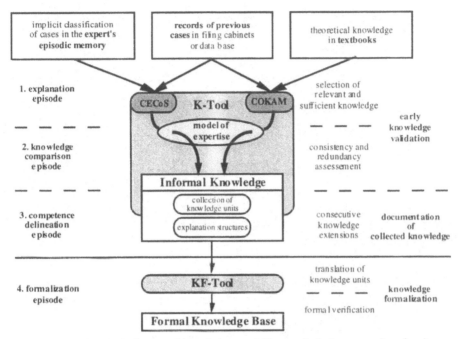

FIG. 12.1. IKAM, the integrated knowledge acquisition method, is a general and quite flexible approach for developing an expert system so that the system is well adjusted to the particular area of application (adapted from Schmalhofer et al., 1991).

The Case-Oriented Expert System

Figure 12.2 shows the general architecture of the COEx system. The upper part shows the *knowledge acquisition component* and the lower part shows the *performance component*. The knowledge acquisition component consists of a model of expertise for skeletal plan refinement (see Aitken, Kühn, Shadbolt, & Schmalhofer, 1993; Kühn & Schmalhofer, 1992), and four knowledge acquisition tools. The Case-Experience Combination System (CECoS; Bergmann & Schmalhofer, 1991; Reinartz & Schmalhofer, 1994) is used to obtain a formalized hierarchy of problem classes from a set of previously solved cases in combination with human expert judgments. The tool for Case-Oriented Knowledge Acquisition from text (COKAM+; Schmidt & Schmalhofer, 1990; Schmidt, 1992) is used for obtaining formalized domain knowledge from written documents (texts) with respect to the specific set of cases that were used for delineating the area of competence of the system (see Schmalhofer, Kühn, & Schmidt, 1991). The machine learning tool PABS (Bergmann & Wilke, 1995; Schmalhofer & Tschaitschian, 1993) is finally used to build procedure schemata by explanation-based abstractions that are also part of the knowledge base. Alternatively, or in addition, one can apply the learning tool SP-GEN that generates skeletal plans from the previously solved cases by explanation-based generalization (see Reinartz & Schmalhofer, 1994; Schmalhofer, Bergmann, Kühn, & Schmidt, 1991).

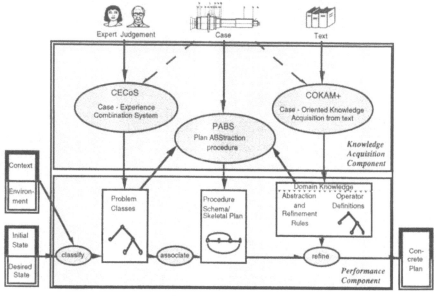

FIG. 12.2. Architecture of the COEx, or case-oriented expert system, consisting of knowledge acquisition and performance components (adapted from Schmalhofer & Thoben, 1992).

The performance component of the COEx system functions in the following way. A new problem description, consisting of the description of the initial and the desired states, is entered into the system. In addition, one may specify a specific context and environment in which the problem is to be solved. The problem is then classified into the most specific problem class that satisfies the problem description. The more novel a specific problem, the higher in the hierarchy of the problem classes will the most specific problem class be (see Reinartz & Schmalhofer, 1994). If a problem has already been solved, the most specific problem class will be a terminal node in the problem hierarchy. After this classification process, the procedure schema (for nonterminal problem classes) or skeletal plan (for terminal nodes) is retrieved and the domain knowledge is used to refine this schematic structure to a concrete plan that solves the specific problem at hand.

An empirical study of the user requirements of such a case-oriented approach to planning has shown that human experts often require a variety of different kinds of solutions to such a planning problem (see Schmalhofer, Globig, & Thoben, 1992). The possibility of entering a specific context and environment together with a planning problem allows for such a flexible way of finding several different plans for solving the same problem.

We have thus presented a general approach to developing expert systems where the knowledge acquisition process is similarly structured to the knowledge acquisition processes of human learners. At first one builds up informal and more material-related representations (see phases 1, 2, and 3 in Fig. 12.1). This informal knowledge is subsequently formalized and abstracted from the specific learning materials. This is quite similar to the more material-related and the material-independent representations that we have observed for the human learners. The different knowledge-acquisition tools are also similarly structured to the respective cognitive processes of template formation (CECoS, SP-GEN), the formation of situation model and procedure schemata (PABS) and building a textbase (COKAM). We have thus shown how a unified theory of cognition can be successfully applied to the area of knowledge engineering and how the COEx-system was thereby developed. As more recent work has shown, the application of such an architecture is not restricted to the field of mechanical engineering but can also be applied in the area of medicine (Birk, Schmalhofer, Thüring, & Gertzen, 1995), as well as for developing a corporate memory (Kühn & Höfling, 1994).

12.3 Summary

We have discussed how the results that were obtained from the psychological experiments on the acquisition of knowledge may be applied in areas such as instructional technology and the development of expert systems. It was shown how instructional sets that may consist of text, examples, and exploration episodes may be designed so that a specific knowledge state will be achieved by the learner. Model-tracing techniques of intelligent tutoring systems basically require a complete representations of the domain, the learner's prior knowledge, and the knowledge state to be achieved. Such representations are expensive and often quite impossible to achieve. It was pointed out that such strict guidance of the student may not even be desirable. On many occasions it may be more appropriate to allow the students to be more creative in their learning activities. Learning environments that do not strictly guide the student but instead provide opportunities for merging different representation spaces may be more adequate for this purpose. We furthermore reported how the results from the psychological research were used as a guideline for developing IKAM, which is a general and quite flexible approach for the design and implementation of expert systems. The COEx system, which was developed according to this approach, was then presented, and correspondences between components of this system and the components of the previously presented cognitive model were pointed out. We have thus demonstrated that results from experimental psychology may yield some useful applications in the areas of instructional technology and expert system development. Obviously, we could not discuss all possible areas of applications and there are several other areas where results from cognitive research can be successfully applied (e.g., human–computer interaction).

13

===

General Discussion, Conclusions, and Future Directions

===

In this book, we have addressed three quite different issues that are nevertheless very closely related in any practice of scientific research on human cognition. The first issue concerns the specific research methodologies that are applied in the area of cognitive experimental psychology. Should such research be conceptualized, performed, and reported solely under the guidance of the traditional principles from experimental design, or should one make the additional effort of building models in the form of computer simulations, which would allow us to unify the empirical findings across different experimental paradigms? The second issue concerns how the experimental psychology research on text comprehension, concept formation, and memory are much more closely related to one another than might appear from the very specialized research paradigms and the highly specific scientific controversies. In particular, we asked whether it would be possible to build a more general theory of *human knowledge acquisition* that would span the areas of text comprehension, concept formation, categorization, memory, and other closely related topics. Such a general theory was intended to include simple and rigorously controlled experimental settings as well as the more real-life-like situations that are studied in instructional and educational psychology. The domain of learning a new programming language was thereby found to be well suited for bridging the gap between simple experimental settings and real-life situations. The experimental investigations of how students with different kinds of prior knowledge would acquire knowledge about a novel subject domain, such as a new programming language, was thus the third topic of our research interest.

13.1 Methodological Issues in Experimental Psychology

The area of experimental psychology has prospered for more than 100 years and is continuing to do so. With its scientific methods, a steadily increasing number of systematic and robust effects is being discovered. This is especially true for the field of cognitive experimental psychology, in which memory, learning, problem solving, judgment, decision making, text comprehension, and similar topics have been thoroughly investigated during the last few decades. In combination with the many interesting research findings, this continuous progress has yielded additional methodological problems that did not exist when the field was first started some 100 years ago.

As the number of well-established experimental effects has increased, it has become quite difficult to maintain an overview of these effects. For example, it may be quite difficult to determine whether the various results about human memory, expert performance, text comprehension, and problem solving are jointly consistent, mutually consistent for some selected areas, or whether results from expert performance and text comprehension do indeed contradict the conclusions about human working memory that were drawn from the memory research with simple learning materials such as word lists (cf. Ericsson & Kintsch, 1995).

In other words, because of its many and continuing successes, the issue of coordinating the conclusions from different lines of research has become a more and more pressing problem in the area of cognitive psychology. Traditionally, the problem of summarizing and thereby coordinating a larger body of research results has been approached in two different ways. Most commonly, a researcher would simply write a review of some body of research and thereby arrive at certain conclusions about what the experimental results would show in general. Obviously the methodological rigor of such verbal summarizations does not even come close to the rigor of the methodology for designing and conducting experiments or the methodology of interpreting empirical data by statistical analyses. The second way of summarizing data is by statistical meta-analyses (cf. Cooper & Hedges, 1994). Such meta-analyses can, however, only be applied where the same (or at least similar) independent and dependent variables have been applied in the different studies. Meta-analyses neither address the commensurability of the theories that have been developed for different experimental paradigms, nor do they provide any support in the planning of coordinated investigations. Statistical meta-analyses are therefore hardly useful for relating the research from different experimental paradigms that appear to be inherently related.

The deeper problem of coordinating the experimental psychology results from different subareas of cognitive psychology lies in the fact that experimental psychologists have quite independently researched various research questions. In different paradigms, different sets of variables were manipulated. Because the research on one particular question was performed in isolation from the other (inherently related) research question, the specific relationships between such research questions remained unclear over the decades. This approach of looking at certain regularities in isolation is quite typical of experimental psychology and it is also the basis for the methodological rigor of the experimental method that is the positive side of the coin. There is, however, another side to this coin, which was pointed out by Newell (1973) more than 20 years ago.

Because human cognition is achieved by one organism or system, one cannot arbitrarily isolate questions when these questions address system attributes that, together, must obviously provide a sufficient description of a functional system. Is information-processing parallel or serial? Is the human knowledge representation propositional or analogue? Are skills represented declaratively or procedurally? Is working memory limited to 7 plus or minus 2 chunks, or is there a relatively large long-term working memory? Should the structure of semantic memory be elicited by independent free associations or by association chains where each generated term is the functional stimulus for the next generated term? These are all questions that may stimulate an experimental psychologist to design experiments, but how can we understand the functioning of the cognitive system when we only look in isolation at the things that obviously go together?

Theories and models are needed for bridging the gaps between different experimental paradigms. Such theories have been termed unified theories of cognition (Anderson, 1976; Newell, 1990). For developing such a model or theory, one could possibly try to inductively infer the general theory from the available experimental results. We may thereby think of an (formal or informal) application of one of the machine learning mechanisms that we described in chapter 2. The basic problem of such a bottom–up or data-driven approach to theory development is that despite all the available data, that data is too sparse for inducing a theory (see Anderson, 1993). On the other hand, one could develop a model in a more top–down fashion. The problem of this top–down or conceptually driven theory development is that it is basically impossible to come up with a theory that fits all the available data.

In a sense, there are too many and too few data available at the same time — not enough data to inductively infer a complete theory and too many data sets (which are often inconsistent) so that a theory would be able to account for all of them. In order to deal with this specific problem, we developed the levels approach to modeling in chapter 3. Instead of a top–down or bottom–up approach to theory development, we have advocated a perspective from evolutionary psychology. Because an organism and its environment evolve together, organism and environment are part and parcel. By describing an organism as being well adapted to its environment, we can thus obtain an appropriate terminology for describing an organism at the knowledge level for some environmental context, so that this description spans the different experimental paradigms that have been used to investigate the cognitive system in more detail. Our rational analyses are thus guided by an environmental and evolutionary perspective and are not driven by normative models or by what has been referred to as *folk psychology* (cf. Cosmides & Tooby, 1994). In a second step, such knowledge-level descriptions are then reified by the symbol level and further operationalized by an implementation on a digital computer. The symbol level is developed so that there is a close correspondence to the data from the psychological experiments. Another way of saying this is that the results from the psychological experiments are used to empirically test the symbol-level description. The implementation level, on the other hand, contains the purely technical details of the theoretical account as well as the technical details of the specific experimental investigations. For the brevity of our exposition, in this book, we also referred to the knowledge level as the *theory*, the symbol level as the *model*, and the implementation level as the *implementation*.

With this levels approach, we are able to resolve some of the inconsistencies that often exist in the data from different experimental paradigms. Basically, inconsistencies are pushed to the technical level. Because only the knowledge and the symbol levels span different experimental paradigms, the specializations that have produced the inconsistencies are now in the technical details. In this manner, we can achieve a paraconsistency across all the experimental data. While the knowledge and symbol-level descriptions are consistent across the different experimental paradigms, the technical details need not be consistent between the different paradigms. An analogy to a simple subject domain may help to clarify the levels approach toward cognitive modeling.

Suppose that, instead of the cognition of humans, we would be researching the auto-motion of cars. Furthermore, assume that traditionally, there are two different ways for evaluating the auto-motion of cars. Assume that one evaluation would address the question of the maximum distance a car would continue after a run down a steep hill. A second evaluation would address the maximum distance a car will drive when going uphill. The first line of evaluation revealed that maximum distance would be positively correlated with the number of persons and the amount of fuel in the car. The second line of evaluation revealed that the maximum distance would be negatively correlated with the number of people in the car and positively correlated with the amount of fuel. The two lines of evaluation would thus have revealed contradictory results. In order to resolve such a contradiction, we need to apply a more appropriate conceptology, which would include terms such as gravity, positional energy, friction, the weight of the vehicle, and so on. In other words, if the whole issue is framed by a better conceptology, we can very well obtain a unified description of seemingly contradictory results. In a quite similar way, we can uniformly describe text comprehension and concept formation from examples in a uniform manner when we assume that the system is well adapted to its natural environment. In this domain, learning goals, prior knowledge, and the available learning materials will provide the more appropriate terminology for describing learning as a constructive knowledge-acquisition process.

Our level approach resembles in many aspects the proposals by Newell and Anderson. From these proposals, Anderson's work is the one that has been the most developed for the purposes of experimental psychology. There is one major difference to Anderson. Anderson (1993) attempted to resolve the identifiability problem by requesting that a cognitive architecture correspond to the human cognitive system at all the levels — the subsymbolic, the symbolic, and the knowledge level (which Anderson called the rational level). Anderson thereby required that the implementation level consist of a neural net. Our approach, on the other hand, views the implementation level only as a technical medium that is not very important other than that it is required for making a model run on a computer or for specifying how some specific experiments were conducted. Whereas Anderson's levels approach sets the goal of completely identifying the human cognitive architecture, our methodology aims at presenting a consistent account of experimental data when such data appear to be inconsistent. With our levels approach, such apparent inconsistencies are then resolved by distinguishing essential assumptions from technical details. With this methodology we developed the comprehension-based model of constructive knowledge acquisition, which was used for unifying research results on concept formation, learning by exploration, and text comprehension into a more general theory of knowledge acquisition from different learning materials.

13.2 Comprehension and Constructive Knowledge Acquisition

The KIWi Model

By the cognitive model that we developed in this research, knowledge acquisition is described as a constructive and possibly creative process. Construction skills that operate on different conceptual spaces retrieve and generate various snippets of knowledge. These knowledge snippets are constructed with respect to the specific learning material (text, examples, etc.), the situations that are referred to by the learning materials, and a learning goal. Subsequently, links are constructed among these knowledge units so that a knowledge network is obtained. This network describes pluralistic views of the learning material in the form of a multilevel representation. It contains contradictory as well as redundant knowledge. In the network, material-related (verbatim, propositional, surface-form, template) and situational units can thereby be distinguished theoretically (see e.g., Figs. 4.1, 4.2, and 6.1) as well as empirically (see e.g., Figs. 7.4, 10.1, 10.4, and 10.7). Integration skills then form a coherent and consistent network by determining that knowledge units jointly fit together well. The other knowledge units which do not fit into this emerging structure are discredited and become disconnected and removed. The resulting knowledge structure is again a multilevel representation. The newly constructed knowledge is thus built from the originally constructed knowledge snippets as a situation-specific circumscription (cf. Figs. 4.2, 4.4, 7.5, and 10.7). Because the situation-specific circumscription is built with knowledge snippets from quite different and previously unrelated conceptual spaces, it may indeed constitute a creative product in the sense of Boden's impossibilist's creativity.

We have furthermore implemented and tested the various components of this model. We also reused simulation programs that were developed by other researchers. The implementation is a hybrid and contains symbolic as well as connectionist components. Basically, one may view the model as a generate-and-test model. Unlike in other generate-and-test models of memory and problem solving (e.g., Schmalhofer & Polson, 1986), the test phase is not sequentially performed on each of the generated items in separation, but instead the various interactions among the different knowledge units determine as a whole which units do or do not pass the test. Unlike in other models, the test phase is therefore contextually determined. The essential characteristics of the proposed model may become more obvious by comparing the model to some alternative models.

Alternative Models

There is not enough space left in this book to compare our model to all the relevant models or even to the most representative models that have been proposed in the last decade. I must therefore restrict myself to comparing the KIWi model to just a few other models. Thereby, I selected models whose basic assumptions were either very close to our model, or models that are quite different in their approach.

The KIWi model shares many theoretical assumptions and several symbol-processing components with the NETWORK model (Mannes & Kintsch, 1991) and UNICOM model (Doane, Kintsch, & Polson, 1989). NETWORK and UNICOM are also based on Kintsch's construction–integration theory and these models were also applied to areas outside the domain of discourse. NETWORK has been applied to describe how subjects solve routine computing tasks. It is similarly concerned with the simulation of contextually driven phenomena. UNICOM has been applied to describe how computer users at different levels of expertise would solve tasks that require the application of single and composite commands in UNIX. Similar to the KIWi model, UNICOM and NETWORK were thus also applied to the area of computer programming. There may be two important differences between KIWi, on the one hand, and NETWORK and UNICOM, on the other hand. Whereas UNICOM and NETWORK are concerned with problem-solving tasks, the KIWi model is a unified model of knowledge acquisition in different situations where problem solving may occur as one of several different criterion test tasks. In NETWORK and UNICOM, the subjects' prior knowledge was independently elicited and the elecited information tokens were then used as external parameters in the model. On the other hand, in the KIWi model, we have theoretically specified the learner's prior knowledge by a formal knowledge base.

Fletcher and Bloom (1988) developed a model of human text processing in which they specified the short-term memory processes that had previously been identified in text comprehension (cf. Fletcher, 1981) in combination with the causal reasoning that occurs with narrative texts (Trabasso & van den Broek, 1985). The architecture and the processes of this model were derived from Kintsch's theory of text comprehension (Kintsch, 1988; van Dijk & Kintsch, 1983) and Kintsch's theory played an equally important role in the development of the KIWi model. Thus there are many similarities between these two models. There are similarities in the representational assumptions, and in that comprehension occurs by a cyclical process. The two models share the assumption that comprehension consists of building up coherent structures consisting of various levels of representation. Even the assumption that the construction of causal structures can be an important part of comprehension is shared by the KIWi model. In the KIWi model, knowledge typing and causal relations occur at the situation level. General coherence, which is based on argument overlap, is represented at the propositional level. In the text comprehension research that was reported in this book, causal structures did not play an important part because we were dealing with expository rather than narrative texts. For narrative texts (Schmalhofer, van Elst, Vogel, & McDaniel, 1995) and even computer programs (Schmalhofer, Bergmann, Boschert & Thoben, 1993), the construction of causal models does, however, play an important part in the KIWi model.

There are also some important differences between the two models. Whereas Fletcher and Bloom made very strict assumptions about the capacity of working memory, which yielded very detailed experimental predictions, in the KIWi model, we were forced to assume that working memory has a much larger capacity than the limitations that were identified by using simple learning materials (cf. Ericsson & Kintsch, 1995; Miller, 1956). As the transition from the view of symbolic cognition further progresses toward a view of situated cognition, it will become more and more appropriate to specify memory and processing limitations in terms of affordances rather than in terms of a system characteristic that could be described in isolation from its environment. With the KIWi model, we attempted to start such a transitional phase. Whereas the model by Fletcher and Bloom unified the processing assumptions about causal reasoning (Trabasso & van den Broek, 1985) and the establishment of local coherence by argument overlap (Miller & Kintsch, 1980) for the area of text comprehension and recall, the intended and achieved scope of unification is quite a bit larger in the KIWi model.

The ELM model (Weber, 1994; Weber, Bögelsack, & Wender, 1993) is similar to the KIWi model in that it also describes how subjects acquire knowledge about the programming language LISP. Whereas the KIWi model has only been applied to the first few hours of learning a programming language, ELM has been used for a much larger curriculum. At the technical level, ELM and KIWi are somewhat similar in that both apply explanation-based learning for establishing an explanatory coherence between programming examples and prior knowledge. But in this respect, ELM and KIWi are at the same time also different. Whereas ELM describes learning as a case-based process and therefore uses only explanation-based generalization, the KIWi model is a comprehension-based learner, which means that it merges knowledge snippets from different conceptual spaces and thus performs true abstractions by explanation based abstraction rather than only generalizations. There is a substantial difference between abstraction and generalization. Whereas a generalization transforms a description along the set–superset dimension, abstraction performs a transformation along a level of detail description (Michalski & Kodratoff, 1990). The learning processes that are described by the ELM model thus occur in a single representation space. The comprehension-based learning processes of the KIWi model, on the other hand, perform translations between representational spaces and may also a create a novel conceptual structure that is tailored to the specific learning context.

The model of *knowledge assessment* by Lukas and Albert (1993), on the other hand, was developed in a quite different research tradition. More specifically, it is based on the theory of knowledge spaces of Doignon and Falmagne (1985). Whereas all of the previously mentioned models postulate dynamic processes and various memory representations for describing a student's cognition, the knowledge-assessment model portrays a learner by a minimal description of the subset of problems that a learner is capable of solving. A particular field of knowledge (e.g., geometry, chess, fault diagnosis of electrical circuits) is thus conceptualized by a finite set of problems that can possibly arise in this field or that a theoretician simply defines to be the relevant set of problems. The theoretician (or domain expert) must furthermore specify which problems build a prerequisite for solving some other problems. The relational structure that is implied by these prerequisites is then used to establish a parsimonious procedure for diagnosing a student's knowledge. The task analyses that Lukas and Albert performed together with their collaborators are performed for establishing the knowledge spaces that are mostly derived from the expert literature of the specific application domain (cf. Korrossy, 1993). For example, the knowledge space about chess is structured according to the writings of chess experts. The knowledge-assessment model is therefore particularly suited for diagnosing a person's performance in a domain with a well structured competence. It is hardly suited for describing how new knowledge may emerge when different conceptual spaces are conjointly viewed. In the light of Lukas and Albert's model, knowledge is viewed as the possession of some set of elementary skills, and knowledge acquisition would thus simply be the process of storing such skills in memory.

As mentioned before, there are many more models to which the KIWi model could be compared. Because of the large number of models, it appears to be more useful to compare the knowledge level assumptions of the KIWi model (i.e., that knowledge acquisition is a comprehension-based process) to alternative theories. This is a comparison among different knowledge-level assumptions.

Alternative Theories and Frameworks

The KIWi model assumes that knowledge acquisition is a comprehension-based process. As we have seen from the comparisons with the ELM and the knowledge-assessment model, there are fundamental differences among different models, and these fundamental differences can be used to define classes of models. Models that assume that knowledge acquisition consists of the search of a conceptual space and a subsequent compilation of the search results builds one such class of models. This class has been termed search-based theories. Models that assume that knowledge acquisition consists of the storage of relatively complex cases in combination with an appropriate indexing structure so that previous cases can be reused for solving novel problems form another class of models. This class has been termed case-based theories. Over the last few years, search-based as well as case-based architectures have been quite extensively researched and elaborated, so that a comparison with these architectures will be quite informative (cf. chapter 2).

The most prominent prototype of a search-based theory of human cognition is Newell's SOAR (Laird, Newell, & Rosenbloom, 1987). SOAR was developed as an architecture for general intelligence. Its intended application is thus much broader than the modeling work presented by our research. On the other hand, SOAR was originally designed to be a nonlearning problem solver and chunking was later on added as SOAR's universal learning mechanism. SOAR was thus originally developed as a theory of problem solving rather than as a theory of human learning. SOAR has been typically applied to toy problems but also to some more complex problems. When SOAR is presented with a problem it searches the problem space to find a solution. Thereby it applies heuristic search strategies. Whenever some impasse is encountered, SOAR dynamically generates a new (sub)goal and a new problem space. The new subgoal is defined so that its solution will resolve the impasse and the new problem space is employed to search for the solution. SOAR can thus generate an arbitrary number of search spaces until it finds a solution to the given problem. Its long-term memory is structured as a production system and all the directly available knowledge is represented by productions.

SOAR's universal learning mechanism is chunking. Whenever a subgoal is generated during problem solving, this subgoal also defines a learning episode that may lead to the generation of a chunk. Chunking consists of the generation of production rules that summarize the processing of a subgoal. In the future, the costly heuristic search in the problem space can thereby be replaced by a direct rule application. The chunk is usually generated when some subgoal is achieved. Quite generally, one may thus conclude that SOAR's learning processes basically consist of knowledge compilation where the most useful knowledge from a problem solving episode is summarized, compiled, or chunked so that these search processes can be avoided when the same problem needs to be solved again.

SOAR and search-based architectures in general, therefore do <u>not</u> learn anything really novel. Everything that can possibly be learned by SOAR is implicitly contained in the definition of the problem spaces. Learning in SOAR thus occurs by explicating those parts of the problem space that are relevant for the specifically presented problem, and by storing the most relevant parts of this solution for future use (chunking or compilation). Knowledge compilation in Anderson's ACT-R architecture functions in a rather similar manner. But ACT-R has also incorporated additional learning mechanisms, such as learning by analogy. Another architecture that combines many different learning mechanisms is the PRODIGY architecture (Veloso, Carbonell, Pérez, Borrajo, Fink, & Blythe, 1995). In search-based architectures, learning and intelligence are assumed to occur by searching a conceptual space, by addressing additional knowledge by some symbol, and by selecting the most relevant parts of some problem solution and forming a respective chunk.

Search-based architectures are thus quite different from comprehension-based theories of learning, like the KIWi model, where knowledge acquisition is seen as a constructive process where new conceptual structures emerge by relating the circumstantially available pieces of information (i.e., the knowledge construction process) and then serendipitiously arranging the form and content of these knowledge units so that a situation-oriented circumscription of some contextually bound knowledge is obtained (the integration process). In the comprehension-based theories, it is thus assumed that intelligence emerges from bottom–up processes, followed by some contextually oriented dialectic structuring process. Learning and knowledge acquisition are thus supposed to be constructive and creative rather than searching in some fixed conceptual space and subsequently producing a short cut for the conducted search. Because search-based theories are usually implemented as production systems, they are often also referred to as rule-based reasoning.

The theory of case-based reasoning assumes that learning consists of the storage of relatively complex real-life episodes and the generation of appropriate indices for storing these episodes so that they can be retrieved later and utilized (cf. Kolodner, 1993). Unlike rules that are general and detached from particular contexts, cases are quite situation-specific representations. Because every detail is potentially relevant, a case is thus stored with all its details. In case-based reasoning, problem solving occurs by intelligently retrieving the most relevant case and then performing local adaptations of the retrieved case so that it can be used for solving a new problem. Case-based reasoning has claimed to achieve creative solutions to a problem (Schank & Leake, 1989). In this respect, case-based reasoning is similar to comprehension-based learning. In case-based reasoning, creative solutions are achieved by analogical reasoning processes, where many details may play an important role. In the comprehension-based theories, on the other hand, creativity arises from merging different representation spaces. Whereas in case-based reasoning the adjustment to a new problem occurs only when a new problem arises, in the KIWi model, specific cases are already abstracted with respect to some anticipated future tasks during knowledge acquisition.

We have thus seen that comprehension-based theories are quite different from search-based and case-based theories. Search-based theories appear to be most appropriate where problem solutions can be obtained by searching a relatively small problem space (such as for toy problems). Case-based theories can be applied to more complex situations when new problems are relatively similar to an older problem at the surface level. Typically, there is no deep-level processing in a case-based reasoner. Comprehension-based models, such as the KIWi model, on the other hand, describe how appropriate abstractions and new conceptualizations can be formed that are situation-oriented, but at the same time are abstracted from the specific details of a case.

13.3 Experimental Evidence

For testing the empirical validity and the usefulness of our theory we performed several experiments that established the relations among text comprehension, concept formation, and categorization tasks according to the guidelines that were provided by the levels approach toward cognitive modeling and the KIWi model as a unifying model. In both areas — text comprehension (cf. Carpenter, Miyake, & Just, 1995) as well as categorization and concept formation (cf. Medin & Heit, in press) — there are competing views about the kind of cognitive processes that are involved in performing the respective tasks. Quite often, pointed scientific controversies flare around competing models or conceptualizations. For example, in the area of text comprehension, it has recently been discussed whether readers would only build local inferences that establish a coherence relation between otherwise unrelated propositions (cf. McKoon & Ratcliff, 1992) or whether readers would indeed construct a causal model from a text (cf. Trabasso & van den Broek, 1985). In the area of categorization, it is for example discussed whether the learning of categories is guided by causal models (Waldmann, Holyoak, & Fratianne, 1995) or whether causal order does not affect cue selection in categorization learning (Shanks & Lopez, 1995). These are just two of many more controversies that are stimulating much additional work in experimental psychology. During the flaring of such controversies, it is quite typical for the participants to point out what they believe would be the basic methodological criteria that need to be met in order to test the critical issue. Previous research experience has, however, often shown that these basic methodological criteria can hardly be established during the heat of a scientific debate. Quite often such debates produce what appears to be an infinite methodological regress and are never clearly resolved.

There are obviously quite serious problems with such a research practice in experimental psychology and these problems have been known for more than 20 years (cf. Newell, 1973). Unless one really wants to restrict the scientific discourse to a rather narrow laboratory setting such as the categorization of artificial stimuli or the processing of texts that consist of two sentences, it becomes obvious that the various controversies in the different fields of specialization in cognitive experimental psychology are closely related.

Therefore they cannot be resolved in isolation from one another and there needs to be a common ground in the form of a theory that sets the basic methodological criteria, long before a scientific debate occurs. In other words, unified theories are needed in cognitive experimental psychology that put the various experimental results in perspective and that allow for a better utilisation of the research results in other areas such as instructional psychology and other disciplines such as artificial intelligence. The most remarkable work on unified theories of cognition has been performed by Anderson (1983, 1993) and Newell (1990). Both researchers have attempted to build a complete theory of the human cognitive system.

But there are also very promising efforts towards unification of various experimental results that are more tightly connected to specific paradigms in experimental psychology. The three-pronged approach of Graesser and his collaborators (cf. Graesser et al., 1994), which attempts to unify the research on inference generation, is an example of such a unification attempt where theory and data are more closely connected than in the more extensive ACT and SOAR theories. The scope of application as well as the granularity of the KIWi model lies somewhere in between the general cognitive architectures of ACT and SOAR and the unification attempts in experimental psychology. The KIWi model provides a unified description of learning from text, the categorization of examples when a learner does or does not have extensive background knowledge available for learning, as well as the activities that occur in learning by exploration. The model also describes the utilisation of the acquired knowledge in various application situations.

The 11 experiments that are reported in this book were designed so that they would test the central assumptions of the KIWi model, and especially with respect to testing the assumptions that relate and thereby unify our scientific knowledge about human knowledge acquisition. The three experiments of chapter 7 clearly show that knowledge acquisition is a goal-driven process and that the representation spaces that are built depend on the anticipated tasks that a learner presumes that she or he will have to solve in the future. The four experiments of chapters 8 and 9 demonstrate how learning from text and learning from examples are related to one another and that the constructed situation representation can be quite independent of the specific learning material. The four experiments of chapter 10 give a clear demonstration that different information sources become integrated during knowledge acquisition by establishing an explanatory coherence among the different sources. These experiments also demonstrate the influence of prior domain knowledge in the different learning modes. It was demonstrated that knowledge acquisition can be a constructive process rather than a pure search or storage process. The experiment in chapter 11 finally shows that the integrated knowledge acquisition assumption of the KIWi model was empirically more adequate than the example-dominance assumptions that supports theories of case-based reasoning. We have thus not only shown that the KIWi model is supported by the experimental studies, but we have also demonstrated how experiments from different areas of specializations in cognitive psychology can be brought together and how the proposed levels approach toward cognitive modeling is thereby applied.

Rather than asking more and more differentiated questions that are then investigated by more and more specialized experimental designs, we have thus shown how experimental psychology could proceed more fruitfully by investigating those aspects that are shared among different areas of specializations such as text comprehension and categorization. A cognitive psychology that becomes increasingly specialized requires a special effort for avoiding an increasing fragmentation into several controversial issues that are independently discussed but indeed inherently related. It has been too long that experimental psychology has been searching for significant differences. We need research that focuses on commonalties in increasingly larger areas of scientific discourse. When applying the levels approach toward cognitive modeling, it turned out that the differences were quite often at a subordinate technical level, whereas commonalties could indeed be established at what has been termed the knowledge and symbol levels. As we have shown, such commonalties are quite important for the application of experimental research results in areas such as instructional psychology or expert system development. I hope that in the future the results from experimental psychology from different areas of specializations will become more closely related to each other by unified theories rather than just being summarized by review articles or by statistical meta-analyses based on the general linear model and cook-book statistics rather than on the domain-specific structures that emerge in the different areas of cognitive research.

13.4 Outlook

In the introductory chapter, I described how psychological research on human knowledge acquisition pertains to more general epistemological issues and, in multifaceted ways, to the well known tensions between empiricist and rationalist research traditions. Our present research has shown that, in the realm of a cognitive science, these tensions can be resolved or at least alleviated when the human cognitive system and its environment are viewed as part and parcel that have evolved together. It was shown that such an evolutionary perspective has clear implications on how the empirical methods of experimental psychology and the technical machinery that is employed for specifying theories of human cognition should be coordinated, modified, and extended. The traditional task analyses, which are usually performed for limited experimental settings (e.g., Simon, 1975) yield normative models. These traditional task analyses were modified and extended into an analysis procedure in which the human cognitive system is viewed as being well adapted to its natural environment. Symbol manipulation mechanisms that had previously been seen as the necessary and sufficient conditions for intelligent behavior were thereby modified into formal description techniques that can describe rather than exert intelligent behavior. The design and the interpretation of psychological experiments were performed at different and joint levels of granularity, so that the essential properties could be shared across different experimental paradigms, while the specific technical differences between these paradigms were described at a subordinate and more technically oriented level. All of these proposed changes were coordinated and the levels approach toward cognitive modeling was thereby obtained as a research methodology that is suited for developing unified theories.

Our research has shown that knowledge acquisition can be a constructive and possibly creative process where snippets, fragments, and almost complete structures from the situational context and from different representation spaces (such as mathematics and commonsense knowledge) are merged and serendipitiously coordinated, and a novel conceptual structure may thereby emerge. New symbol structures are thus formed that are grounded in the environment rather than being only compositions of previously defined symbols.

The symbol-level hypothesis, as it was originally stated by Newell, is too restrictive for modeling human cognition, which is often bound to its context and environment. An evolutionary perspective, in which a task environment and the cognitive system evolve together and are therefore well adapted to one another, provides a valuable addition and generalization for cognitive theorizing. With an evolutionary perspective, we attempted to perform research that would yield a transition from the conventional cognitive research that is moulded by the formative influences of the information-processing and the computer metaphor (cf. Gigerenzer & Goldstein, 1995) to a view of situated cognition, in which the computer metaphor will have been deconstructed. Rather than juxtaposing the view of symbolic cognition and the view of situated cognition, which has been the current way of framing the relation between symbolic and situated cognition, we have thus identified the occasions in which the view of symbolic cognition is appropriate and where the assumptions of situated cognition are more adequate.

Basically, we have identified that models of symbolic cognition are appropriate when an area of research or application is so small, self-contained, and closed that a subject's operational knowledge about a domain can be completely represented. This is often true for toy domains. But already in an area like computer programming, it can be seen that the knowledge that the subjects bring into solving a task interacts with circumstantial entities so that new knowledge is being constructed in a manner that cannot be predicted by symbolic information-processing models. Symbolic models cannot produce anything really new in the sense that the produced concepts or the produced behavior would not simply be some explication of what was already represented before. Even when learning a programming language, knowledge snippets from different representation spaces and circumstantial entities are merged to build new representation spaces. In such a situated account, we are therefore dealing with an open system where new conceptual spaces and new behavior emerges over time. The transition from novice to expert behavior is thus explained by the emergence of a conceptual structure at the situational level. Whereas the novices use the peripheral representations as the conceptual space, expert behavior is explained by the formation of an appropriate situational representation, which may also include schematic structures.

With appropriate adjustments being made, computer simulation techniques and experimental methods will, on the other hand, continue to be useful techniques, even for researching situated cognition. Such adjustments are mostly motivated by the assumption that a cognitive system and its natural environment should be viewed as part and parcel, rather than viewing the cognitive system and its environment as completely separate parts that would interact by a locally defined interface (such as perception and action). Therefore, I hope that the future research on knowledge acquisition and cognitive psychology in general will not only benefit from the heritage of Hermann Ebbinghaus and the heritage of Alan Turing but that it will be built on a joint heritage that will also include the inheritance from Charles Darwin.

References

Agre, P. E. (1993). The symbolic worldview: Reply to Vera and Simon. *Cognitive Science, 17,* 61-69.

Aitken, J. S., Kühn, O., Shadbolt, N., & Schmalhofer, F. (1993). A conceptual model of hierarchical skeletal planning and its formalization. In: G. Löckenhoff (Ed.), *Proceedings of the 3rd KADS User Meeting* (pp. 229-247). Munich: Siemens AG.

Albert, D., Aschenbrenner, M., & Schmalhofer, F. (1989). Cognitive choice processes and the attitude-behavior relation. In A. Upmeyer (Ed.), *Attitudes and Behavioral Decisions* (pp. 61-100). New York: Springer-Verlag.

Allwood, C. M. (1986). Novices on the computer: A review of the literature. *International Journal of Man-Machine Studies, 25,* 633-658.

Anderson, J. R. (1976). *Language, memory, and thought.* Hillsdale, NJ: Lawrence Erlbaum Associates.

Anderson, J. R. (1978). Arguments concerning representations for mental images. *Psychological Review, 85,* 249-279.

Anderson, J. R. (1983). *The architecture of cognition.* Cambridge, MA: Harvard University Press.

Anderson, J. R. (1989). A theory of the origins of human knowledge. *Artificial Intelligence, 40,* 313-351.

Anderson, J. R. (1990a). *The adaptive character of thought.* Hillsdale, NJ: Lawrence Erlbaum Associates.

Anderson, J. R. (1990b). Cognitive modeling and intelligent tutoring. *Artificial Intelligence, 42,* 7-49.

Anderson, J. R. (1993). *Rules of the mind.* Hillsdale, NJ: Lawrence Erlbaum Associates.

Anderson, J. R., Boyle, C. F., Corbett, A. T., & Lewis, M. W. (1990). Cognitive modeling and intelligent tutoring. *Artificial Intelligence, 42,* 7-49.

275

Anderson, J. R., & Corbett, A. T. (1993). Acquisition of LISP programming skill. In S. Chipman & A. L. Meyrowitz (Eds.), *Foundations of knowledge acquisition: Cognitive models of complex learning* (pp. 1-24). Boston: Kluwer Academic Publishers.

Anderson, J. R., Farrell, R., & Sauers, R. (1984). Learning to program in LISP. *Cognitive Science, 8,* 87-129.

Anderson, J. R., & Fincham, J. M. (1994). Acquisition of procedural skills from examples. *Journal of Experimental Psychology: Learning, Memory, and Cognition, 20,* 1322-1340.

Anderson, J. R., & Skwarecki, E. (1986). The automated tutoring of introductory computer programming. *Communications of the ACM, 29,* 842-849.

Angele, J., Fensel, D., Landes, D., & Studer, R. (1991). KARL: An executable language for the conceptual model. In J. H. Boose & B. R. Gainers (Eds.), *Proceedings of the 6th Banff Knowledge Acquisition for Knowledge-Based Systems Workshop* (pp.1.1-1.20). Calgary: SRDG Publications. Department of Computer Science, University of Calgary.

Atkinson, R. C., Bower, G., & Crothers, E.J. (1965). *An introduction to mathematical learning theory.* New York: Wiley.

Atkinson, R. C., & Shiffrin, R. M. (1968). Human memory: A proposed system and its control processes. In K. Spence & J. Spence (Eds.), *The psychology of learning and motivation* (Vol. 2, pp. 89-105). New York: Academic Press.

Bain, W. M. (1986). *Case-based reasoning: A computer model of subjective assessment.* Unpublished doctoral dissertation, Yale University.

Baird, C. B., & Noma, E. (1978). *Fundamentals of scaling and psychophysics.* New York: John Wiley & Sons.

Bergmann, R. (1990). *Generierung von Skelettplänen als Problem der Wissensakquisition.* [The generation of skeletal plans as a knowledge acquisition problem]. Unpublished master's thesis, Universität Kaiserslautern.

Bergmann, R., Boschert, S., & Schmalhofer, F. (1992). Das Erlernen einer Programmiersprache: Wissenserwerb aus Texten, Beispielen und komplexen Programmen. [The learning of a programming language: Knowledge acquisition from texts, examples and complex programs]. In K. Reiss, M. Reiss, & H. Spandl (Eds.), *Maschinelles Lernen - Modellierung von Lernen mit Maschinen* [Machine learning - The modeling of learning by machines]. (pp. 204-224). Berlin: Springer-Verlag.

Bergmann, R., & Schmalhofer, F. (1991). CECoS: A case experience combination system for knowledge acquisition for expert systems. *Behavior Research Methods, Instruments, & Computers, 23,* 142-148.

Bergmann, R., & Wilke, W. (1995). Learning Abstract Planning Cases. In N. Lavrac & S. Wrobel (Eds), *Machine Learning: ECML-95* (pp. 55-76). Berlin: Springer-Verlag.

Birk, A., Schmalhofer, F., Thüring, M., & Gertzen, H. (1995). Architecture and user-interface of the IDEAS intelligent documentation system. In W. Schuler, J. Hannemann, & N. Streitz (Eds.), *Designing User Interfaces for Hypermedia* (pp. 78-94). Heidelberg: Springer-Verlag.

Blumberg, M. S., & Wasserman, E. A. (1995). Animal mind and the argument from design. *American Psychologist, 50,* 133-144.

Boden, M. A. (1991) *The creative mind: Myths and mechanisms.* New York: Basic Books, Inc., Publishers.

Bourne, L. E., Jr., Ekstrand, B. R., & Dominowski, R. L. (1971). *The psychology of thinking.* Englewood Cliffs, NJ: Prentice-Hall.

Bourne, L. E. Jr., & Restle, F. (1959). Mathematical theory of concept identification. *Psychological Review, 66,* 278-296.

Bovair, S., & Kieras, D. E. (1983). A guide to propositional analysis for research on technical prose. In B. K. Britton & J. B. Black (Eds.), *Understanding expository prose* (pp. 315-362). Hillsdale, NJ: Lawrence Erlbaum Associates.

Bower, G. H. (1970). Imagery as a relational organizer in associate learning. *Journal of Verbal Learning and Verbal Behavior, 9,* 529-533.

Bower, G. H., Black, J. B., & Turner, T. J. (1979). Scripts in memory for text. *Cognitive Psychology, 11,* 177-220.

Bower, G. H., & Trabasso, T. (1964). Concept identification. In R. C. Atkinson (Ed.), *Studies in mathematicl psychology* (pp. 32-94). Stanford, CA: Stanford Univeristy Press.

Brachman, R. J., McGuiness, D. L., Patel-Schneider, P. F., Resnick, L. A., & Borgida, A. (1990). Living with CLASSIC: When and how to use a KL-ONE-like language. In J. Sowa (Ed.), *Principles of semantic networks* (pp. 401-456). San Mateo: Morgan Kaufmann Publishers.

Brachman, R. J., & Schmolze, J. G. (1985). An overview of the KL-ONE knowledge representation system. *Cognitive Science, 9,* 171-216.

Bransford, J. D., Barclay, J. R., & Franks, J. J. (1972). Sentence memory: A constructive versus interpretive approach. *Cognitive Psychology, 3,* 193-209.

Breuker, J. A., & Van de Velde, W. (Eds.). (1994). *The Common-KADS library for expertise modelling.* Amsterdam, Netherlands: IOS Press.

Breuker, J. A., & Wielinga, W. J. (1989). Model driven knowledge acquisition. In P. Guida & G. Tasso (Eds.), *Topics in the design of expert systems* (pp. 265-296). Amsterdam, North-Holland: Elsevier.

Britton, B. K., & Eisenhart, F. J. (1993). Expertise, text coherence, and constraint satisfaction: Effects on harmony and settling rate. In *Proceedings of the Fifteenth Annual Conference of the Cognitive Science Society* (pp. 266-271). Hillsdale, NJ: Lawrence Erlbaum Associates.

Britton, B. K., & Gülgöz, S. (1991). Using Kintsch's computational model to improve instructional text: Effects of repairing inference calls on recall and cognitive structures. *Journal of Educational Psychology, 83,* 329-404.

Brooks, R. A. (1991). Intelligence without representation. *Artificial Intelligence, 47,* 139-159.

Bruner, J. S., Goodnow, J. J., & Austin, G. A. (1956). *A study of thinking.* New York: Wiley.

Bürckert, H.-J., Hollunder, B., & Laux, A. (1993). *Concept logics with function symbols* (Research Report RR-93-07). Kaiserslautern: German Research Center for Artificial Intelligence GmbH.

Carbonell, J. G. (1986). Derivational analogy: A theory of reconstructive problem solving and expertise acquisition. In R. S.Michalski, J. G. Carbonell, & T. M. Mitchell (Eds.), *Machine Learning: An Artificial Intelligence Approach* (Vol. 2, pp. 371-392). Los Altos, CA: Morgan Kaufmann.

Carbonell, J. G. (1989). Introduction: Paradigms for machine learning. *Artificial Intelligence, 40*, 1-9.

Carnap, R. (1928). *The logical structure of the world; Pseudoproblems in philosophy.* Berkeley: University of California Press. Republication in 1967.

Carpenter, P. A., Miyake, A., & Just, M. A. (1995). Language comprehension: Sentence and discourse processing. *Annual Review of Psychology, 46*, 91-120.

Carroll, J. M., Mack, R. L., Lewis, C. H., Grischkowsky, N. L., & Robertson, S. R. (1985). Exploring exploring a word processor. *Human Computer Interaction, 1*, 283-307.

Catrambone, R. (1995). Improving examples to improve transfer to novel problems. *Memory and Cognition, 22*, 606-615.

Chandler, P. J. (1965). *Subroutine STEPIT: An algorithm that finds the values of the parameters which minimize a given continous function.* Bloomington: Indiana University, Quantum Chemistry Program Exchange.

Charniak, E., & McDermott, D. (1985). *Introduction to artificial intelligence.* Reading, Mass: Addison-Wesley Publishing Company.

Chase, W. G., & Simon, H. A. (1973). Perception in chess. *Cognitive Psychology, 4*, 55-81.

Chi, M. T. H., Bassok, M., Lewis, M., Reimann, P., & Glaser, R. (1989). Self-explanations: How students study and use examples in learning to solve problems. *Cognitive Science, 13*, 145-182.

Chi, M. T. H., Feltovich, P., & Glaser, R. (1981). Categorization and representation of physics problems by experts and novices. *Cognitive Science, 5*, 121-152.

Chi, M. T. H., de Leeuw, N., Chiu, M.-H., & LaVancher, Ch. (1994). Eliciting self-explanations improves understanding. *Cognitive Science, 18*, 439-478.

Chipman, S., & Meyrowitz, A. L. (1993). *Foundations of knowledge acquisition: Cognitive models of complex learning.* Boston: Kluwer Academic Publishers.

Chomsky, A. N. (1956). Three models for the description of language. *IRE Transactions on information theory, IT*-2, 113-124.

Cirilo, R. K., & Foss, D. J. (1980). Text structure and reading time for sentences. *Journal of Verbal Learning and Verbal Behavior, 19*, 96-109.

Clancey, W. J. (1983). The epistemology of a rule-based expert system - Framework for explanation. *Artificial Intelligence, 20*, 215-251.

Clancey, W. J. (1985). Heuristic classification. *Artificial Intelligence, 27*, 289-350.

Clancey, W. J. (1989). The knowledge level reconsidered: Modeling how systems interact. *Machine Learning, 4*, 285-292.

Clancey, W. J. (1991). The Frame of reference problem in the design of intelligent machines. In K. VanLehn (Ed.), *Architectures for intelligence. The Twenty-second Carnegie Mellon symposium on cognition* (pp. 357-423). Hillsdale, NJ: Lawrence Erlbaum Associates.

Clancey, W. J. (1993). Situated action: A neuropsychological interpretation response to Vera and Simon. *Cognitive Science, 17*, 87-116.

Coombs, C. H., Dawes, R., & Tversky, A. (1970). *Mathematical psychology: An elementary introduction.* Englewood Cliffs, New Jersey: Prentice Hall Inc.

Cooper, H., & Hedges, L. V. (Eds.). (1994). *The handbook of research synthesis.* New York: Russell Sage Foundation.

Cosmides, L, & Tooby, J. (1994). Beyond intuition and instinct blindness: Toward an evolutionarily rigorous cognitive science. *Cognition, 50*, 41-77.

Dee-Lucas, D., & Larkin, J. H. (1988). Attentional strategies for studying scientific texts. *Memory and Cognition, 16*, 469-479.

DeJong, G., & Mooney, R. (1986). Explanation-based learning: An alternative view. *Machine Learning, 1*, 145-176.

Dennett, D. C. (1987). *The intentional stance.* Cambridge, MA: MIT Press/A Bradford Book.

Dietterich, T. G. (1986). Learning at the knowledge level. *Machine Learning, 1*, 287-316.

Doane, S. M., Kintsch, W., & Polson, P. (1989). Action planning: Producing UNIX commands. In *Proceedings of the Eleventh Annual Conference of the Cognitive Science Society* (pp. 458-465). Hillsdale, NJ: Lawrence Erlbaum Associates.

Doane, S. M., McNamara, D. S., Kintsch, W., Polson, P. G., & Clawson, D. (1992). Prompt comprehension in UNIX command production. *Memory and Cognition, 20*, 327-343.

Doignon, J.-P., & Falmagne, J.-C. (1985). Spaces for the assessment of knowledge. *International Journal of Man-Machine Studies, 23*, 175-196.

Dorffner, G., & Prem, E. (1993). Connectionism, symbol grounding, and autonomous agents. In *Proceedings of the Fifteenth Annual Conference of the Cognitive Science Society* (pp. 144-148). Hillsdale, NJ: Lawrence Erlbaum Associates.

Dörner, D. (1989). Die kleinen grünen Schildkröten und die Methoden der experimentellen Psychologie. [The small green turtles and the methods of experimental psychology]. *Sprache und Kognition,* [Language and Cognition], *8*, 86-97.

Dosher, B. A. (1982). Effect of sentence size and network distance on retrieval speed. *Journal of Experimental Psychology: Learning, Memory, and Cognition, 8*, 173-207.

Dosher, B. A., & Rosedale, G. (1991). Judgments of semantic and episodic relatedness: Common time-course and failure of segregation. *Journal of Memory and Language, 30*, 125-160.

Dyer, M. (1983). *In Depth Understanding.* Cambridge, MA: MIT Press.

Ebbinghaus, E. (1885). *Über das Gedächtnis: Untersuchungen zur experimentellen Psychologie.* Leipzig: Dunker. Reprinted by Wissenschaftliche Buchgesellschaft, Darmstadt in 1971. [Translation by H. Ruyer and C. E. Bussenius, *Memory,* New York, Teachers College, Columbia University. 1913.]

Eckes, Th. (1996). Begriffsbildung. [Concept formation]. In J. Hoffmann & W. Kintsch (Eds.), *Enzyklopädie der Psychologie. Serie Kognition, Band Lernen* (pp. 273-319). Göttingen: Hogrefe.

Egan, J. P. (1975). *Signal detection theory and ROC analysis.* New York: Academic Press.

Einstein, G. O., McDaniel, M. A., Owen P. D., & Coté, N. C. (1990). Encoding and recall of texts: The importance of material appropriate processing. *Journal of Memory and Language, 29*, 566-581.

Ellman, T. (1989). Explanation-based learning: A survey of programs and perspectives. *ACM Computing Surveys, 21*, 163-222.

Ericsson, K. A., & Chase, W. G. (1982). Exceptional Memory. *American Scientist, 70*, 607-615.

Ericsson, K. A., & Kintsch, W. (1995). Long-term working memory. *Psychological Review, 102*, 211-245.

Ericsson, K. A., & Simon, H. A. (1984). *Protocol analysis. Verbal reports as data.* Cambridge, MA: MIT Press.

Falmagne, R. J., & Gonsalves, J. (1995). Deductive inference. *Annual Review of Psychology, 46*, 525-559.

Fandel, G., Dyckhoff, H., & Reese, J. (1990). *Industrielle Produktionsentwicklung.* (Industrial development of manufacturing). Heidelberg: Springer-Verlag.

Feldman, D. H., Csikszentmihalyi, & Gardner, H. (1994) *Changing the World: A Framework for the Study of Creativity.* Westport, CT: Praeger Publishers.

Finke, R. A. (1995). Creative insight and preinventive forms. In R. J. Sternberg & J. E. Davidson (Eds.), *The nature of insight* (pp. 255-280). Cambridge, MA: MIT Press.

Fischer, G., McCall, R., Ostwald, J., Reeves, B., & Shipman, F. (1994). Seeding, evolutionary growth and reseeding: Supporting the incremental development of design environments. In *CHI'94 Conference Proceedings* (pp. 292-298). Reading, MA: Addison-Wesley.

Fischer, G., & Reeves, B. (in press). Beyond intelligent interfaces: Exploring, analyzing and creating success models of cooperative problem solving. *Applied Intelligence Journal.*

Fischer, U., & Schmalhofer, F. (1990). *Historische, soziologische und kognitive Aspekte der Fertigungstechnik* [Historical, sociological and cognitive aspects of manufacturing techniques] (ARC-TEC Projekt Report). Unpublished manuscript, Kaiserslautern: German Research Center for Artificial Intelligence GmbH.

Fletcher, C. R. (1981). Short-term memory processes in text comprehension. *Journal of Verbal Learning and Behavior, 20*, 564-574.

Fletcher, C. R., & Bloom, C. P. (1988). Causal reasoning in the comprehension of simple narrative texts. *Journal of Memory and Language, 27*, 235-244.

Freuder, E. C. (1978). Synthesizing constraint expressions. *Communications of the ACM, 21*, 958-966.

Galambos, J. A. (1983). Normative studies of six characteristics of our knowledge of common activities. *Behavior Research Methods & Instrumentation, 15*, 327-340.

Gardner, H. (1987). *The mind's new science: A history of the cognitive revolution.* New York: Basic Books, Inc., Publishers.

Garnham, A., & Oakhill, J. V. (1992). Discourse representation and text processing from a "mental models" perspective. *Language and Cognitive Processes, 7*, 193-204.

Gentner, D. (1983). Structure-mapping: A theoretical framework for analogy. *Cognitive Science, 7*, 155-170.

Gernsbacher, M. A. (1990). *Language comprehension as structure building.* Hillsdale, New Jersey: Lawrence Erlbaum Associates.

Gibson, J. J. (1954). The visual perception of objective motion and subjective movement. *Psychological Review, 61*, 304-314. Reprinted in *Psychological Review, 101*, 318-323, 1994.

Gigerenzer, G. (1991). From tools to theories: A heuristic of discovery in cognitive psychology. *Psychological Review, 98*, 254-267.

Gigerenzer, G., & Goldstein, D. G. (1995). *Mind as computer: The birth of a metaphor.* Manuscript, Department of Psychology, University of Chicago.

Gillund, G., & Shiffrin, R. M. (1984). A retrieval model for both recognition and recall. *Psychological Review, 91,* 1-67.

Glenberg, A. M. & Langston, W. E., (1992). Comprehension of illustrated text: Pictures help to build mental models. *Journal of Memory and Language, 31,* 129-151.

Goldman, S. R., & Varma S. (1995). CAPping the construction-integration model of discourse comprehension. In C. A. Weaver, III, S. Mannes, & C. R. Fletcher (Eds.), *Discourse Comprehension: Essays in Honor of Walter Kintsch* (pp. 337-358). Hillsdale: Lawrence Erlbaum Associates.

Gong, R., & Elkerton, J. (1990). Designing minimal documentation using a GOMS model: A usability evaluation of an engineering approach. In *Proceedings of CHI'90: Conference on Human Factors in Computing Systems* (pp. 99-106). Reading, MA: Addison Wesley Publishing.

Graesser, A. C., & McMahen, C. L. (1993). Anomalous information triggers questions when adults solve quantitative problems and comprehend stories. *Journal of Educational Psychology, 85,* 136-151.

Graesser, A. C., Singer, M., & Trabasso, T. (1994). Constructing inferences during narrative text comprehension. *Psychological Review, 101,* 371-395.

Graesser, A. C., & Zwaan, R. A. (1995). Inference generation and the construction of situation models. In C.A. Weaver, III, S. Mannes, & C. R. Fletcher (Eds.), *Discourse Comprehension: Essays in Honor of Walter Kintsch* (pp. 117-139). Hillsdale: Lawrence Erlbaum Associates.

Greeno, J. G. (1994). Gibson's affordances. *Psychological Review, 101,* 336-342.

Greeno, J. G. (1995). Understanding concepts in activity. In C.A. Weaver, III, S. Mannes, & C. R. Fletcher (Eds.), *Discourse Comprehension: Essays in Honor of Walter Kintsch* (pp. 65-95.). Hillsdale, NJ: Lawrence Erlbaum Associates.

Greeno, J. G., & Moore, J. L. (1993). Situativity and symbols: Response to Vera and Simon. *Cognitive Science, 17,* 49-59.

Greeno, J. G., & Steiner, T. E. (1964). Markovian processes with identifiable states: General considerations and application to all-or-none learning. *Psychometrika, 29,* 309-333.

Gregg, L. W., & Simon H. A. (1967). Process models and stochastic theories of simple concept formation. *Journal of Mathematical Psychology, 4,* 246-276.

Grice, H. P. (1967). *The logic of conversation.* William James Lectures, Cambridge, MA: Harvard University Press.

Gruber, T. R. (1994). Towards principles for the design of ontologies used for knowledge sharing. In Guarino & Poli (Eds.) *Formal Ontology in Conceptual Analysis and Knowledge Representation.* Boston: Kluwer Academic Publishers.

Guindon, R., & Kintsch, W. (1984). Priming macropropositions: Evidence for the primacy of macropropositions in the memory for text. *Journal of Verbal Learning and Verbal Behavior, 23,* 508-518.

Hanschke, P., Abecker, A., & Drollinger, D. (1991). TAXON: A concept language with concrete domains. In H. Boley & M. M. Richter (Eds.), *Processing Declarative Knowledge* (pp.411-413). Heidelberg: Springer-Verlag.

Harnad, S. (1990). The symbol grounding problem. *Physica, 42,* 335-346.

Hayes, P. J., Ford, K. M. & Agnew, N. (1994). On babies and bathwater: A cautionary tale. *Artificial Intelligence Magazine, 15,* 14-26.

Hegarty, M., & Just, M. A. (1993). Constructing mental models of machines from text and diagrams. *Journal of Memory and Language, 32,* 717-742.

Heit, E. (1992). Categorization using chains of examples. *Cognitive Psychology, 24,* 341-380.

Heit, E. (1994). Models of the effects of prior knowledge on category learning. *Journal of Experimental Psychology: Learning, Memory, and Cognition, 20,* 1264-1282.

Herrmann, Th. (1990). Die Experimentiermethodik in der Defensive? [Is the experimental methodology in a defensive position?] *Sprache und Kognition,* [Language and Cognition] *9,* 1-11.

Hintzman, D. L. (1988). Judgements of frequency and recognition memory in a multiple-trace memory model. *Psychological Review, 95,* 528-551.

Hintzman, D. L. (1990). Human learning and memory: Connections and dissociations. *Annual Review of Psychology, 41* 109-139.

Holyoak, K. J., & Thargard, P. R. (1989). Analogical mapping by constraint satisfaction. *Cognitive Science, 13,* 295-356.

Jäger, St. (1992). *Erstellung und Anwendung einer PROLOG/C Schnittstelle zur Simulation des Constuction-Integration Modells.* [Implementation and application of a PROLOG/C interface for simulations with the construction-integration model]. Unpublished manuscript, Department of Computer Science, University of Kaiserslautern.

Jacoby, L. L. (1991). A process dissociation framework: Separating automatic from intentional uses of memory. *Journal of Memory and Language, 30,* 513-541.

Johnson-Laird, P. N. (1980). Mental models in cognitive science. *Cognitive Science, 4,* 71-115.

Johnson-Laird, P. N. (1983). *Mental models: Towards a cognitive science of language, inference, and consciousness.* Cambridge, MA: Harvard University Press.

Kant, I. (1781). *Kritik der reinen Vernunft [Critique of pure reason].* Stuttgart, 1966: Reclam.

Kieras, D. E. (1985). The why, when, and how of cognitive simulation: A tutorial. *Behavior Research Methods, Instruments, & Computers, 17,* 279-285.

Kieras, D. E., & Bovair, S. (1984). The role of a mental model in learning to operate a device. *Cognitive Science, 8,* 191-219.

Kieras, D. E., & Polson, P. (1985). An approach to the formal analysis of user complexity. *International Journal of Man-Machine Studies, 22,* 365-394.

Killin, J. (1992). The management and maintenance of an operational KADS system development. In T. Wetter, K.-D. Althoff, J. Boose, B. R. Gaines, M. Linster, & F. Schmalhofer (Eds.), *Current developments in knowledge acquisition - EKAW '92* (pp. 6). Heidelberg: Springer-Verlag.

Kintsch, W. (1974). *The representation of meaning in memory.* Hillsdale, NJ: Lawrence Erlbaum Associates.

Kintsch, W. (1986). Learning from text. *Cognition and Instruction. 3,* 87-108.

Kintsch, W. (1988). The role of knowledge in discourse comprehension: A construction-integration model. *Psychological Review, 95,* 163-182.

Kintsch, W. (1992). A cognitive architecture for comprehension. In H. Pick, P. van den Broek, & D. Knill (Eds.), *The study of cognition: Conceptual and methodological issues* (pp. 143-164). Washington, DC: APA Press.

Kintsch, W. (1994). Text comprehension, memory, and learning. *American Psychologist, 49,* 294-303.

Kintsch, W., & van Dijk, T. A. (1978). Toward a model of text comprehension and production. *Psychological Review, 85,* 363-394.

Kintsch, W., & Welsch, D. M. (1991). The construction-integration model: A framework for studying memory for text. In W. Hockley & S. Lewandowsky (Eds.), *Relating theory and data: Essays on human memory in honor of Bennet B. Murdock* (pp. 367-386). Hillsdale, NJ: Lawrence Erlbaum Associates.

Kintsch, W., Welsch, D. M., Schmalhofer, F., & Zimny, S. (1990). Sentence memory: A theoretical analysis. *Journal of Memory and Language, 29,* 133-159.

Kitajima, M., & Polson, P. G. (1995). A comprehension-based model of correct performance and errors in skilled, display-bassed, human-computer interaction. *International Journal of Human-Computer Studies, 43,* 65-99.

Kitajima, M., & Polson, P. G. (in press). A Comprehesion-based Model of Exploration. *Human-Computer Interaction.*

Klahr, D., & Dunbar, K. (1988). Dual space search during scientific reasoning. *Cognitive Science, 12,* 1-48.

Klayman, J., & Ha, Y. (1987). Confirmation, disconfirmation and information in hypothesis testing. *Psychological Review, 94,* 211-228.

Kliegl, R., Mayr, U., & Krampe, R. Th., (1994). Time-accuracy functions for determining process and person differences: An application to cognitive aging. *Cognitive Psychology, 26,* 134-164.

Kliegl, R., & Olson, R. K. (1981). Reduction and calibration of eye monitor data. *Behavior Research Methods and Instrumentation, 13,* 107-111.

Kobsa, A., & Wahlster, W. (Eds.) (1989). *User models in dialog systems.* New York: Springer-Verlag.

Kolodner, J. L. (1993). *Case-based reasoning.* San Mateo, CA: Morgan Kaufmann.

Korrossy, K. (1993). *Modellierung von Wissen als Kompetenz und Performanz.* [Knowledge modeling as competence and performance modeling]. Unpublished doctoral dissertation, Fakultät für Sozial- und Verhaltenswissenschaften, Universität Heidelberg.

Kozma, R. B. (1987). The implications of cognitive psychology for computer-based learning tools. *Educational Technology, 27,* 20-25.

Kozma, R. B. (1991). Learning with media. *Review of Educational Research, 61,* 179-212.

Krämer, S. (1988). *Symbolische Maschinen: Die Idee der Formalisierung im geschichtlichem Abriß.* [Symbolic machines: A brief history of the idea of formalization]. Darmstadt: Wissenschaftliche Buchgesellschaft.

Krantz, D. H., Luce, R. D., Suppes, P., & Tversky, A. (1971). *Foundations of measurement.* Vol. 1., New York: Academic Press.

Krems, J., & Pfeiffer, T. (1992). Verstehen und Erinnern einfacher Kommandosequenzen in Abhängigkeit von Erfahrung und Kompetenz: Mustervorteil oder effizientere bereichsspezifische Fertigkeiten? [The understanding and remembering of simple command sequences as a function of experience and competence]. *Zeitschrift für Psychologie, 200,* 45-60.

Kühn, O. (1987). *Wissenserwerb durch Explorieren eines Computersystems im Vergleich zu Lernen durch Instruktion in Abhängigkeit unterschiedlicher Vorkenntnisse.* [Knowledge acquisition by the exploration of a computer system in comparison to learning by instruction as a function of a learner's prior knowledge]. Unpublished master's thesis, Universität Heidelberg.

Kühn, O. (1991). *KIWi-1: Eine integrative Simulation von Lernen aus Text, aus Beispielen und durch Explorieren.* [KIWi-1: An integrative simulation of learning from text, from examples and by exploration]. Unpublished program documentation, Kaiserslautern: German Research Center for Artificial Intelligence GmbH.

Kühn, O., & Höfling, B. (1994). Conserving corporate knowledge for crankshaft design. In F. D. Auger, R. V. Rodriguez, & M. Ali (Eds.), *Seventh international conference on industrial and engineering applications of artificial intelligence and expert systems* (pp. 475-484). Yverdon, Switzerland: Gordon and Breach Science Publishers.

Kühn, O., & Schmalhofer, F. (1987). Erlernen der Computerbenutzung durch gezielt sequenzierte Instruktion oder durch Explorieren. [Learning how to use computers by orderly sequenced instructions and by exploration]. In W. Schönpflug & M. Wittstock (Eds.), *Software Ergonomie* [Software ergonomics]. (pp. 387-398), Stuttgart: Teubner Verlag.

Kühn, O., & Schmalhofer, F. (1992). Hierachical skeletal plan refinement: Task-and inference structures. In C. Bauer & W. Karbach (Eds.), *Interpretation Models for KADS - Proceedings of the 2nd KADS User Meeting (KUM'92)* (GMD Studie 212). Sankt Augustin: Gesellschaft für Mathematik und Datenverarbeitung (GMD).

Kuhn, Th. (1970). *The structure of scientific revolutions.* Chicago: Chicago University Press.

Kutas, M., & Hillyard, S. A. (1980). Reading senseless sentences: Brain potentials reflect semantic incongruity. *Science, 207,* 203-205.

Laird, J. E., Newell, A., & Rosenbloom, P. S. (1987). Soar: An architecture for general intelligence. *Artificial Intelligence, 24,* 169-203.

Lajoie, S., & Lesgold, A. (1989). Apprenticeship training in the workplace: Computer coached practice environment as a new form of apprenticeship. *Machine-Mediated Learning, 3,* 7-28.

Langley, P., Simon, H. A., & Bradshaw, G. L. (1983). Heuristics for empirical discovery. In L. Bolc (Ed.), *Computational Models of Learning* (pp. 21-54), New York: Springer-Verlag.

Langley, P., Simon, H. A., Bradshaw, G. L., & Zytkow, J. M. (1987). *Scientific discovery: Computational explorations of the creative process.* New York: Cambridge University Press.

Larkin, J. H., & Simon, H. A. (1987). Why a diagram is (sometimes) worth ten thousand words. *Cognitive Science, 11,* 65-100.

Lassez, C. (1987, August). Constraint logic programming. *BYTE,* 171-176.

LeFevre, J., & Dixon, P. (1986). Do written instructions need examples? *Cognition and Instruction, 3,* 1-30.

Lesgold, A. M. (1993). Beyond a commodity view of knowledge in instruction. In G. Strube & K. F. Wender (Eds.), *The cognitive psychology of knowledge* (pp. 425-433). Amsterdam, North-Holland: Elsevier.

Lesgold, A. M., & Schmalhofer, F. (Eds.). (1994). *Expert- and tutoring systems as media for embodying and sharing knowledge* (Dagstuhl-Seminar-Report; 9431). Wadern, Germany: IBFI Schloß Dagstuhl.

Levine, M. (1975). *A cognitive theory of learning: Research on hypothesis testing.* New York: Wiley.

Lewis, C. (1988). Why and how to learn why: Analysis-based generalization of procedures. *Cognitive Science, 12*, 211-256.

Lewis, C., Polson, P. , Wharton, C., & Rieman, J. (1990). Testing a walkthrough methodology for theory-based design of walk-up-and-use interfaces. *CHI'90 Conference Proceedings*, Reading, MA: Addison-Wesley, 235-242.

Lukas, J., & Albert, D. (1993). Knowledge assessment based on skill assignment and psychological task analysis. In G. Strube & K. F. Wender (Eds.), *The cognitive psychology of knowledge* (pp. 139-159). Amsterdam, North-Holland: Elsevier.

Mackworth, A. K. (1977). Consistency in networks of relations. *Journal on Artificial Intelligence, 8*, 99-118.

Mandl, H., & Lesgold, A. (1988). *Learning issues for intelligent tutoring systems.* NewYork: Springer-Verlag.

Mannes, S., & Kintsch, W. (1987). Knowledge organization and text organization. *Cognition and Instruction, 4*, 91-115.

Mannes, S., & Kintsch, W. (1991). Routine computing tasks: Planning as understanding. *Cognitive Science, 15*, 305-342.

Maturana, H. R., & Varela, F. J. (1990). *Der Baum der Erkenntnis.* [The tree of knowledge]. München: Goldmann Verlag.

McCarthy, J., Abrahams, P. W., Edwards, D. J., Hart, T. P., & Levin, M. I., (1976). *LISP 1.5 programmer's manual.* Cambridge, MA: M.I.T. Press.

McDaniel, M. A., Einstein, G. O., Dunay, P. K., & Cobb, R. E. (1986). Encoding difficulty and memory: Toward a unifying theory. *Journal of Memory and Language, 25*, 645-656.

McDaniel, M. A., & Schlager, M. S. (1990). Discovery learning and transfer of problem solving skills. *Cognition and Instruction, 7*, 129-159.

McDaniel, M. A., & Waddill, P. J. (1990). Generation effect for context words: Implications for item-specific and multifactor theories. *Journal of Memory and Language, 29*, 201-211.

McKoon, G., & Ratcliff, R. (1992). Inference during reading. *Psychological Review, 99*, 440-466.

McKoon, G., & Ratcliff, R. (1995). The minimalist hypothesis: Directions for research. In C.A. Weaver, III, S. Mannes, & C. R. Fletcher (Eds.), *Discourse Comprehension: Essays in Honor of Walter Kintsch* (pp. 97-116). Hillsdale, NJ: Lawrence Erlbaum Associates.

McKoon, G., Ward, G., Ratcliff, R., & Sproat, R. (1993). Morphosyntactic and pragmatic factors affecting the accessibility of discourse entities. *Journal of Memory and Language, 32*, 56-75.

McMillan, C., & Smolensky, P. (1988). Analyzing a connectionist model as a system of soft rules. In *The Tenth Annual Conference of the Cognitive Science Society* (pp. 62-68). Hillsdale, NJ: Lawrence Erlbaum Associates.

McNamara, D. S. (1995, January). *A history text revisited: Effects of prior knowledge and text coherence.* Poster presented at the Sixth Annual Winter Text Conference, Jackson Hole.

McNamara, D. S., Kintsch, E., Songer, N. B., & Kintsch, W. (in press). Are good texts always better? Interactions of text coherence, background knowledge, and levels of understanding in learning from text. *Cognition and Instruction.*

McNamara, T. (1994). Priming and theories of memory: A reply to Ratcliff and McKoon. *Psychological Review, 101,* 185-187.

Medin, D. L., & Heit E. (in press). Categorization. In D. E. Rumelhart & B. O. Martin (Eds.), *Handbook of Cognition and Perception: Cognitive Science.* San Diego: Academic Press.

Medin, D. L., Wattenmaker, W. D., & Michalski R. S. (1987). Constraints and preferences in inductive learning: An experimental study of human and machine performance. *Cognitive Science, 11,* 299-339.

Meyer, M. (1994). *Finite domain constraints: Declarativity meets efficiency, theory meets application.* Unpublished doctoral dissertation, Computer Science Department, University of Kaiserslautern.

Michalski, R. S. (1983). A theory and methodology of inductive learning. *Artificial Intelligence, 20,* 111-161.

Michalski, R. S. (1993). Toward a unified theory of learning: Multistrategy task-adaptive learning. In B. G. Buchanan & D. C. Wilkins (Eds.), *Readings in knowledge acquisition and learning* (pp. 7-38). San Mateo, CA: Morgan Kaufmann.

Michalski, R. S., & Kodratoff, Y. (1990). Research in machine learning: Recent progress, classification of methods, and future directions. In Y. Kodratoff & R. S. Michalski (Eds.), *Machine learning: An artificial intelligence approach, Vol. 3* (pp. 3-30). San Mateo, CA: Morgan Kaufmann.

Miller, G. A. (1956). The magical number seven, plus or minus two: Some limits on our capacity for processing information. *Psychological Review, 63,* 81-97.

Miller, J. R., & Kintsch, W. (1980). Readability and recall of short prose passages: A theoretical analysis. *Journal of Experimental Psychology: Human Learning and Memory, 6,* 335-354.

Minsky, M., L. & Papert, S. A. (1988). *Perceptrons.* Cambridge MA: MIT Press.

Mitchell, T. M., Keller, R., & Kedar-Cabelli, S. (1986). Explanation-based generalization: A unifying view. *Machine Learning, 1,* 47-80.

Mooney, R., & DeJong, G. (1985). Learning schemata for natural language processing. *Proceedings of the Ninth International Joint Conference on Artificial Intelligence* (pp. 681-687). Los Angeles, CA: Morgan Kaufmann.

Moorman, K., & Ram, A. (1994). A model of creative understanding. In *Proceedings of the 12th National AAAI Conference.*

Morik, K. (1993). Maschinelles Lernen. [Machine learning] In G. Görz (Ed.) *Einführung in die Künstliche Intelligenz* [Introduction to artificial intelligence]. (pp. 247-301). Bonn: Addison-Wesley.

Morrow, D., Bower, G., & Greenspan, S. (1989). Updating situation models during narrative comprehension. *Journal of Memory and Language, 28,* 292-312.

Mross, E. F., & Roberts, J. O. (1992). *The construction-integration model: A program and manual.* (Technical Report, ICS, No. 92-14). Boulder, CO: Institute of Cognitive Science, University of Colorado.

Murdock, B. B. Jr. (1974). *Human memory: Theory and data.* Potomac, Maryland: Lawrence Erlbaum Associates.

Narens, L., & Mausfeld, R. (1992). On the relationship of the psychological and the physical in psychophysics. *Psychological Review, 99,* 467-479.

Nathan, M., Kintsch, W., & Young, E. (1992). A theory of algebra-word-problem comprehension and its implications for the design of learning enviroments. *Cognition and Instruction, 9,* 329-389.

Nelson, R. R., Whitener, E. M., & Philcox, H. H. (1995). The assessment of end-user training needs. *Communications of the ACM, 38,* 27-39.

Neubert, S., & Studer, R. (1992). The *KEEP* model, a *K*nowledge *E*ngin*E*ering *P*rocess model. In T. Wetter, K.-D. Althoff, J. Boose, B. R. Gaines, M. Linster, & F. Schmalhofer (Eds.), *Current developments in knowledge acquisition - EKAW '92.* Heidelberg: Springer-Verlag.

Newell, A. (1973). Production systems: Models of control structure. In W.G. Chase (Ed.), *Visual information processing* (pp 463-526). New York: Academic Press.

Newell, A. (1980). Physical symbol systems. *Cognitive Science, 4,* 135-183.

Newell, A. (1982). The knowledge level. *Artificial intelligence, 18,* 87-127.

Newell, A. (1990). *Unified theories of cognition.* Cambridge, MA: Harvard University Press.

Newell, A. (1992). Precis of unified theories of cognition. *Behavioral and Brain Sciences, 15,* 425-437.

Newell, A., & Simon, H. A. (1956). The logic theory machine: A complex information processing system. *IRE Transactions on information theory, IT-2,* 61-79.

Newell, A., & Simon, H. A. (1972). *Human problem solving.* Englewood Cliffs, N.J.: Prentice-Hall.

Noordman, L. G. M., Vonk, W., & Kempff, H. J. (1992). Causal inferences during the reading of expository texts. *Journal of Memory and Language, 31,* 573-590.

Norman, D. A. (1993). Cognition in the head and in the world: An Introduction to the special issue on situated action. *Cognitive Science, 17,* 1-6.

Norvig, P. (1989). Marker passing as a weak method for text inferencing. *Cognitive Science, 13,* 569-620.

Nosofsky, R. M. (1988). Exemplar-based accounts of relations between classification, recognition and typicality. *Journal of Experimental Psychology: Learning Memory and Cognition, 14,* 700-708.

Novick L. R. (1988). Analogical transfer, problem similarity, and expertise. *Journal of Experimental Psychology: Learning, Memory, and Cognition, 14,* 510-520.

Novick L. R., & Holyoak, K. J. (1991). Mathematical problem solving by analogy. *Journal of Experimental Psychology: Learning, Memory, and Cognition, 17,* 398-415.

Ohlsson, S., & Jewett, J. J. (1995). Abstract computer models: Towards a new method for theorizing about adaptive agents. In N. Lavrac & S. Wrobel (Eds.), *Machine Learning: ECML-95* (pp. 33-52). Berlin: Springer-Verlag.

Patel, V., & Groen, G. (1986). Knowledge based solution strategies in medical reasoning. *Cognitive Science, 10*, 91-116.

Pennington, N., & Hastie, R. (1981). *Juror decision making: Story structure and verdict choice.* Technical report, American Psychological Association.

Perfetti, C. A., & Britt, M. A. (1995). Where do propositions come from? In: C. A. Weaver, III, S. Mannes, & C. R. Fletcher (Eds.), *Discourse comprehension: Essays in honor of Walter Kintsch* (pp. 11-34). Hillsdale: Lawrence Erlbaum Associates.

Pirolli, P. L. (1991). Effects of examples and their explanation in a lesson on recursion: A production system analysis. *Cognition and Instruction, 8*, 207-259

Pirolli, P. L., & Recker, M. (1994). Learning strategies and transfer in the domain of programming. *Cognition and Instruction, 12*, 235-275.

Puppe, F. (1991). *Einführung in Expertensysteme.* [Introduction to expert systems]. Berlin: Springer-Verlag.

Puppe, F., & Reinhardt, B. (1994). *Generating case-oriented training from diagnostic expert systems.* Unpublished manuscript, Universität Würzburg.

Ram, A. (1993). Creative conceptual change. In *Proceedings of the Fifteenth Annual Conference of the Cognitive Science Society* (pp. 17-26). Hillsdale, NJ: Lawrence Erlbaum Associates.

Ratcliff, R., & McKoon, G. (1978). Priming in item recognition: Evidence for the propositional structure of sentences. *Journal of Verbal Learning and Verbal Behavior, 17*, 403-417.

Ratcliff, R., & McKoon, G. (1988). A retrieval theory of priming in memory. *Psychological Review, 95*, 385-408.

Ratcliff, R., & McKoon, G. (1989). Similarity information versus relational information: Differences in the time course of retrieval. *Cognitive Psychology, 21*, 139-155.

Ratcliff, R., & McKoon, G. (1994). Retrieving information from memory: Spreading-activation theories versus compound-cue theories. *Psychological Review, 101*, 177-184.

Reder, L. M. (1982). Plausibility judgments versus fact retrieval: Alternative strategies for sentence verification. *Psychological Review, 89*, 250-280.

Reder, L. M. (1987). Strategy-selection in question answering. *Cognitive Psychology, 19*, 90-134.

Reder, L. M., Charney, D. H., & Morgan, K. I. (1986). The role of elaborations in learning a skill from an instructional text. *Memory & Cognition, 14*, 64-78.

Reed, A. V. (1973). Speed-accuracy trade-off in recognition memory. *Science, 181*, 574-576.

Reinartz, Th., & Schmalhofer, F. (1994). An integration of knowledge acquisition techniques and EBL for real-world production planning, *Knowledge Acquisition Journal, 6*, 115-136.

Rendell, L. (1986). A general framework for induction and a study of selective induction. *Machine Learning, 1*, 177-226.

Richards, B.L., & Mooney, R.J. (1991). First-order theory revision. In *Proceedings of the Eighth International Workshop on Machine Learning* (pp. 447-451). Evanston, IL.

Richter, M. M. (1989). *Prinzipien der Künstlichen Intelligenz*. [Principles of artificial intelligence]. Stuttgart: Teubner.

Riesbeck, C. K., & Schank, R. C. (1989). *Inside case-based reasoning*. Hillsdale, NJ: Lawrence Erlbaum Associates.

Rinck, M., & Bower, G. H. (1995). Anaphora resolution and the focus of attention in situation models. *Journal of Memory and Language, 34*, 110-131.

Rodenhausen, H. (1992). Mathematical aspects of Kintsch's model of discourse comprehension. *Psychological Review, 33*, 547-549.

Rosch, E., & Mervis, C. B. (1975). Family resemblance: Studies in the internal structure of categories. *Cognitive Psychology, 7*, 573-605.

Ross, B. H., & Kennedy, P. T., (1990). Generalizing from the use of earlier examples in problem solving. *Journal of Experimental Psychology, 16*, 42-55.

Rumelhart, D. E., & McClelland, J. E. (1986). *Parallel distributed processing*. Cambridge, MA: MIT Press.

Sahakian, W. S. (1975). *History and systems of psychology*. New York: John Wiley & Sons, Inc.

Samuel, A. L. (1959). Some studies in machine learning using the game of checkers. *IBM Journal Research and Development, 3*, 210-229. Reprinted in: E. A. Feigenbaum, & J. Feldman (Eds.), *Computers and Thought*. New York: McGraw-Hill, 1963.

Sandoval, J. (1995). Teaching in subject matter areas: Science. *Annual Review of Psychology, 46*, 355-374.

Schank, R. C. (1982). *Dynamic memory: A theory of learning and computers and people*. New York: Cambridge University Press.

Schank, R. C., & Abelson, R. (1977). *Scripts, plans, goals and understanding*. Northvale, NJ: Lawrence Erlbaum Associates.

Schank, R. C., & Leake, D. B. (1989). Creativity and learning in a case-based explainer. *Artificial Intelligence, 40*, 353-385.

Schiefele, U. (1991). Interesse und Textrepräsentation - Zur Auswirkung des thematischen Interesses auf unterschiedliche Komponenten der Textrepräsentation unter Berücksichtigung kognitiver und motivationaler Kontrollvariablen. [Interest and text representation - The influence of thematic interest on various text representation components including cognitive and motivational control variables] *Zeitschrift für Pädagogische Psychologie, 5*, 245-259.

Schlenker, B., Schmalhofer, F., Kühn, O., & Rohr, M. (1989, November). *Wissensanalyse für medizinische Erklärungen*. [The analysis of knowledge for medical explanations]. Poster presented at the 22nd Arbeitstreffen der Gedächtnispsychologie und Informationsverarbeitung, Weschnitz, Odw.

Schmalhofer, F. (1982). Comprehension of a technical text as a function of expertise (Doctoral dissertation, University of Colorado, 1982). *University Microfilms International*, Pub. No.: 83-09,879.

Schmalhofer, F. (1983). *Text processing with and without prior knowledge: Knowledge-versus heuristic-dependent representations* (Diskussionspapier Nr. 32). Heidelberg: University of Heidelberg, Department of Psychology.

Schmalhofer, F. (1986a). Verlaufscharakteristiken des Informationsabrufs beim Wiedererkennen und Verifizieren von Sätzen. [The time course of information retrieval in the recognition and verification of sentences]. *Zeitschrift für experimentelle und angewandte Psychologie, 18*, 133-149.

Schmalhofer, F. (1986b). The construction of programming knowledge from system explorations and explanatory text: A cognitive model. In C.R. Rollinger & W. Horn (Eds.), *GWAI-86 and 2nd Austrian Artificial Intelligence Conference* (pp. 152-163). Heidelberg: Springer-Verlag.

Schmalhofer, F. (1987a). Mental model and procedural elements approaches as guidelines for designing word processing instructions. In H.-J. Bullinger & B. Shakel (Eds.), *Human-Computer Interaction INTERACT '87* (pp. 269-288). Amsterdam: North-Holland.

Schmalhofer, F. (1995). The acquisition of knowledge from text and example-situations: An extension to the construction-integration model. In C.A. Weaver, III, S. Mannes, & C. R. Fletcher (Eds.), *Discourse Comprehension: Essays in Honor of Walter Kintsch* (pp. 257-283). Hillsdale, NJ: Lawrence Erlbaum Associates.

Schmalhofer, F. (1996). Maschinelles Lernen: Eine kognitionswissenschaftliche Betrachtung. [Machine learning: A cognitive science perspective]. In J. Hoffmann & W. Kintsch (Eds.), *Enzyklopädie der Psychologie. Serie Kognition, Band Lernen* (pp. 445-501). Göttingen: Hogrefe.

Schmalhofer, F., Aitken, S., & Bourne, L.E. (1994). Beyond the knowledge level: Descriptions of rational behavior for sharing and reuse. In L. Steels, G. Schreiber & W. Van de Velde (Eds.), *A Future for Knowledge Acquisition, EKAW '94 Proceedings* (pp. 83-103). Berlin: Springer-Verlag.

Schmalhofer, F., & Auerswald, M. (1994). Zur Beschreibung von menschlichem und maschinellem Lernen auf der Wissensebene. [Knowledge level descriptions of human and machine learning]. In K. Opwis (Ed.) *Proceedings der 1. Fachtagung der Gesellschaft für Kognitionswissenschaft* (pp.100-102). Freiburg i. Br.: Psychologisches Institut der Universität.

Schmalhofer, F., Bergmann, R., Boschert, S., & Thoben, J. (1993). Learning program abstractions: Model and empirical validation. In G. Strube & K. F. Wender (Eds.), *The cognitive psychology of knowledge* (pp. 203-231). Amsterdam, North-Holland: Elsevier.

Schmalhofer, F., Bergmann, R., Kühn, O., & Schmidt, G. (1991). Using integrated knowledge acquisition to prepare sophisticated expert plans for their re-use in novel situations. In Th. Christaller (Ed.), *GWAI-91: 15. Fachtagung für Künstliche Intelligenz* (pp. 62-73). Heidelberg: Springer-Verlag.

Schmalhofer, F., & Boschert, S. (1988). Differences in verbalizations during knowledge acquisition from texts, and discovery learning from example situations. *Text, 8*, 369-393.

Schmalhofer, F., Boschert, S., & Kühn, O. (1990). Der Aufbau allgemeinen Situationswissens aus Text und Beispielen. [The formation of general situation knowledge from text and examples]. *Zeitschrift für Pädagogische Psychologie, 4*, 177-186.

Schmalhofer, F., & Glavanov, D. (1986). Three components of understanding a programmer's manual: Verbatim, propositional, and situational representations. *Journal of Memory and Language, 25*, 279-294.

Schmalhofer, F., Globig, Ch., & Thoben, J. (1992). The refitting of plans by a human expert. In F. Schmalhofer, G. Strube, & Th. Wetter (Eds.), *Contemporary knowledge engineering and cognition* (pp. 115-124). Heidelberg: Springer-Verlag.

Schmalhofer, F., & Kühn, O. (1988). Acquiring computer skills by exploration versus demonstration. In *The Tenth Annual Conference of the Cognitive Science Society* (pp. 724-730). Hillsdale, NJ: Lawrence Erlbaum Associates.

Schmalhofer, F., & Kühn, O. (1991). The psychological processes of constructing a mental model when learning by being told, from examples and by exploration. In M. J. Tauber & D. Ackermann (Eds.), *Mental models and human-computer interaction 2* (pp. 337-360). Amsterdam: North-Holland.

Schmalhofer, F., Kühn, O., Charron, R., & Messamer, P. (1990). An implementation and empirical evaluation of an exploration environment with different tutoring strategies. *Behavior Research Methods, Instruments, & Computers, 22*, 179-183.

Schmalhofer, F., Kühn, O., Messamer, P., & Charron, R. (1990). An experimental evaluation of different amounts of receptive and exploratory learning in a tutoring system. *Computers in Human Behavior, 6*, 51-68.

Schmalhofer, F., Kühn, O., & Schmidt, G. (1991). Integrated knowledge acquisition from text, previously solved cases and expert memories. *Applied Artificial Intelligence: An International Journal, 5*, 311-337.

Schmalhofer, F., & Polson, P. G. (1986). A production system model for human problem solving. *Psychological Research, 48*, 113-122.

Schmalhofer, F., Reinartz, T., & Tschaitschian, B. (1995). A unified approach to learning for complex real world domains. *Applied Artificial Intelligence, 9*, 127-156.

Schmalhofer, F., Schlei, J., & Farin, E. (1986). *Eine Anpassung der Assembler-Routinen der CMU-Button Box an Turbo-Pascal* [An adaptation of the assembly language routines of the CMU-Button Box to Turbo-Pascal]. (Forschungsbericht 36). Freiburg i. Br.: Psychologisches Institut der Universität Freiburg.

Schmalhofer, F., & Thoben, J. (1992). The model-based construction of a case-oriented expert system, *AI Communications, 5*, 3-18.

Schmalhofer, F., & Tschaitschian, B. (1993). The acquisition of a procedure schema from text and experiences. In *Proceedings of the 15th Annual Conference of the Cognitive Science Society* (pp. 883-888). Hillsdale, NJ: Lawrence Erlbaum Associates.

Schmalhofer, F., & van Elst, L. (1995). Entwicklung von Expertensystemen: Prototypen, Tiefenmodellierung und kooperative Wissensevolution. [The development of expert systems: Prototypes, deep modeling and cooperative knowledge evolution]. In W. Dzida & U. Konradt (Eds.), *Psychologie des Software-Entwurfs* (pp. 223-244). Göttingen: Verlag für Angewandte Psychologie.

Schmalhofer, F., van Elst, L., Vogel, R., & McDaniel, M. (1995, September). *Die Generierung von Inferenzen und ihre Stabilität über die Zeit.* [The generation of inferences and their stability over time]. Paper presented at the workshop Künstliche Intelligenz und Kognitionswissenschaft, Bielefeld, Germany.

Schmalhofer, F., & Wetter, T. (1988). Kognitive Modellierung: Menschliche Wissensrepräsentation und Verarbeitungsstrategien. [Cognitive modeling: Human knowledge representation and processing strategies]. In T. Christaller, H.-W. Hein, & M. M. Richter (Eds.), *Künstliche Intelligenz: Theoretische Grundlagen und Anwendungsfelder* (pp. 245-291). Berlin: Springer-Verlag.

Schmid, U. (1994). *Implementation eines kognitionspsychologischen Modells zum Textverstehen.* [Implementation of a psychological model of human text comprehension]. Unpublished master's thesis, Institut für Software und Theoretische Informatik, Fachbereich 13, Technische Universität Berlin.

Schmidt, G. (1992). Knowledge acquisition from text in a complex domain. In *Proceedings of the Fifth International Conference on Industrial and Engineering Applications of Artificial Intelligence and Expert Systems* (pp. 529-538). Berlin: Springer-Verlag.

Schmidt, G., & Schmalhofer, F. (1990). Case-oriented knowledge acquisition from texts. In B. Wielinga, J. Boose, B. Gaines, G. Schreiber & M. van Someren (Eds.), *Current Trends in Knowledge Acquisition* (pp. 302-312). Amsterdam: IOS Press.

Schneider, W., Gruber, H., Gold, A., & Opwis, K. (1993). Chess expertise and memory for chess positions in children and adults. *Journal of Experimental Child Psychology, 56,* 328-349.

Schneider, W., Körkel, J., & Weinert, F. E., (1989). Domain-specific knowledge and memory performance: A Comparison of high- and low-aptitude children. *Journal of Educational Psychology, 81,* 306-312.

Schneider, W., & Oliver, W. L. (1991). An instructable connectionist/control architecture: Using rule-based instructions to accomplish connectionist learning in a human time scale. In K. VanLehn (Ed.) *Architectures for intelligence. The Twenty-second Carnegie Mellon Symposium on Cognition* (pp. 113-146). Hillsdale, NJ: Lawrence Erlbaum Associates.

Schooler, L. J., & Anderson, J. R. (1990). The disruptive potential of immediate feedback. In *Proceedings of the Twelfth Annual Conference of the Cognitive Science Society* (pp. 702-708). Hillsdale, NJ: Lawrence Erlbaum Associates.

Searle, J. (1983). *Intentionality: An essay in the philosophy of mind.* Cambridge: Cambridge University Press.

Shanks, D. R., & Lopez, F. J. (1995). Causal order does not affect cue selection in human associative learning. *Memory & Cognition.*

Shavlik, J. W., & Dietterich, T. G. (Eds.) (1990). *Readings in machine learning.* San Mateo, CA: Morgan Kaufmann.

Shoben, E. J., Wescourt, K. T., & Smith, E. E. (1978). Sentence verification, sentence recognition, and the semantic-episodic distinction. *Journal of Experimental Psychology: Human Learning and Memory, 4,* 304-317.

Shortliffe, E. H. (1976). *Computer-based medical consulting: MYCIN.* New York: Elsevier/ North Holland.

Simon, H. A. (1975). The functional equivalence of problem solving skills. *Cognitive Psychology, 7,* 268-288.

Simon, H. A. (1991). *Models of my life.* New York: Basic Books, Inc. Publishers.

Singer, M. (1991). Independence of question-answering and searched representation. *Memory & Cognition, 19,* 189-196.

Singer, M., & Ferreira, F. (1983). Inferrring consequences in story comprehension. *Journal of Verbal Learning and Verbal Behavior, 22,* 437-448.

Singer, M., & Halldorson, M. (1996). Constructing and validating motive bridging inferences. *Cognitive Psychology, 30,* 1-38.

Slamecka, N. J., & Graf, P. (1978). The generation effect: Delineation of a phenomenon. *Journal of Experimental Psychology: Human Learning and Memory, 4,* 592-604.

Smith, E. E., & Medin, D. L. (1981). *Categories and concepts*. Cambridge, MA: Harvard University Press.

Smolensky, P. (1988). On the proper treatment of connectionism. *Behavioral and Brain Sciences, 11*, 1-74.

Snow, R. E., & Swanson, J. (1992). Instructional psychology: Aptitude, adaption, and assessment. *Annual Review of Psychology, 43*, 583-626.

Soloway, E. (1985). From problems to programs via plans: The content and structure of knowledge for introductory LISP programming. *Journal of Educational Research, 1*, 157-172.

Spada, H., Stumpf, M., & Opwis, K. (1989). The constructive process of knowledge acquisition: Student modelling. In H. Maurer (Ed.), *Computer-assisted learning* (pp. 486-499). Berlin: Springer-Verlag.

Spur, G. (1979). *Produktionstechnik im Wandel*. [Changes in manufacturing technology]. München: Carl Hanser.

Stegmüller, W. (1969). *Wissenschaftliche Erklärung und Begründung*. [Scientific explanation and justification]. Berlin: Springer-Verlag.

Sterling, L., & Shapiro, E. (1986). *The art of PROLOG*. Cambridge, MA: MIT Press.

Sternberg, R. J. (1996). *Cognitive Psychology*. Fort Worth, TX: Harcourt Brace College Publishers.

Sternberg, S. (1969). Memory scanning: Mental processes revealed by reaction time experiments. *American Scientist, 57*, 421-457.

Sticklen, J. (1989). Problem solving architecture at the knowledge level. *Journal of Experimental and Theoretical Artificial Intelligence, 1*, 1-52.

Strube, G. (1990). Neokonnektionismus: Eine neue Basis für die Theorie und Modellierung menschlicher Kognition? [Neoconnectionism: A new basis for the theory and modeling of human cognition]. *Psychologische Rundschau, 41*, 129-143.

Suchman, L. (1987). *Plans and situated actions*. Cambridge, MA: Cambridge University Press.

Suppes, P., & Zinnes, J. L. (1963). Basic measurement theory. In R. D. Luce, R.R. Bush & E. Galanter (Eds.), *Handbook of mathematical psycholoy. Vol. I* (pp. 1-76). New York: Wiley.

Tenenberg, J. (1987). Preserving consistency across abstraction mappings. In *Proceedings of the 10th international joint conference on artificial intelligence* (pp. 1011-1014). San Mateo, CA: Morgan Kaufmann.

Theios, J., Smith, P. G., Haviland, S. E., Troupman, J., & Moy, C. (1973). Memory scanning as a serial self-terminating process. *Journal of Experimental Psychology, 97*, 323-336.

Till, R. E., Mross, E. F., & Kintsch, W. (1988). Time course of priming for associate and inference words in a discourse context. *Memory and Cognition, 16*, 283-298.

Touretzky, D. S. (1993). The hearts of symbols: Why symbol grounding is irrelevant. In *Proceedings of the Fifteenth Annual Conference of the Cognitive Science Society* (pp. 165-168). Hillsdale, NJ: Lawrence Erlbaum Associates.

Townsend, J. T. (1974). Issues and models concerning the processing of a finite number of inputs. In B. H. Kantowitz (Ed.), *Human information processing: Tutorials in performance and cognition* (pp. 133-186). Hillsdale, NJ: Lawrence Erlbaum Associates.

Trabasso, T., & van den Broek, P. (1985). Causal thinking and the representation of narrative events. *Journal of Memory and Language, 24,* 612-630.

Tschaitschian, B. (1993). *Multiple Abstraktion und Rekonkretisierung verschiedenartiger Erfahrungen.* [Multiple abstraction and re-instantiation of different kinds of experiences]. Unpublished master's thesis, Department of computer science, Universität Kaiserslautern.

Turing, A. M. (1936). On computable numbers, with an application to the Entscheidungsproblem. In *Proceedings of the London Mathematical Society, Series 2, 42,* 230-265.

Turing, A. M. (1963). Computing machinery and intelligence. In E. A. Feigenbaum & J. Feldman (Eds.), *Computers and Thought.* New York: Mc Graw Hill. Original work published 1950.

Turner, A. A. (1987). *The propositional analysis system version 1.0* (Technical Report No. 87-2). Boulder, CO: Institute of Cognitive Science, University of Colorado.

van Dijk, T. A., & Kintsch, W. (1983). *Strategies of discourse comprehension.* San Diego, CA: Academic Press.

VanLehn, K., Brown, J. S., & Greeno, J. (1984). Competitive argumentation in computational theories of cognition. In W. Kintsch, J. R. Miller, & P. G. Polson (Eds.) *Methods and tactics in cognitive science* (pp. 235-262). Hillsdale, NJ: Lawrence Erlbaum Associates.

VanLehn, K., & Jones, R. M. (1993). Learning by explaining examples to oneself: A computational model. In S. Chipman & A. L. Meyrowitz (Eds), *Foundations of knowledge acquisition: Cognitive models of complex learning* (pp. 25-82). Boston: Kluwer Academic Publishers.

van Petten, C., & Kutas, M. (1990). Interactions between sentence context and word frequency in event-related potentials. *Memory and Cognition, 18,* 380-393.

Veloso, M. M. & Carbonell, J. G. (1993). Derivational analogy in PRODIGY: Automating case acquisition, storage, and utilization. *Machine Learning, 10,* 249-278.

Veloso, M., Carbonell, J., Pérez, A., Borrajo, D., Fink, E., & Blythe, J. (1995). Integrating planning and learning: The PRODIGY architecture. *Journal of Experimental and Theoretical Artificial Intelligence, 7,* 81-12.

Vera, A. H., & Simon, H. A. (1993a). Situated action: A symbolic interpretation. *Cognitive Science, 17,* 7-48.

Vera, A. H., & Simon, H. A. (1993b). Situated action: Reply to William Clancey. *Cognitive Science, 17,* 117-133.

von Savigny, E. (1969). *Philosophie und normale Sprache.* [Philosophy and ordinary language]. Freiburg i. Br.: Verlag Karl Alber.

Vorberg, D., & Ulrich, R. (1987). Random search with unequal search rates: Serial and parallel generalizations of McGill's model. *Journal of Mathematical Psychology, 31,* 1-23.

Waldmann, M. R., Holoyak, K. J., & Fratianne, A. (1995). Causal models and the acquisition of category structure. *Journal of Experimental Psychology: General, 124,* 181-206.

Wason, P. C. (1960). On the failure to eliminate hypotheses in a conceptual task. *Quarterly Journal of Experimental Psychology, 32,* 109-123.

Watson, J. B. (1913). Psychology as the behaviorist views it. *Psychological Review, 20*, 158-177. (Reprinted in *Psychological Review, 101,* 2, 248-253, 1994).

Weaver, C. A. III, Mannes, S., & Fletcher, C. R. (Eds.). (1995). *Discourse comprehension: Essays in honor of Walter Kintsch.* Hillsdale, NJ: Lawrence Erlbaum Associates.

Weber, G. (1994). *Fallbasiertes Lernen und Analogien.* [Case-based learning and analogies]. Weinheim: Psychologie Verlags Union.

Weber, G., Bögelsack, A., & Wender, K. F. (1993). When can individual student models be useful. In G. Strube & K. F. Wender (Eds.), *The cognitive psychology of knowledge* (pp. 263-284). Amsterdam, North-Holland: Elsevier.

Weinert, F. E. (1993). Wissenschaftliche Kreativität: Mythen, Fakten und Perspektiven. [Scientific creativity: Myths, facts and perspectives]. In P. Freese (Ed.), *Paderborner Universitätsreden* (pp. 1-24). Paderborn: Verlag der Universität Paderborn.

Weinert, F. E., & Helmke, A. (1995). Learning from wise mother nature or big brother instructor: The wrong choice as seen from an educational perspective. *Educational Psychologist, 30*, 135-142.

Weinert, F. E., Schrader, F. W., & Helmke, A. (1990). Educational expertise: Closing the gap between educational research and classroom practice. *School Psychology International, 11*, 163-180.

Weisberg, R. W. (1995). Prolegomena to theories of insight in problem solving: A taxonomy of problems. In R. J. Sternberg & J. E. Davidson (Eds.), *The nature of insight* (pp. 157-196). Cambridge, MA: MIT Press.

Wertheimer, M. (1945). *Productive Thinking.* New York: Harper & Brothers.

Westermann, R., & Gerjets, P. (1994). Induktion. [Induction]. In Th. Herrmann & W. H. Tack (Eds.), Enzyklopädie der Psychologie. Serie Forschungsmethoden der Psychologie. Band 1: *Methodologische Grundlagen der Psychologie* (pp. 428-471) Göttingen: Hogrefe.

Wetter, Th. (1990). First-order logic foundation of the KADS conceptual model. In B. J. Wielinga, B. Gaines, A. T. Schreiber, & M. van Someren (Eds.), *Current Trends in Knowledge Acquisition* (pp. 356-375) Amsterdam: IOS Press.

Wickelgren, W. A., Corbett, A. T., & Dosher, B. A. (1980). Priming and retrieval from short-term memory: A speed accuracy trade-off analysis. *Journal of Verbal Learning and Verbal Behavior, 19*, 387-404.

Wielinga, B. J., Schreiber, A. Th., & Breuker, J. A. (1992). KADS: A modelling approach to knowledge engineering. *Knowledge Acquisition Journal, 4*, 5-53.

Winograd, T. (1995). From programming environments to environments for designing. *Communications of the ACM, 38*, 65-74.

Winston, P. H. (1984). *Artificial intelligence.* Reading, Massachusetts: Addison-Wesley.

Wisniewski, E. J., & Medin, D. L. (1994). On the interaction of theory and data in concept learning. *Cognitive Science, 18*, 221-281.

Wittgenstein, L. (1971). *Philosophische Untersuchungen.* [Philosphical investigations]. Frankfurt: Suhrkamp Taschenbuch. (First published by Basil Blackwell in 1958).

Wrobel, St. (1991). Die Umweltverankerung von Begriffsbildungsprozessen. [The environmental anchoring of concept formation processes]. *Künstliche Intelligenz, 1*, 22-26.

Zimny, S. T. (1987). *Recognition of memory for sentences from a discourse*. Unpublished doctoral dissertation, University of Colorado, Boulder, CO.

Zwaan, R. A. (1994). Effect of genre: Expectations on text comprehension. *Journal of Experimental Psychology: Learning, Memory, and Cognition*, 20, 920-933.

Zwaan, R. A., Magliano, J. P., & Graesser, A. C. (1995). Dimensions of situation model construction in narrative comprehension. *Journal of Experimental Psychology: Learning, Memory, and Cognition, 21*, 386-397.

Author Index

Subject Index